The Economic Novel in America

WALTER FULLER TAYLOR

OCTAGON BOOKS

A DIVISION OF FARRAR, STRAUS AND GIROUX

New York 1973

Copyright 1942, by The University of North Carolina Press

Reprinted 1964
by special arrangement with The University of North Carolina Press

Second Octagon printing 1969

Third Octagon printing 1973

OCTAGON BOOKS
A DIVISION OF FARRAR, STRAUS & GIROUX, INC.
19 Union Square West
New York, N. Y. 10003

LIBRARY OF CONGRESS CATALOG CARD NUMBER: 64-24845
ISBN 0-374-97790-9

Printed in U.S.A. by
NOBLE OFFSET PRINTERS, INC.
NEW YORK, N.Y. 10003

PREFACE

In the following pages, my aim has been to describe and interpret the response given by American authorship to one of the major social forces of the latter nineteenth century— the rapid industrialization of our American society, the sudden maturation of the Machine Age. More specifically, I have proposed to show how, between the Civil War and the turn of the century, certain democratic and middle-class ideals, which had hitherto been applied chiefly to politics, were so extended as to apply to economics as well; how that democratic ideology found voice in our published fiction; and how, consequently, there developed within that fiction a coherent and incisive *critique* of capitalistic industrialism.

During my examination of this body of critical literature, I have been led, by the clear indications of historical evidence, into strenuous disagreement with certain widely held ideas about the complacency and cultural enervation of the so-called Gilded Age; so that the general drift of my work is toward the rehabilitation of that somewhat maligned era. Although this outcome was not my original intention, I am far from regretting it. Indeed, I only hope that others will find a pleasure equal to my own in the assurance that our democratic tradition in America has been more continuously dynamic, and that our cultural inheritance from the latter nineteenth century is richer, than has often been supposed.

In the preparation of this book, I have had the aid of many kindnesses from members of my family, from colleagues, and from other friends, to all of whom I am sincerely grateful. I am particularly indebted to Professor Howard Mumford Jones, under whose supervision I began this study, as a doctoral investigation, at the University of North Carolina in 1928, and under whose teaching I first became really aware of the possibilities of an historical approach to the study of literature. I am indebted also to Professor Gregory Lansing Paine, of the University of North Carolina, for certain kind and valuable suggestions; to Professor Eldon Cleon Hill, of Miami University, for the reading and criticizing of the fifth and sixth sections of the chapter on Hamlin Garland; and to Mrs. Rosa Dykes Quisenberry, of the Mississippi College Library, for unfailingly courteous and efficient coöperation.

For permission to quote from copyrighted material, I should like to make grateful acknowledgment to the following:

E. P. Dutton and Company, for permission to quote from Van Wyck Brooks's *Letters and Leadership* and *The Ordeal of Mark Twain.*

Mr. Henry A. Dwire, Editor of the *South Atlantic Quarterly,* for permission to use, with slight changes, pp. 393-6 of my article, "Mark Twain and the Machine Age," *The South Atlantic Quarterly,* XXXVII: 384-96 (October, 1938).

Mrs. Constance Garland Harper, of the Hamlin Garland Literary Estate, for permission to quote from Mr. Garland's *Prairie Folks.*

Harper and Brothers, for permission to quote from Mark Twain's *A Connecticut Yankee in King Arthur's Court* and from *Mark Twain's Letters,* edited by Albert Bigelow Paine.

Houghton-Mifflin Company, for permission to quote from Edward Bellamy's *Looking Backward.*

Miss Mildred Howells, for permission to quote from her edition of *The Life in Letters of William Dean Howells,* and from Mr. Howells' *A Hazard of New Fortunes, The Landlord at Lion's Head,* and *Years of My Youth.*

Dr. Jay B. Hubbell, Editor of *American Literature,* for permission to use, with slight changes, a passage, pp. 4-6, of my article, "On the Origin of Howells' Interest in Economic Reform," *American Literature,* II: 3-14 (March, 1930).

Alfred A. Knopf, Inc., for permission to quote from Stephen Crane's *Maggie.*

The Macmillan Company, for permission to quote from
Hamlin Garland's *A Daughter of the Middle Border*, and
from Robert Herrick's *Memoirs of an American Citizen* and
The Web of Life.

W. F. T.

CONTENTS

THE ECONOMIC NOVEL

CHAPTER ONE: THE ENVIRONMENT

I

Of the interaction of literature and society, much has been said, little is definitely known. Since the time of Taine, the sociological interpretation of literature has borne, with singular persistence, a relatively scant fruitage of historical fact and a luxuriant foliage of speculation. Among such speculations, some of the most interesting, provocative, and even sensational have dealt with American literature of a period not so very remote from our own time—the period to which, in its very infancy, Mark Twain and Charles Dudley Warner affixed the unforgettable nickname of the Gilded Age. In that confused and turbulent generation, America first felt the entire social impact of the Machine, with the consequence that a society mainly decentralized and agrarian gave way, with catastrophic suddenness, to one that was highly centralized, urban, industrial. That our literature should have been deeply affected by such a cultural revolution, and that in time a sociological interpretation of that literature should arise, were both, no doubt, inevitable.

What seems less inevitable—indeed, almost fortuitous—is the particular drift and coloring of those critical interpretations of the Gilded Age which, through more than two decades, have prevailed most widely. Vague anticipations of this entire body of critical theory are to be found as early as Van Wyck Brooks's *America's Coming-of-Age* (1915). Throughout this early volume, Mr. Brooks's conclusions are reasoned from certain premises which only his other writings make fully articulate:—the premise that business interests are necessarily

3

hostile to the creative life [1]; the further premise that something of final aesthetic weight and authority has been consistently lacking in American literature; and the related premise that our abundant creative talent has been thwarted by the hostile environment of an over-acquisitive society.—"Those of our writers who have possessed a vivid personal talent have been paralyzed by the want of a social background." [2]

The hypotheses that are mostly implicit or nebulous in *America's Coming-of-Age* appear, fully matured, in *Letters and Leadership* (1918). In the latter volume, the history of the creative life in America, as portrayed in the rich, finely-colored medium of Mr. Brooks's sensitively persuasive style, takes on something of the august proportions of a slowly developing tragedy, with the Gilded Age as its inescapable catastrophe. Our culture, always ingrained with Yankee business acumen, weakened by the long repressions of Puritanism, malnourished by the barrenness of the frontier, yielded, we are told, to the first attacks of a value-destroying industrialism; yielded indeed—unlike the cultures of Europe—without so much as an articulate protest.

The industrialism that bowled us over . . . was no sooner well under way in Europe than human nature began to get its back up, so to speak; and a long line of great rebels reacted violently against its desiccating influences. Philologists like Nietzsche and Renan, digging among the roots of Greek and Semitic thought, artists like Morris and Rodin, rediscovering the beautiful and happy art of the Middle Ages, economists like Marx and Mill, revolting against the facts of their environment, kept alive the tradition of a great society and great ways of living and thus were able to assimilate for human uses the positive by-products of industrialism itself, science and democracy.

. . . For us, individually and socially, as I have tried to show, nothing of this kind has been possible. [3]

---

[1] Observe, for instance, the implications of the passage on Emerson, *America's Coming-of-Age*, pp. 84-5. Compare with this passage the statement, "the creative impulses of men are always at war with their possessive impulses," in the same author's *Letters and Leadership*, p. 25.

[2] Van Wyck Brooks, *America's Coming-of-Age*, p. 109.

[3] Van Wyck Brooks, *Letters and Leadership*, pp. 50-1. Reprinted by permission of E. P. Dutton and Company, publishers.

The Ordeal of Mark Twain (1920) not only applies to the greatest literary personality of the age Mr. Brooks's hypothesis of the thwarting of high creative talent by a merely industrial and acquisitive society; it reasserts the dictum that the America of the Gilded Age produced no critique of industrialism:

In an age when every sensitive mind in England was in full revolt against the blind, mechanical, devastating forces of a "progress" that promised nothing but the ultimate collapse of civilization; when all Europe was alive with prophets, aristocratic prophets, proletarian prophets, religious and philosophical and humanitarian and economic and artistic prophets, crying out, in the name of the human spirit, against the cruel advance of capitalistic industrialism; in an age glorified by little but the beautiful anger of the Tolstoys and the Marxes, the Nietzsches and the Renans, the Ruskins and the Morris's—in that age America, innocent, ignorant, profoundly untroubled, slept the righteous sleep of its own manifest and peculiar destiny.[4]

So far, indeed, as the literary fraternity were aware of sociological issues at all, they were, Mr. Brooks claims, solidly in league with the financial fraternity.[5] And within so hostile a milieu, even our American abundance of talent was not able to effectuate itself. "The blighted career, the arrested career, the diverted career are, with us, the rule. The chronic state of our literature is that of a youthful promise which is never redeemed." [6]

---

[4] Van Wyck Brooks, *The Ordeal of Mark Twain,* pp. 89-90. Reprinted by permission of E. P. Dutton and Company, publishers.

[5] *Ibid.,* p. 275.

[6] Van Wyck Brooks, "The Literary Life in America"; *Emerson and Others,* pp. 222-3. It is interesting to observe that in his recent *New England: Indian Summer* (1940) Mr. Brooks views the Gilded Age with a profound tolerance, even a sympathy, that are sharply at variance with the caustic severity of his earlier writing. The change is, on the whole, one of emotional tone rather than of explicit statement, and the earlier generalizations about the complacency of the Gilded Age are not withdrawn. See, however, for a brief treatment of the interest in social reform awakened by Edward Bellamy and Henry George, and of the democratic influence in the social criticism of William Dean Howells, pp. 380-94.

Quite obviously, such sweeping, condemnatory generalizations neither were, nor are, established historical truth. No doubt they are highly original, interesting, and provocative speculation; but they are *only* speculation, or, at most, hypothesis—nothing more. Nevertheless, they have won ready support among a number of our ablest critics and historians, and have had wide general circulation as well.

For example, Lewis Mumford, in his beautifully written study, *The Golden Day* (1926), advances, alongside the thesis that American culture came to its finest flowering during the "Golden Day" before the Civil War, the complementary thesis that during the following generation it suffered a decadence so severe as to vitiate its literary effort. The Gilded Age, absorbed in "mad exploitation" and "boomtown optimism," interested in no activity but business, devoted to no aim but that of material comfort, brought forth a futile society which "denied, starved, frustrated its imaginative life"; in consequence, "each of the principal literary figures of postbellum America, Mark Twain, Ambrose Bierce, Henry James, William Dean Howells, William James, was the remains of a man." [7]

More deeply than has yet been pointed out, this same assumption of the cultural wrong-doing of the Gilded Age permeates the most erudite and influential study of that period that has yet appeared—Vernon Louis Parrington's *The Beginnings of Critical Realism in America* (1930). To be sure, Parrington's very title testifies to his disagreement with one of the principal Brooksian theories—the theory of the passiveness of the Gilded Age and of its barrenness of any literature of critical protest. Nevertheless, Parrington does assume that the society of the Gilded Age was such as to discourage both fine living and creative expression. The entrance into the Gilded Age of a keen young mind like Godkin's becomes

[7] Lewis Mumford, *The Golden Day*, pp. 87, 159-64, 177. It is noteworthy that in a later work, *The Brown Decades* (1931), Mr. Mumford profoundly modifies this attitude, and even insists that the error of belittling the Gilded Age not be continued. See especially, in *The Brown Decades*, pp. 20-1.

thus, in Parrington's judgment, "a cold plunge into a dirty pool," and Godkin's ultimate discouragement appears to have grown out of his oversensitiveness to the misbehavior of "certain blackguard years." [8] The corroding pessimism of Mark Twain appears, to Parrington, to have followed inevitably upon his failure to outgrow the "jerry-built" spiritual home afforded by his times—"What a commentary on the Gilded Age!" [9] And, still seen in this same perspective, the enemies of the current Philistinism, like Wendell Phillips, take on, in Parrington's imagination, the giant-like stature of heroes, courageous as King Arthur in his last dim weird battle of the West.[10]

In regard to this devaluation of an entire period in our cultural history, the majority of scholars acquainted with American literature have apparently felt it wise to reserve judgment. No such assumptions as those of Van Wyck Brooks color the discussions in the symposium, *The Reinterpretation of American Literature* (1928); no such hypotheses are sanctioned by the various articles and reviews published in the scholarly journal, *American Literature;* no such interpretation is to be found in the surveys of American literature prepared by such students as Leisy and Boynton, or in anthologies such as those edited by Foerster and Hubbell.[11] Nevertheless, a steadily accumulating body of reasearch has so far brought forth no thoroughgoing study of the problems which Mr. Brooks and others have so strikingly presented. Individual articles have appeared, and even monographs, but no systematic assembly of evidence copious enough, and significant enough, to show what degree of truth dwells in the charges levied against the

[8] Vernon Louis Parrington, *The Beginnings of Critical Realism in America,* pp. 160, 168.

[9] *Ibid.,* pp. 89, 101.

[10] *Ibid.,* p. 142.

[11] Norman Foerster (Editor), *The Reinterpretation of American Literature* (New York, 1928); Ernest E. Leisy, *American Literature, an Interpretative Survey* (New York, 1929); Percy Holmes Boynton, *Literature and American Life* (Boston, 1936); Norman Foerster (Editor), *American Poetry and Prose* (Boston and New York, 1934); Jay B. Hubbell (Editor), *American Life in Literature* (New York, 1936).

Gilded Age. Meanwhile, in the absence of any adequate check from the exacting discipline of historical research, critical and journalisitc speculations about the period have multiplied.

In the early nineteen-thirties, there appeared, indeed, an entire group of such treatises, all of which, however they might otherwise differ, agreed in their condemnatory tone. In his *Portrait of the Artist as American* (1930), Matthew Josephson greatly elaborates the Brooksian theory of the hostility of the Gilded Age to creative art. Whereas the antebellum generation had encouraged the development of individual talent, the Gilded Age impaled such talent on one or the other horn of an inescapable dilemma—frustration or escape. Those men who remained artists had to flee; those who remained Americans had to face artistic failure. A James became a *deraciné;* a Howells suffered the loss of imaginative freshness and deep moral conviction. The general result of the tragedy was "an appalling and uncalculated destruction of talent." [12] In *Expression in America* (1932), Ludwig Lewisohn is less concerned with the plight of the American artist than with the general complacency and emasculation of our post-bellum culture.[13] In *The Liberation of American Literature* (1932), V. F. Calverton assumes that the art of the Gilded Age was shaped by a "petty-bourgeois ideology," the impotence of which has become so apparent that it is soon to be replaced by "a definitely crystallized proletarian ideology." [14] In *The Great Tradition* (1933), Granville Hicks finds in our post-Civil-War literature a series of worthy but unsuccessful efforts to grapple with the facts of contemporary life—unsuccessful, that is, in the sense that no author of that age arrived at a Marxian understanding of class conflict.

Similarly adverse interpretations of the Gilded Age were, during these same years, finding their way into college and university textbooks. In *American Literature as an Expression of the National Mind* (1931), Russell Blankenship maintains

[12] Matthew Josephson, *Portrait of the Artist as American,* especially pp. xxii, 163-5, 231, 290.

[13] *Expression in America,* pp. 238, 296-9.

[14] V. F. Calverton, *The Liberation of American Literature,* p. 370.

that in the Gilded Age "money was the sole criterion by which everything was judged," and that the sins of the period were "numerous and grave." [15] And in *American Literature and Culture* (1932), Grant C. Knight describes the American literary chronicle from 1870 to 1900 as "a desert dotted with many bleached bones." [16]—Attitudes like these, while they would hardly gain unqualified acceptance from any considerable body of historians, have discernibly colored the contemporary interpretation of an entire era in American literary history. Indeed the very name by which that period continues to be known—a name that originated in satire and condenses in brilliant epithet an adverse moral judgment—tends to perpetuate that coloring. Now this entire attitude, it should be evident, has grown out of a method of thought which is at bottom theoretical, speculative, perhaps even *a priori*. The condemnation of an important era in the American past rests on no groundwork of exact historical study, but, at most, upon general unsystematized observations; and those observations have been more than a little influenced both by the exigencies of journalism and by the perennial human tendency toward myth-making.

The following treatise will approach the problem of the interrelationship of literature and society through the quite different avenue of historical investigation. Although it will not avoid the task of critically appraising purely literary values, it will distinguish that appraisal sharply from historical study, and will postpone it until a certain groundwork of historical fact has been established. It will arrive at no ultimate laws, no basic principles; it will disclose no complete articulation of literary and social forces, or even of literary and economic forces, within even the single generation to which it is devoted. But it will put on historical record, with

[15] Russell Blankenship, *American Literature as an Expression of the National Mind*, pp. 391, 457. See also pp. 404, 410, 429, 433. Among the "numerous and grave" sins of the period, Mr. Blankenship includes responsibility for what might be called the spiritual nihilism of Henry Adams and Mark Twain.

[16] *American Literature and Culture*, p. 290.

the support of adequate evidence, the American *critique* of capitalistic industrialism, as that *critique* is expressed in published fiction, and as that fiction articulates with its contemporary social framework of events, ideas, and literary tastes.

The following discussions will, in their progress toward this goal, (1) survey briefly the environment within which our *critique* of the Machine Age developed; (2) fix on the materials and the ideas characteristic of the work of a number of lesser novelists; (3) examine individually, and at much greater length, the economic criticism of Mark Twain, Hamlin Garland, Edward Bellamy, William Dean Howells, and Frank Norris; and (4) describe in resumé the salient traits of the entire movement and arrive at an estimate of its degree of literary worth. The effect of these studies will be to show that our post-Civil-War literature treats, with seriousness and vigor, precisely the same problem that occupied the great Victorian social critics from Carlyle through William Morris —the problem of assimilating into a previously existent humane culture the disruptive forces of capitalistic industrialism; that our literature attacks that problem from viewpoints and according to methods already deeply ingrained into our middle class and democratic civilization; and that therefore our American cultural tradition is, particularly in its exploration of the possibilities of democracy, more continuous than has often been supposed.

II

If, after 1865, American Literature did indeed suffer strangulation at the hands of a bourgeois materialism, that fact would indicate a catastrophic break in our literary tradition. Before the Civil War, symptoms of any such disaster were few indeed; the time-spirit of the generation which produced Thoreau and Whittier was, as the critics of the Gilded Age are ready enough to admit, of quite another kind. Yet the temper of that previous era must inescapably have had some effect upon that of the Gilded Age;—indeed, an understanding of it, and of its repercussions after the Civil War, might well prove to be a *sine qua non* in the understanding of the latter period. And therefore it will be necessary, even at the risk of platitude, to recall, in brief resumé, some of its main elements; and, in so doing, to fix on certain landmarks in the former era, by which to chart the literary history of the latter.[17]

And if, at the beginning, we look impartially on the entire composite of ideas—economic, political, ethical—expressed in our pre-Civil-War literature, we must observe at once that those ideas not only sanction the material acquisition which Mr. Brooks has thought so dangerous to art, but even emphasize its value. *Getting* and *owning* have always appeared important, not only to the typical American citizen, but also to the typical American writer.[18] Even so early a writing as Franklin's "The Way to Wealth" testifies, in its universal popularity, to a general American agreement with such dicta as "Get all you can, and what you get, hold." To Freneau, part of the future "Rising Glory" of the American nation was to be its prosperity as an agrarian commonwealth. According to Timothy Flint, somewhat later, the desire of the typical frontiersman was "to be a freeholder, to have plenty of rich land, and to be able to settle his children about him."

Moreover, such hopes were, in considerable degree, actually realized. Were St. Jean de Crévecoeur the only writer to conceive of early America as a land of "fair cities, substantial

[17] In any such resumé—and especially in one that is of necessity brief—it is essential to know the precise grounds of one's study, and to remain rigidly within them. In the following pages, neither the conventions of *belles-lettres* on the one hand, nor the vast and complex body of social practice or even theory on the other, is of *primary* concern. The territory to be surveyed is, rather, that dubious area where literature and society overlap; the area in which literature appears to grow naturally out of the germinal ideas of a social order, and at once to articulate and creatively mold those ideas. This resumé is, in short, concerned with the composite body of ideas and assumptions about social living which motivated, and are expressed in, our pre-Civil-War literature.

[18] There have been, of course, such notable exceptions as Thoreau. But American objections to acquisition have usually been pointed not against the ownership of property in itself, but against failure to develop other and presumably superior interests. See below, pp. 84-90.

villages, extensive fields,... decent houses, good roads, orchards, meadows, and bridges," a land distinguished by a "pleasing uniformity of decent competence," such roseate colorings might be dismissed as fanciful; but similar testimony is abundant. Joel Barlow, a person much less sentimentally exuberant than Crévecoeur, speaks of Americans as "less numerous, less indigent, and better instructed" than the mass of Europeans. Timothy Dwight portrays an American village as a seat of peace and pleasure, where one might

> hear the voice of Industry resound
> And mark the smile of Competence, around;

and the ornithologist Alexander Wilson found that in America an industrious rural people might enjoy "Plenty's smiling cup, without its woe." By the early nineteenth century, in short, the United States was already looked on, with considerable justification, as a land of material abundance—so much so that the editors of a recent American anthology could speak, as of a thing already established and to be taken for granted, of "the American hope of universally diffused economic security." [19]

Now that American hope, for all its concern over property, is more unlike than like bourgeois materialism, as the latter is usually understood. It agrees with bourgeois materialism, of course, in its stress on thrift, acquisition, individual effort, and freedom from governmental control. Yet in the very midst of these likenesses it owns a native American flavor, a social consciousness, even an altruism which make of it so novel a concept that the vocabulary of European class divisions is, when applied to it, misleading or futile.

Such individuality was stimulated, no doubt, both by the frontier and by our formerly agrarian mode of living. To the frontier, to the rich resources of a continent, was owing the fact that opportunity could knock at the doors of the many instead of the few. To an agrarian environment, where a prosperous and all but classless people could live as a com-

[19] Harry R. Warfel, Ralph H. Gabriel, and Stanley T. Williams, *The American Mind* (New York, 1937), I, 395.

munity, bound to the land and to one another by a host of common experiences in shop and field, was owing the perceptive quality, the folk-flavor, common to a Lincoln, a Garland, a Clemens. That agrarian way of life, fostered as it was both by natural conditions and by the low-tariff policies of the government, held its dominance long. And therefore, until well after the Civil War, the typical middle-class American was from his earliest years differently conditioned from, say, a London bourgeois. Not only did an informal democracy—economic, political, social—fix itself in his mind as the norm of social order; the very texture of his thinking—his entire stock of basic childhood images, feelings, adventures—was necessarily of a different cast from that of his old-world kinsman.

Out of this soil there grew, therefore, something quite different from bourgeois materialism. Out of this soil there grew what may be called the *democratic* materialism of America—a tradition, a way of thinking, an ideal according to which the gaining of property is to be not selfishly individual, but general. This ideal renders great wealth and undeserved poverty both suspect, thrusts them both outside the pale of the socially desirable; it requires that no one have too much, and that everyone have enough. But its main emphasis falls, no doubt, on the latter demand. That the humblest person might have an income sufficient to assure him of a certain minimum of the physical decencies and comforts—this was the economic goal set up, consciously or unconsciously, by the thought of early America. Later, therefore, when such a writer as Edward Bellamy portrayed in *Looking Backward* (1888) a prosperous, highly industrialized Utopian society, it is quite possible that he was no more indulging a daydream of bourgeois luxury than he was predicting the rule of the proletariat; that he was, instead, only transferring from the geographical to the industrial frontier the old American dream of the release of an entire people from want.—But this is to anticipate.

In its strongly democratic coloring, this American view of material wealth typifies many phases of American culture.

Prior to the Civil War, a surprisingly large area of our literary thought was infused with a fresh, a living interest in the democratic ideal. Democracy was no mere catchword, no mere fragment of a platitude; it was still a comparatively young, a vital, a militant movement, with a thousand challenging possibilities still unexplored. To an interest so challenging, so pervasive, American authorship was bound to respond; from the Revolution to the Civil War, in fact, hardly an important American writer failed to respond to it, and to put on record, somewhere, his political philosophy. From the Right, the conservative Poe and Melville looked with distrust on the exuberances of the People. At the Center, Irving, Cooper, Hawthorne, the mature Lowell, and occasionally Longfellow upheld a dignified republicanism. But on the Left-Center and Left were ranged the largest and by far the most distinctly American group, from Revolutionists like Freneau to nineteenth-century liberals like Bryant, Whittier, the youthful Lowell, and Whitman.[20] Bryant, indeed, might very well be chosen out of all our antebellum authors as the most typical champion of a liberal democratic idealism. In his loyalty to democratic leaders such as Lincoln, in his extension of democratic theory into such socio-economic fields as the slavery question, in his interest in the progress of democracy in Europe and South America, and in his hopes for a world-leadership, political and even spiritual, to be exercised by America—in all this Bryant sums up as fully as does Whitman, and without Whitman's idiosyncrasies, the most central aims and hopes of the American democracy.[21]

[20] In this same group should be placed, no doubt, Thoreau and even Emerson, although they stood somewhat apart from the others in their distrust of the democratic mass and their tendencies toward philosophical anarchy.

[21] Among the poems in which Bryant expressed these ideas are "The Death of Lincoln," "The Greek Boy," "Romero," "Hymn of the Waldenses," "The Winds," "To the Memory of William Leggett," and "The Lapse of Time."

For an interpretation of democratic idealism with reference to its agrarian setting, see Henry Douglas Wild's doctoral dissertation, *Democratic Idealism in American Literature from Penn to Whitman*. The University of Chicago, 1924. Among the lesser authors quoted or re-

Such power as that wielded by the democratic ideal could hardly have been gained without the aid of strong philosophical allies. For a movement of thought languishes in isolation, and flourishes most as a member of some community of ideas, supported by its integration within some view of life larger and more general than itself. To this principle, the democratic idealism of America was no exception; it lay suspended, as it were, within the medium of a still larger philosophy, as a cloud is held suspended within the enveloping atmosphere. That larger philosophy, which quietly, persistently gave shape to the thought of many an author who never took the trouble to systematize it or perhaps even recognize it in himself, was the cosmic optimism made current by the eighteenth-century Enlightenment.

Deep in the consciousness of our earlier national writers there dwelt, as the very source and life-spring of their philosophy, something of the old deistic vision of a rational mankind dwelling within an orderly, benevolent Cosmos. Not many, to be sure, were so explicit as was Freneau in speaking of the created world as "thoughts, on Reason's scale combined," or as Whitman in his reference to the great natural laws that "take and effuse without argument." But the great majority—Bryant and Emerson and Longfellow no less than Freneau—took implicitly for granted that the cosmic scheme favors those qualities in man that man has usually most prized in himself. They took for granted that the Universe supports the cause of order against disorder; reason against unreason; integration against disintegration; admiration, hope, and love [22] against stolidity, despair, and hate. They held, in short, the optimism which assumes that humane values are created not in despite of Nature's indifference or hostility, but with Nature's active aid. [23]

---

ferred to by Wild are Timothy Flint, James Hall, Charles Fenno Hoffman, James Kirke Paulding, and Alexander Wilson. See particularly the bibliography, pp. 124 ff.

[22] The phrase is, of course, Ruskin's.

[23] Such exceptions as Hawthorne and Melville naturally suggest themselves. It might be observed, too, that Whittier, Longfellow, and others found in Christianity additional sanction for optimism.

From such premises may be inferred, easily and naturally, that passionate romantic faith in the natural man which now, a century later, appears so extraordinary. Mankind, twinned with a benevolent Cosmos as offspring of an all-wise Creator, must be innately worthy and potentially perfectible—worthy, at the very least, of a voice in his own government; perfectible enough, in all likelihood, to insure a marvellous future for self-governing humanity. To Freneau, man was, even when "debased in dust" before Tyranny, "that Being, active, great, sublime." To Emerson, individual man was "greater than all the geography and all the government of the world." To democratic leaders from Paine through Jefferson and Lincoln, there appeared to be no question of the intelligence and essential justice of the average mind.

Along with so complete a faith in man, there developed, naturally enough, a similar faith in the continued progress of both the individual and the race.[24] The fair eighteenth-century vision of human perfectibility often became, to the American romanticist, more than a vision; it became an unquestioned assumption, a basal premise from whose hidden taproot might emerge a dozen separate branches of thought. Within such a climate of opinion even Thoreau, for all his distrust of humanity in the mass, could express a hope for a "yet more perfect state," which he had imagined, but never anywhere seen, and could believe that "there is more day to dawn. The sun is but a morning star." And the more socially minded Whittier could write, even after the tragic disruptions of the Civil War,

> A glory shines before me
> Of what mankind shall be,
> Pure, generous, brave, and free,

And the numerous political and social reformers of Whittier's generation, if they could not altogether share his vision of an

[24] The idea of progress had, obviously, other sanctions as well—among them, the quite general acceptance of evolution as meaning progressive improvement.

idyllically perfect mankind, could mostly agree, nevertheless, that both the individual and the social life tended naturally toward improvement—the individual, toward an ever larger and finer experience of living; society, toward a rational, more nearly perfect order in which the individual mind could flower most abundantly.

In some such all-inclusive optimism lies the philosophical sanction for the aggressive support which the men of our romantic generation gave to democracy; for their deep assurance that their labors for the improvement of human life would prove neither barren nor unfruitful; and for that vigorous prosecution of numerous social reforms by which they hoped to extend democracy into other fields than the merely political.

For democracy rapidly became—indeed, in some measure had always been—much more than just a means of carrying on the government; its thousandfold applications proved as broad, as deep, as richly complex as its philosophical sources. Once possessed of an ideal so broad in scope, and withal so fascinating, an energetic people could hardly have passed by the chance to explore all its possibilities—educational, social, and economic as well as governmental. Universal education, for example, obviously developed in this country under the aura of democracy. Hardly was the national government established when Joel Barlow pointed out the responsibility of the state for the enlightenment of its future voting citizenry; and during the following century it became the task of some thousands of teachers and organizers, of whom Horace Mann was only the most notable, to bring that theory to some realization.

Like universal education, an agrarian social structure appeared to American thinkers to be a natural accompaniment of democracy. In judging cities to be "pestilential to the morals, the health, and the liberties of man," in regarding farmers as the state's most valuable citizens, and in thinking of democracy as the natural form of government for a village and rural people, Jefferson was only forming into logical clarity the ideas which his contemporaries mostly took for granted.[25] Prior to the Civil War, such an agrarian society was fostered both by natural conditions and by the prevailing low-tariff policies of the government. It not only came into being; it developed a characteristic way of life and no little intellectual energy, both in the older-settled regions along the Atlantic slope and in the newer communities beyond the Appalachians.[26]

Yet all the while, however idyllic might be the agrarian dream, in actuality social injustice persisted in cropping out. Short of the creation of a Utopia inhabited altogether by affluent freeholders, there appeared to be no way of preventing the exploitation of man by man—the renter by the landlord, the wage-earner by the employer. In some measure there existed even in youthful America, a class of the socially submerged, a class who appeared to be victims not so much of their own shiftlessness as of social arrangements which favored exploitation. Since these people were denied many of the fruits of democracy, they became a natural object of concern to the democratic idealist; and in that concern democracy was reinforced by one of the great pervasive sentiments of the romantic period—humanitarianism.

In the writings of Freneau and Paine, among others, the bearing of democracy on economic justice become abundantly clear. It appears in Freneau's attack on the exploitation which delivers "all earthly good" into the hands of "the few, the proud, the first." It appears more fully in Paine's attack on inequalities in the distribution of wealth, for in that curiously prescient treatise, *Agrarian Justice* (1797), Paine dwells on the undemocratic contrast between "affluence and wretchedness," sets up the prevention of poverty as a legitimate goal of government, shows that much of the wealth in any society

[25] This is not to deny, of course, the existence of a strong minority who were of a different persuasion—those, for instance, who agreed with the party policy of the Federalists and the Whigs. It is only to insist that the *main* current of American political thought was the agrarian-democratic one represented by Jefferson.

[26] See Wild, *op. cit.*, pp. 88 ff., for a survey of testimony about the West offered by a number of writers, particularly Charles Fenno Hoffman and James Hall.

is socially rather than individually created, and proposes that
the state, by taxation, take a part of this socially created
wealth for redistribution among the poor and old. But the
carry-over of democracy into economics appears most characteristically in the large body of anti-slavery writings from
Jefferson through Whittier and Lowell. The economic system
of slavery, as a denial of the democratic equality of mankind,
is treated as *ipse facto* wrong; and in behalf of the human
beings whose natural rights are so rudely denied, all resources
of moral indignation and humane feeling are appealed to.[27]
Slavery is inconsistent with democracy; therefore slavery
must go.—In short, there runs through a large body of American writing done prior to the Civil War the basic though
unspoken assumption that a democratic polity requires also
a democratic economy. Political democracy alone is not
enough to insure the welfare of the average man, and must
therefore be reinforced by some measure of economic democracy.

Some such way of thought underlies not only a great deal
of the anti-slavery sentiment of the pre-War generation; it
underlies also, many of the general reform movements of the
times, and especially the founding of the numerous socialized
communities whose aim was to provide for their members
economic security and equality. In a number of these communities the dominant motives were, of course, religious; and
in most, some ethical or social objective went along with the
merely economic one. Nevertheless, the economic aim did
exist. Communities like the Owenite settlement at New Harmony or the Fourieristic group at Brook Farm did provide,
during the brief day of their florescence, the material and
physical democracy toward which our political theory naturally inclined. They awakened, moreover, discussions which
were heard far beyond the circle of their direct influence;

[27] There were, to be sure, many other grounds of argument against
slavery, some of them perhaps more influential than this one. It is noteworthy, however, that the defenders of slavery—Calhoun and Fitzhugh,
for example—were compelled to found their arguments on the opposite
and undemocratic principle of the inequality of men.

even an adverse *critique*, like that of Horace Greeley in *Hints Toward Reforms* (1850), increased the number of those who were made aware of their experiments in social order. American society could not yet be looked on as a thing immutably crystallized, the possibilities of democracy were still being explored; and the institutions that would best embody the democratic ideal were still in process of discovery.

Would America's nascent industrialism prove to be hindrance or aid to this half-emerged scheme of universal democracy? With almost the first appearance of the Industrial Revolution on these shores, opinion on that subject sharply divided. Most Americans, to be sure, took to the Machine without foresight—indeed, almost without thought—as it proved useful in their immediate practical business, or revealed its enormous potentialities for the physical conquest of a continent. Among the more thoughtful, a number looked on the Machine favorably, as a means of realizing the high level of popular material comfort at which democracy was aimed.[28] Others, on the contrary, were quick to observe that however valuable the Machine might be in itself, its social by-products were inconsistent with and dangerous to democracy. Neither the abuse of woman and child labor, nor the rapid growth of the slums, nor yet the creation of a class of landless wage slaves, could have any place in the scheme of the democratic idealist; and all of these conditions drew a recurrent fire of sharp criticism. Timothy Flint's observation of the "blanched cheeks" and "tender forms" of factory girls; Horace Greeley's interest in the regulation of factory labor; Theodore

[28] See, in this connection, the suggestive article by Broadus A. Mitchell, "American Radicals Nobody Knows," *The South Atlantic Quarterly*, XXXIV, 394-401 (October, 1935). Among those Americans who were "radical" in their treatment of industrialization and prosperity were Alexander Hamilton, Matthew Carey, Daniel Raymond, J. N. Cardozo, John Rae, Friedrich List and Henry C. Carey. The composite opinion of these men Mr. Mitchell sums up as follows: "Peace, stability, a high general level of education and intelligence, a rising standard of living, the fostering of mechanical proficiencies, excellent means of internal transportation and communication, the minimum of political difference—these were the conditions of national advance."

Parker's Christian concern over the "perishing classes" in Boston—these and many other straws show at least one way in which the wind of social criticism was blowing. Long before the Machine was generally recognized as a dominant social force, American thinking had grown aware that its social effects might become a grave threat to democratic well-being, and had also put that judgment abundantly on record.[29]

The democracy that gave aim and form to our pre-Civil-War culture was more therefore by far than just a method of government; it was also a tradition, a philosophy, almost an entire way of life in itself. It was a dynamic ideology, which broke through any narrow political boundaries to make itself felt in education, in economics, in the entire range of American society, setting up everywhere the standards by which the new industrialism was to be judged, pressing onward everywhere toward the generous end of the enlargement of all the possibilities of life for the common man.

In that democratic scheme of living, material aims were, as has been frankly admitted, important; but they were by no means *all*-important. Alongside our materialism appears everywhere our immaterialism. Almost invariably the American thinker takes for granted that mere acquisition does not satisfy human nature; that man has aesthetic or spiritual needs as well as material ones; and that between these two realms of experience there is no essential conflict.[30]

Among most Americans, those immaterial needs were no doubt mainly fulfilled by religion; or, more precisely, by Prostestant Christianity. Not the least remarkable phase of our remarkable history was the Protestant evangelization of the Frontier—the successful work of some thousands of circuit riders who underwent hardship and danger in order to cleanse lives and save souls; the intertwining within our na-

[29] See, for corroboration, the opinion expressed by the editors, Harry R. Warfel, Ralph H. Gabriel, and Stanley T. Williams, in *The American Mind*, I, 389.

[30] These sentences—need it be emphasized?—are meant to apply, as does the remainder of this passage, to the period *before* the Civil War.

tional consciousness of all the church's spiritual aspiration, its moral earnestness, its age-old folkways and humane ameliorations. So established, the Church rapidly became both complement and curb of the prevailing materialism, satisfying needs that property alone could not satisfy, and employing its moral force to ameliorate social evils. In the South, for instance, religious leaders sought to lessen the harshness of slavery by encouraging Christian conduct between master and slave; in the North, such men as Theodore Parker called for the application of Christianity to social problems and thus anticipated the "social gospel" of two generations later.

Not even in the iron age of early Puritanism, however, did religion wholly exclude other nonmaterial values; and from the Revolutionary period onward, evidences of a widespread and often intense interest in humane culture are so abundant and so obvious that it would be pointless to dwell long upon them. The feeling that the ultimate flowering of democratic life must be in personalities rather than possessions, the eager belief that American democracy would find its highest expression in the fine arts and the humanities—this hope, these standards of value have been continuously present in the national mind. To the Revolutionary generation, America was to become, in the words of John Trumbull, "the first in letters, as the first in arms." To less enthusiastic democrats, like Fenimore Cooper, democracy was at least to leave unhampered the sizeable minority who desired to obtain "manners, education, and refinement," and thereby to cultivate those "innocent tastes which are productive of high enjoyments." To Whittier, whose words have something of the significance of those of a natural bard or folk poet, the best achievements of New England had been not in the outward life but in the inward; her treasures were not material wealth, but the schoolhouse and her Pilgrim stock.

Such an emphasis on ideal values furnished a natural vantage-ground from which to survey and critically evaluate the workings of actual American society; and that vantage-ground, though occupied at one time or another by most major American authors, became in unusual degree the property of the Transcendentalists. To the Transcendentalist, indeed, the merely acquisitive life often seemed not only an inadequate one, but one actually hostile to the finest human possibilities.[31] In Emerson's judgment, the American Scholar, Man Thinking, must not only grow beyond but actively resist "the vulgar prosperity that retrogrades ever to barbarism;" the reformer, if he would improve the state, must strike deeper than some mere institution, such as slavery, and attack the fundamental evil of the tyranny of "Things." In Thoreau's opinion, possessions were, at their worst, a deadly enemy of the mind that would live "free and uncommitted," and, at their best, only instruments, not finalities. The well-known passages in *Walden* in which Thoreau evaluates the railway, the postal service, and the telegraph, not only are among the deepest-searching American judgments of the Machine, but anticipate by more than a decade Matthew Arnold's dictum that such things as wealth, coal, and "population" are only means, not ends; only the instrumentalities of complete living, not the elusive and immaterial life itself.

In brief, America had developed, by the middle of the nineteenth century, a clearly defined ideology, wide-ranging, inclusive, immensely dynamic. That American cultural pattern had, for its philosophic groundwork, the cosmic optimism of the eighteenth century, together with the associated ideas of progress and perfectibility. Its core-idea and motive was a democratic equalitarianism that had already found natural expression in a middle-class, agrarian way of life, and that was already reaching beyond merely political applications into economic. Its economic goal was a moderate, well-diffused prosperity, free from extremes of poverty and wealth. Its ultimate cultural aim was the flowering of American personality in religious experience, in the fine arts, and in the humanities.

With the coming of the Machine Age, that ideology, together with the antebellum pattern of actual life in which it

[31] But, as has been pointed out above, the feeling of an essential clash between acquisition and the humanities is a minority, not a majority, opinion.

had already been partially realized, was threatened with swift destruction.

III

But it is necessary to remember always that the industrial revolution in America was not wrought by the Machine alone, but by the Machine in combination with other factors. For industrialism developed in this country not just in and of itself, but as the tool and instrument of Capitalism—a capitalism, moreover, that was committed to a politico-economic scheme of free enterprise, competition, and *laissez-faire*. It developed, furthermore, in a nation whose rapid growth enormously stimulated production, and whose tradition of minimized government joined with the *laissez-faire* theory to preclude any state control of that production in the general interest. With us, therefore, the immediate net product of the Machine Age was an uncontrolled capitalistic industrialism, a gigantic, unpruned socio-economic growth that sprawled over the national life at random, and shed off indiscriminately both healthful and poisonous fruits.

The bourgeoning of industrialism in America is usually, and rightly, associated with the decade following the Civil War. Actually, of course, the plant had already been long in growth; the system had already, before the war, brought forth all the evils that were to cause dismay in sensitive minds later. The multiplication of corporate businesses, the influx of cheap immigrant labor, the low wage and the long workday, the rapid growth of cities, the springing-up of labor organizations—all these concomitants of industrialism had appeared before 1860.[32] But the industrial scale was relatively a small one; the tariff and banking policies of the government continued to foster an agrarian rather than an industrial state, the economic safety-valve of the frontier was still operative, and the coming-of-age of industrialism was correspondingly delayed.

[32] See, in this connection, Ernest Ludlow Bogart, *An Economic History of the United States*, pp. 244-52, and John Bach McMaster, *A History of the People of the United States*, VIII, 96-9.

Almost overnight, however, the exigencies of the Civil War virtually created a number of large-scale industries, and struck the restraints of a pro-agrarian policy from still others. The closing of Mississippi River traffic shunted Midwestern business eastward and stimulated the east-west railways; the shortage of civilian manpower hastened the mechanization of farming; the needs of the army called for tremendous developments in meat-packing, shoe-making, and other industries. Meanwhile, an entire reversal in governmental economic policy was taking place. The agrarian control of Congress had been destroyed by secession; the government, if it would win the war, had compelling need of the support of the northern industrial interest; and, in consequence, a series of laws were passed which committed the nation to an industrial policy. A national banking system was established; the immigration laws were relaxed to permit the wholesale importation of labor under contract; the tariff was more than doubled. These laws, moreover, continued in effect after the war, and joined with other forces, such as the continued rapid expansion of the country, to act as powerful stimulants to industrial growth.

The result was an all but incredible skyrocketing of industrial production. From the Civil War to 1900, capital invested in manufactures increased, at the most conservative estimate, five or six times over; the money value of factory products mounted with similar speed; and in certain basic industries, such as steel, the growth in productive output was immensely larger even than this. Correspondingly, the number of cities of 8,000 or more inhabitants at least trebled.[33] And yet mere statistics tell only the smallest part of the story. For they can only record, not really picture, the flinging out of great railroads across prairie and mountain, the bulking-up of great smoke-enveloped jungles of factories, the spawning of great industrial cities overrun with warehouses and railway yards and millionaires' palaces and unspeakable slums, the bewilderingly swift consolidation of businesses into great national

[33] These estimates are based on tables and expository passages in Bogart, *op. cit.*, pp. 381-2, 400-2.

monopolies. The rapidity of these changes long outstripped all efforts to keep mental pace with them; and even now, in the long perspective of another half-century, they appear "the most amazing economic transformation the world has ever known." [34]

The differences in volume between post-War and pre-War business were no more striking than the differences in kind. Until as late as 1865, business had mostly followed a distributist, small-unit pattern; by 1900 the pattern had shifted, in a number of important fields, to one of concentration or even monopoly. The natural search for an escape from the harsh pressures of competition, the largeness of the home market, the rapid introduction of machinery and the demands of the Machine process for quantity production—all these and other forces joined to compel rapid consolidation in such industries as iron and steel, farm implements, and oil. Moreover, concentration in any one major industry tended to force concentration in various dependent and subsidiary industries, as well as in associated financial groups, and thereby to constrain business as a whole into the moulds of standardization and large-scale production. Big Business came to set the pace and the pattern for all business; and this "extraordinary unification of the nation's economic life" became, in the judgment of a recent historian, the "most notable development" of our latter-nineteenth-century history.[35]

This tremendous growth and concentration were won only in the face of the suspicion and often the bitter hostility of the middle classes whose independence, whose very livelihood even, they threatened. They were won often by practices to which the entire middle-class theory of life was in deadly enmity. For, instead of the stability, prudence, and thrift demanded by the middle-class mind, the whole expansive force of the times—the headlong exploitation of the frontier, the mushrooming of huge corporate urban businesses, all the playing-for-high-stakes of the feverish business game—demanded a spirit of daring, speculation, and risk-taking. Often

[34] Burton J. Hendrick, *The Age of Big Business*, p. 3.
[35] Ida M. Tarbell, *The Nationalizing of Business*, pp. 266-7.

the wildest risks were justified, the longest chance-taking paid off handsomely; and the speculative spirit, in consequence, flooded into every area of American business, from the gathering-in of public lands to the investment policies of remote provincial banks.

In such an environment, all the abuses of an uncontrolled investment system multiplied with the speed of bacteria. Characteristic if not universal in the launching of new large-scale businesses were the practices of stock-watering, the issuing of bogus dividends to induce investment, and even the fleecing of a company by its own promoters. Perhaps the most notorious swindles took place in the semipublic utilities, and particularly in the various city traction systems. Promoters of the Metropolitan in New York, for instance, formed a construction company and overcharged the Metropolitan four hundred per cent, bought or leased other companies at similarly exorbitant rates, issued false dividends to run the stock up to two hundred sixty-nine, and quietly sold out. The company went bankrupt; the leading promoter left an estate of forty million, which included not one share of Metropolitan stock.[36]

The Gilded Age was prolific in scandals still more public and notorious than that of Metropolitan traction. The attempted gold corner in the Black Friday episode, the stock-manipulation and thug warfare carried on by Fisk and Gould in their manipulation of the Erie railway, the Credit Mobilier —these and a thousand other business piracies ran counter to the conviction if not always to the practice of the middle classes. But more dangerous to the middle-class regime than any isolated or sensational scandals was the unremitting pressure, legitimate and illegitimate, which Big Business exercised on all branches of government. By persuasion, economic pressure, intimidation, and straightout bribery, railways, utilities, and other businesses recurrently dominated city councils, state legislatures, and even the Congress and courts of the federal government. Thereby they wrested the State away from the service of the general welfare; they forced it

[36] Hendrick, *op. cit.*, pp. 140-7.

into the service of small and often wholly unscrupulous cliques of financiers and speculators; and in so doing they threatened the whole working effectiveness of democracy.

But the evils of speculation and political corruption, serious as they were, by no means exhausted the resources of business piracy. By many another practice, often legal enough but none the less opposed to the unwritten *mores* of the country, Big Business sought to beat the competitive game. Indeed, a business often *became* big by just such practices, throttling its competitors by the use of railway rate discriminations, secret rebates, local price wars, and "fighting brands" of goods, or perhaps overwhelming them by mere ingenuity of combination. And all the while a business was dealing thus with the middle class, it might also be clamping down on the proletariat, by breaking up labor unions and systematically evading social legislation.

By 1900, in short, Big Business, urged on by various pressures—technological, speculative, competitive—had smashed the unwritten middle-class code of free competition among equals; had rolled over it, indeed, with the indifferent ruthlessness of an avalanche. In the process, it had elevated the age-old petty chicaneries and treacheries of commerce into major social problems, and had unintentionally made the behavior of industry a main concern of the democratic state.

Other social ramifications of industrialism proved just as far-reaching. In some of its results—and in the critical literature of the times perhaps too little attention is paid to this fact—industrialism did tend to help realize the aims of democracy. It did increase man's power over nature; it did, among much of the population, help make the old democratic dream of material abundance and physical comfort come true. In that midwestern region where three out of every four farmers were putting in telephones, for instance, the conveniences of the Machine Age were obviously not *all* being monopolized by an exploiting class. But what the Machine offered with one hand it often struck away with the other. While it was padding the middle classes with physical comforts, it was also disrupting the entire social pattern they had laboriously laid out. For example, it was plainly transforming even the racial make-up of the republic. Industrialism demanded abundant cheap labor; that labor could be had only by means of the tidal waves of immigration that swept into the country at the rate of a half-million aliens each year; and those aliens were no longer mainly British or even Teutonic, but Slavic and Italian folk who stolidly resisted assimilation and herded into compact, foreign-language-speaking communities of their own.

The flooding-in of immigration hastened a change that industrialism must in any case have brought about—the rapid growth of cities. In 1860, about one-sixth of the population lived in cities of eight thousand people or more; by 1900, the proportion had risen to one-third—an exact doubling. And of the total population, in the latter year, perhaps as few as two-fifths were actually living on the farm. Even so, the numerical growth of the cities hardly kept pace with their growth in social and economic power. For the first time, the communities which Jefferson had looked on as pestilential to morals, health, and liberty were in position to dominate the American pattern of living.

Meanwhile there appeared, in those sprawling unorganized urban growths, many a symptom that justified Jefferson's most serious fears. To many a city dweller, the decent physical existence demanded by democracy was as unattainable as Utopia. Wages were too little, hours too long. In New York in 1890, cash-girls were receiving as little as $1.75 per week for work that sometimes dragged on to sixteen hours a day; and in the sweated industries, women's pay might fall as low as thirty cents daily, with the average at sixty cents.[37] Such pittances, while not typical of American wage levels, were sufficiently frequent; consequently whole masses of people, reduced to living upon them, herded together within noxious slums, found themselves wholly deprived of the usual physical decencies of life. Of the slums, and the lethargic squalor that enveloped them, nineteenth-century social workers have

[37] Jacob Riis, *How the Other Half Lives*, pp. 109, 236-7. See also, for corroboration, Bogart, *op. cit.*, p. 407.

left accounts that are hardly the more believable for being quite true. They tell of the crowding which sometimes thrust twelve or thirteen people for sleeping quarters into a small, lamplighted, unventilated room; they tell of the universal filth, the universal lack of sanitation; they tell of a death rate nearly forty per cent higher than that of the city population as a whole.[38] They sum up the entire picture in words like these:

Scene after scene is the same. Rags, dirt, filth, wretchedness, the same figures, the same faces, the same old story of one room unfit for habitation yet inhabited by a dozen people, the same complaint of a ruinous rent exacted by a merciless landlord, the same shameful neglect of all sanitary precautions; rotten floors, oozing walls, vermin everywhere, broken windows, crazy staircases. . . .[39]

And, with reference to the human material involved, they conclude that

a little more than half the population of New York are living under conditions which murder the children, degrade and ruin the young, corrupt every aspiration and stifle every hope.[40]

Obviously, the continued growth of such areas of life would destroy democracy, as democracy had been conceived of by a Jefferson, a Whittier, a Lincoln.

Equally menacing to democracy was the far-reaching, thoroughgoing realignment of social classes which was being wrought by industrialism. This is not to suggest, of course, that all of the bitter class struggles of the Gilded Age were altogether evoked by the Machine; for many of the older factional issues lived on—became, indeed, the foci of the most sensational political battles of the time. The issue of the tariff pitted producer against consumer, farmer against manufacturer, and fixed the line of conflict in at least one presidential election. The issue of the currency, arising as it did out of a deflationary policy that at least doubled the value of the

[38] Riis, *op. cit.*, pp. 19, 62.
[39] Mrs. Helen Campbell, *Darkness and Daylight*, p. 102.
[40] Mrs. Helen Campbell, *The Problem of the Poor*, p. 114.

dollar in thirty years and bore with frightful severity on the mortgage-burdened Midwestern farmer, pitted debtor and silver producer against creditor. The currency issue awakened perhaps the most numerous and heated debates of that generation; it erupted and re-erupted in Greenbackism, the Farmers' Alliance, Populism; it resounded in such rallying cries as "the crime against silver," "sixteen to one," and "cross of gold."—In all these struggles, however, the outcome rested usually in favor of the real or supposed interests of Big Business, sometimes at frightful emotional and social cost to other classes. The new industrial alignment into plutocracy, middle classes, and proletariat had already become, it appeared, the most fundamental class division of all.[41]

Of the three classes, it was the newest, the plutocracy, that controlled the economics of our first industrial era. That class was not large. Its nucleus consisted of a few great industrial and financial organizers—Rockefeller, Harriman, Carnegie— and of a somewhat larger number of manipulators and promoters on the order of the genially piratical traction magnate Charles T. Yerkes. Besides these, the plutocracy included an able group of high-salaried executives, and a miscellany of lesser *nouveaux riches,* investors, speculators, climbers, and general hangers-on. But for all the smallness of the class, the members of the plutocracy wielded a force which, within the limits where they chose to use it, and in spite of the heavy attacks it suffered, was all but absolute. Holding the compelling weapon of economic and financial power, they wrested into their favor all important decisions on the tariff, immigration, the currency, and even the disposal of the public lands, and at the same time either forestalled or evaded most legislation aimed at industrial control or social welfare. The plutocracy were, in short, the one class that could afford to be wholly satisfied with the American politico-economic set-up, because they got therefrom precisely what they wanted.

[41] The conventional Marxian division into capitalist, bourgeois, and proletarian classes is somewhat misleading when applied to nineteenth-century America. The word *bourgeois,* in particular, carries with it suggestions that are quite inapplicable to our agrarian-derived middle class.

Inescapably, the lot of the other two classes was less fortunate. Labor had to deal on the one hand with a stronger employing unit, and on the other with the competitive torrent of immigration. The middle-class merchant or small manufacturer found himself under the dominance of the trust; the farmer was pulled into the industrial marketing cycle and there caught between the two millstones of mortgage and deflation. Inevitably, both labor and the middle classes suffered, and their suffering was rendered the more acute by two major financial panics that struck within twenty years, bringing with them their usual accompaniments of widespread anxiety, insecurity, and disorganization.[42]

Faced with these conditions, Labor adopted, partially and under great difficulties, the only method by which it might ever expect to cope with the plutocracy—organization. Existing unions were enlarged, others were created. The vaguely altruistic Knights of Labor, founded in 1869, gained a national and largely sympathetic hearing for its cause; the American Federation of Labor, founded in 1886 with a more limited and definite program, was perhaps more practically effective. In practices, the labor organizations ranged all the way from orderly negotiation to outright crime. Characteristically, they used the strike, and used it, quite literally, in tens of thousands of industrial clashes, of which the violent railway strikes of 1877, the Homestead Steel strike of 1892, and the Pullman strike of 1894 were only the most notorious.[43] Generally associated in the public mind with labor troubles were, moreover, such events as the sensational Haymarket Riot of Chicago, the first important outbreak in America of proletarian revolutionary violence.

Faced with many of the same dangers that beset Labor, the middle classes found it hard to decide whether Labor was

[42] See, in this connection, the comprehensive and striking summary of the causes of industrial unrest, 1870-1900, in Mark Sullivan, *Our Times*, I, 149.

[43] The average yearly number of strikes from 1886 to 1894 was nearly six thousand. See the table in Frank J. Sullivan's chapter, "Twenty Years of Strikes and Lockouts," in Robert Marion Lafollette (Ed.), *The Making of America*, VIII, 148-51.

their enemy or ally; and, as Labor appeared to them now a
victim of society, now a violent disturber of the peace, their
attitude varied from sympathy to outspoken opposition. But
toward the Plutocracy, and toward the entire pattern of life
the Plutocracy stood for, middle-class opinion showed no
such vacillation. Against the Plutocratic power, the middle
classes, urged on by their emotional revulsion against social
evils like the slum, urged on by the defeats they had suffered
in the competitive struggle, urged on sometimes by the harsh
pressures of actual poverty, waged consistent and powerful
warfare.[44]

In that warfare, one plain and urgent task was that of alleviating the worst evils of industrialism, of giving immediate
aid to suffering people of the submerged classes. In part, the
humanitarianism of the middle classes expressed itself in voluntary charity, which now had not only to be done, but to
be systematically organized on a scale the country had not
previously known. In part, it expressed itself in the building
up in tenement areas of religious centers like the Bowery
Mission of Jerry McAuley, and of settlement houses like the
Neighborhood Guild of New York. In part, it fixed attention
on a series of exposures of how the "Other Half" lived, and
provided such vigorous efforts at slum clearance as those recorded in Jacob Riis's *A Ten Year's War* (1900). And in part
the same humanitarian spirit led to the organization of nuclei
of reform like the anti-poverty clubs and the Christian Socialist groups, whose common aim it was to build up the social
consciousness, to strengthen the ethical motives, that might
lead to ultimate social justice.

Meanwhile, the middle classes also attacked what many
of them regarded as the very core and central source of
America's economic ills—the unfair competition, the political
corruption, the general exploitation practiced by Big Busi-

---

[44] This is not to claim, of course, that the middle classes were quite
clear, deliberate, and purposeful in the conflict. Allowance must be
made for their very gradual awakening to the situation, for a good deal
of fumbling in the discovery of the real issues at stake, and for the
natural limitations of human intelligence.

ness. They attempted, that is, to impose on business enough governmental control to insure at least a certain amount of fair play in the competitive game, at least a certain amount of consideration for the general welfare. Consequently, in state after state, legislation appeared which was aimed at the regulation of hours and working conditions [45] or at the control of railways and trusts. Moreover, with the passage of the Interstate Commerce Act and the Sherman Anti-Trust Act, the Federal government was made—theoretically at least—an agency for the control of railway and trust on a national scale. All this while, the recapture for the people of the agencies of government themselves was the objective of still other efforts—campaigns for the purification of politics, agitations in behalf of the initiative and referendum, proposals for the direct election of United States senators. And back of these political struggles lay the massive motivating force of widespread popular indignation over hard times and social injustice, of rousing agitations that tossed up slogans like Mary Ellen Lease's "less corn and more hell," of great popular organizations such as the Grange and the Farmers' Alliance. Among these various movements, the Populist Party of 1892 and the Populist-Democratic fusion of 1896 most successfully welded into a single program all the social objectives aimed at by the militant middle classes.

The social history of the Gilded Age is largely, in short, a story of class conflict between various middle-class groups and the plutocracy. It is a story of the sudden bourgeoning of a capitalistic industrialism which challenged the cultural dominance of our agrarian-nurtured, democratic middle classes. It is a story of the strenuous efforts of the middle classes to meet that challenge and to assimilate into their established culture the new, disruptive forces loosed by the Machine. The first large phase of that class struggle came to an end in the latter nineties with the defeat of the Populist-Democratic coalition led by Bryan, the outbreak of the Spanish-American war, and the temporary diversion of the national interest into other channels than that of economic

[45] In this legislation, Labor was, of course, also influential.

reform. The temporary lull in social conflict found the plutocracy with its immediate aims wholly realized. Its great fortunes were established; its command over the national economy had grown all but absolute; the potentially restraining
arm of the federal government was still held off.

On the other hand, the middle classes still held an economic
power which, taken in the aggregate, was considerable. More
important, they still held virtually complete control of the
nation's cultural tradition and of its social ideology, together
with all the literary and journalistic resources needful to dis-
seminate those ideas. Furthermore, in the course of their life-
or-death struggle to control and assimilate the new forces that
threatened to engulf them, they had been driven to apply to
the nascent Machine society the old ideals and social standards of our agrarian democracy, and thereby both to achieve
and to put on composite record a strikingly consistent *critique*
of capitalistic industrialism.

IV

That American *critique* of industrialism overflowed into
many channels besides the one—prose fiction—which is to be
fully charted in the following pages. Occasionally it lapped
over into *belles lettres*—into poetry and the literary essay. For
the pre-Civil-War generation of romantic poets mostly lived
on into the post-Civil-War world, where the ills of industrialism invited the same reforming zeal, the same humanitarian
fervor, which these poets had formerly brought to bear on
the ills of slavery. They could not, to be sure, wholly respond
to that invitation; they had neither the reserves of energy,
nor the steadily intense awareness of new conditions, which
would have been needful in a second great crusade. But some
such energy, some such awareness they did have. Sometimes
their romantic idealism did clash with the raw injustices of
the Machine Age, and out of the friction was born a spark
of poetry.

For example, in 1877, the year of the first great American
railway strikes, Whittier spoke out briefly but clearly on the

conflict between Labor and Capital. In "The Problem," he preaches, with characteristic simplicity and directness, a plain gospel of fair dealing, justice, and consideration on the part of both employer and employee:

Solution is there none
Save in the Golden Rule of Christ alone.

Longfellow, though he had no message so forthright as Whittier's, still owned the gentle humanitarianism with which he had suffused his antislavery poems of the forties; and in "The Challenge" he invested it with a new object of pity, the "starving, numberless army" of the slums. And Lowell, although his youthful radicalisms were long since past, nevertheless denounced the "parasitic greed" of the Reconstruction era, observed with regret the growth of a "proletary" population, and pointed out the need for mitigating the evils that flowed from vast inequalities in wealth.[46]

On occasion, too, a younger generation of romantic poets spoke with equal disfavor of the social fruitage of capitalistic industrialism. Lanier, an ideal Southern patrician in his contempt for commerce, wrote into his novel, *Tiger-Lilies* (1867), a story of the corruption of character by "Trade," and planned to include in the unfinished *Jacquerie* a treatment of the overthrow of medieval chivalry by capitalism. In "The Symphony," he denounced the heartlessness of Trade, touched ironically on the idea that economic science is only a rationalization of injustice, and called for a return to the immaterial values of chivalric love, the enjoyment of Nature, the enjoyment of Art, and, above all, Christian kindness:—"The Time needs heart—'tis tired of head." [47] Somewhat later, Edwin Markham wrote, in "The Man with the

[46] See also, in regard to the carry-over of romantic idealism from the slavery controversy to the treatment of industrialism, Vernon Louis Parrington's discussion of Wendell Phillips in *The Beginnings of Critical Realism in America*, pp. 140-7.

[47] A suggestive comparison with Lanier is afforded by Lafcadio Hearn's reaction against Western—that is, capitalistic—civilization. See the provocative discussion of Hearn in Granville Hicks, *The Great Tradition*, pp. 148-52.

Hoe," a tremendous indictment of social injustice that had obvious applications to the contemporary, capitalistic world. In "The Brute," William Vaughn Moody wrote a parable on the need for social control of the Machine; and in "Gloucester Moors" he gave more powerful voice to the humanitarian sentiment of Longfellow's "The Challenge."

Of all our nineteenth-century poets, however, it was Whitman who first became really aware of the economic practices of the Gilded Age, who reacted against them most vigorously, and who voiced the critical ideas that were to become most typically American.[48] At no time, then or later, did Whitman ever pronounce against the Machine *per se*. In the "labor of engines" as well as that of trades, in the factory as well as the craftsman's shop, he found "developments" and "eternal meanings"; the "fierce-throated beauty" of a locomotive, he celebrated equally with that of Blue Ontario's shore. Even in the midst of the powerful critical blasts of *Democratic Vistas*, he continued to celebrate the mechanical progress and the "business materialism" of "these states." The thing he did object to, the thing he would if possible have destroyed wholly, was the national absorption in a tawdry struggle for wealth which had already honeycombed the social fabric with corruption, which estopped the growth of fine personalities, which threatened to make of America's most prosperous classes only "a mob of fashionably dressed vulgarians."

The depravity of the business classes of our country is not less than has been supposed, but infinitely greater. The official services of America, national, state, and municipal, in all their branches and departments, except the judiciary, are saturated in corruption, bribery, falsehood, maladministration; and the judiciary is tainted.

As a cure for "these lamentable conditions," Whitman called for a new American literature, vigorous enough to reawaken in Americans "the breath recuperative of sane and heroic life." And in sane and heroic life, as he understood it, the best good was identical with the total, not partial, growth of the

[48] Compare with Whitman's ideas those characteristic of the entire movement here treated, as summarized below, pp. 323-31.

individual personality. *Getting* and *having* were of far less importance than *being;* the material, however important in itself, was to be held rigidly subordinate to the spiritual. "As fuel to flame, and flame to the heavens, so must wealth, science, materialism—even this democracy of which we make so much—unerringly feed the highest mind, the soul."

V

But the belletristic passages in Lanier and Moody and Whitman, however significant in themselves, suggest only faintly the tremendous volume of economic discussion that went on during the Gilded Age. During that entire period, American thought on economics was active and vigorous; and economic treatises, American and British, circulated in large numbers. An exhaustive list of titles of these polemic writings, including articles and editorials as well as books, would no doubt extend to quite literally tens of thousands of entries. Obviously, no list of this sort exists. Nevertheless, by means of even a general and cursory survey some certainties about those voluminous discussions can be reached; and among those certainties none are more immediately clear than the intense interest taken in economics by the middle classes, and the dominance of the middle classes in the critical thought of the times.

The proletariat and the plutocracy were not, of course, wholly without spokesmen. The former were represented, for example, by their own gifted organizer, Terence V. Powderly, in *Thirty Years of Labor* (1889), and by the theorist Laurence Gronlund, whose *The Coöperative Commonwealth* (1884) envisages the extinction of the middle class and the creation, along Marxian lines, of a proletarian state.[49] The latter, the plutocracy, were somewhat unintentionally represented by Andrew Carnegie in *Triumphant Democracy* (1885). *Triumphant Democracy,* although designed to impress on the British the value of American institutions, is actually not a defense of popular government so much as a

[49] *The Coöperative Commonwealth,* pp. 70-6.

paean of the splendid material progress wrought by free capitalistic enterprise:

The old nations of the earth creep on at a snail's pace; the Republic thunders past with the rush of the express. The United States, the growth of a single century, has already reached the foremost rank among nations, and is destined soon to outdistance all others in the race. In population, in wealth, in annual savings, and in public credit; in freedom from debt, in agriculture, and in manufactures, America already leads the civilized world.[50]

But definitely proletarian or definitely plutocratic writing was equally the exception, not the rule. The great mass of economic discussion available to American readers in the seventies, eighties, and nineties was a middle-class discussion, which gave voice to ideas that might appeal to an agrarian, professional, or small-capitalist audience. Within the mental range of this one class there existed, however, an astonishing variety of viewpoints and literary types:—heavy treatises of economic theory, serious textbooks, popularizations, partisan arguments, journalistic sketches of proletarian life, pamphlets by crackpot reformers. The same current of economic discussion embraces, near opposite shores, General Francis A. Walker's textbook, *Political Economy* (1883) and Frank Rosewater's polemic, *No More Free Rides on This Jackass, or Protection Forever and Everywhere* (1882).

Even the theoretical, quasi-scientific economic treatises that circulated in the post-Civil-War United States are surprisingly numerous, surprisingly varied. Their range of interest, their occasional turn toward popularization, and something even of their usual approach to economics are suggested by such representative titles as Edward Atkinson's *The Distribution of Products* or *The Mechanism and Metaphysics of Exchange* (1885); Fred B. Hawley's *Capital and Population* (1882); L. D. Mason and John J. Labor's *The Primer of Political Economy; in Sixteen Definitions and Forty Propositions* (1875); J. E. Thorold Rogers' edition of Adam Smith's *The Wealth of Nations* (1870); J. C. Shadwell's *Politi-*

[50] *Triumphant Democracy*, p. 1.

cal Economy for the People (1880); Robert H. Smith's *The Science of Business, a Study of the Principles Controlling the Laws of Social Exchange* (1885); and Francis A. Walker's *The Wages Question* (1876).

Evidently, informed Americans of the period were quite generally familiar with the methods of the classical economists, but quite unwilling to rest satisfied in their conclusions. On the one hand, the ideas of Adam Smith, Malthus, Ricardo, and Mill were in general circulation; the concepts of *laissez-faire*, of the pressure of population on subsistence, of economic rent, and of the wages fund were current intellectual coinage. On the other, sharp criticism of these same ideas circulated with equal freedom. Before the Civil War, Henry C. Carey had already opposed Malthus's theory of population; in the seventies, Francis Walker attacked the wages-fund theory. In the eighties, Richard T. Ely pointed out that much of the work of Smith and Ricardo and even Mill, written as it was before the maturity of the industrial revolution, was already antiquated. Instead of the free competition envisaged by the classical economists, Ely maintained, there had developed a concentration of capital which tended toward monopoly and "economic feudalism," and which therefore made it necessary to obtain by artificial means such alleviations as better housing for the poor and a larger relative return for labor.

Many as were these examinations of economic theory, they were far outnumbered by works devoted to more immediately practical issues. After all, the concept of marginal utility might very well seem somewhat thin and far away to a people faced with, let us say, the chaotic violence of the great railway strikes of seventy-seven. Among contemporary economic discussions, the immediate, urgent issue of class struggle echoes through such titles as Albert O. Dulles's *The Conflict between Capital and Labor* (1876), Simon Newcomb's *A Plain Man's Talk on the Labor Question* (1886), and E. M. Chamberlin's account of the organization of labor unions in *The Sovereigns of Industry* (1887). The issue of class conflict reaches also, though indirectly, into the many treatises whose objective is to suggest some amelioration of social evils: for example, Charles M. Richardson's *Large Fortunes, or Christianity and the Labor Problem* (1888), or H. D. Lloyd's *Labour Copartnership* (1898), or Nicholas P. Gilman's *Profit-Sharing between Employer and Employee; a Study in the Evolution of the Wages System* (1889). Still more voluminous, apparently, is the literature on political and party questions like the tariff, railways, trusts, currency, and the corruption of the government by business interests. Within even this one area of writing there is, moreover, immense variety, the range including F. W. Taussig's dignified *History of the Tariff* (1885), H. D. Lloyd's impressive exposure of the tactics of Standard Oil in *Wealth against Commonwealth* (1894), and W. H. Harvey's popular pedagogy in *Coin's Financial School* (1894).

Out of the awakening of the national mind to the existence of the slum grew another clearly defined body of literature— a literature devoted partly to a muckraking exposure of social evils, partly to discussion of the improvement of tenement housing and the conduct of organized charity. An interest that was maintained steadily throughout that entire generation speaks in the titles of Charles L. Brace's *The Dangerous Classes of New York, and Twenty Years' Work Among Them* (1872) and the Charity Organization Society of New York's *Handbook for Friendly Visitors among the Poor* (1883). An immensely quickened interest, a far deeper concern, characteristic of the latter eighties and early nineties, speaks in Jacob Riis's *How the Other Half Lives* (1890). A certain romantic curiosity about the slums, which developed alongside much genuine humanitarianism, and which presently made of the picturesqueness of low life a kind of literary fad, appears in A. F. Sanborn's *Moody's Lodging House and Other Tenement Sketches* (1895).

Reconstructive programs outlined in the great mass of anti-poverty literature are, on the whole, surprisingly mild, comprising as they do only housing reform, instruction in crafts and home economics, and various other alleviations. But proposals for the radical and thoroughgoing reorganization of society were by no means lacking. The genuine economic radicalisms of the Gilded Age followed one or the other of the two routes—individualism and collectivism—charted by the two most widely read advocates of social change, Henry George and Edward Bellamy. Henry George's attack on land-monopoly through the proposal of the Single Tax in *Progress and Poverty* (1879, '80), provoked a debate which reverberated throughout the entire generation, producing such tracts as W. A. Phillips' *Labor, Land, and Law, a Search for the Missing Wealth of the Working Poor* (1889) and M. W. Mcagher's *Alluring Absurdities, Fallacies of Henry George* (1889). The socialism of Bellamy's *Looking Backward* (1888), although it awakened a discussion only less universal than did George's anti-monopoly crusade, was by no means so original. From Charles Nordhoff's *Communistic Societies in the United States . . . their Religious Creeds, Social Practices, Numbers, Industries, and Present Condition* (1875), from Richard T. Ely's *French and German Socialism in Modern Times* (1883), from Laurence Gronlund's *The Coöperative Commonwealth* (1884), and from still other sources, readers could, prior to the publication of *Looking Backward,* have come to know of several types of socialistic theory and practice.

The foregoing are only a few titles from the hundreds of book-length treatises on economics which were circulated in the United States between the Civil War and 1900. Yet not even in all these hundreds of volumes is the recorded American *critique* of industrialism fully comprised. Nationwide, urgent, intense in its interest, the economic debate found many and varied avenues of expression: magazine articles, personal letters, political speeches, editorials published in many a city and country newspaper, *obiter dicta* scattered through many a work of autobiography and reminiscence. Yet even a brief glance over a few of these critical materials should not be without value. It should go far toward dispelling the myth of the complacency of the Gilded Age. It should go far toward suggesting, instead, the volume, the complexity, the sheer energy of the American critical response to indus-

trialism. It should indicate that the economic fiction which is
the main subject of the following pages is only one phase of a
more inclusive movement of ideas, only one province of a
larger area of intellectual history, much of which has yet to be
accurately charted.

VI

Of the numerous American critics of the economic order,
the one who most nearly summed up within himself the controlling ideas of the whole movement was, no doubt, the
philosopher, economist, and protagonist of the Single Tax,
Henry George. But the significance of Henry George—it must
at once be added—is not to be found in his devotion to the
Single-Tax panacea. It is to be found, instead, in his general
and underlying social philosophy, that sturdy trunk out of
which the Single-Tax proposal grew as an eccentric though
favored bough. Product of the democratic mass, identified
until middle life with the everyday, workaday American
world, George intuitively felt and thought along the same
channels as did other Americans. But he felt more keenly,
and thought more systematically. Because his mind was
larger than the minds of his contemporaries, it gathered into
the unity of his recorded work many concepts that lie scattered piecemeal among those others. And because that mind
was clearer, more precise, and more analytical, it often made
explicit and orderly the relationships which others only
fumbled at, or implied, or took for granted. And therefore—
because George is at the same time great and representative
—his writing discloses with unique clarity the cultural sources
of our *critique* of industrialism, the intimate relationship
which knits together our pre-Civil-War and post-Civil-War
culture, and the unbroken continuity in our tradition which
links the era of the Revolution with the era of the Populist
Party.

The mind of Henry George was essentially a product of
our antebellum culture—of that romantic, expansive, energetic, and fluid era which Lewis Mumford has called the

Golden Day. As intimately as a Whitman, George knew both the daily life and the great controlling ideas of that time. Its moral earnestness came to him naturally through the disciplines which his father, a strict churchman, maintained in his childhood home at Philadelphia. The texture of its daily work-world, the feel of "the labor of engines and trades," came to him through the *wanderjähre* during which he worked as printer's devil, ordinary seaman, storekeeper, and California goldseeker. It was in California, whither he had been driven by the hard times of fifty-seven, that he first found a truly congenial profession; and it was there, also, that his struggles with the Western Union and the Associated Press first brought home to him the menacing power of monopoly.[51]

There, too, at times, he knew poverty—undeserved and desperate poverty. At the time of the birth of his second child, when there was no food in his house, only a gift of five dollars, begged from the first man he chanced upon in the street, withheld him from committing a robbery.[52] Moreover, the deprivation he found so unbearable appeared—stern and tragic fact—to be not the occasional, but the continuous, the inescapable condition of life for large masses of the population. America's magnificent material progress, as George observed during a memorable journey back East in 1868-9, appeared only to deepen the hopeless squalor in which the lowest classes were submerged. To ignore these evils, or stolidly to take them for granted, as others were doing, was to him impossible. The common sufferings of humanity were not common to him, but particular. And so, moved by his own experience, by his general awareness of life, and by a kind of Christian compassion, he came finally to a solemn resolution to search out the cause and the cure of poverty.[53]

The direction of that search was being determined, all this

[51] Henry George, Jr., *The Life of Henry George*, pp. 5, 19, 42, 51-2 77-8, 183; G. R. Geiger, *The Philosophy of Henry George*, pp. 23-30, 38-9.

[52] George's own testimony. See Henry George, Jr., *op. cit.*, p. 148, and G. R. Geiger, *op. cit.*, p. 36.

[53] Henry George, Jr., *op. cit.*, p. 191; G. R. Geiger, *op. cit.*, pp. 41-2.

while, by several forces, not the least of which was his continued experience with the social order in California. For in California George had observed almost the entire process of frontier settlement—the entire transition of mankind from a "state of nature" to that of government under a social compact. He had once talked, for example, with an old miner, who had suggested to him that, as settlement thickened, the high wages then paid to laborers would necessarily decline. He had seen, and was still seeing, how rapidly the public domain was being squandered in prodigal gifts to railways, or allowed to fall in huge blocks into the hands of speculators who never lifted a finger to bring it into cultivation. And when, finally, a popular agitation against land-monopoly arose, George, as editor and speaker, took a conspicuous part in the movement.[54]

George's interpretation of these frontier experiences was being controlled, all this while, by the dominant ideology of an earlier, a pre-Civil-War America, which in his youth he had assimilated as naturally as he had breathed the common air. Deep within the subsoil of his philosophy, heritage from another generation, lay still the cosmic optimism of the Enlightenment, instructing him, as it had instructed a Paine or a Shelley, that the World-Order is kindly disposed toward reasoning men, that by the reason human life may be adjusted to an orderly regimen of beneficent natural law, that evil is superficial and curable, and that the human race may therefore look forward to a future of infinite progress. George could feel, therefore, that the misery and vice of the slums, against which he had resolved to wage continuous war, were not attributable to "the laws of the All-Wise and All-Beneficent," but only to "the short-sighted and selfish enactments of men." And he could derive even from Political Economy, at a time when that study was still referred to as the dismal science, the lesson that most of the bad and the perplexing in our social conditions "grows simply from our ignorance of law," and the realization of how much "better and happier

[54] Henry George, Jr., *op. cit.*, pp. 80, 210; Geiger *op. cit.*, pp. 81-2, 224.

men might make the life of man." [55] Upon vigorous and rational efforts to improve the human lot there would rest, it appeared, the approving smile of the Cosmos itself.

And just as George inherited the optimism of an earlier time, so he inherited its democratic humanitarianism. Notwithstanding his indifference toward the Civil War—an indifference common enough among Californians—George had been consistently sympathetic with the great expression of pre-Civil-War humanitarianism, the anti-slavery movement. To him, however, the destruction of Negro slavery closed only a single battle in the march of humanitarianism, not the entire campaign. In the victorious North there had arisen a slavery which, though less gross in appearance than chattel slavery, was not less cruel:

What is the difference, whether my body is legally held by another, or whether he legally holds that by which alone I can live? Hunger is as cruel as the lash. The essence of slavery consists in taking from a man all the fruits of his labor except a bare living, and of how many thousands miscalled free is this the lot? Where wealth most abounds there are classes with whom the average plantation negro would have lost in comfort by exchanging.[56]

Whatever humanitarian sympathy had been extended to the Negro slave might now be extended as justly to the wage-slaves of the Northern factories. As the ideals of democracy had been expressed in the destruction of Negro slavery, so they must be realized in the destruction of wage slavery and the setting-up in its place of a regimen of social justice.[57]

Not only in his optimistic faith in progress, not only in his humanitarianism, was George a child of our pre-Civil-War culture, but also in his philosophy of government.

[55] Henry George, *Progress and Poverty*, in George's collected *Works* (New York, 1898), I, 285. See also "The Study of Political Economy," a lecture delivered at the University of California, March 9, 1877, *Works*, IX, 153.

[56] Henry George, a Fourth of July Oration, delivered at San Francisco in 1877. *Works*, IX, 174.

[57] See, in this connection, besides the reference above, the article "Slavery and Slavery" in *Social Problems*. *Works*, III, 148-60; also Henry George, Jr., *op. cit.*, p. 267.

Within the field of political theory proper, he accepted a Jeffersonian democracy [58] which gave sanction to his intuitive sympathy with the masses, taught him the old democratic ideal of the minimized state,[59] and gave him as the groundwork of his entire governmental philosophy the doctrine of natural rights. In dealing with the theory of natural rights, George saw clearly—as indeed Jefferson had seen before him —that natural rights cannot be upheld on the fragile support of politics alone, but must be rested on the solid foundation of economic well-being. Since neither life, nor liberty, nor the pursuit of happiness can be maintained without a certain minimum of material wealth, the doctrine of natural rights necessitates, as its support and corollary, the doctrine of the security of property. But property is, after all, only labor embodied in tangible form; and labor cannot possibly be carried on without access to natural resources—that is, to land. And therefore, from the postulate of a natural right to life, liberty, and the pursuit of happiness, both Jefferson and George are led, inescapably, to the postulate of a natural right in land. After speaking of man's right to the product of his own labor, George, for instance, continues as follows:

But man has also another right, declared by the fact of his existence —the right to the use of so much of the free gifts of nature as may be necessary to supply all the wants of that existence, and as he may use without interfering with the equal rights of anyone else, and to this he has a title as against all the world.

This right is natural; it cannot be alienated. It is the free gift of his Creator to every man that comes into the world—a right as sacred, as indefeasible as his right to life itself.[60]

[58] See, in this connection, G. R. Geiger's statement that George was, in general, familiar and sympathetic with the doctrine of the Revolutionary thinkers, and that Jefferson, in particular, was his "recognized idol" (*Op. cit.*, pp. 190-1). See also George's claim, in a speech delivered at Cooper Union during the Pullman strike, that his democracy was "the democracy of Thomas Jefferson" (*Works*, IX, 336).

[59] See his "Fourth of July Oration" of 1877, *Works*, IX, 172.

[60] Henry George, *Our Land and Land Policy*, p. 85. See, for other statements of the sphere of natural rights in economics, George's "Fourth of July Oration" of 1877, *Works*, IX, 173, and "The Rights of Man," *Social Problems, Works*, III, 92-104.

In the maintaining of this inalienable right in land, the United States had been, during its first century of existence, peculiarly fortunate; for, while that right had been neglected by the government, it had been upheld by the natural effects of an open frontier:

We have hitherto had an advantage over older nations which we can hardly overestimate. It has been our public domain, our background of unfenced land, that made our social conditions better than those of Europe; that relieved the labour market and maintained wages; that kept open a door of escape from the increasing pressure in older sections, and acting and reacting in many ways on our national character, gave it freedom and independence, elasticity and hope.[61]

When George had equipped himself with the Jeffersonian idea of a natural right in land, when he had become deeply concerned over the cause and cure of poverty, when he had observed that the growth of socially submerged classes accompanied the decline of the public domain, he had come upon the very threshold of his great social discovery. His one final step—outcome of the fusion of these three trends of thought—came at some time during the latter eighteen-sixties. The major cause of poverty, he concluded, is a monopoly which deprives the majority of people of the free use of land, and enables the few to attach, in the form of rent, the earnings of the many. To destroy that monopoly, by taxation, would be to destroy poverty too.

George's first important effort to propagandize his new doctrine was the treatise of California land tenure entitled *Our Land and Land Policy* (1871).[62] Within this early pamphlet exist, in summary, all of George's significant ideas. Upon even so young a state as California, George points out, the evil of land-monopoly has already become fixed. The public domain, potentially the home of a prosperous agrarian people

[61] The "Fourth of July Oration," *Works*, IX, 168.

[62] George had approached some of the ideas of *Our Land and Land Policy* in such earlier works as the article "What the Railroad Will Bring Us," written in 1868 for the *Overland* magazine. See the quotation in Henry George, Jr., *op. cit.*, p. 178.

dwelling upon moderate-sized farms,[63] has already passed into the hands of a small, favored, exploitive class, many of whose estates are so vast that across them (as George quaintly words it) a strong horse cannot gallop in a day. The ownership of these great estates is, of course, only a means of attaching, through rent and unearned increment, the earnings of other people. The immediate effects are the relative enrichment of the owners, and the impoverishment of all others. The remoter effects are the concentration of capital within a few hands, the reduction of wages, the decline of independence of thought and action, and, presently, the creation of widely, permanently separated classes of rich and poor.[64] This cleavage of classes is bound to spell, in time, the doom of democracy; for political power derives from economic power, and the actual control of the state will inevitably pass from the impoverished many to the wealthy and dominant few. Under their regime, the forms of popular government may be preserved; but "the real government which clothes itself with these forms, as if in mockery, will be many degrees worse than an avowed and intelligent despotism." [65]

Nevertheless, by a clear, simple course of action on the part of the state, this disaster to democracy may be averted. The entire destruction of land-monopoly is both ethical and practical. It is ethical because land-monopoly is founded on injustice, the injustice of denying to men their natural right to the use of the earth. It is ethical because, also, the value of land in a civilized commonwealth is not the product of any individual but of society itself; [66] for that value hinges on the total productive power of a civilized people, most of which arises from coöperation rather than from individual effort. Justly, therefore, the state may take back for the people

[63] George agrees with Jefferson, of course, in his preference for what has come to be called an "agrarian-distributist" economy.

[64] Henry George, *Our Land and Land Policy*, pp. 14, 20 ff., 33-7, 69.

[65] *Ibid.*, p. 97.

[66] George's thought here parallels the argument of Thomas Paine in *Agrarian Justice*, as has been observed by G. R. Geiger, *op. cit.*, p. 189. Although it is entirely possible that George had read Paine's treatise, no adequate evidence to that effect is at hand.

at large that which the people themselves have created. It may do so by the simple, practical device of levying upon land a tax sufficient to make speculative holdings unprofitable and thus to destroy any monopolistic tendencies in land tenure.[67] This is, in essentials, the Single-Tax program which was later to awaken an all but world-wide controversy.[68]

But that controversy was still a decade in the future. *Our Land and Land Policy,* however important its thesis, however original and cogent its reasoning, was after all a limited work, hardly more ambitious in scope than a seventeenth-century controversial pamphlet; and it failed of any large audience. To awaken widespread debate over the deeply-rooted land-tenure customs of a whole people, some more ambitious work, built along larger and more powerful lines, would, George realized, be needed. And in this larger work, his land-tenure program, to which he was coming to give an almost religious devotion, must rest not only on the sanctions of politics and ethics, but also upon those of economic science. Already interested in the study of economics, George now made it his task to master the content and method of the classical economists from Smith through Mill.

The matrix of George's thinking was, however, already fixed. Whatever economic studies he might undertake must inevitably be absorbed into that closely integrated philosophy, traditionally American and democratic, which already dominated his mind. The thought-methods of the classical economists—their elaborate analyses, comparisons, and simplifications, along with the technical vocabulary that passed among them as current coinage—all these came to flow from the mind of George as naturally as they had from that of Ricardo, but with a difference. In the classical economy, that method, that vocabulary had commonly been used in the support of concepts such as the wages-fund theory or Mal-

[67] Henry George, *Our Land and Land Policy,* pp. 104-7.

[68] George's later pronouncements in *Progress and Poverty* are, of course, more precise in expressing his intention to limit all taxation to this one form, and to take by taxation *all* the rent-value inherent in the land itself or in its situation, as distinguished from the value of the improvements wrought by the owner's labor.

thus' theory of population, which made any general improvement in the economic condition of the masses appear impossible. In George, the same vocabulary, the same method, are
used to destroy these very theories and thus to smash the
obstacles which economics had thrust athwart the high
American hope of a widely diffused material welfare. Understood in this perspective, George's magnificent argument
in *Progress and Poverty* takes on the character of an elaborate
rationalization, in which the entire system of classical economy is wrested from its former allegiance to English capitalism, and is devoted, instead, to that American, that democratic ideology which looks toward the economic well-being
of the whole populace.

To speak of *Progress and Poverty* as a rationalization is not
to belittle it; for even rationalization has its undoubted uses,
and the book is, after all, much more than that. It is, and has
been continuously, an immense intellectual force. As one advances, page by page, through its perfectly turned analyses,
the impression steadily deepens that George is one of the
most singularly persuasive, one of the most impressively convincing, of writers. He has lucidity, earnestness, imagination.
He is master of a logic so closely integrated that, once his
premise of natural rights is admitted, it seems invulnerable.
Above all, he achieves, in the marshalling of his multitudinous materials, a classic symmetry which gives to his work
an effect of cumulative power. His first task is, of course, to
impress on his readers, as powerfully as possible, the shock-
ing anomaly of want in the midst of wealth, and, by consequence, the need for his own inquiry into the cause and cure
of poverty. His next task, a negative one, is to destroy the
two economic doctrines which had hitherto been used as
weapons to parry every important demand for reform—the
wages-fund theory and the Malthusian theory of population.
Having disposed of these theories, George enters next an
analysis of the factors in the creation and disposal of wealth.
In this analysis, his intention is to show that there is no real
conflict of interest between capital and labor; that there is,
however, a fundamental conflict between labor and capital

on the one hand and land-monopoly on the other; that the demands of wages and interest are in fundamental conflict with the demands of economic rent; and that the last of these —economic rent—is the principal device by which one class may exploit another and therefore the cause of the anomaly of poverty in the midst of progress.

To destroy poverty, then, George's argument continues, it is necessary to destroy monopoly in land. To destroy monopoly in land, it is necessary to confiscate economic rent. To confiscate rent, it is necessary only to levy upon land a Single Tax sufficient to take back to Society all income which flows from the land itself, as distinguished from the user's own labor or improvements. This done, speculation and exploitation will cease. Once more, as in the elder days of limitless free land, the resources of the earth will be available to every human being. The immediate effect will be to release the entire productive energies of the people, to create a broadly diffused prosperity—in short, to abolish poverty. But the remoter effects may well be even more glorious. Whereas modern civilization, still ground under the weight of terrible injustices, shows many a symptom of lapsing like its predecessors back into the chaos of some dark age, a reformed society, cleansed of injustices, freed from the shackles of want, might in its splendid advance revive the dying dream of human perfectibility:

With want destroyed; with greed changed to noble passions; with the fraternity that is born of equality taking the place of the jealousy and fear that now array men against each other; with mental power loosed by conditions that give to the humblest comfort and leisure; and who shall measure the heights to which our civilization may soar? Words fail the thought! It is the Golden Age of which poets have sung and high-raised seers have told in metaphor! It is the glorious vision which has always haunted men with gleams of fitful splendor. It is what he saw whose eyes at Patmos were closed in a trance. It is the culmination of Christianity—the City of God on earth, with its walls of jasper and its gates of pearl! It is the reign of the Prince of Peace.[69]

[69] *Progress and Poverty* (Henry George and Company, n. d.), p. 496.

It is doubtful whether any treatise so intricate and difficult as *Progress and Poverty* has ever had so wide a hearing. After a few months of limited sale, during which the general public remained unaware of it, the book "caught on"; discussions about it multiplied; circulation mounted into tens and hundreds of thousands, and finally into millions; [70] and George himself rapidly became an international figure. This tremendous popular response virtually fixed the role which, for the remainder of his life, George was to play. Thenceforward he was to be a propagandist; a crusader; a missionary carrying to all men the ideal of social justice and the gospel of social salvation through faith in the Single Tax. For nearly two decades, unfaltering, he carried on his campaign—lecturing both in America and abroad; aiding in the establishment of antipoverty societies; editing for three years the organ of the Single-Tax movement, *The Standard;* spinning out economic expositions that ranged from brief editorials to his massive *Science of Political Economy* (1898); conducting two vigorous campaigns for the mayoralty of his adopted city, New York; and continuously awakening, by all these means, a spirited and all but universal debate.[71]

The innumerable controversies over George have only one thing in common—their involuntary testimony to his power to stimulate, to provoke, to awaken. The various attitudes toward George and his proposals range from impassioned defense to bitter attack. To the youthful Hamlin Garland, George was the masterful leader of a great social crusade, a Messiah to whom he was proud to own discipleship.[72] To Thomas Henry Huxley, on the other hand, George

[70] Henry George, Junior, estimates, in the preface to the Twenty-fifth Anniversary Edition of *Progress and Poverty* that by 1905 the circulation of the *"Progress and Poverty* literature" had reached five million copies. This figure includes copies of the book itself, and also separately published excerpts and supporting pamphlets.

[71] See, for a very full account of this period in George's life, Henry George, Junior, *op. cit.*, pp. 335 ff.

[72] It is interesting to observe that John Dewey has placed an even higher estimate on George than did Garland, though for a different reason:—"It would require less than the fingers of two hands to enu-

was merely the collector of "that interesting museum of political delusions," *Progress and Poverty*.[73] Yet the mere duration and severity of the debate are sufficient proof that George, right or wrong, had hit on something vital. As one of the controversialists puts it,

Crushed by the Duke of Argyll, refuted by Mr. Mallock, extinguished by Mayor Hewitt, undermined by Mr. Edward Atkinson, exploded by Professor Harris, excommunicated by archbishops, consigned to eternal damnation by countless doctors of divinity, put outside the pale of the Constitution by numerous legal pundits, waved out of existence by a million Podsnaps, still Henry George's theories seem to have a miraculous faculty of rising from the dead.[74]

Discussion, however, does not always signify agreement, and agreement itself does not always mean willingness to take positive action. When the immense volume of debate over the Single Tax is sifted, the number of George's actual disciples appears surprisingly small. When search is made for the actual, practical effects of the Single-Tax program on American land tenure, the result is practically nil.[75] Nothing is clearer than that the influence of Henry George—and it has been a large one—is not to be found in the sphere of immediate practical achievement. And no doubt this is well; for, seen even in the brief perspective of a half-century, George's program of reform appears to have grown prematurely rigid, to have remained fatally simple. During the very height of his outward success, George was succumbing to inward failure. At the very crest of his popularity, he was

merate those who, from Plato down, rank with Henry George among the world's social philosophers." (Introduction to *Significant Paragraphs from Progress and Poverty*, selected by Harry G. Brown. New York, 1928.)

[73] Thomas Henry Huxley, "Capital—the Mother of Labour," *The Nineteenth Century*, 27:513-32 (March, 1890).

[74] Thomas G. Shearman, "The Mistakes of Henry George," *The Forum*, 8:40-52 (September, 1889).

[75] This subject is thoroughly treated in Arthur N. Young, *The Single Tax Movement in America* (Princeton, 1916).

suffering, unrealized by himself, that subtlest and most pain-
less of all tragedies, the tragedy of the closed mind. The keen
observation, the brilliant induction of his frontier youth had
gradually hardened into the rationalization characteristic of
his middle age; and rationalization had, in turn, hardened
into a rigid mental fixation upon the one reformative device
of the Single Tax.

But the Single-Tax panacea fell far short of treating the
entire question of poverty. It dealt far too cavalierly with the
basic problem of increasing the productive power of the
laborer; it passed far too easily over the possibility that the
laborer may be exploited by many another class than that of
the landowner—by the merchant, for instance, or by the capitalist.[76] Above all, it substituted, for the forward-looking
realism that was needful, a scheme of reform which, although
radical enough in appearance, was in fact most subtly reac-
tionary; which was not progressive, but wistfully, profoundly
nostalgic. For the Single-Tax agitation was, in essence, simply
an effort to restore and to fix permanently, by artificial means,
the vanishing frontier era of free opportunity; and its deep
human appeal inhered mainly in its promise of recalling, from
just beyond the horizon, an American Golden Age so recent
that the memory of it was dwelling, still undimmed, within
the national consciousness.

It was in the intellectual and moral sphere, then, rather
than in any practical initiation of his program, that the immense energies of George were chiefly felt. Few men have
had so large a power to awaken and to stimulate; "Mr.
George's great merit," a contemporary accurately observed,
"is as an alarm bell."[77] Among those upper-middle-class
people who had been most influenced by our older cultural

[76] George was acquainted with socialism, including Marxian socialism,
but felt that it did not get at the root of economic injustice. "There is
no conflict between labor and capital; the true conflict is between labor
and monopoly. Abolish the monopoly that forbids men to employ themselves, and capital could not possibly oppress labor." (*Protection or
Free Trade,* pp. 299-306. The quotation is from p. 306.)

[77] W. H. Babcock, "The George Movement and Property," *Lippincott's Magazine,* 39:133-9 (January, 1887).

disciplines, the decade from 1885 to 1895 was, indeed, a time
of extraordinary concern over the entire problem of economic
injustice and economic reform. "The men and women I met,"
reports one observer, "filled me with astonishment. They were
all self-conscious and introspective. Most of them were brooding over wrongs—the concrete wrongs of others, and their
own abstract injuries—in a world that hid from them the great
secret of existence. And they were all devising ways and
means to correct the misdeeds of man and of God." [78] Of this
quite unusual focusing of the middle-class mind on the problem of social justice, George was at once a type and an important cause.

And not only in his humanitarianism, but in his entire social
philosophy (his absorption in the Single Tax always ex-
cepted), George typifies and sums up the critical movement
of which he was a part, so that we may discern within his
recorded thought, integrated and articulate and clear, those
central trends of development which other minds indeed felt
powerfully, but which they often left beclouded or unex-
pressed. Into the late afternoon of the nineteenth century he
brought, as did his fellow critics, the auroral glow of its hopeful dawn—the cosmic optimism of the Enlightenment, with all
which that optimism implied of trust in the benevolence of
Nature and faith in the perfectibility of man. Into the twilight
of an era he brought, as they did, the buoyant middle-class
ideology of America's clear workaday morning before the
Civil War—the Revolutionary credo of equality and natural
rights; the desire to create a larger and richer life for the
average man; the clear recognition that a certain minimum
of material well-being is not only a value in itself, but a necessary groundwork for aesthetic and spiritual growth; and the
conviction that whatever dangers threatened this democratic
way of life should be met by militant ethical crusade. Upon
the social evils of the Gilded Age, then, George and his
contemporaries alike brought to bear a criticism founded in
its every part upon the ideals of the Golden Day; and in so
doing they carried on, from one generation to another, a

[78] Margaret Sherwood Pollock, *An Experiment in Altruism*, pp. 6-7.

native American tradition, mature and clearly defined; a tradition strong enough to grapple powerfully with the disintegrative forces of the Machine Age, in Titanic effort to control them, to subdue them, and to assimilate them into itself.

I

The first American novelist to treat the social problems of the Machine Age seriously and at length was Elizabeth Stuart Phelps, who wrote, in *The Silent Partner* (1871), a vivid, somewhat sentimental study of the physical suffering and moral atrophy of a group of New England mill hands. Three years later, Rebecca Harding Davis illustrated, in *John Andross*, the corruption of a state legislature by financial interests; and in the following year Dr. J. G. Holland treated, in *Sevenoaks*, such commercial episodes as the theft of inventions and the sale of stock in a fake oil company.

During the latter seventies and early eighties, such economic novels appeared intermittently; during the latter eighties, in a steady, though slender, stream. But during the early nineties, the current of economic fiction rose to flood levels; seven volumes appeared in '88, eleven in '89, fifteen in '90, twenty-two in '91, twenty-four in '92, seventeen in '93, twenty-two in '94, and seventeen in '95.[1] In '96 and '7, publication remained at seventeen novels in each year; but in the Spanish War era of '98 and '9, it declined to eleven and twelve novels respectively. When, in 1900, the number of new economic novels again rose to seventeen, their character had undergone a distinct change; novels conditioned by the middle class interest in economic reform were fewer, and in their room were appearing amoral romances of economic struggle

[1] These numbers are based on the list of economic novels in the bibliography, below, pp. 346-53. In all likelihood, they fall short of entire accuracy, but they show clearly enough the concentration of interest in economic fiction between the middle eighties and the middle nineties.

such as Merwin and Webster's *The Short Line War* (1899).
Altogether, between 1870 and 1901, some two hundred and
fifty volumes of economic fiction—mostly novels—were published in the United States. In view of the number of these
novels, and in view of the coherent social philosophy that can
be shown to exist in them, it is not too much to say that during
the so-called Gilded Age American writers so dealt with
industrialism as to create a well-defined, clearly recognizable
literary movement—a movement whose influence was felt
intermittently throughout that generation, but whose chief
concentration was reached between 1888 and 1897.

A number of the economic novels are, and were even at
the time of their publication, of negligible importance. On
the other hand, a number are significant as the work of
talented minor, or even potential major, authors. Thomas
Bailey Aldrich in *The Stillwater Tragedy* (1880), John Hay
in *The Breadwinners* (1884-5), Henry Francis Keenan in *The
Money-Makers* (1885), Stephen Crane in *Maggie* (1892),
H. H. Boyesen in *Social Strugglers* (1893), Francis Hopkinson Smith in *Tom Grogan* (1896), Charles Dudley Warner in
That Fortune (1899),[2] and David Graham Phillips in *The
Great God Success* (1901), all brought to the treatment of
social and economic themes sound craftsmanship and considerable ability; and in *The Gospel of Freedom* (1898), *The
Web of Life* (1900), and *The Real World* (1901), Robert
Herrick was already employing in the treatment of industrialism not only sound craftsmanship, but a fine, consistent
sense of humane value.[3] Furthermore, in contrast with both
the negligible run-of-the-mine novels and those of a respectable second rank, a few others are clearly of principal importance in American literary history, either in themselves or

[2] For other economic novels by Boyesen and Warner, see the bibliography, pp. 346 and 353 respectively.

[3] There can be no doubt that Herrick's work is of sufficient importance
to warrant detailed, individual consideration, such as that given below
to Mark Twain, Garland, Bellamy, Howells, and Norris. However, since
his principal work belongs clearly in the twentieth century, it has
seemed inappropriate to consider him, along with these other five, in
a historical study devoted altogether to the Gilded Age.

in their relation to the work of a potential major author. These few are the work of Mark Twain, Hamlin Garland, Edward Bellamy, William Dean Howells, and Frank Norris.

It will be the object of later chapters to follow out, in its genetic development, the economic writing of each one of these five principal authors. It is the object of the present chapter to treat, collectively, the economic fiction of the lesser novelists and thereby to place in view a kind of cross-section of the treatment of economic forces in the fiction of the Gilded Age.

A glance at the many variations, at the wide disparities among these economic novels might indeed, at first, make the hope of evoking any clear pattern from their confusion appear illusory. In popularity, for example, the variation extends from Reverend Charles Monroe Sheldon's *In His Steps* (1897), some eight million copies of which have been distributed in the United States alone, down to works so obscure that there appears to be no record of their sales at all. Moreover, in manner of publication the divergence is almost as wide as in popularity.

A clear majority of the economic novels—60 per cent at the most conservative estimate possible—were issued by commercial publishers of some general reputation. Of the remaining minority, some were issued by publishing houses devoted to some special and perhaps noncommercial policy—for example, the humanitarian Arena Publishing Company of Boston or the socialistic Charles H. Kerr and Company of Chicago. Others were issued by publishers whose standing and policy are now doubtful or unknown; and some few were issued directly by the authors themselves. Naturally this last group contains relatively more amateur writing and eccentric thinking than the others; and yet the entire range in viewpoint from conservatism to radicalism, and almost the entire range in literary skill, may be found in books which came to the public through the most orthodox commercial channels.

But disparities in literary merit, in popularity, and in manner of publication cannot conceal the underlying threads of unity that run through our economic fiction. They cannot

conceal the fact that that economic criticism is largely a
native, an American product. To be sure, American economic
novelists occasionally allude to or echo Ruskin or Morris
or Tolstoy; and the ideas of Marx are still discernible, though
so changed that Marx himself might well have disowned
them, in the collectivism of Edward Bellamy and his followers. But most of our economic fiction is quite plainly a direct
response of American authorship to American materials.
Many of our authors appear to have written quite without
benefit of the European example; and on the whole the conclusion is inescapable that the United States would have
had some literary *critique* of industrialism, not immeasurably
different from the actual one, had there been in Europe no
corresponding literary movement whatever.

And just as our economic fiction is mainly native and
American, so it is mainly—indeed, almost totally—middle
class. Prior to 1900, nothing resembling the recent wave of
proletarian fiction existed. Sentiment inclined rather toward
liberal reform than toward radicalism, and even the radicalism of the age was of the middle class, not of the proletariat.
The majority of our novelists held a position that may properly be defined as "Left-Center." Such novelists, although
aware of the obvious evils of capitalistic industrialism, although capable of the sharpest examination of the corrupt
practices of Big Business, although deeply concerned over
certain disintegrating effects of industrialism in the lives of
both the rich and the poor, nevertheless stopped short of
advocating any fundamental change in the economic system.
Moderate politico-economic reforms, or the alleviations
offered by settlement work and slum-clearance, appeared to
them sufficient.

Clearly demarked from the dominant Left-Center, two
minority groups made up different branches of a middle-class
"Left." Both groups resembled the Left-Center in their sensitiveness to the evils of industrialism; they resembled each
other in their readiness for thoroughgoing instead of merely
partial change. But one wing of the Left, individualists after
the fashion of Henry George, wished to retain competitive

capitalism and at the same time to destroy all monopoly of natural resources. Another, collectivists after the fashion of Edward Bellamy, wished to destroy capitalism and replace it by socialism. Both types of radical program were, however, most carefully articulated with American middle class and democratic modes of thought.

Other minority groups made up, taken collectively, a kind of Right-Center. An extreme Right—a defense of Plutocracy— was as lacking in our literature before 1900 as a proletarian Left. The great corporate organizers, being overwhelmingly successful, needed no literary defense, and had, in any case, no literary tradition. Moreover, our middle-class authorship was still most imperfectly aware of the intricate corporate structure of Big Business; and, to the limited extent of its information, was, both by tradition and by temperament, hostile. A conservatively inclined author might, however, illustrate and idealize the virtues of the old-fashioned middle-class business man; or he might attack a potential enemy of both the middle class and the plutocracy—organized labor. Or, overlooking the entire field of politico-economic discussion, even forgetting any considerations of ethics, he might become absorbed in the thrill of economic conflict, and create from it an amoral romance of economic struggle closely akin to the old romance of heroic adventure. Novels of business adventure, novels illustrating the dangers of organized labor, novels idealizing the middle-class business man, constitute the Right-Center of our economic fiction.[4]

It is now pertinent to describe, in order, the work of each of these groups; and in the presentation of the Left-Center, it will be necessary to deal first with the authors' exposure of the evils of industrialism, and afterwards with the several remedies which they proposed.

II

To most of our economic novelists, and especially to the authors of the Left-Center group, the cut-throat tactics prev-

---

[4] Naturally, these classes are not perfectly defined or mutually exclusive.

alent in business were about equally of fascinating interest and of grave concern. Our economic fiction from 1870 to 1900 is frequently sprinkled, sometimes flooded, with episodes revealing the corrupt business practices of an era that produced its Fisk and Gould, its Credit Mobilier, its South Improvement Company.

For example, in *Sevenoaks,* published as early as 1875, Dr. J. G. Holland tells the story of a financial magnate who enriches himself by the sale of stock of a fake oil company, by the rejuvenation of an old railroad for speculative purposes, and by the theft of certain inventions.[5] In *The Autocrats,* published as late as 1901, Charles K. Lush tells the story of a business adventurer who attempts to get a fifty-year franchise for a traction company in order to increase the value of his stock, and whose tactics range from outright bribery to virtual blackmail.[6] And throughout the time intervening between these two publications, novelists recurrently dealt with the practices of stock-watering, false capitalization, dishonest promotion, and criminal pseudo-investment schemes; with attacks on the reputations of business opponents; and with a number of abuses belonging peculiarly to the railways.[7] Among these latter abuses, some amount merely to the familiar practice of charging all the traffic will bear; some consist of rebating and other discriminations among shippers; and some involve the "wrecking" of a railway system by the maintaining of dishonest employees to misdirect freight and falsify financial statements, the object being to beat down the

[5] Josiah Gilbert Holland, *Sevenoaks,* pp. 10, 149, 158, 204, 277.

[6] Charles Keeler Lush, *The Autocrats,* pp. 19-22, 100, 108.

[7] For a series of episodes illustrating the practices of blackmail, stock-watering, booming fraudulent stock, and "unloading," see H. H. Boyesen, *A Daughter of the Philistines* (1883), pp. 244-300. For other fictional treatments of business piracy, see Thomas Scott Denison, *An Iron Crown* (1885), pp. 77-8, 410, 464-5; Henry Francis Keenan, *The Money-Makers* (1885), pp. 37, 242 ff.; Charles K. Lush, *The Federal Judge* (1897), p. 12; Caroline Walch, *Doctor Sphinx* (1899), p. 332. See, for a clever satire on promotion in general, William Hawley Smith, *The Promoters* (1904).

These and succeeding footnote citations in this chapter are intended to be only representative, not exhaustive.

railway's stock and thus enable the wreckers to gain control.[8]

Occasionally, some novelist portrays a big business man engaged in honest dealing;[9] but the overwhelming majority leave the impression that honesty and business—at least the modern speculative, exploitive, industrial forms of business —are total strangers. Typical of the majority attitude is the passage in *The Victors* (1901) where Robert Barr tells with a lightness bordering on humor of the dealings of four business adventurers about a railway franchise. Mitchell, the original owner, thinking it worthless, sells it to the youthful Munro and McAllister for $1000.00; they in turn sell it to the experienced capitalist Van Ness for $100,000.00. Every one of the parties in the deal feels with pleasure that he has been smart enough to fleece the other. As Van Ness interprets the situation,

"What hardened villains business makes of us. . . . It's a shame to take advantage of the simple ignorance of that young man. The franchise is cheap at half a million, but, alas! business is business."[10]

Plainly, knavery among business men could hardly be limited to the game of fleecing one another; it was bound to touch the general public as well, and in no way more directly than in making business so largely speculative in character. The American economic novelists were frequently concerned with speculation in stocks, sometimes with speculative business in general; and, with the exception of a few romancers of economic struggle, their attitude is uniformly hostile. A typical illustration of the evils of the stock market occurs in Agnes Maule Machar's *Roland Graeme, Knight* (1892). Here, the youth Waldberg plays the stock market in order to get money to enable him to marry Kitty Farrell. A novice at the specula-

[8] See, for examples, Thomas Scott Denison, *op. cit.*, pp. 400-1, 466-9; Edward Everett Hale, *Sybil Knox* (1892), pp. 96-7, 110-5; Robert Herrick, *Memoirs of an American Citizen*, (1905), pp. 66, 138; Charles Dudley Warner, *A Little Journey in the World* (1889), p. 164.

[9] E. g., Robert Herrick, *op. cit.*, pp. 274, 290.

[10] Robert Barr, *The Victors*, pp. 330 ff.

tive game, he loses, commits a virtual forgery to recoup his loss, and escapes moral collapse only through the timely help given him by the hero, Roland Graeme.[11] In her portrayal of the financial and moral dangers of stock-speculation, Miss Machar was only following conventions that were already well established in American fiction, and that have persisted into the fiction of our own time.

The fictional indictment of speculation, however, reveals considerable variety. In some novels, the condemnation is on the ground of the insecurity which speculation causes, whether to the poor clerk who loses his own and his loved ones' savings gambling on the stock market,[12] or to the wealthy financier who with his family may be left without resource when his entire fortune is puffed away by a single breath of change.[13] In others, the moral effects of speculation are treated, as in Thomas Scott Denison's story of the young man who, after losing his own money, takes his sister's, without her knowledge, and loses it as well.[14] Speculation is thus made to appear a root of such evils as forgery, embezzlement, betrayal of confidence, and plain thievery. In such a game, the newcomer is obviously at the mercy of the shrewd inside manipulator, a person quite indifferent to the injury his deals may cause other people. "Do you think I have time to attend to every poor duck? Why don't people look where they put their money?" [15] says one successful speculator, apropos of his responsibility to the public. Speculation is, moreover, harmful to legitimate businesses such as banking,[16] and, even at its very best, unproductive. The workman and manufacturer

[11] Agnes Maule Machar, *Roland Graeme, Knight,* pp. 259-66.

[12] Robert Herrick, *The Web of Life,* p. 339.

[13] Clinton Scollard Ross, *The Speculator* (1891), entire, but especially pp. 69, 122. See also the same author's *The Silent Workman* (1886), pp. 19-20, and Thomas Scott Denison's *An Iron Crown,* pp. 150-1, 323-4. Of course, the most powerful story of the effects of speculation is that in Frank Norris's *The Pit* (1903), for a discussion of which, see below, pp. 300 ff.

[14] Denison, *op. cit.,* pp. 334-5.

[15] Charles Dudley Warner, *A Little Journey in the World,* p. 304.

[16] Mary H. Ford, *Which Wins?* (1891), p. 80.

create; the speculator only manipulates. "Why should they have the lion's share?" asks one producer in regard to the winnings of successful speculators. "The lion's share belongs to the lion. *They* are nothing but jackals." [17]

The speculative conduct of business in general fares no better in the economic novel than speculation in stocks. For instance, Caroline Walch, in *Doctor Sphinx* (1899), objects to the degree to which "our whole American life is being pervaded by this restless desire of immediate unheard-of returns for a non-equivalent expenditure of honest labor." [18] In *Hope Mills,* Amanda Douglas builds her plot about the rehabilitation of a New England mill town out of the economic chaos into which it has been plunged by speculative business. Wild business gambles which wrecked the main factory and bank, and brought discomfort and even disaster to thousands of people, the author refers to as "a sickening mass of selfishness and corruption." [19] Of the economics of speculation, she says, in the words of one of her characters,

There's just one thing that makes a man or a country rich, ... and that's industry, good, honest labor. Marking one's goods up before breakfast, as the Frenchman did, realizes no absolute money.... When a man makes money simply by another person's loss, he has not created anything, or made any more of it; and the world's no better, that I can see. [20]

For this hostility to all forms of speculation, the causative factors are as easily discernible as they are fundamental. They lie at the very core of the thought-habits and folk-ethic of our American middle class. For a hundred years and more, that

[17] Alice French, *The Lion's Share* (1907), p. 183. Italics not in the original. See also p. 309.

[18] Caroline Walch, *Doctor Sphinx*, p. 339.

[19] Amanda M. Douglas, *Hope Mills* (1880), pp. 92, 108.

[20] *Ibid.*, p. 137. See, for other treatments of speculative business, Rebecca Harding Davis, *John Andross* (1874), p. 261, and the episodes in H. H. Boyesen's *A Daughter of the Philistines,* pp. 244-300, referred to above. Of course, by far and away the best literary exposé of the entire speculative game is Twain's and Warner's *The Gilded Age* (1873), for a discussion of which, see below, pp. 123 ff.

class had theoretically, and often actually, upheld the virtues
of honesty, diligence, prudence, and thrift. As far back as the
mid-eighteenth century, Franklin had made their philosophy
articulate in such maxims as "Honesty is the best policy,"
"Drive thy business, let not that drive thee," "Diligence is the
mother of good luck," and "Lying rides upon debt's back";
and the widespread, enduring popularity of Franklin's pru-
dential maxims is sufficient evidence that he continued to
speak *for* his readers, as well as to them.

But in a new country, bent on the parcelling-out of an in-
conceivably rich public domain, speculative plunging was
inevitable; frequently the middle-class code voiced by Franklin was violated on every main count. Presently, however,
spokesmen for the thrifty middle class denounced such violations and lashed them with satire. For instance, Joseph Glover
Baldwin in his *Flush Times in Alabama and Mississippi*
(1853) told all that was necessary about the speculative fever
in the pioneer deep South; and Artemus Ward, in sketches
like "William Barker, the Young Patriot" (1862), flayed the
profiteer of Civil War times. Indeed, native American humorists, perhaps the most popular of our literary spokesmen
shortly after the mid-century, customarily assumed the pru-
dential code of the middle class, and often explicitly satirized
violations of that code. Now stock speculation, and the speculative conduct of big business enterprises, are obvious and
flagrant violations of the middle-class code of honesty,
diligence, prudence, and thrift; and in denouncing them the
economic novelists were, whether spontaneously or by deliberate choice, working within the grooves of an established
tradition.

In the fiction which so vigorously exposed general business
rascality and the dangers of the speculative game, the reader
might well expect an even more vigorous exposé of the injustices done by the great corporation to the individual, middle-
class producer. Stories of this kind do indeed exist, though in
surprisingly small number. In a representative one, Gertrude
Potter Daniels' *The Warners* (1901), the common situation of
the crowding-out of an independent producer by unfair com-

petition is wrought into a sensational melodrama which approaches, without ever quite reaching, the qualities of genuine tragedy. Cyrus and Betty Warner, their business ruined by the price-cutting of the oil magnate Fellows, go to work in a northern city as common laborer and sweatshop slave. Their daughter, Betty Junior, rebelling against poverty, leaves home and becomes the mistress of Fellows' son, Ted. During a depression, while Cyrus is unemployed, Betty Senior collapses from overwork and malnutrition, and, when her returning daughter acknowledges that she has murdered Ted, dies of shock. Intermingled with this principal story, a subplot relates in lurid apologue how the "Red," Kirby, half-crazed by injustices, enters into a bombing plot which, miscarrying, results in the death of his wife and child.[21]

Yet, in general, the seriousness of the Trust problem did not call forth a correspondingly important movement in fiction.[22] Novelists apparently failed to grasp the enormous extent and power of the drive toward consolidation. In the birth-era of such leviathans as Standard Oil and United States Steel, many a writer continued to lay the scene of his economic problem-novel in a mid-century New England mill town, and to treat the capital-labor conflict as if it were solely a struggle between individual employer and local employee.

But if the economic novelists failed to grasp the increasing corporateness of business, they did not fail to grasp the close relationship of economics and politics; they did not fail to expose the frequent perversion of democratic government into the service of Big Business. In actual life, business had

[21] Gertrude Potter Daniels, *The Warners*, pp. 108-9, 116.

[22] For other examples of the treatment of monopoly by the lesser novelists, see Thomas Scott Denison, *op. cit.*, p. 437; Francis N. Thorpe, *The Divining Rod* (1905), pp. 48 ff.; Robert Upton Collins, *John Halsey, the Anti-Monopolist* (1884); and Charles Cyrel Post, *Driven from Sea to Sea* (1884). No doubt the ablest illustration of the antitrust movement is in Frank Norris's *The Octopus* (1901), for a discussion of which, see below, pp. 294 ff. For a quite different kind of treatment, in which the trusts are regarded as a natural stage in an evolutionary growth toward socialism, see the works of Bellamy and Howells, discussed below, pp. 192 ff. and 260 ff., respectively.

to come to legislatures and city councils for franchises, grants of land, and favorable legislation; and in literature, the plot of many a novel turns on the efforts of business men, whether by legitimate means or illegitimate, to gain these necessities. In J. W. De Forest's *Honest John Vane* (1875), the ironic title refers to a legislator who is led first into a scheme resembling that of the notorious Credit Mobilier, and later into outright bribery,[23] and thereby becomes the servant of special interests instead of the general welfare. In F. Marion Crawford's *An American Politician* (1885), Patrick Ballymolly—a political boss who holds the balance of power in a state legislature and who is also an owner of interests in iron—deliberately weighs the attitudes of two senatorial candidates towards the tariff, and turns the election in favor of the high-protectionist.[24] In Paul Leicester Ford's *The Honorable Peter Stirling* (1894), although the novel is mainly a political one, the enveloping action at least is furnished by economic forces; indeed, it is largely Peter's protection of the public interest against the special interests of certain business corporations that gives his actions their significance.[25]

The narratives of De Forest, Crawford, and Ford are representative of the variety of superficial detail with which they and numerous other novelists treated a single fundamental theme. Rebecca Harding Davis in *John Andross,* which tells of the rebellion of a young legislator against the whiskey ring he has been forced to serve; Thomas Scott Denison in *An Iron Crown,* which deals with the railways' manipulation of both state and national legislatures—these and still other novelists, however they may vary in details of plot and character and method, all agree in portraying the corruption

[23] John W. De Forest, *Honest John Vane,* pp. 85, 90, 168. Besides the treatment of political corruption in the novels referred to here, noteworthy examples are to be found in Twain's and Warner's *The Gilded Age,* Garland's *A Member of the Third House* and *A Spoil of Office* (both 1892), and Norris's *The Octopus.* See below, respectively, pp. 165-71 and 294-300.

[24] F. Marion Crawford, *An American Politician,* pp. 227 ff.

[25] See, for example, the passage including his speech on a corporation and its record for bribery, pp. 287 ff.

of the government either by the personal forces of unscrupulous business leadership or by the impersonal forces of ruthless business struggle.[26] In all, the central charge is that representative government, which ought to look to the welfare of the whole democratic group, is often turned into an agency of favoritism to the few. As Robert Herrick says of one state, in the words of his capitalist, Van Harrington,

The legislature might be said, in a general way, to represent the people of the state of Illinois, but it represented also the railroad interests, the traction and gas interests, and the packers, and when it came to a matter of importance it pretty generally did what it was told by its real bosses.[27]

But such an indictment as this is never brought against the judiciary, state or federal. The administration of the courts is criticized in only a few cases, and in them only with some vague suggestion of intimidation or the exerting of undue influence. All this while, the courts were, to be sure, pursuing a policy that now appears almost startlingly pro-capitalist; they had, for example, wrested the fourteenth amendment from its original intent, and were employing as a ban on even the most moderate social legislation the clause guaranteeing freedom of contract to the black freedman! Such facts, however significant, the writers of the economic novel mostly neglected. The single significant story bearing on the judiciary is Charles K. Lush's *The Federal Judge* (1897). Here, the author tries to account for the capitalistic leanings of the judiciary on the theory that a judge may, through long association with capitalist or executive, unconsciously assimi-

[26] Rebecca Harding Davis, *John Andross*, pp. 72-3, 131, 222, 300; Denison, *op. cit.*, pp. 37-40, 76-8, 312 ff. See, for other treatments of the same theme, Guy W. Carryl, *The Lieutenant Governor* (1903); Arnold A. Clark, *Beneath the Dome* (1894); Elliott Flower, *Slaves of Success* (1905), especially pp. 00-1; Henry Francis Keenan, *The Money-Makers* (1885); Charles K. Lush, *The Autocrats*; especially pp. 19-22; Francis Lynde, *The Grafters* (1904); and David Graham Phillips' *The Plum Tree* (1905). Carryl's *The Lieutenant Governor* is unusual in that the corrupting influence is the labor union, not the capitalist.

[27] Robert Herrick, *Memoirs of an American Citizen*, pp. 315-6.

late the latter's point of view. Lush's principal character, Judge Dunn, a tough, honest, anticorporation man, is gradually so changed by the influence of the railway magnate Gardwell that, when the latter faces a strike, the judge protects him by issuing against the labor group an injunction of unprecedented severity:

It is strictly charged and commanded that you do absolutely refrain from combining and conspiring to quit, *with or without notice,* the service of the road, and from interfering with the agents or employees of the receiver in any manner, by actual violence, by intimidation, or *otherwise.*[28]

And yet, extensively as the left-center novelists dealt with the unethical practices of Big Business and the effect of those practices on government, they did not make of such matters their sole concern—indeed, hardly their majority concern. They employed, besides these lines of attack, numerous others, some of which are of major importance. Among the miscellaneous problems they touched on, and yet did not fully consider, are the possible interference of capitalistic interests with the distribution of the news,[29] the economic position of woman,[30] the monotony and physical discomforts of farm work, and the ill effects of the Western mortgage system.[31] More frequently mentioned than any of these is the bearing of the money power on higher education. To be sure, no novelist of the period put together a phrase quite as neatly turned as Robert Frost's "I think he owns some shares in Harvard College"; but several said much the same thing. H. H. Boyesen, Herbert Hopkins, and Vida D. Scudder all point out the danger to academic freedom in the pressure that a wealthy man may exert, through personal influence or donations, on the college or university.[32] More fully, Margaret

[28] *The Federal Judge,* p. 247. See also pp. 15-6, 36 ff., 232-6, 355.
[29] Keenan, *op. cit.,* p. 269
[30] Mrs. Mary H. Ford, *Which Wins?* pp. 230-1.
[31] *Ibid.,* p. 88; also Denison, *op. cit.,* pp. 400-1. Economic problems connected with the agrarian West were, of course, most ably treated by Hamlin Garland. See below, pp. 159 ff.
[32] H. H. Boyesen, *The Mammon of Unrighteousness* (1891), pp.

Sherwood Pollock tells in *Henry Worthington, Idealist* (1899) how a young professor, in the course of making his study of urban poverty both serious and practical, awakens among some wealthier, more conservative people an opposition that finally causes his dismissal.[33]

Of other miscellaneous subjects treated by the authors of the Left-Center, none lent themselves to vivid dramatization more easily than the recurrent business depressions, along with their dark shadow of cyclical unemployment. The literary treatment of the business crisis is, it should be admitted, a partial affair; in regard to the deeper causes of depression, the Left-Center had little to say.[34] But the human results—the strain, the suffering, and the actual privation involved—they show vividly. The depression of the seventies, which had far-reaching indirect results on a number of novels, is an immediate subject in Amanda Douglas's *Hope Mills* and Henry Francis Keenan's *The Money-Makers*. In the former, the author describes the groups of "anxious, moody-eyed men walking the streets, or grouped on corners, their coats and hats shabby, their beards untrimmed"; and "young men and boys offering to do any kind of work for any kind of pay."[35] In the latter, the author relates that "as the winter advanced, the misery of the unemployed became more pitiable. In Valedo, thousands were on the verge of starvation, and the most alarming threats were openly uttered."[36] The depression of the nineties appears in almost strictly historical form in Robert

---

10 ff.; Herbert M. Hopkins, *The Torch* (1903), pp. 140-1, 218; Vida D. Scudder, *A Listener in Babel* (1904), pp. 190 ff. See also, in this general connection, Ellen Glasgow's *Phases of an Inferior Planet* (1898), for its implications in regard to the financial rewards of pure scholarship.

[33] *Henry Worthington, Idealist,* pp. 38, 278.

[34] For an exception, see Amanda Douglas, *op. cit.*, pp. 77-82, a discussion of the possible relation between low wages, underconsumption, and depression. The authors of the Left, especially Bellamy, traced the cause of recurring depressions directly to competition and the effects of the profit system.

[35] Douglas, *op. cit.*, p. 116.

[36] Keenan, *op. cit.*, p. 261.

Barr's *The Victors*,[37] as part of the background of the plot in Herrick's *The Web of Life* (1898), in occasional allusions in Caroline Walch's *Dr. Sphinx*,[38] and by implication at least in Hervey White's *Differences* (1899). In *Differences*, the heroine, Genevieve Carr, an earnest and compassionate settlement worker, finds her most nearly insoluble problem in involuntary unemployment:

> To get work, only to get work for the people, was the one question that kept the young girl awake and thinking long into the night. It was the one mission that kept her moving through the day, for work was the only test of sincerity. . . . The men said they could not get work, and who could say they were not speaking the truth, when she knew that many of the most active and earnest men had been tramping the streets hopeless for months, and when she herself, with her influence and rich friends, could not find vacancies for one in a hundred of the applicants.[39]

And yet, when the novelist wrote of cyclical unemployment, he treated at most a symptom of industrialism, not a major trait or force. When, however, he turned from unemployment to the kindred theme of class conflict, he touched one of the three or four basic forces of his century. The break-up of the middle-class hegemony that had obtained in our country until after the Civil War; the emergence of the hostile, embattled forces of capital and labor—this was a fundamental change indeed. That the novelists of the time understood it is too much to claim. But they did observe it; they did, though somewhat bewildered, grasp its importance; and they did put the new spectacle of class warfare on literary record as a thing they deeply suspected and profoundly disliked.

Among their numerous stories of strikes, there is often genuine sympathy for both the laborer and the capitalist, seldom or never for the strike as a weapon of class warfare. Without any important exceptions, these stories emphasize the disorder, the suffering, and the brutality caused by strikes; the

[37] Pp. 484-5.
[38] *E. g.*, pp. 48, 343-4.
[39] P. 44.

release which strikes, like other forms of war, give to the
violent, treacherous, nether side of human nature. A typical
picture of the labor-capital struggle occurs in Robert Herrick's
The Web of Life, where the drama of the physician Sommers'
rebellion against a life of prosperous Philistine self-satisfaction
is played out against the background of the economic
struggles of the nineties:—the sullenness of capital, the
violence of labor, the clatter of tongues preaching conflicting
solutions, the outbreak of the Pullman strike, the railway
union's boycott of Pullman products, menacing mob violence,
incendiarism and, finally, martial law.[40]

Ordinarily, the treatment of the Strike fails to achieve any
deepseated probing into motives and causes. Sometimes the
arbitrary attitude of a capitalist—his refusal to conciliate or
even to negotiate—is played up;[41] sometimes it is charged that
owners deliberately provoke rioting as a means of discrediting
a strike.[42] Often, on the other hand, strikes are attributed
chiefly to the work of a walking delegate or other agitator—
a type of person who is always unsympathetically presented.[43]
But at times an author abandons or plays down such polemic
phases of his story, and fixes on some situation of deep human
interest which is brought into relief by a strike. Alice French's
story of the grocer Race Battles, and of his struggle to keep
solvent while carrying the accounts of his idle workman
friends, owns an interest which is quite independent of the
author's economic message.[44]

[40] Herrick, *op. cit.,* pp. 135-8, 190 ff., 218, 226 ff. For some of the
numerous other treatments of strikes, see Florence Converse, *The
Burden of Christopher* (1900), pp. 171-2; Thomas Scott Denison, *An
Iron Crown,* pp. 470 ff.; Alice French, *The Heart of Toil* (1898), pp.
159 ff.; Clinton Scollard Ross, *The Silent Workman,* p. 41; Charles
Dudley Warner, *A Little Journey in the World,* p. 243.

[41] Clinton Scollard Ross, *The Silent Workman,* p. 36; Paul Leicester
Ford, *The Honorable Peter Stirling,* pp. 300-1.

[42] Dan Beard, *Moonblight* (1892), pp. 165, 190; Keenan, *op. cit.,*
pp. 292 ff.

[43] For an example, see Douglas, *op. cit.,* p. 322. In regard to the
characterization of the walking delegate, see below, pp. 10-11, 313.

[44] *The Heart of Toil,* pp. 1-44. See, for other examples of human interest stories connected with strikes, the stories of lovers separated by

Ordinarily, however, the new class-division in our society was not interpreted as a conflict between proletarian and capitalist. Apparently easier, more comfortably familiar, was the old distinction between the rich and the poor. The apparent widening of the gulf between the Haves and the Have-Nots, the dilemma of poverty in the midst of progress, troubled the novelists of the Left-Center only less seriously than it troubled Henry George. Hence they not only dramatized the contrast between riches and poverty; they judged both extremes in the light of the middle-class ideal of a moderate prosperity, and condemned them as breeders of the most serious moral and social problems.[45] "If I were only sure," replies the heroine of Hervey White's *Differences*, in answer to the charge that her views made "civilization" and "progress" appear futile—"If I were only sure that our specialized civilization were progress. It seems to me now only one-sided idleness and pleasure with the rich, and drudgery and suffering with the poor."[46]

Such words as those pose the most searching, profound, and extensive questions asked by the authors of the Left-Center. Granted that one effect of capitalistic industrialism is to fix in permanently stratified classes the wealthy capitalist on the one hand, and the poor laborer on the other, into what kind of life is each of the two groups to be conditioned? What are the possibilities of life, what are the realizable human values, first, among the very poor, and second, among the very rich? To present the answer given by the Left-Center to these questions is the object of the following two sections.[47]

---

industrial conflict in Lynn Boyd Porter's *Speaking of Ellen* (1890) and Mary Wilkins Freeman's *The Portion of Labor* (1901).

[45] For some among many available examples, see Margaret Deland, *The Wisdom of Fools* (1897), p. 188; Robert Herrick, *The Common Lot*, (1904), pp. 211-2; Agnes Maule Machar, *Roland Graeme, Knight*, pp. 52-3; Clinton Scollard Ross, *The Silent Workman*, p. 45, and *The Speculator*, pp. 76-7; Albion W. Tourgée, *Murvale Eastman, Christian Socialist*, (1890), p. 270.

[46] *Differences*, p. 289.

[47] One noticeable fact about the novels of the Left-Center is their neglect of certain forces and ideas that have since attracted attention.

III

If it were possible to gather within a historical study the entire growth of America's awareness of life (as distinguished from that more limited and formal thing called American thought), few developments would look more dramatic than the sudden awakening of the national mind to the fact of widespread, undeserved, and hopeless poverty. In the literary indictment that accompanied that awakening, few counts are more impressively driven home than that against the working-conditions inflicted upon the submerged poor. To a middle-class American mind—a mind used to the quieter, old-fashioned labors of farm and shop and store—work in the midst of such a perfect flower of industrialism as a steel mill might well seem a condemnation to an inferno. To Margaret Deland's Mrs. Eaton—a character created as a type of honesty and clear perception—it appears as follows:

As she understood the situation, this misery [from a strike] existed because her brother would no longer give even fourteen cents an hour to human beings who had to stand half naked in the scorch of intense furnaces, reeking with sweat, taking a breathless moment to plunge waist deep into tanks of cold water; to men who worked where the crash of exploding slag or the accidental tipping of a ladle might mean death; to gaunt and stunted creatures, hollow-eyed, with bleared and sodden faces, whose incessant toil to keep alive had crushed out the look of manhood, and left them

---

For instance, F. Marion Crawford's *An American Politician* (1885) is almost alone in its recognition (p. 65) of the economic effects of the frontier. The superior importance of human rights over property rights—an important matter for the liberal—although often assumed, is rarely made even as explicit as in Henry Francis Keenan's remark that the tariff enabled owners to "exact enormous returns on money invested, while the human capital invested got the smallest possible rewards" (*The Money-Makers*, p. 262). Any thoroughgoing attack on the competitive system as a whole is hardly to be expected in a literature whose temper is merely liberal rather than radical. Separate instances may, however, be found, as in Florence Converse, *The Burden of Christopher*, pp. 180, 259, and Alvah M. Kerr, *An Honest Lawyer* (1892) p. 97.

silent, hopeless, brutish, with only one certainty in their stupefied souls: *"men don't grow old in the mills."* [48]

The literary indictment of bad working conditions is, on the whole, complete, though quite sporadic and unsystematized. It touches on the petty persecutions a laborer may suffer.[49] It portrays such evils as occupational disease—the cotton cough or wool-picker's blindness—and the industrial accident, from which, it is shown, child laborers are by no means exempt.[50] It portrays the abuse of child labor,[51] and the evasion of even such limited child-labor laws as were then in existence; "Yes; I'm independent now . . . ," says an idle tenement father in one of these stories. "I put the last of my kids to work this morning. She's only eleven, but I swore her past the factory act as fourteen." [52] It dwells on the humdrum monotony of sweatshop and low-grade-factory work, at best a thing destructive to many values and enjoyments, at worst a crushing slavery;[53] and, finally, it suggests the futility of a life which, sufficiently barren itself, leads only to some equally barren end such as unemployment, the blacklist, or premature superannuation.[54]

Such indictments of the working-conditions of the poor have, of course, no extensive bearing on the employees of prosperous, intelligently managed businesses. They deal somewhat with the steel mills and mining; but for the most

[48] Margaret Deland, *The Wisdom of Fools,* p. 96.

[49] James W. Sullivan, *Tenement Tales of New York* (1895), p. 179.

[50] Agnes Maule Machar, *Roland Graeme, Knight,* p. 249; R. L. Makin, *The Beaten Path* (1903), pp. 1-3; Gwendolen Overton, *Captains of the World* (1904), pp. 26-8; Elizabeth Stuart Phelps, *The Silent Partner,* pp. 82, 186, 215.

[51] Phelps, *op. cit.,* p. 213; Jacob Riis, *Out of Mulberry Street* (1897), p. 166; Marie Van Vorst, *Amanda of the Mill* (1905), pp. 120 ff.

[52] Sullivan, *op. cit.,* pp. 181-2.

[53] *Ibid.,* pp. 49-50, 70. See also Edward Fuller, *The Complaining Millions of Men* (1893), p. 57; Elizabeth Stuart Phelps, *op. cit.,* pp. 70 ff.; Jacob Riis, *Nibsy's Christmas* (1893), p. 9.

[54] Robert Herrick, *The Web of Life,* p. 249; Jacob Riis, *Out of Mulberry Street,* pp. 91-3; Mary Wilkins Freeman, *The Portion of Labor* (1901), p. 155.

part they apply to the small, ill-managed, even "marginal" factory and—with especial force—to the sweatshop. Quite similar, in its concentration on the slum industries, is the literary attack on the very core of the problem of poverty—the combination of long hours and low pay, of a maximum workday with a minimum wage. Typical of the descriptions of the deadening routine of the sweated worker is Gertrude Potter Daniels' passage in *The Warners*:

One can get through with the finishing of many shirts a day, provided one's back holds out. Betty ... crouched over a machine hour after hour, stitching, stitching, always stitching; and the pile of garments at her side grew higher. There was always the same number to send each night. Faster work never increased it; slower she never did. The routine of her days was relentless.[55]

Other authors, in dealing with the wage question, come to grips with actual figures—the sixty cents per day earned in piece-work sewing in New York City; the dollar a day earned in mining in Pennsylvania, to be spent for groceries at the company store and for rent of one of the company's houses.[56] The dollar wage appears also in Helen Campbell's *Mrs. Herndon's Income* (1886), in which a liberal capitalist, reared in luxury, learns, by investigation, of the impossibility of keeping up the decencies of life in an American city upon such a wage scale, and of the relentless struggle with poverty which it necessitates.[57] Other novels suggest, instead of the more immediate privations, the later inescapable fruitage of long hours and low wages:—the slow drying-up of the joy of living;[58] the slow undermining of physical stamina and its consequences in disease;[59] and, upon the slightest mischance, the erasure of the workman's thin margin of security and the

[55] P. 229. See, for an additional example, Agnes Maule Machar, *op. cit.*, pp. 66-7.

[56] Edgar Fawcett, *The Evil That Men Do* (1889), pp. 8-9; Dan Beard, *Moonblight*, p. 111.

[57] Pp. 332 ff.

[58] Stephen Crane, *Maggie* (1892), pp. 61-2.

[59] Gertrude Potter Daniels, *The Warners*, p. 173; Amanda Douglas, *Hope Mills*, p. 91.

coming of actual destitution.[60] "The truth is"—so one character sums up the matter—"a large proportion of our laboring classes are always living next door to starvation, and if sickness or want comes, it is next door no longer." [61]

Yet it was not the working conditions of the urban poor, nor even the combination of exhaustion-hours and starvation-wages, that the middle-class mind found most repellent. It was rather the environment into which the poor were herded by the requirements of the factory system—an environment that was noisy, squalid, crowded, filthy, indecent. It was, in short, the Slum.

Not until the latter eighties and early nineties did the American consciousness really awaken to the existence of the Slum. Prior to that time, the subject had aroused, to be sure, a good deal of sporadic comment; Rebecca Harding Davis's remarkable story, "Life in the Iron Mills," had touched on the home life of factory workers as early as 1861, and Helen Campbell's thoughtfully written treatise, *The Problem of the Poor*, had appeared in 1882.[62] During the early eighties, Henry George and his followers had been active in persuasion and propaganda; during the latter eighties, Edward Bellamy and other Nationalists joined them in the attack on poverty. In 1890 appeared the key-book of the entire anti-slum movement, Jacob Riis's *How the Other Half Lives*, a reporter-

[60] Jacob Riis, *Out of Mulberry Street*, p. 18; Mary Wilkins Freeman, *The Portion of Labor*, p. 514.

[61] Roland Graeme, in Agnes Maule Machar's *Roland Graeme, Knight*, p. 35. The poverty described in this and other books referred to in the above paragraph is, it will be observed, urban, not rural; a poverty of the slums, not of the farms. Stories illustrating rural poverty are not numerous, even in the work of Hamlin Garland, who was most seriously concerned about it. For a treatment of rural poverty by one of the "lesser" novelists, see Mary H. Ford, *Which Wins?*, pp. 57-60, 66, 72-8, 162-76. See also, for comparable treatments of rural life, Adam Blake, *The Man with the Hoe* (1904); Harold Frederic, *Seth's Brother's Wife* (1887), especially pp. 33-4, 45-6, 387-8, 396; and Joseph Kirkland, *Zury* (1887).

[62] For early references in fiction to the slums, see Josiah Gilbert Holland, *Nicholas Minturn* (1876), pp. 281 ff.; and Charles Joseph Bellamy, *The Breton Mills* (1879), pp. 30-1, 75.

reformer's exposé of the squalor of East-Side New York, accurate, earnest, restrained, quietly eloquent. Thenceforward —and especially for the next five years—the slum was in effect a fresh literary field, strange to the readers of the eighteen-nineties as the solitary forests and great lakes of interior America had been to the reader of Fenimore Cooper's time; and both writers and readers appear to have explored that new area with an intense curiosity in which were mingled compassion, morbid fascination, and something akin to horror.

By no means all of the literature of the slum is humanitarian. Some is merely sensational journalism of human-interest appeal; some is a rendering, Wordsworthian fashion, of the romance of low life; some is the literary counterpart of a leisure-class slumming party. But insofar as such literature *is* humanitarian, its immediate object and method are well stated by Margaret Sherwood Pollock:

There was much to hope for . . . from the spread of information concerning the slum population, . . . from the awakening interest of the upper classes in its condition, and from all our new and intelligent methods of doing good.

. . . Each board-meeting, conference, committee meeting to which I went as guest or member, gave me fresh proof of the growth of knowledge about the destitute.[63]

The plain, truthful portrayal of the slum—so it was evidently thought—offers an indictment powerful enough to awaken public opinion to the need for reform.

Accordingly, slum literature abounds in descriptions of the vileness of tenement districts—rooms, houses, entire streets. A score of contemporary novels could yield up passages similar to Stephen Crane's description of the home of his heroine Maggie as

a dark region where, from a careening building, a dozen gruesome doorways gave up loads of babies to the street and the gutter. A wind of early autumn raised yellow dust from cobbles and swirled it against a hundred windows. Long streamers of garments fluttered from fire-escapes. In all unhandy places there were buckets,

[63] *An Experiment in Altruism*, p. 93.

brooms, rags, and bottles. On the street infants played or fought
with other infants or sat stupidly in the way of vehicles. Formidable women, with uncombed hair and disordered dress, gossiped
while leaning on railings, or screamed in frantic quarrels. Withered persons, in curious postures of submission to something, sat
smoking pipes in obscure corners. A thousand odors of cooking
food came forth to the street. The building quivered and creaked
from the weight of humanity stamping about in its bowels.[64]

And still other novels could offer passages similar to Helen
Campbell's description of a tenement house, as expressed by
her character, Mrs. Biggs:

"Water in the cellars, filth and mould and damp on the walls;
boards rottin' under the feet that tread 'em; dark rooms that never
get air nor a gleam o' sunshine, an' that smell . . . !" [65]

From these two treatments, H. H. Boyesen's differs chiefly
in his heavier emphasis on the rowdiness, foulness, and hatred
liberated by the slum environment; Charles Dudley Warner's,
in his sense of the extreme difficulty of alleviating poverty;
Paul Leicester Ford's, in his ironic comment on the relative
importance of property rights and human rights, the careful
storage of goods in great warehouses and the careless storage
of labor in the tenements—"any place serves to pack humanity." [66] But whatever the differences among such descriptions,
they all agree in creating an impression of darkness, foulness,

---

[64] *Maggie,* pp. 9-10. Reprinted by permission of Alfred A. Knopf, Inc.
The use of this quotation is not intended to suggest any reforming or
humanitarian interest in Crane. It is perhaps worthy of observation, in
passing, that it could hardly have been the *materials* of Crane's *Maggie*
that publishers found objectionable. These, including the theme of
poverty as a factor in prostitution, were simply the commonplaces of
antipoverty literature. Crane's naturalistic, amoral attitude was, however, new.

[65] Helen Campbell, *Mrs. Herndon's Income,* pp. 240 ff.

[66] H. H. Boyesen, *Social Strugglers* (1893), pp. 260 ff.; Charles
Dudley Warner, *The Golden House* (1885), p. 74; Paul Leicester
Ford, *The Honorable Peter Stirling,* pp. 48-9. For some among numer-
ous other fictional descriptions of the slum, see Campbell, *op. cit.,* pp.
43-4; Machar, *op. cit.,* p. 18; Riis, *Nibsy's Christmas,* pp. 11, 25; Kate
Douglas Wiggin, *Timothy's Quest* (1890), pp. 7, 10.

dampness, noise, crowding, squalor, smell, general ugliness, and brutalizing struggle. They all agree in demonstrating that society in a supposedly democratic country compels a considerable aggregate of its members to live under conditions that ought to be intolerable, but are not.

And yet the most searching indictment of urban poverty does not rest on the ground of any humanitarian tenderness for the suffering. It rests, instead, on the ground of the social harm done by the slum, as a breeder of physical and moral weakness. In its treatment of health, tenement fiction ranges from stories of individual illness under conditions that forbid any privacy, any of the decencies of life, or any effective medical care, through stories of the sapping of children's physiques by malnutrition and near-starvation, to descriptions of the tenements as source and cause of general epidemics.[67] But the attack does not stop with the demonstration of such obvious social dangers as these. In antipoverty literature there is also a genuine concern for the creation of human values, for the development of fine lives, and consequently for the elimination of the slum because of its destructiveness to both.

Of the moral dangers of the slum, the one given most frequent and definite fictional treatment is its influence in fostering prostitution—a theme easily dramatized, easily invested with sentiment. For example, in Edgar Fawcett's *The Evil That Men Do,* the virtuous heroine, Cora Strang, is pursued, betrayed, and ruined by men, quite as in an old-fashioned Richardsonian novel of sentiment, but with the important difference that, in the making of Cora's tragedy, the main force is the barren, unprotected, joyless life of the tenement working girl.[68] In *Maggie,* Stephen Crane's heroine follows the same course as Fawcett's Cora Strang—first a virtuous girl, then a mistress, then a prostitute—and follows it because of

[67] Amanda Douglas, *op. cit.,* p. 129; Paul Leicester Ford, *op. cit.,* pp. 54, 58; Machar, *op. cit.,* p. 230; Margaret Sherwood Pollock, *An Experiment in Altruism,* p. 67; Jacob Riis, *Nibsy's Christmas,* pp. 27, 35-8; Clinton Scollard Ross, *The Silent Workman,* p. 43.

[68] For certain key passages, see pp. 8-9, 18-19, 74-9, 89, 96, 107, 306, and especially, on the economic implications of the story, p. 117.

much the same social and economic compulsions.[69] The two novels differ widely, to be sure, in manner; for where Fawcett is verbose, flaccid, sentimental, and didactic, Crane is concise, vigorous, unsentimental, and amoral. But they wholly agree with each other, and with other writings,[70] in their controlling thesis. Moreover, the slum environment is charged with being responsible, not only for the encouragement of prostitution, but also for the general fostering of juvenile delinquency,[71] and for the moulding of potentially normal youth into criminals. Jacob Riis, in interpreting the story of a tenement boy who grows up into a gangster and gunman, concludes that the environment, not the boy, is to blame. "The real reckoning of outraged society is not with him, but with Scrabble Alley." [72]

The most serious and far reaching charge made against an environment of extreme poverty is, in short, that it virtually destroys the possibility of creating fine lives. Of the slum population, later writers often merely reiterate, in different words, what Elizabeth Stuart Phelps had earlier said of the stunted lives of a community of mill hands. In *The Silent Partner*, her character, Catty Garth, a deaf-mute who is going blind from an occupational disease, becomes a

type of the world from which she sprang—the world of exhausted and corrupted body, of exhausted and corrupted brain, of exhausted and corrupted soul, the world of the laboring poor as man has made it, and as Christ has died for it, a world deaf, dumb, blind, doomed, stepping cheerfully to its destruction before our eyes.[73]

[69] For Crane's interpretation of the influence of the slum environment, see, in *Maggie*, pp. 39-62.

[70] For example, James William Sullivan, *op. cit.*, pp. 74-87; Margaret Sherwood Pollock, *An Experiment in Altruism*, pp. 184-5.

[71] Elizabeth Stuart Phelps, *op. cit.*, p. 211.

[72] Jacob Riis, *Nibsy's Christmas*, pp. 43-52.

[73] Elizabeth Stuart Phelps, *op. cit.*, p. 277.

The fact that our literature dealing with the urban poor contains the above-outlined indictment does not mean, of course, that the picture is one of unrelieved gloom. For pictures of the cheerful side of tenement life, see especially Jacob Riis, *Out of Mulberry Street*, pp. 4, 5,

IV

If the typical Left-Center novelist condemned industrialism as a cause of undeserved poverty, he also condemned it as a cause of undeserved wealth. And the chief ground of his latter condemnation is, paradoxically enough, the same—that abnormal wealth, like abnormal poverty, thwarts the creation of the finer human values. To him, the ideal of Success, in the sense of the rapid heaping-up of riches, appeared tawdry and unsatisfying, and he subjected it to sharp criticism. Sinclair Lewis and Willa Cather were, in short, by no means the first American novelists to object to our acquisitive materialism; *Babbitt* and *The Professor's House* were, in this respect, anticipated by a number of novels published before 1900.

The philosophy underlying the attack on Success—a philosophy implicit in most of the novels and explicit in some—is a kind of informal humanism. Success—that is, victory in the business struggle—is looked on as simply a phase in the natu-

---

25 ff., 41, and others. For stories in which the general interest exceeds the sociological, see Abraham Cahan, *The Imported Bridegroom* (1898) and *Yekl* (1896); Alvin Francis Sanborn, *Meg McIntyre's Raffle* (1896); Kate Douglas Wiggin, *Timothy's Quest;* and, especially, Isaac K. Friedman's charming romance, *Poor People* (1900). For a novel dealing with a related subject, the life of the tramp, see Josiah Flynt, *The Little Brother* (1902). For works not mentioned above in the text, but concerned in one way or another with the problem of urban poverty, see the list below. Dates are given for those titles that have not previously occurred in this chapter:
  Barr, Mrs. Amelia, *The King's Highway* (1897)
  Bellamy, Charles Joseph, *The Breton Mills*
  Betts, Lilian W., *The Story of an East Side Family* (1903)
  Harriman, K. E., *The Homebuilders* (1904)
  Holland, Josiah Gilbert, *Nicholas Minturn,* pp. 281 ff. especially
  King, Edward, *Joseph Zalmonah* (1893)
  McCardell, Roy L., *The Wage Slaves of New York* (1899)
  Mead, Mrs. Lucia True, *Memoirs of a Millionaire*, pp. 84-5 especially
  Riis, Jacob, *Children of the Tenements* (1903)
  Scudder, Vida D., *A Listener in Babel* (1904)
  Smith, Edgar Maurice, *A Daughter of Humanity* (1895)
  Stanton, Edward, *Dreams of the Dead* (1892)

ral struggle for survival, the brutality of which is repellent to man's aspiration to be *above,* as well as *in,* Nature. In Robert Herrick's *The Web of Life,* the rebellious physician, Sommers, speaks of it as "a brutal game, this business success,—a good deal worse than war, where you line up in the open at least," [74] and comes to feel, in some moods, that the struggle for success is worse than anarchy:

> The brutal axioms of the economists urged men to climb, to dominate, and held out as the noblest ideal of the great commonwealth the right of every man to triumph over his brother. If the world could not be run on any less brutal plan than this creed of *success, success,* then let there be anarchy—anything.[75]

Even more concretely put is the judgment of Will Payne's character, Nidstrom:

> What can you expect? With everybody scrambling and clutching, even if you're lucky enough to grab something you must take the chance of somebody else grabbing it away while you're reaching for another piece. It's part of the plan.[76]

Success, then, as realized in the ownership of great wealth, is only proof of the possession of sharper beak and longer claw, not of any peculiarly human grace, intelligence, or virtue.[77]

For the most part, the critics of wealth go at their attack pragmatically, by showing the harmful effects of riches both on the owners and on other people whose lives the wealthier folk affect. They charge, characteristically, that wealth may

[74] Robert Herrick, *The Web of Life,* p. 154.

[75] *Ibid.,* pp. 201-2. Reprinted by permission of The Macmillan Company, publishers. See also p. 40, and, for Sommers' opinion that the possession of wealth is largely a matter of chance, p. 105.

[76] Will Payne, *The Money Captain* (1898), p. 159. For still another identification of Success with the struggle for survival, see H. H. Boyesen, *The Mammon of Unrighteousness* (1891), pp. 165, 241, 318.

[77] The most carefully wrought elaboration of this idea is in the work of Edward Bellamy, for which see below, pp. 197, 202. Occasionally, one comes on a passage in which the opposition to Success appears to stem from the old aristocratic feeling that Trade is inherently cheapening. See, for example, Charles K. Lush, *The Autocrats,* pp. 6-7.

destroy character by fostering "bestial indulgence"; [78] that, by removing any stimulus to effort, it may cause a man to become a soft, uncreative dilettante [79] or even a wastrel; [80] that it may, by undermining the character of a single person, destroy the happiness of an entire family.[81] Perhaps the most powerful story illustrating this thesis, George Cary Eggleston's and Mary Shell Bacon's *Juggernaut* (1891), tells how Edgar Braine, in the midst of a feverishly intense struggle for wealth and power, attempts to use his wife as a financial tool, and in so doing brings about the destruction both of her character and of their mutual happiness. "Juggernaut"—the craze for quickly gained, immense wealth—"has passed over his soul and Helen's." [82]

On the other hand, in Charles Dudley Warner's *A Little Journey in the World,* the destruction of character does not take the form of spectacular catastrophe, but rather that of slow enervation in the midst of a cloying materialism. Margaret Debree is, in her early youth, a girl of charm, warm human sympathy, sensitive perception, and spirituality.[83] But after her marriage to the wealthy speculator Henderson, she drifts apart from her old friends, falls in with a group of the idle rich at Newport, and finally sinks passively into the luxury of a new palatial home. "What I saw in a vision of her future," the narrator says of her, "was a dead soul—a beautiful woman in all the success of envied prosperity, with a dead soul." [84]

The loss of sympathy with mankind, the growth of callousness toward suffering, the ennui and the spiritual barrenness that follow the limiting of one's interest to the narrow range

[78] Henry Francis Keenan, *The Money-Makers,* p. 156.

[79] For example, Fred Lawrence in Amanda Douglas's *Hope Mills.* See especially p. 61.

[80] For example, Walter Hampton in H. H. Boyesen's *A Daughter of the Philistines.*

[81] This is the theme of David Graham Phillips' *The Master Rogue* (1904).

[82] George Cary Eggleston and Mary Shell Bacon, *Juggernaut,* p. 343. See also pp. 225, 281, 312-6.

[83] Charles Dudley Warner, *A Little Journey in the World,* p. 45.

[84] *Ibid.,* p. 383. See also pp. 242, 287, 322-3, 351.

of material comfort [85]—these effects are, however serious in themselves, among the milder evils charged against great wealth; but the charges are not always mildly expressed. Philip Warburton, in H. H. Boyesen's *Social Strugglers,* puts the case as follows:

If wealth entails the loss of human sympathy, as in nine cases out of ten it seems to do, I regard it as a misfortune. If it means, as in this country it seems to mean, the loss of vital contact with humanity, the contraction of one's mental and spiritual horizon, a callous insensibility to social wrongs and individual sorrows, a brutal induration in creature comforts and mere animal well-being, the loss of that divine discontent and noble aspiration which alone makes us human—if it means this or any part of it, it is the greatest calamity which can befall a man.[86]

Nor is it only the wealthy themselves who are injured by wealth. Others, through subservience to the wealthy, may become their tools and dupes in the search for Success; others may, in short, be diverted from more humanly valuable pursuits into less valuable. The social climber, the capitalist's tool, the young professional man forced to choose between integrity and prosperity, all figure as types in the literature of the Gilded Age. With practically no exceptions, the portrayal of the social climber is a hostile one. In Robert Grant's *Unleavened Bread* (1900), the climber Selma White contrives, by an unscrupulous following of the main chance through three marriages, to arrive at Success as the wife of a United States senator, after first making him sacrifice his honor to win the nomination. But the bread of Selma's character is not at all leavened by her "rise," and at the close of her story

[85] For additional instances of the treatment of these subjects, see Robert Herrick, *The Web of Life,* pp. 151-2; David Graham Phillips, *The Great God Success* (1901); Clinton Scollard Ross, *The Speculator,* p. 37.

[86] Hjalmar Hjorth Boyesen, *Social Strugglers,* pp. 84-5. See also, for treatments of wealth or "Society" not referred to above, Mrs. Ellen Warner Kirk, *Queen Money* (1888), and *A Daughter of Eve* (1889); Charles Dudley Warner, *The Golden House* and *That Fortune.* Similar to those novels, but far less definitely didactic, is Henry Blake Fuller's *With the Procession* (1895).

she is still suffering from the tragedy—or rather the high comedy—of being the thing she is.[87] In Edgar Fawcett's *An Ambitious Woman* (1884), Claire Twining finds merely social and worldly success unsatisfying. In H. H. Boyesen's *Social Strugglers*, the complacent Philistinism of Sally Bulkley and her wealthy husband Marston Fancher is clearly evaluated by Maud Bulkley and her fiancé Philip Warburton: "The satisfactions which it (social success) yields are not even remotely in proportion to the expenditure of time, money, and energy which it involves." [88]

Other novels deal with the character of the man who succeeds by making himself useful as a tool to the capitalist, as do the brilliant Hilliard in H. F. Keenan's *The Money-Makers* [89] and John Andross in Rebecca Harding Davis's novel of that name. The authors' social criticism turns, in both novels, on the undue subservience paid to wealth [90] and the prostituting of truly fine talents to unworthy ends. Always unfortunate, the surrender to commercialism may become tragic when the fine standards of some creative profession are compromised for the sake of immediate gain. To choose prosperity at the expense of integrity is to invite disaster. The ultimate logic of such a choice is most strikingly dramatized, no doubt, in Robert Herrick's *The Common Lot*. Jackson Hart, a young architect, allows himself to become involved, for the sake of quick financial success, in a scheme of jerry-building. Gradually he wears away his talent in uncreative work; and finally he suffers the terrible retribution of watching human beings burn to death in a hotel which he had designed in the full knowledge that it might become a fire-trap.[91]

[87] In this novel, Grant strikingly anticipates Sinclair Lewis in his satire of the pseudo-education of a certain type of American woman, and in his ridicule of "Methodists," politicians, and small-town boosters. For passages treating specifically of economics, see pp. 110, 100.

[88] H. H. Boyesen, *Social Strugglers*, pp. 287-9.

[89] Pp. 14-6, 27, 181 ff.

[90] See, especially, *John Andross*, p. 135. Cf. with this Josiah Gilbert Holland, *Sevenoaks*, pp. 15, 19, 160.

[91] For Herrick's clearest presentation in the novel of the choice between sound work and commercialization, see pp. 54-5. Compare with

To the degree that the social climber and capitalist's tool are unfavorably treated, the idealist and liberal who rebel against the dominance of wealth are portrayed sympathetically. In Margaret Deland's "The House of Rimmon," the heroine, Mrs. Eaton, rebels by simply refusing to accept any support whatever from a family business she knows to be based on dishonesty and injustice.[92] In H. H. Boyesen's *Social Strugglers,* Maud Bulkley and Philip Warburton give up the luxurious life of their class simply because they find it barren of satisfactions. In Robert Herrick's *The Gospel of Freedom* (1898), Adela Wilbur rebels not only against the meaningless round of social functions in which she is engaged, but also against the dubious business ethics of her husband and the emptiness of a life cut to the patterns of a thrifty, religious, and dull "bourgeoisie." Her solution of the problem—a solution far less buttressed with certainty than that of Boyesen's hero and heroine—leaves her only with the desire that, having freed herself, she may "learn how to live." [93]

In Herrick's *The Web of Life,* the profoundest and most dramatically powerful novel of this kind, the rebel is the idealistic, inarticulate young physician, Sommers, who is unable to reconcile himself to the shallowness and futility of life among his wealthy clientele in Chicago. During the Pullman strike, he casts his sympathies definitely on the side of the worker, enters into a *liaison* with the teacher Alves Preston, and wholly estranges himself from his class. But his sym-

---

this story David Graham Phillips's *The Great God Success,* especially pp. 122, 167-8, 266-74, 294. For other treatments of the possible harmful effects of industrialism on the professions, see Florence Converse, *The Burden of Christopher,* pp. 195-6; Ellen Glasgow, *Phases of an Inferior Planet,* especially pp. 142-3, 165-76; Robert Herrick, *Memoirs of an American Citizen,* the character of the minister, Hardman, especially p. 213.

[92] Margaret Deland, "The House of Rimmon," in *The Wisdom of Fools,* especially pp. 92-5, 120. Mrs. Eaton's pattern of conduct is, it might be observed in passing, precisely that advocated by Thoreau in "Civil Disobedience."

[93] Robert Herrick, *The Gospel of Freedom,* p. 202. For other significant passages in the novel, see pp. 104 ff., 112, 123-4, 195, 202.

pathy with the common people is too heavily burdened with disillusion, too darkly colored by a mystical, poetic fatalism,[94] to incite him to active leadership in reform. He finds peace, after a time, in the somewhat strangely twinned satisfactions of renunciation and craftsmanship; in the resolution to forget himself in giving his best to his profession, with the expectation of only a moderate financial return.

In summary view, the left-center *critique* of the evils of industrialism appears searching, extensive, and, considering the varieties of story and personality involved, surprisingly coherent. In virtually its every expression, that *critique* is a product of our American, democratic, middle-class culture. From the viewpoint of the middle-class ethical theory of honesty, prudence, and thrift, it exposes and condemns the unethical practices of Big Business, especially as these latter tend to undermine the integrity of our democratic government. From the viewpoint of democratic equality, it examines, exposes, and condemns the effect of capitalistic industrialism in creating sharply defined classes of the very rich and the very poor. It presents, frankly and honestly, the distressing squalor of life in the slums, and illustrates how such an environment destroys rather than creates value. And it criticizes also the life of the very rich, inculcating the barrenness of merely material success, and insisting that not acquisition but fine living is the genuinely worthy goal of life.

It is now pertinent to examine the remedies that were proposed for the cure of these evils.

V

The constructive suggestions of the Left-Center novelists are as scattered and unintegrated as their destructive *critique* is pointed and coherent. The evils of industrialism, as they appeared to a typical middle-class, democratic mind, were clear enough; the possible remedy was not at all clear, and was a subject of wide disagreement. For, while certain novelists would have had America seek reform by some rearrange-

[94] For typical expressions, see pp. 168-9, 348.

ment of the social machinery, a second group looked for reform rather to the organization of labor; a third, to the humanitarian leadership of the prosperous classes; and a fourth, to some gradual, deep-seated change in the motives or psychology of the race, such as the extension of the motive of brotherly love. Furthermore, since these various proposals for reform are not mutually exclusive, a novelist might at the same time advocate two or more of them, as Agnes Maule Machar supported at the same time Christian socialism and the organization of labor. But on one subject—the very one which designates their position as a "Left-Center" and not a true "Left"—the novelists were in complete agreement. Uniformly, they opposed the adoption of radical methods of reform—the mild, middle-class socialism of some of their own compatriots only less than the tougher-minded Marxian socialism which looked toward a violent proletarian revolution.

The Left-Center's hostility to socialism often found expression in the very *genre* which the work of Bellamy and others was linking indissolubly with the collectivist ideal—the Utopia. Obviously, a Utopian story-framework could be used as easily to ridicule socialism as to defend it. For example, Anna Bowman Dodd, in *The Republic of the Future* (1887), pictures satirically a "Utopian" state where socialism has brought forth its perfect fruit; a state where paternalistic regimentation has gone so far that even food may be taken only on medical prescription; a state in which the people, because of the very *ennui* of entire security, have sunk into cureless melancholy.[95] And, just as easily, the Utopia could be made to illustrate, along with the errors of collectivism, the rightness of a liberal, individualistic social program. In Richard Michaelis's *Looking Forward* (1890)—one of the numerous replies to Bellamy's *Looking Backward*[96]—the author claims that a realistic view of human nature would reveal

[95] Anna Bowman Dodd, *The Republic of the Future*, pp. 23, 30, 35-40, 58, 63-6.

[96] For a brief account of the controversy, with additional references, see below, pp. 205-7.

Bellamy's collective state as a thing as fantastic as the experiences of his hero Julian West:

> The surmise, that men and women in a communistic state, would put off all selfishness, envy, hate, jealousy, wrangling and desire to rule is just as reasonable as the supposition, that a man can sleep one hundred and thirteen years and rise thereafter as fresh and young as when he went to bed.[97]

Accordingly, Bellamy's machinery of state socialism, were it operated by average human beings, would eventually produce more serious evils even than the present one. Productive efficiency would decline; a corrupt bureaucracy would develop; and the authoritarian state, so administered, would evoke in opposition a violent, destructive radicalism.[98] On the other hand, a sound program of liberal reform, suited to both the needs and the limitations of human nature, might practically include an attack on monopolies, the taxation of large inheritances, the better organization of labor, and the scientific study of demand and production.[99]

Such opposition to any radical change in society is characteristic of the novels of the Left-Center, no less than of the Utopias; and in proportion as that change is associated with lawlessness and violence, the opposition becomes more uncompromising, the denunciation more severe. The danger of violence is shown, for example, in the story of the agitator Kirby in Gertrude Potter Daniels' *The Warners*. Kirby, fanatical, desperate, throws a bomb at a detachment of police; it falls short and explodes among the bystanders; and the flight of the crowd leaves exposed in the street the bodies of two innocent victims—Kirby's wife and child.[100] Although few scenes in anti-radical fiction are quite as melodramatic as this, both the radical agitator and the various -*isms* he may stand for are constantly portrayed in the same hostile light.[101] The

[97] *Looking Forward*, Preface, p. iv.

[98] *Ibid.*, pp. 22, 37-47, 57-9, 78, 85-9.

[99] *Ibid.*, pp. 96 ff.

[100] *The Warners*, pp. 103, 172-80.

[101] See, for example, Helen Campbell, *Mrs. Herndon's Income*, pp. 78, 457; Amanda Douglas, *Hope Mills*, pp. 112-4; Mary Wilkins Free-

typical novelist of the Left-Center, serious as he thought the evils of capitalistic industrialism, looked for their correction not to the entire rebuilding of society, but to other and milder measures.[102]

In a nation committed in theory to a government of, by, and for the people, it was only natural that some novelists should look for reform to some legislated change in the social machinery. In *An Iron Crown*, Thomas Scott Denison answers his question "What must we do?" in the two words, "Purify politics." The purification of politics is to be secured (it presently appears) by depriving the illiterate of the vote, awakening public interest in politics and public honesty, and reforming the jury system; it is to result in—among other outcomes—governmental regulation of the common carriers.[103] A somewhat more paternalistic program appears in Richard Michaelis's *Looking Forward*, in the advocacy of governmental action against trusts, and of government ownership of natural monopolies.[104] Dwight Tilton's still more ambitious program, in *On Satan's Mount* (1903), looks toward the organization of a national party composed of all who labor.[105]

---

man, *The Portion of Labor*, pp. 100, 413-9. An exception is the sympathetic forecast of a proletarian revolution in Henry Francis Keenan's *The Money-Makers*, pp. 245-7.

[102] The union of opposition to socialism with support of liberal reform is to be found in the following Utopian stories, not mentioned above:

Bachelder, John, *A.D. 2050* (1890), especially pp. 3-5
Caswell, Edward A., *Toil and Self* (1900)
Hale, Edward Everett, *How they Lived at Hampton* (1888), especially pp. 260 ff.
Leland, Samuel Phelps, *Peculiar People* (1892)
Roberts, J. W., *Looking Within* (1893)
Van Deventer, Emma M., *Moina*, or *Against the Mighty* (1891)
Welcome, S. Byron, *From Earth's Center* (1894).

[103] Denison, *op. cit.*, pp. 128-9, 467-8.

[104] Michaelis, *op. cit.*, pp. 96 ff.

[105] Dwight Tilton, *On Satan's Mount*, p. 328. See also F. Marion Crawford's *An American Politician*, pp. 65-7; and, for an attitude rather skeptical of the value of political action, Isaac K. Friedman, *The Radical* (1907), pp. 360-2.

The subject of the control of the currency, so bitterly fought over in the political struggles of the nineties, appears in a number of novels, which range in viewpoint from Ignatius Donnelly's Populist, anti-gold-standard position in *The Golden Bottle* (1892) to the sound-money thesis of Garrett P. Serviss's *The Moon Metal* (1900).[106]—And yet, on the whole, proposals for liberal economic legislation are less numerous, less significant, than the actual history of the period, plus the long conditioning of the American mind in political thought, might lead one to expect.[107]

While some novelists of the Left-Center expected reform to come through political action, others looked rather to such nonpolitical methods as the organization of Labor. The idealistic aims of the Knights of Labor are illustrated by Agnes Maule Machar, who has the labor leader Jeffrey express his hope that laborers will "maintain an unselfish policy.... They must be generous to unorganized labor also. Their cause must be the cause of labor as a whole." [108] Grant M. Overton stresses, on the other hand, the growing divergence between rich and poor, and in consequence the practical need of an organization of labor to combat the organization of capital.[109] Overton, Leroy Scott, and Marie Van Vorst all stress the need of able leadership, and idealize the labor leader who is honest,

[106] For other treatments of the currency question, see:
Adams, Frederick Upham, *President John Smith* (1897)
Chamberlain, Henry A., *Six Thousand Tons of Gold* (1894)
Dement, R. S., *Ronbar* (1895)
Hill, Beveridge, *The Story of a Canyon* (1895)
Phelps, Corwin, *An Ideal Republic* (1896)
Tibbles, T. H., and Mrs. Elia W. Peattie, *The American Peasant* (1892)

[107] The comparatively limited treatment of social legislation by the authors of the Left-Center should not be taken to indicate a *general* neglect of the subject in our fiction. Authors of the socialistic Left (see below, pp. 104-7) were necessarily concerned with politics. See also the analysis of the relation between economic and political thought in the writings of Clemens, Garland, Bellamy, and Howells, below, pp. 123 and 133 ff., 155 ff., 193 ff., 250 ff., respectively.

[108] Machar, *op. cit.*, p. 189.

[109] Grant M. Overton, *Captains of the World*, pp. 25, 74.

moderate, courageous, and faithful to his class.[110] Leroy Scott's Tom Keating, the finest character of this sort, meets his severest test not when he exposes a corrupt walking delegate or when he wins a strike, but when he refuses an excellent offer of promotion in order to remain faithful to the proletariat.[111]

Somewhat more frequently than to some social rearrangement or to the organization of labor, authors of the Left-Center looked for economic reform to the voluntary leadership of the more prosperous classes. And that leadership, they hoped, would find some more fruitful expression than the mere supporting of charity. To them, charity was an immediate necessity, if many of the poor were not to starve; but its usefulness could be only that of temporary alleviation, not of genuine cure. Typical of this attitude toward charity is the feeling of the social worker, Genevieve Radcliffe, in Hervey White's *Differences*. Genevieve, during a week of terrible cold, that came when unemployment was at its peak,

was growing hardened and dazed for lack of time to despair in. . . . There was no time for the stipulated investigation. It was give, give, recklessly to all now. . . . Here was work to be done, or fellow-beings would die of cold and hunger. She knew that the method was a bad one; but for the time it was her best, and she could not stop to criticize.[112]

Many of the objections to charity turn upon the harm presumably done to both parties involved: to the giver, in that his motives may be cheapened by condescension and pride of class, or that his object in giving may be only the purchase

[110] *Ibid.*, p. 190; Leroy Scott, *The Walking Delegate* (1905), the portions of the story relating to Tom Keating, and especially pp. 82, 327, 363; Marie Van Vorst, *Amanda of the Mill*, the portions relating to Henry Euston.

[111] Scott, *op. cit.*, pp. 367-8. For other writings sympathetic with organized labor, see Martin A. Foran's *From the Other Side* (1886) and Charles M. Sheldon's *The Crucifixion of Philip Strong* (1894). See also, in regard to Mark Twain's support of organized labor, below, pp. 134 ff. For a discussion of anti-labor fiction, see below, pp. 109 ff.

[112] *Differences*, p. 51.

of good will; [113] to the recipient, in that charity forces upon him a type of aid he does not want, humiliates him, sets him apart in a "class," and tends to enervate him morally.[114] At least one story approaches the problem from another viewpoint—that of showing the confusing pressures brought to bear upon a philanthropist, and the difficulty of sorting out worthy from unworthy causes.[115] Evidently, the typical American novelist could not envisage or countenance the need for organized charity as a permanent part of the American social scheme; he desired, rather, the reform of those conditions which had made charity necessary. Charities for children, however, he generally approved; and the usefulness of charity as a means of immediate relief, he always recognized.

Charity is not, then, to be the main social concern of the prosperous classes; the principal thing, fundamental, underlying all others, is their recognition of their responsibility for social leadership. With the luxuries enjoyed by the wealthy go corresponding obligations. In Elizabeth Stuart Phelps' *The Silent Partner*, the heroine, Perley Kelso, insists that when she inherits the wealth of her father's factory holdings, she inherits the responsibilities too. Denied an active part in the management of the mills, she nevertheless undertakes, as a social worker, to introduce into the lives of the mill hands as many humane elements as possible.[116] Similarly, Mrs. Lucia Mead, in *Memoirs of a Millionaire*, deals with the use of wealth for social betterment, particularly in the erection of improved tenements; and David Graham Phillips includes in *The Deluge* a lesson on "responsibility in possession." [117]

But when the novelist faced the question, "Just what defi-

[113] Margaret Sherwood Pollock, *An Experiment in Altruism*, p. 100; Morrison I. Swift, *The Monarch Billionaire* (1903), pp. 187 ff.; Charles Dudley Warner, *A Little Journey in the World*, p. 374.

[114] Florence Converse, *The Burden of Christopher*, p. 59; Paul Leicester Ford, *The Honorable Peter Stirling*, p. 259; Hervey White, *Differences*, pp. 3, 15.

[115] Helen Campbell, *Mrs. Herndon's Income*, pp. 169 ff.

[116] Phelps, *op. cit.*, pp. 61, 230 ff.

[117] Mrs. Lucia True Ames Mead, *Memoirs of a Millionaire*, pp. 119 ff.; David Graham Phillips, *The Deluge* (1905), p. 262. See also, in connec-

nite, practical work may a wealthy person do in order to fulfill his social responsibilities?" his answer was not always adequate. Of his two most frequent replies, one is that such a person might well enter some humanitarian work in the slums. The fictional counterparts of Toynbee Hall and Hull House are numerous. One frequently repeated plot, for example, turns on the revolt of some socially minded youth of means against the acquisitive life of his social group, and his discovery of spiritual peace in some effort toward the improvement of the tenements. In H. H. Boyesen's *Social Strugglers*, Maud Bulkley comes to see the hollowness of an exclusively social career, gives up the expectation of making a wealthy marriage, and, accepting the love of a man in only moderate circumstances, shares his interest in the development of a group of tenement boys at a social center. Variations of this typical story appear in Elizabeth Stuart Phelps' *The Silent Partner*, Amanda Douglas' *Hope Mills*, Margaret Sherwood Pollock's *An Experiment in Altruism*, Vida D. Scudder's *A Listener in Babel*, and other novels. The humanitarian activities proposed in these stories are sufficiently various: industrial education; the maintaining of church mission centers; the teaching of home economics, especially with regard to budgeting and cooking; the maintaining of coffeehouses, club-rooms, classes for small children, and club-groupings for older boys and girls; and the fostering of various quasi-charitable endeavors.[118] The fictional picture of the

---

tion with the treatment of the responsibilities attendant on wealth, Thomas and Anna M. Fitch, *Better Days, or A Millionaire's Tomorrow* (1892), and Alvah Milton Kerr, *An Honest Lawyer* (1892), especially pp. 129, 261.

[118] Helen Campbell, *Mrs. Herndon's Income*, pp. 236, 428, with which compare the discussion in the same author's social study, *The Problem of the Poor*, pp. 214 ff.; Amanda Douglas, *Hope Mills*, pp. 172-3, 214-8; Agnes Maule Machar, *Roland Graeme, Knight*, pp. 126, 159; Margaret Sherwood Pollock, *An Experiment in Altruism*, pp. 37-47; Vida D. Scudder, *A Listener in Babel*, pp. 127-8; Albion W. Tourgée, *Murvale Eastman, Christian Socialist*, p. 524. In somewhat the same class of fiction belong Helen Campbell's *Miss Melinda's Opportunity* (1886), Kate Douglas Wiggin's *The Story of Patsy* (1889), and portions of other novels.

Settlement may, in short, be deficient in profundity and drama; it is not lacking in abundance, or in frequency of repetition.

If the leadership of the prosperous classes is often portrayed as taking the form of Settlement or other humanitarian work, it is even more frequently pictured as initiating some form of capital-labor coöperation, particularly profit-sharing. Just as one frequently used plot portrays the wealthy young humanitarian turning settlement worker, so another portrays him introducing into his factory some plan of coöperative management. For instance, Florence Converse's ably written novel, *The Burden of Christopher*, presents the tragic breakdown of a man whose introduction of profit-sharing eventuates, paradoxically, in personal dishonor. Christopher Kenyon, having inherited a shoe factory, resolves to operate it on an eight-hour day, profit-sharing basis.[119] For several years he meets, though with great difficulty, the competition of low-wage, long-hour shops. Finally, acting under great emotional strain, he takes money from a trust fund to invest in his own tottering business; and, when discovered, he escapes public humiliation by suicide. But his experiment, because of its fruits in the lives of his workmen, has been far from a failure. According to Christopher's friend Philip Starr,

"It was well worth while giving twelve hundred men and women and their children eleven years of breathing space and good food. It was well worth while letting up the pressure. These men have minds; they are reasonable; more than that, they are thoughtful, and, in the best sense of the term, ambitious." [120]

Other novels of profit-sharing differ from *The Burden of Christopher* in story, or in the details of the profit-sharing scheme, not in underlying philosophy. In most, the great difficulty of conducting a partly humanitarian enterprise in the midst of an exclusively profit-making economy is made abundantly plain; [121] in most, the initiative is taken by some indi-

[119] *The Burden of Christopher*, p. 44.
[120] *Ibid.*, pp. 298-9.
[121] See, for an additional example, Amanda Douglas, *Hope Mills*, especially pp. 340-67.

vidual capitalist, usually a youth, who is impelled into the task by humanitarian motives. The socio-ethical principle involved is the superiority of coöperation over unmodified competition. Usually implicit, it is put into words by the character Wilkinson in David N. Beach's *The Annie Laurie Mine* (1902):

> "The way out is not in the opposition of class to class, of capital to labor, of wealth to poverty; but in their getting together; in their understanding one another; in a large forbearance toward one another."[122]

At times, coöperation through profit-sharing is fused with that rather vague sentiment called Christian socialism; through profit-sharing, the Christian ideal of brotherly helpfulness can find practical realization.[123] In several novels—such as Helen Campbell's *Mrs. Herndon's Income,* Alice Prescott Smith's *The Legatee* (1903), George Kibbe Turner's *The Taskmasters* (1902), and Marie Van Vorst's *Philip Longstreth* (1902)— while no formal scheme of profit-sharing is presented, the same effects follow from kindred means—the enlightened, just, and honest conduct of business, or a benevolent paternalism on the part of the capitalist. Novels of this kind are, however, greatly outnumbered by those in which profit-sharing is advocated outright.[124]

But during the same years when novels illustrative of political reform, or labor organization, or settlement work, or the sharing of profits, were appearing, other novels, of comparable number, were being built about the core-idea that economic reform is to come, not through any social device, but only

[122] Pp. 216-7.

[123] See, for example, Machar, *op. cit.,* especially p. 101; Tourgée, *op. cit.,* pp. 536-7.

[124] For other treatments of profit-sharing, not referred to in the above discussion, see the following:

Bellamy, Charles Joseph, *The Breton Mills,* especially pp. 230 ff.

Bennett, Mary E., *Asaph's Ten Thousand* (1890), especially pp. 285 ff.

Martin, James W., *Which Way, Sirs, the Better?* (1895)

Porter, Lynn Boyd, *Speaking of Ellen*

Warner, Beverley E., *Troubled Waters* (1885), especially pp. 116-7, 317 ff.

through some gradual human development in motives and racial character. To stimulate such inward growth was the principal object of those who called themselves Christian socialists. To their thinking, it was only logical that the Christian ethic of kindliness to one's neighbor should be broadened from a merely individual application to a social one. By a sufficiently widespread practice of Christian consideration for others, they assumed, the evils of industrialism would be automatically cured.

The most carefully considered novel of Christian socialism is, perhaps, Albion W. Tourgée's *Murvale Eastman, Christian Socialist.* The social task of Christianity, as defined by Tourgée's minister-hero, Murvale Eastman, is not that of striving for any particular economic system, but rather that of Christianizing the human nature that underlies all mechanisms.

The function of the Church as an element of civilization, is not to prescribe methods, not to devise remedies; that is the function of government, the duty of society. The function of the Church is only to inspire action, to provide impulse, to exalt and purify motive, to incline men to apply the Christ-spirit to collective human relations.

Accordingly,

As the Lord of the Sabbath devoted his life on earth to doing good, so he demands that his followers, of all classes and conditions, shall make the welfare of their fellows the first and highest object in life, after their own wants and the comfort of those dependent upon them. *This is Christian Socialism.*[125]

As to the practical work in which such motives might eventuate, Judge Tourgée suggests the possibility of social legislation, of the placing of social burdens principally on the strong, of profit-sharing, and of the further study of social questions; [126] but in all instances he consistently subordinates social machinery to motivation.

All this is, of course, more Christian than socialistic. A better equilibrium is maintained in Katharine Pearson Woods' *Metze-*

[125] Tourgée, *op. cit.*, pp. 273, 123-4.
[126] *Ibid.*, pp. 318, 536-7.

rott, *Shoemaker* (1889), the story of Karl Metzerott's development away from a non-Christian to a Christian sanction for
socialism; or in Caroline A. Mason's *A Woman of Yesterday*
(1900), in which Christian morality furnishes the social motive of the coöperative colony Fraternia.[127]

Other novelists, without speaking formally of Christian Socialism, worked, along with the Christian Socialists, toward
the goal of refining human motives. New laws, new labor organizations would alike be unnecessary among a people moved
by a Christian sense of brotherhood; no injustice could long
survive the practice of the simple altruism of Jesus, "the most
revolutionary element that could possibly be introduced into
society." [128] This elementary but dynamic Social Gospel [129] is
the message of one of the most widely read books in literary
history, Charles Monroe Sheldon's *In His Steps* (1897). In
this story, a number of leaders in Reverend Henry Maxwell's
church in the industrial city of Raymond agree to regulate
their entire conduct according to the one question, "What
would Jesus do?" In obedience to the ethics of Jesus, the
minister himself goes into the uncongenial task of preaching
to workingmen; a superintendent of railway shops, learning
of his railway's violation of Federal law, resigns his place and
reveals the facts; a wealthy merchant resolves to conduct his
business on principles of unselfishness and helpfulness, and to
use his wealth as a trust for the good of humanity; an heiress
plans to devote her money to the establishment of settlement
work and model tenements in the slums; and a famous bishop

[127] Katharine Pearson Woods, *Metzerott, Shoemaker*, pp. 44-5, 370;
Caroline A. Mason, *A Woman of Yesterday*, pp. 261 ff. For other treatments of Christian socialism in fiction, see:
> Lubin, David, *Let There be Light* (1900), especially pp. 141-8,
> 153-61
> McCowan, Archibald, *Christ the Socialist* (1894)
> Machar, Agnes Maule, *Roland Graeme, Knight*, especially p. 279
> Woods, Katharine Pearson, *A Web of Gold* (1890)

[128] Margaret Deland, *The Wisdom of Fools*, p. 132.

[129] The phrase is employed here in the same sense as in Harry R.
Warfel, Ralph H. Gabriel, and Stanley T. Williams, *The American
Mind*, *II*, 1092. See the editors' introduction to and selections from
Charles Monroe Sheldon and Walter Rauschenbusch, pp. 1088-96.

not only helps establish, but lives in, a settlement in the midst of the direst poverty in his city.[130] The thesis illustrated in all these episodes, the author has condensed into a single question:

Would it not be true, think you, that if every Christian in America did as Jesus would do, society itself, the business world, yes, the very political system under which our commercial and governmental activity is carried on, would be so changed that human suffering would be reduced to a minimum? [131]

Other novelists, less ethically specific than Sheldon, inculcate the value of Christian love as a social motive. Helen Campbell, in *Mrs. Herndon's Income,* illustrates in her character Mr. Featherstone a bare, intellectual system of ethics founded on natural law, which proves unsatisfying, while, in attractive contrast, she illustrates in Lessing and Mrs. Herndon and Dr. Strothers a more satisfying dependence on an ethics of brotherly love, creation of a personal God—"Love, Divine Love, that guides the world in its course and cares for sparrow as truly as for human soul."[132] Amanda Douglas, in *Hope Mills,* has a spokesman character inculcate the teaching that the modern industrial world needs to relearn a very old lesson, "the essence of all knowledge, all religion, briefly comprehended in this, 'Love thy neighbor as thyself.' "[133] And numerous other novels resemble these in their emphasis on Christian ethics.[134]

[130] Charles Monroe Sheldon, *In His Steps,* pp. 45, 78-9, 86-7, 143, 216-7. Since the book is primarily a Christian rather than a sociological tract, it is natural that many moral problems, besides those suggested above, are illustrated. These, however, should indicate the extensive bearing of Christian ethics on economic reform.

[131] *Ibid.,* p. 266; spoken in a sermon by Reverend Henry Maxwell.

[132] Helen Campbell, *Mrs. Herndon's Income,* p. 422. See also pp. 275, 425, 442, 515.

[133] Douglas, *op. cit.,* p. 134.

[134] See, for further examples:

Beard, Dan, *Moonblight* (1892), especially p. 139
Bennett, Mary E., *Asaph's Ten Thousand*
Brooks, Byron A., *Earth Revisited* (1894)
Converse, Florence, *The Burden of Christopher,* especially p. 309
Cruger, Mary, *Brotherhood* (1891)
Dowling, George T., *The Wreckers* (1886), pp. 223-4, 255

And, finally, a few writers, who felt with the Christian Socialists that trustworthy reform could be had only as the fruit of sound racial character, conceived of that growth in character in broadly humanistic rather than in merely Christian terms. In the thoughtful novels of Robert Herrick, the solution of the individual's struggle to adapt himself to industrialism is often his growth toward spiritual poise in the process of doing some truly creative work. In the words of Jennings in *The Gospel of Freedom,* "To accept the world as it comes to our hands, to shape it painfully without regard for self,—that brings the soul to peace." [135] —And it was also possible, at least to a believer in progress, to look beyond the growth of the individual to a future growth in the character of the entire race—to such a growth, indeed, as would lift human life forever above the sufferings and the injustice of the first industrial era. Some such anticipation is the social message of Joaquin Miller in that curious romantic Utopia, *The Building of the City Beautiful* (1893). Human nature, the author assumes, is originally good; and the gradual development of the race, releasing it from the pressure of the struggle for survival, will one day allow that goodness to assert itself in a society devoted to democratic equality, to leisure, to rational abundance without luxury, to whatever enjoyments are to be found in beauty and in creative workmanship.[136]

Ford, Mary H., *Which Wins?*, p. 299
Grigsby, Alcanoan A., *Nequa* (1900), p. 283
Hale, Edward Everett, *How They Lived at Hampton*, pp. 260 ff.
Sheldon, Charles Monroe, *The Crucifixion of Philip Strong*
————, *His Brother's Keeper* (1896)
Woods, Katharine P., *John, A Tale of the Messiah* (1896)
————, *The Son of Ingar* (1897)

[135] See, for comparable expressions, Herrick's *The Web of Life,* p. 329, and *The Real World* (1901), pp. 333 ff. Cf. H. H. Boyesen, *A Daughter of the Philistines*, p. 324.

[136] Joaquin Miller, *The Building of the City Beautiful*, pp. 110, 155, 170 ff. See also Amos K. Fiske, *Beyond the Bourn* (1891), especially pp. 103-14, in regard to racial development and eugenics; and Albert Merrill, *The Great Awakening* (1899).

A unique "solution" of the ethics of industrialism, not paralleled, seemingly, in any other work, is that of Mary Wilkins Freeman in *The*

VI

But while the majority of our economic novelists were content with the advocacy of moderate and liberal reforms, sizeable minorities demanded that the social organization be subjected to radical and thoroughgoing change. It is proper to speak of these minorities as comprising, in an informal sense, a Left Wing of American economic criticism. But the American Left, thus defined, is not to be associated with European leftist groups or with European revolutionary philosophies. Radicalisms of the latter sort did, to be sure, exist in America, and did attain, even before 1900, some literary expression. For example, John Henry Mackay's *The Anarchists*, translated from the German by George Schumm, was published in Boston in 1891 by Benjamin R. Tucker, who was acting, apparently, with the encouragement of an Anarchists' club. Certain scenes in Mackay's book portray the poverty of the proletariat in east London; others (coherence is not the author's forte), the execution of the Chicago anarchists. As a remedy for economic injustice, Mackay explicitly rejects communism, and proposes, instead, anarchy, to be secured by violent revolution. —But expressions of this nihilistic sort are utterly uncharacteristic of American radicalism.

The Left of our economic fiction is, accordingly, a very American, a very middle-class Left. In even its most radical proposals, it preserves with little change the basic ideals of middle-class civilization:—material abundance, moral stability, democracy, and a large measure of intellectual freedom. In its exposure of the evils of industrialism, the fiction of the Left closely resembles that of the Left-center, unrolling as it does the same panorama of business piracy, the corruption of government, the splitting of the social community into the

Portion of Labor. Her prematurely aged workman, Andrew Brewster, "seemed to see that labor is not alone for itself, not for what it accomplishes of the tasks of the world, not for its equivalent in silver and gold, not even for the end of human happiness and love, but for the growth in character of the laborer.

"'That is the portion of labor,' he said." (p. 563).

"two nations" of rich and poor; but in its treatment of causes it strikes, necessarily, into more individual paths. Some Leftist writers, obviously of the persuasion of Henry George, discover the root of all social evils in land-monopoly; others, obviously of the school of Edward Bellamy, discover it in competition.

The middle-class Left diverges, in short, into two widely disparate groups, equally desirous of far-reaching reform, but held apart by diametrically opposed views of society, the individual and the collective. The individualistic group derives, as might be expected, almost wholly from Henry George, although their literary tool is the one chiefly popularized by the arch-collectivist Edward Bellamy—the Utopia. In non-Utopian novels, it is possible, of course, to discover support for Henry George's aim of abolishing poverty; [137] but for specific inculcation, by the lesser novelists, of George's land-tenure ideas, it is usually necessary to turn to some such Utopia as Henry Olerich's *A Cityless and Countryless World* (1893), in which the Georgian idea of the use of land for the benefit of all, not for the monopolistic advantages of a few, is made the starting point of an ideal economy.[138] Altogether, however, fiction dealing with land-tenure is less voluminous than the world-wide interest awakened by George might lead one to expect. The single important body of creative writing directly connected with the Georgian crusade is that of Hamlin Garland.[139]

The lesser fiction of the collectivist Left is more voluminous

[137] See, for example, Edgar Fawcett, *The Evil That Men Do*, p. 117; A. W. Tourgée, *Murvale Eastman*, p. 14.

[138] Henry Olerich, *A Cityless and Countryless World*, pp. 4-5. The economic scheme described by Olerich is that of voluntary coöperation among *individuals*. Olerich's individualism is evidently owing in part to the influence of Herbert Spencer (for which see *ibid.*, p. 39) as well as to that of George.

[139] For which see below, pp. 155 ff. For other works of fiction illustrative of the Single Tax or related ideas, see Arnold A. Clark's novel, *Beneath the Dome*, and the following Utopias:

Crocker, Samuel, *That Island* (1892)

Hertzka, Theodore, *Freeland, A Social Anticipation* (1891)

Holford, Costello N., *Aristopia, A Romance History of the New World* (1895)

Simpson, William, *The Man from Mars* (1891)

than that of the individualist, without being superior in intellectual or literary quality. Like the fiction of the Georgites, it consists mostly of Utopias. Among the lesser writers, not one produced a *novel*, in the genuine sense of that word, the controlling thesis of which is socialistic; their treatment of socialism extends, at most, the length of passing mention or an occasional sympathetic passage.[140] But the scarcity of socialistic novels is matched by the abundance of Utopias. From 1890 through 1900, not less than twenty Utopias, exclusive of the writings of Bellamy and Howells, were devoted to the case for a middle-class socialism, either in its entirety, or in some substantial part.[141] Most of the twenty derive, as obviously in ideas as in form, from Edward Bellamy.

Fairly representative of this entire body of writing—though perhaps below the average in literary skill—is Bradford M. Peck's *The World a Department Store* (1900). The book is an attenuated version of Bellamy's *Looking Backward*. The ideal society portrayed therein is a thinner, more mechanized version of the fair coöperative world of Bellamy; the romance, a faint echo of the strange and tender love of Bellamy's Edith Leete and Julian West. As in Bellamy, the causative change in society is that from competition to coöperation; the effect, that of material abundance in place of scarcity; the ethical sanction

[140] See, for passages of this kind, Lynn Boyd Porter, *Speaking of Ellen*, p. 22, and Leroy Scott, *The Walking Delegate*, p. 102. Some socialistic influence is discernible in Morrison I. Swift's *The Monarch Billionaire* and perhaps in Dwight Tilton's *On Satan's Mount*. Because of their fantastic temper, these two stories have as much in common with the Utopia as with the novel.

[141] See, in the bibliography below, the entries under Adams, Allen, Caryl, Chavannes (two entries), Cowan, Crocker, Emmons, Forbush, Fuller, Galloway, Geissler, Grigsby, Mason, Peck, Rosewater, Salisbury, Schindler, Wellman, and Worley. The classification of the works by Adams and Mason as Utopias is perhaps questionable. Antedating Bellamy's *Looking Backward*, and differing from that work and from most of the others in its defense of violence, is Alfred Denton Cridge's *Utopia; or The History of an Extinct Planet* (1884). For a general study of American Utopias, see Robert L. Shurter, *The Utopian Novel in America, 1865-1900*, An Unpublished Doctoral Dissertation, Western Reserve University (Cleveland, 1936).

for the new society, a Christian altruism.[142] In *The World a Department Store*, these ideas are rendered by a quality of mind, in an imaginative medium, which can be suggested by two brief quotations. Of his hero's visit to a factory, the author says, "Here he observed artistic work in the finishing of the interior of all these rooms"; of the climax of his hero's romance, "Mr. Brantford and Miss Brown, with blissful contentment, watched the rising moon shed its silver rays upon the water." [143]

The other collectivist Utopias all agree with Peck's in their devotion to the goals of abundance and economic security; and, as the proper means toward that end, they mostly agree on the partial or complete nationalization of industry. Like his, the others are, in both form and ideas, "written down" from Bellamy. Like his, they are inferior in writing-quality— the work of earnest people, unused to literary expression, but apparently moved by devotion to a Cause to write, and, in some cases, also to publish at their own expense. Obviously, such writings are literature only in the most elastic sense of that term; primarily they are tracts, significant only in what they illustrate, not in what they are. To come upon any adequate literary treatment of middle-class collectivism, the reader must turn to the two larger figures, Bellamy and Howells, whose fiction not only contains everything of moment to be found in the lesser collectivist writings, but much that cannot be duplicated there.

VII

The clearly marked Left in our economic fiction is not balanced by a clearly marked Right. There exists, in short, no literary defense of the class that had most at stake in the preservation of capitalism—the new Plutocracy. Nor is this surprising. The Harrimans and Rockefellers of the Gilded Age were too enormously successful to have need of a literary defense. The great magnates were lacking, moreover, in a literary

[142] Bradford Peck, *The World a Department Store*, pp. 23-35, 54, 181.

[143] *Ibid., op. cit.*, pp. 132, 281 respectively.

tradition; and the established middle classes, who did have one, were either unaware of them or suspiciously hostile. On the other hand, a measurable quantity of our fiction does veer somewhat Right from Center; a measurable quantity does have the social flavor of a conservative upper bourgeoisie, satisfied with its achieved values, hostile to such potential dangers as organized labor, and interested in the thrill of successful economic struggle. In such novels it is only natural to find, as a characteristic hero, an individual *entrepreneur* of the old middle-class type, a man grown wealthy—though not wealthy enough to be set apart from his middle-class social group— from the solid creative work of the building of bank or factory.

In the stories of Alice French—notably those in the volume *The Heart of Toil*—some such character appears again and again, delineated, apparently, with a kind of reiterative tenderness. Miss French's typical business man is shrewd, hardheaded, reticent, deliberately competent in leadership, honest, responsible, stubborn in a fight, crusty-tempered upon the surface, kindly and even somewhat sentimental at the core. Personally acquainted with his employees, he meets them with bluff friendliness, as well as with a condescension of which neither he nor his author is aware. He is even willing to make sacrifices, within reasonable limits, for the workmen's collective good. In "The Conscience of a Business Man," the owner, Rivers, protects his employees during a depression by operating his mill at a loss, even though that policy means the giving up of a cherished plan to repurchase his childhood home.

In perfect keeping with such an owner are Miss French's types of workingmen and labor leaders. Her ideal proletarians are solid, abstemious, hard-working Anglo-Saxon yeomen, of precisely the same hardy breed as the Mayflower Pilgrims or the soldiery of Cromwell. Her ideal labor leader directs his Union toward the goals of good fellowship and mutual humanitarian helpfulness.[144] Strikes, Miss French teaches, are painful and destructive, and they cause men to be violent and law-

[144] See, in this connection, the novel, *The Man of the Hour*, pp. 260 ff., 343-8.

less. Therefore the bad labor leader is one who foments strikes, and the good labor leader is one who preserves law and order —that is, the established middle-class way of life comfortably directed by the property owner—by preventing strikes. In "The Moment of Clear Vision," the leader Harry Leroy prevents a strike by abducting the agitator Victor West—a felony which, wrought upon by Miss French's alchemy, takes on the glow of pure ethical gold. The philosophy which conditions the entire disposal of plot, character, and thesis in Miss French's stories, is in short, identical with the economic interests of a conservative upper bourgeoisie.[145]

If the mere number of publications about a subject is a criterion of popular interest, middle-class conservatives cared less for the idealizing of their own business men than for the exposure of the dangers threatened by another social group—organized labor. The controversy over the Trade-Union was a recurrent one; and if organized labor awakened able defenders in Grant Overton and Leroy Scott, it awakened even abler enemies in Thomas Bailey Aldrich, John Hay, and F. Hopkinson Smith. The last of these three, although not so well known as the others, surpasses them in the skillful weaving of an anti-labor thesis into the very texture of fiction. In his *Tom Grogan* (1896), a woman, who is forced by her husband's illness and death to carry on his work as a stevedore, and who cannot accept the conditions of trade-union membership, attempts to operate as an independent. Union men thereupon subject her to persecutions that extend finally into crime. They bring pressure on dealers to refuse her business, and on workmen to leave her employment. They try to have her contracts invalidated; they burn her property; and, in an episode which appears more credible in the original novel than in summary, they attempt to kill her.[146] But all persecutions fail, and in the end the courts tardily dispose of Tom's principal enemy, the criminal labor

[145] The book that most closely resembles Miss French's work is Helen Choate Prince's *The Story of Christine Rochefort* (1895), in which see particularly the characterization of Gaston Rochefort, p. 67 *et. al.*

[146] F. Hopkinson Smith, *Tom Grogan*, especially pp. 60-7, 166, 204, 239-47.

leader McGaw. The story remains, all the while, simply a story—terse, swift-moving, wholly free from moralistic comment. Because of the very absence of doctrinal inculcation, the controlling thesis—the threat of the Union to the independent workingman—is perhaps the more powerfully driven home.

The typical case against Labor includes, as an important count, the charge that the Union is dangerous to the independence of the laborer or small operator. The Union is only less menacing to a middle-class democracy than is the Trust; the tyranny of Proletarian might well be as distasteful as the tyranny of Plutocrat. Moreover, the labor organization, even more fully than unscrupulous Big Business, is to be identified with crime. In Aldrich's *The Stillwater Tragedy* (1880), the striker Durgin is a murderer; in Hay's *The Breadwinners* (1884), the labor organization known as the Breadwinners is as violent and lawless as the historical Molly Maguires. And finally—the anti-labor case concludes—labor is easily and frequently misdirected by unscrupulous leadership.

Although honest, responsible labor leaders appear sometimes even in the hostile pages of anti-labor fiction,[147] the overwhelming majority range in moral hue from the irresponsible to the criminal. The walking delegate in Aldrich's *The Stillwater Tragedy* is, in the words of the author,

a glib person disguised as The Workingman's Friend—no workingman himself, mind you, but a ghoul that lives upon subscriptions and sucks the senses out of innocent human beings.[148]

Durgin in the same novel, Offitt and Sleeny in Hay's *The Breadwinners*, McGaw in Smith's *Tom Grogan*, are all simply and plainly criminals; Baretta in Fuller's *The Complaining Millions of Men* is the victim of a persecution mania.[149] Typical

[147] See, for an example, Edward Fuller, *The Complaining Millions of Men*, p. 48.

[148] Thomas Bailey Aldrich, *The Stillwater Tragedy*, p. 171.

[149] Pp. 317-20, 390 ff. The character of the agitator is painted in almost as dark colors, in fiction that is not noticeably antagonistic to labor. See, for examples, the characterization of Walker in Edward Everett Hale's *Sybil Knox*, especially pp. 233 ff., or of Dressler in Robert Her-

of the anti-labor novelist appears to be the attitude of John Hay, as interpreted by his biographer, William Roscoe Thayer:

"Honest" labor has nothing to complain of; . . . social and anarchistic panaceas, instead of curing would poison society; and . . . those persons who engineer a social war are either actual or potential criminals, having the gullible masses for their dupes.[150]

Besides the anti-labor novel, support for the conservative interests came, at least indirectly, from another type of fiction —the romance of economic struggle. Struggle—or, more technically, conflict—is traditionally the essence of plot; and it was no doubt inevitable that novelists, in an era when the Machine was remaking so many of the conditions of living, should discover that conflict in contemporary life, should come to think of it in industrial and not in feudal terms. Where a Scott had found the thrill of adventurous conflict in feudal warfare, where a Cooper had found it in the hardships of pioneering, the novelist of a capitalistic machine age might find it in the struggle of rancher against railroad, or of speculator against speculator in the stock market. Conceivably the word "romance," applied to novels of this latter kind, is a misnomer; for often there is much of the feel of actuality about them, and certainly there is far less of the fantastic than in the typical romance of the times. Underneath all superficies, however, their genuine core of interest is adventure, staple fare of the romantic reader from time immemorial. And just as the adventure-interest predominates over realism, so it predominates over—indeed, obliterates—any interest in the improvement of society. The typical romance of business struggle delivers no

---

rick's *The Web of Life*, pp. 187, 257-8. See also George T. Dowling's *The Wreckers*, pp. 250-1.

[150] William Roscoe Thayer, *The Life and Letters of John Hay*, II, 14.
Besides the novels mentioned above, others which might reasonably be classed as anti-labor fiction are:

Barr, Mrs. Amelia, *The King's Highway* (1897)
Barr, Robert, *The Mutable Many* (1896)
Foote, Mary Hallock, *Coeur D'Alene* (1894), especially pp. 46-7.
French, Alice, *The Man of the Hour* (1905)

criticism, proposes no reform; its conservatism lies in an acceptance rather than an explicit defense of the industrial *status quo*.

An occasional dribbling of such fiction, beginning certainly as far back as Mary Hallock Foote's *John Bodewin's Testimony* (1886),[151] increased to a veritable flood about the turn of the century, a time which significantly coincides with a revival of interest in another kind of romance, the historical.[152] To these latter years belong the business romances of Harold Frederic, Robert Barr, Will Payne, Charles K. Lush, Samuel Merwin, and H. K. Webster.

Representative of a simple type of story of economic struggle is Merwin and Webster's *Calumet K* (1901), the story of the building of a grain elevator. The conflict in the story is that between the Boss, Charlie Bannon, and the all but insuperable obstacles in the way of his getting the job done on time; the romance lies in the age-old thrill of smashing victoriously through difficulties. By sheer intelligence, force, and drive, Bannon steers through labor troubles, overcomes the drag of his foreman's half-loyalty, and gets his materials moved in spite of a hostile railway. Shrewd, cool-headed, dynamic, wholly absorbed in his job, Bannon is as much at home in the wilderness of industrial conflict as Cooper's Leatherstocking is at home in the wilderness of forest and hostile Indian. As completely as Leatherstocking is the hero of *The Last of the Mohicans*, so he, in his slighter stature, is the hero of Merwin and Webster's romance of business; an idealization, like Leatherstocking, but one brought forth by a different era and a different set of social needs. That, after all, his life is barren of

[151] Certain earlier works, already mentioned in another connection, might possibly be looked on as, in part, romances of business. Thomas Bailey Aldrich's *The Stillwater Tragedy* (1880) includes a romantic success-story. George H. Bartlett's *A Commercial Trip with an Uncommercial Ending* (1884), in which a young travelling salesman neglects his work for a love affair, is a romance, but hardly a romance of business.

[152] For a fuller discussion of the shift in popular interest from reform to romance, a change which apparently took place not long after 1895, see below, in the discussion of Hamlin Garland, pp. 174 ff.

all human values but one, that the end his remarkable job is to serve is only the manipulation of a corner in wheat [153]—all this troubles Bannon as little as it apparently troubled his creators. The remoter social and moral implications of the story, they overlook; for them, the thrill of the immediate struggle is sufficient.

A far richer story, and one far more suggestive of the intricacies of a complex modern society, is Will Payne's *The Money Captain* (1898), a novel curiously prophetic of Theodore Dreiser's larger achievement in *The Titan*. Like Dreiser's Cowperwood, Payne's Dexter, "Duke of Gas," is a powerful corporate organizer whose energies, consciously or unconsciously exercised, dominate the lives of dozens of other people, so that, with equal unconcern, he bribes a group of aldermen, or breaks the speculator Gregg and the banker Brouillard,[154] indifferent to the losses of Brouillard's depositors. Dexter is successfully opposed only by a man of equal energy, Leggett, an editor who is reviving a moribund newspaper by miscellaneous attacks and exposures. Leggett, possessed of evidence of Dexter's bribery, is witheld from publishing it by his fiancée, Mrs. Isabella Wilder, whose friends, the Deeres, are certain to be involved in the scandal. Instead, Leggett attacks Dexter by criminal libel, and escapes prosecution and probable imprisonment only because of Dexter's premature breakdown and death from overwork.

The Money Captain is rich in incidents, is skillfully managed, heightened, and complicated. It is rich in dramatic conflict; scenes such as that in which Isabella Wilder pleads with Leggett to withhold the evidence against Dexter come alive as if powerfully acted on the stage. And it is rich also in individual characters, one of whom, Dexter, falls only just short of enduring worth. Motivated not merely by desire for wealth, but also by a desire to see his plans achieved, and by a sense of the obligations his wealth has created; [155] quiet, reserved, affectionate, unscrupulous, enormously energetic, Dexter is

[153] For this angle of the story, see p. 286.
[154] Will Payne, *The Money Captain*, pp. 146, 152 ff.
[155] *Ibid.*, pp. 273 ff.

immensely more than the stilted conventional figure which, in the typical economic novel, passes for the Capitalist. He is an individual, and, with the exception of Harrington in Herrick's *Memoirs of an American Citizen,* the most arresting individual of his kind prior to Dreiser's Cowperwood.

The broad differences between *Calumet K* and *The Money Captain* suggest the diversity and wealth of the materials to be found in the fiction of economic struggle. In one group of such novels, the plot turns on a struggle for the ownership of some business:—in Edward Everett Hale's *Sybil Knox* and Merwin and Webster's *The Short Line War* (1899) for the possession of railroads; in Lush's *The Autocrats* and Barr's *The Victors,* for the possession of franchises. In another type of story, such as Webster's *Roger Drake, Captain of Industry* (1902), the plot turns on the effort of some business man to "rise," often by unethical methods. Speculative struggles in the stock-market are the focal interest of such other volumes as Harold Frederic's *The Market Place* (1898), Webster's *The Banker and the Bear* (1900), and Will Payne's *On Fortune's Road* (1902).[156] In short, the romances of economic struggle, although they are deficient in general ideas, are abundantly outfitted with stories and people. Immeasurably more than the amateur, tractarian writings of the Left, and somewhat more than even the novels of the Left-Center, the novels of economic struggle fulfill the historical purposes of fiction—namely, to entertain the reader and at the same time to enlarge his awareness of life by showing him credible, interesting human beings doing interesting and credible things. And although such men as Merwin and Webster and Payne produced no absolutely first-rank work, there can be no question that they discovered the general field of materials and in large measure established the conventions that entered into the

[156] It is characteristic of such stories that the love interest, if any at all is present, is subordinated to the interest in business adventure. But in another kind of plot, the love interest is integral with the economic theme. For instance, the obstacle between two lovers may be that they belong in different and perhaps hostile economic classes, as in Mary Wilkins Freeman's *The Portion of Labor* and Lynn Boyd Porter's *Speaking of Ellen.*

making of two finer stories—Frank Norris's *The Octopus* and *The Pit*.[157]

With the consideration of the romances of economic conflict, our survey of the lesser economic novels is complete. But before forming any conclusions about the entire movement of economic criticism in fiction, we must turn to that part of it which is, to literary history as distinguished from social history, the most important. We must turn to the work of five men—Mark Twain, Hamlin Garland, Edward Bellamy, William Dean Howells, and Frank Norris—each of whom has some claim to major rank in our literature. And because of the importance of these men, we shall examine their work with some thoroughness, in regard to its origins, its content and meaning, its critical and literary values. In so doing, we shall find among them, though in different proportion, precisely the same critical viewpoints as among the lesser novelists. The liberal Left-Center is represented by Mark Twain; the radical middle-class Left is represented in its individualistic bearings by Garland and in its collectivist by Bellamy and Howells; and the conservative Right-Center is represented by Frank Norris.

---

[157] See below, pp. 294 ff. For other novels of economic struggle, not mentioned in the preceding discussion, see:

Foote, Mary Hallock, *Coeur D'Alene,* a novel the anti-labor bearing of which has already been mentioned
———, *John Bodewin's Testimony*
———, *The Led-Horse Claim* (1883)
Hamblen, Herbert Elliott, *The General Manager's Story* (1897)
Kester, Vaughan, *The Manager of the B. and A.* (1901)
Lefevre, Edwin, *Wall Street Stories* (1901)
Thurber, Alwyn H., *Quaint Crippen, Commercial Traveller* (1896)
Waterloo, Stanley, *The Launching of a Man* (1899)

I

From the currents of thought which swept along so many of our secondary and subliterary authors, the principal creative writers of the Gilded Age could hardly have escaped. To some of these men—Henry James, for instance—economic criticism was only a passing and casual matter; to others, such as Hamlin Garland, it was for a while not only an important, but a dominant, concern. In the mind of Mark Twain, it was not a dominant concern; it was not a constant, or even a systematically considered one. And yet Mark Twain's utterances on economics are, taken in the aggregate, surprisingly extensive. The importance of these expressions lies, in part, in the light they throw on the response of a sensitive creative mind to its environment. It lies, even more, in the fact that even the casual utterances of a major writer develop, in the process of being reread and reabsorbed from generation to generation, a significance that cannot possibly attach to more transitory writings.

If one may judge by the luxuriant growth of theory that has sprung up about the subject, the importance of Mark Twain's relation to the Machine Age has been recognized for some two decades. In *The Ordeal of Mark Twain* (1920), Van Wyck Brooks spoke of industrialism as one of the several forces which, by thwarting the natural expression of Mark Twain's genius, provoked the corroding pessimism of his latter years. By nature a satirist, contemptuous of the standards and practices of the Gilded Age, Mark Twain, for the sake of success, suppressed his convictions, assumed "the whole character and point of view of the typical American magnate," and became,

116

after a time, merely "the spokesman of the Philistine majority." [1] Consequently, "to degrade beauty, to debase distinction and thus to simplify the life of the man with an eye single
to the main chance" came to be the chief object of his humor. [2]
This miscarriage of his creative life, caused in large part by
his surrender to capitalistic industrialism, destroyed for him
the meaning of existence. "The spirit of the artist in him, like
the genii at last released from the bottle, overspread in a
gloomy vapour the mind it had never quite been able to possess." [3] Seen in the light of this interpretation, the career of
Mark Twain takes on something of the symmetry of tragic
drama. Our principal humorist, in many ways the most robust
literary figure of his generation, becomes the central personage
in a story of moral failure, of nemesis, and of retribution as
strangely, beautifully romantic, as darkly fascinating, as any
in the pages of Hawthorne.

Now the mere appearance of this sort of critical view is not,
just in itself, cause for surprise. The disturbing fact is, rather,
the extent to which this and similarly romantic interpretations
have for twenty years colored the entire critical and historical
treatment of Mark Twain. According to Lewis Mumford, for
instance, Mark Twain failed to see that his Yankee exponent
of industrialism was as absurd as his King Arthur, and that
social injustice was still distressingly prevalent; to Mark Twain,
"industrialism was an end-in-itself, and to fail to take it seriously and magniloquently was to rob life of its chief felicities." [4]
According to Vernon Louis Parrington, Mark Twain failed to
discern, even while writing *The Gilded Age,* the *liaison* between political corruption and the commercial exploitation of
the frontier. [5] According to Russell Blankenship, he was aware
of social injustice, but "though he raged in private, he never
unsheathed his pen"; as a consequence, he looked back upon

[1] Van Wyck Brooks, *The Ordeal of Mark Twain,* pp. 173-9.
[2] *Ibid.,* p. 261.
[3] *Ibid.,* pp. 26-7.
[4] Lewis Mumford, *The Golden Day,* p. 172.
[5] Vernon Louis Parrington, *The Beginnings of Critical Realism in
America,* p. 93.

his life as "a record of utter futility." [6] According to Matthew Josephson, the corruption, the materialism of the Gilded Age caused him to become "cynical at heart." [7] And according to Fred Lewis Pattee, he considered his literary vocation as "merely a money-making affair"; he "lacked honesty, lacked detachment, lacked ability to see himself in perspective"; "an industrialist he was with the ethics of the Gilded Age." [8]

Such critical views are, on the whole, less inaccurate than inadequate. A diamond may not be known by the color it flashes from a single facet; nor, likewise, may a personality as resourceful as that of Mark Twain be summed up in any simple formula. Until the whole story of Mark Twain's attitude toward economics is in hand, we will do well to withhold opinion. We will do well, also, to deny ourselves the pleasure of passing moral judgments, and to assume, instead, the more exacting task of historical interpretation. Meanwhile, although we recognize that Mark Twain was first of all a humorist, we need feel no inappropriateness in treating his work seriously, inasmuch as he himself insisted upon the seriousness of his aims, and upon the usefulness of laughter as a satirical weapon. [9] We shall first inquire how Mark Twain's theory and practice of economics developed, and what, in their entirety, those opinions and practices were; we shall then ask to what extent, and in what way, his economic philosophy found expression in his published work; and, having done so, we will be led finally to certain conclusions about Mark Twain's personality, his significance, his value.

[6] Russell Blankenship, *American Literature as an Expression of the National Mind*, pp. 457, 470.

[7] Matthew Josephson, *Portrait of the Artist as American* p. 160.

[8] Fred Lewis Pattee (Ed.), *Mark Twain: Representative Selections*, Introduction, pp. xxx, xliii.

By no means all of the recent criticism of Mark Twain takes the tack indicated by the above quotations. The studies by Minnie Brashear, Bernard DeVoto, and Edward Wagenknecht adopt a quite different approach. These, however, have little to say about Mark Twain's relation to industrialism.

[9] *The Mysterious Stranger*, p. 142.

II

For the satire of the *Gilded Age* and the *Connecticut Yankee*, much of the groundwork was laid during Mark Twain's youth in antebellum Missouri. His lifelong interest in speculative enterprise, for instance, was sufficiently natural to a man whose youth had been brought so closely in touch with the speculative opportunities afforded by the frontier. During his childhood, his own region in Missouri had known the excitement of a land boom. His father, like Squire Hawkins in *The Gilded Age*, had actually purchased a tract of land among the Tennessee "knobs." [10] But the speculative fever was by no means his only heritage from the frontier. The passionate democracy of the *Connecticut Yankee* was an equally natural product of the back-country—an idealization of the entire social equality in which the author had moved as a youth among the Missouri villagers.

Along broader lines, Mark Twain's view of life was at first formed under the influence of evangelical Christianity; and much of the Christian ethic, much of the Christian attitude toward the judging of right and wrong, remained embedded within him even after he had adopted a fatalistic philosophy which theoretically negated it. The Christian concepts of biblical history, of salvation and damnation, of heaven and hell, he retained for imaginative uses after he had abandoned any actual belief in them. That abandonment came, apparently, during his early manhood, and was accompanied, if not caused, by his reading in the works of the eighteenth-century rationalists. At some time prior to the Civil War, he read Paine's *The Age of Reason*, and marvelled at the author's "fearlessness and wonderful power." He evidently read, too, in Voltaire, whose pessimism, and whose indictment of the cruelties of a nominally Christian civilization, he was later to repeat. [11]

[10] Minnie L. Brashear, *Mark Twain, Son of Missouri*, pp. 40, 88.
[11] For a treatment of these and other readings of Mark Twain, see Brashear, *op. cit.*, pp. 164, 245 ff.

The juxtaposition in Mark Twain's early thought of these two influences—Paine and Voltaire—suggests that his later pessimism might well be the product of other causes than a surrender to the industrialism of the Gilded Age. From Paine, or at least from the movement of thought which Paine exemplified, he got the simple mechanistic philosophy which he kept for the remainder of his life. In his old age, no less than in his youth, he held the deistic view that the universe is a nicely assembled machine, handiwork of some cosmic Engineer who exercises no special providence in behalf of human happiness or unhappiness.[12] But, to a nature as tender-minded as his, to a mind as sensitive to evil and suffering, it would be not only natural, but almost inevitable, to disjoin the mechanism of Paine from his optimism, to retain only the former, and to unite with it a pessimism comparable to that of Voltaire. In his blasts at hypocrisy and cruelty, in his feeling for the prevalence of crime and misfortune in the human story, Mark Twain is the spiritual descendent of the French rather than of the Anglo-American rationalist.[13] The idea of an impersonal cosmic mechanism, fused with the pessimism of Voltaire instead of the optimism of Paine, may quite possibly mark the beginning of the path whose end is the view that the whole life-scheme, only a dream itself, is "frankly and hysterically insane, like all dreams."

But all this is to anticipate. What is more pertinent, for the present, is the observation that Mark Twain's response to Voltaire and Paine is only one of many evidences that he was intellectually a child of the eighteenth century. In literature, his was the eighteenth-century preference for such types as the character-study, the informal essay, the apologue, the maxim, the picaresque narrative. In philosophy, his was not only the eighteenth-century fondness for a mechanistic deism, but also the eighteenth century habit of attacking the profoundest problems of life by means of that heightened common

[12] Albert Bigelow Paine, *Mark Twain: A Biography*, pp. 1352, 1582-3.
[13] Compare, for example, Voltaire's treatment of war in *Candide* with Mark Twain's "The War Prayer" in *Europe and Elsewhere*, pp. 397-8.

sense called Reason, operating upon the tangible materials of actual experience.[14] Like Paine, he had only the most limited understanding of an approach to social and ethical truth through tradition, or intuition, or the more precise methods of the social sciences. Accordingly, his social and moral inquiries are mostly direct, pragmatic, rational. "I believe," he once wrote, "that the world's moral laws are the outcome of the world's experience. It needed no God to come down out of heaven to tell men that murder and theft and the other immoralities were bad, both for the individual who commits them and for the society that suffers from them." [15] Hence the direct application of reason to experience—the whole mental process being colored, of course, by his individal tastes and prejudices —became the means by which he gave his social philosophy such order as it possessed.

More directly, and upon more immediate issues, the sociological writing of Mark Twain stemmed from the *milieu* of back-country humor in which his methods of composition crystallized. Like his fellow humorists, he came to compose in short, discontinuous units; to write a book was to put together a string of anecdotes. Like them, again, he adopted the informal, quasi-oral manner of a fireside *raconteur;* like them, he could employ humor as a means of social criticism; like some of them, he found in a superb gusto the natural expression of his own abounding zest for life. Such political and social interests as his fellow-humorists owned were not dominant in their work or even systematically followed up; and yet the critical passages in back-country humor are, in the aggregate, extensive, and they deal with much the same subjects, and in much the same way, as do the early critical passages in Mark Twain. Frontier speculation and political jobbery are, for example, of obvious interest; but they are condemned, as in Mark Twain,

[14] In these respects, Mark Twain did not differ from a number of other Americans of his century, especially such other humorists as, say, A. B. Longstreet. See Brashear, *op. cit.*, pp. 225 ff.

[15] Paine, *op. cit.*, p. 1583. See also, for an example of his use of such pragmatic reasoning, the apologue entitled, "Was It Heaven? or Hell?" *The Writings of Mark Twain* (Author's National Edition), 24: 65-9.

by the standards of prudence, thrift, and, above all, honesty.[16] To be sure, Mark Twain did not necessarily adopt these traits, these interests, because of his acquaintance with the other back-country humorists. Rather, he developed them, directly, out of the same folkways and as an expression of the same civilization.

Out of all this agrarian, middle-class, individualistic code, the standard that was to be most important for Mark Twain and his work was that of plain, old-fashioned honesty. In his exuberant, often confused, often erratic nature, the passion for honesty was one of the ·few qualities absolutely stable and constant. His dislike of the common scoundrelism of the era of reconstruction; his refusal to support the compromised Blaine for president, and his disgust with men who placed party above integrity; [17] his resolution to pay the publishers' debts for which he was not legally liable; his scorn of the hypocrisies that accompanied the march of European imperialism—these feelings, these attitudes, are all constant and all of a piece. To Mark Twain, "a man's first duty is to his own honor," even though honor may be "a harder master than the law." [18]

It is noteworthy that Mark Twain's first experiences on the frontier evoked that curiously dual, curiously self-contradictory attitude toward speculation which he was to preserve as long as he lived. On the one hand was his feverish enthusiasm for all sorts of speculative enterprises and get-rich-quick schemes; on the other, a capacity for self-criticism, product of his common sense and honesty, which showed him the absurdity of even his own speculative undertakings. On the one hand, he could search out a timber claim, or excitedly prospect for silver ore, or write enthusiastically to his brother about the

---

[16] See, for example, Joseph Glover Baldwin, *Flush Times in Alabama and Mississippi* (New York, 1853), pp. 83-6. For expressions on prudence and thrift, see Henry Wheeler Shaw, *Everybody's Friend...* (Hartford, 1874), p. 593.

[17] *Mark Twain's Letters*, I, 443; letters of August 21 and September 17, 1884, to William Dean Howells.

[18] *Ibid*. See also Paine, *op. cit.*, pp. 1005 ff.

Monitor Ledge, "I know it to contain our fortune." [19] On the other, he could soberly caution his mother and sister against the contagion of his own enthusiasm. "Pamela, don't you know that undemonstrated human calculations won't do to bet on? Don't you know that I have only *talked* as yet, but proved nothing? Don't you know that I have expended money in this country but have made none myself? . . . Don't you know that people who always feel jolly, no matter where they are or what happens to them—who have the organ of hope preposterously developed— . . . are very apt to go to extremes, and exaggerate with 40-horse microscopic power?" [20]

The young man who could thus ridicule his own speculative enthusiasms was father to the satirist who, a decade later, collaborated in that exuberant attack on speculation, *The Gilded Age*. His development from the one period to the other led, as we know, through his work as journalist and humorist in Nevada and California and Hawaii; his part in the *Quaker City* excursion, and the tremendous success of *The Innocents Abroad* and *Roughing It;* his marriage to Olivia Langdon; their settlement in Connecticut; their friendship with the Warners; and the plan of Clemens and Warner to write a satirical novel. Of all his experiences during these years, perhaps the one that lies closest to his work in *The Gilded Age* was his residence in Washington in '68 and his disillusion with the spectacle of the federal government. "There are more pitiful intellects in Congress!" he exclaimed, in a letter to Orion Clemens; and, again, in a sentence curiously prophetic of *The Gilded Age*, "This is a place to get a poor opinion of everybody in." [21]

III

The Gilded Age [22] is the only important novel in which our back-country humor is brought to bear on our national eco-

[19] See his various letters, chiefly to Orion Clemens, *Letters*, I, 56-79.

[20] *Letters*, I: 63-8; a letter of February 8, 1862, to Mrs. Jane Clemens and Mrs. Pamela Clemens Moffett.

[21] *Letters*, I, 150; a letter of February 21, 1868, to Orion Clemens.

[22] Any consideration of *The Gilded Age* as an illustration of Mark

nomics. And yet the economy portrayed in *The Gilded Age* is not quite genuinely that of our latter nineteenth century. For, although capitalistic, it is not primarily industrial; the entire novel, notwithstanding the late date of its appearance, is curiously pre-machine. Essentially, it is the novel of a frontier democracy, in which the frontier practices of speculative plunging and dishonesty, together with their reactions upon the government and, indeed, the entire life of the nation, are satirized from the viewpoint afforded by middle-class ideals of prudence, thrift, and honesty.

The social origin of the novel was, no doubt, the orgy of speculation, of money-grabbing, of political corruption which the nation witnessed during the decade that followed the Civil War—the same unsightly spectacle that had drawn down the denunciatory blasts of Whitman's *Democratic Vistas*. To a degree that is astonishing, even in view of Clemens' explicit claim that he had "hurled in the facts," [23] the actual persons and doings of the early Gilded Age pass in review in the novel which has given that era its derogatory name. Of the characters, Laura Hawkins was certainly suggested by Mrs. Laura Fair of California, who had recently been acquitted of murder on the ground of emotional insanity.[24] Senator Dilworthy was

---

Twain's thought brings up, necessarily, the complicated question of the joint authorship of the book. Details regarding the exact portions actually written by Mark Twain may be found in the following sources: *Letters*, I, 205, a letter of April 17, 1873 to the editor of the *Daily Graphic*, New York City; *Ibid.*, 1, 214-5, a letter of February 28, 1874 to Dr. John Brown of Edinburgh; Franklin Walker, "An Influence from San Francisco on Mark Twain's *The Gilded Age*," *American Literature*, VIII, 65, footnote (March, 1936); E. E. Leisy, "Mark Twain's Part in *The Gilded Age*," *American Literature*, VIII: 445-7 (January, 1937). What appears plain from all these treatments is that the entire book passed under the surveillance of both authors, that they were in substantial agreement, and that therefore its principal objectives may be taken to indicate the point of view of either author.

[23] *Letters*, I, 205; a letter of April 17, 1873, to the editor of the New York *Daily Graphic*.

[24] Franklin Walker, "An Influence from San Francisco on Mark Twain's *The Gilded Age*," *American Literature*, VIII: 61-6 (March, 1936).

drawn from Senator Pomeroy of Kansas; [25] and the activities of William M. Weed and his associates so closely resemble those of the Tweed Ring of New York that the picture is practically undisguised. Among the dupes of the speculative game, Washington Hawkins was suggested by Orion Clemens; and the effervescent Colonel Sellers, in all probability, by a relative of Mark Twain's, James Lampton.[26]

Of the forms of business and political piracy that were generally prevalent during the early seventies, the overwhelming majority are exposed in *The Gilded Age*. The dishonest promotion of railways; the graft in railway construction; the jobbery in real-estate values that accompanied the surveying of railway routes; the misuse of such federal agencies as the Indian Bureau; the absurd overexpansion of credit; the maneuvering of "corners," eight of which were attempted in a single year; the issuing of wild-cat bank notes; the blackmailing and the outright bribing of legislators; the dividing among legislators of the stock of favored corporations; improper lobbying—all these exuberances of the Reconstruction decade appear in *The Gilded Age*. Even Laura Hawkins' career at the Capital has some basis in fact, for in Washington, during the seventies, "the woman lobbyist was seen everywhere, making the streets and hotels disreputably gay." [27] In fact, comparatively few of the cut-throat practices of post-Civil-War business escaped Warner and Clemens:—the Black Friday incident and other escapades of Fisk and Gould; railway rebating and other forms of discrimination; and, most important, the growth, still

[25] Paine, *op. cit.*, pp. 477-9. See also, for a contemporary recognition of these portraits, the review in *Old and New*, IX: 386-8 (March, 1874).

[26] Paine, *op. cit.*, pp. 477-9. For another explanation of the original of Sellers, see John W. Chapman, "The Germ of a Book," *Atlantic*, 150: 720-1 (December, 1932). In regard to Warner's possible contribution to the character, see Arthur Hobson Quinn, *American Fiction: an Historical and Critical Survey*, pp. 246-7.

[27] Allen Nevins, *The Emergence of Modern America*, p. 96. For instances of business piracy paralleling those satirized in *The Gilded Age*, see *ibid.*, pp. 60-3, 120, 164-200, 293; also Ellis P. Oberholzer, *A History of the United States Since the Civil War*, II, 585; III, 71-2; or any extensive history of the period.

not generally known, of the control of the Rockefeller interests over oil. In regard to the *general* speculative conduct of business, the case of the satirists is not only complete, but overwhelming. Moreover, in such episodes as Henry Brierly's education in the ways of lobbying, blackmail, and bribery, the reaction of the speculative spirit on politics is perfectly indicated.[28]

To grasp firmly the idea that *The Gilded Age* is, in its critical phases, primarily an attack on the evils of speculation, including the political evils; that it is, in the words of a contemporary reviewer, a "determined and bitter satire," written "to expose speculators, lobbyists, and corrupt legislators," [29] is to do away with two serious misconceptions about the book: Parrington's curious idea that Mark Twain satirized the corrupt office-holder without seeing his relation to the frontier speculator, that he damned the "agent," Senator Dilworthy, and overlooked the "principal," Colonel Sellers; and Van Wyck Brook's even more curious idea that the philosophy of the book is a wholly acquisitive one, and that the main incident is Philip Sterling's discovery of a coal mine.[30] But to Clemens and Warner, Sellers was nothing so practically effective as a "principal" in wrong-doing. The "principal" force for evil in the novel is an intangible one—the Spirit of Speculation; and his immediate agents are such hard-boiled promoters, grafters, and general knaves as Duff Brown, Rodney Shaick, Bigler, and Patrick O'Riley. Others—Laura Hawkins, Washington Hawkins, Sellers, even Philip Sterling—occupy the position either of victims or of dupes. Indeed, it was Mark Twain's opinion that only *as a failure* could such a person as Sellers be harmless; "it would be clearly a crime against society to make him a 'success' in life, since this would be to add another Jay Gould to the world's burdens." [31] And of Philip Sterling, the

---

[28] *The Gilded Age*, I, 306 ff.

[29] *Old and New*, IX: 386-8 (March, 1874)

[30] See, respectively, *The Beginnings of Critical Realism*, pp. 93 ff.; *The Ordeal of Mark Twain*, pp. 79 ff.

[31] John W. Chapman, "The Germ of a Book," *The Atlantic Monthly*, 150: 720-1 (December, 1932). The quotation is from a letter of Mark Twain's to the author, February 15, 1887.

text of *The Gilded Age* itself points out that his handicap is the lack of any specific, creative profession, born, as he had been, "into a time when all young men of his age caught the fever of speculation." [32]

Clemens' and Warner's attack on the speculative spirit is executed with a union of gusto and of satirical insight which makes of it a significant, if not a finally great, work. The superb nonsense of Colonel Sellers is, of course, too well known to require elaboration. What is less often noticed is that even the minor passages in the book are often salty with satirical thrust and epigram. To have Senator Dilworthy begin by asking the government for only two or three hundred thousand dollars for Sellers' project—"You can begin to sell town lots on that appropriation, you know"; to give the Senator's home the name of Saint's Rest; [33] to have the Knobs University proposed with the object of the moral and spiritual advancement of the colored race; to have a credit shark matter-of-factly announce, "I wasn't worth a cent two years ago, and now I owe two millions of dollars"; above all, to have a Congressional bill labeled the "National Internal Improvement Directors' Relief Measure" [34]—all these minor eddies in the current of the story are of the essence of robust satire.

For all its gusto, for all its abundance of detail, *The Gilded Age* is a simple illustration of a simple code. That is the code of middle-class prudence, thrift, and honesty that had already been applied to the speculative game by many of the American people and by some of the native American humorists. Of the more intricate social problems of the era just then beginning —the workings of the Machine, the operation of capitalism on the larger, more dangerous scale which the Machine was making possible, the difficulty of achieving social justice in an industrialized society of all these, the authors of *The Gilded Age* were, in 1873, not keenly aware.

[32] *The Gilded Age*, II, 191.
[33] The same name had been previously used by Petroleum V. Nasby.
[34] *The Gilded Age*, I: 230, 291-2; II: 103-4, 135-6.

IV

On these more intricate subjects, Mark Twain long had little
to say. Most of his expressions on them date from the latter
eighties—that time when the national thought so curiously
and suddenly awakened to the social problems raised by industrialism—through about 1905. It is Mark Twain's utterances
during these years that, joined with certain facts of his life,
have given color to the critical assertion that he himself became
a typical capitalist of the Gilded Age, or, at least, that he failed
to speak his real feelings about social injustice. But none of
these matters need remain speculative or theoretical. From
an examination of Mark Twain's correspondence and of the
course of his private life, it should be possible to discover just
what were his private views on several major questions of
sociology. And from an examination of his public utterances
on each of these questions, it should be possible to discover
to what extent he gave these views a public hearing.

That Mark Twain shared largely in the commercial spirit of
his age, that he enjoyed it, that as a man he plunged into many
a speculative venture that as a satirist he would have ridiculed
—none of this is open to doubt. With some exceptions and reserves, to be noted below, he carried on even his own profession of letters as a commercial project. *The Innocents Abroad,*
for example, he deliberately planned with the object of making
money; "I had my mind made up to *one* thing—I wasn't going
to touch a book unless there was money in it, and a good deal
of it." [35] And even though he recurrently looked forward to
the time when he could lay the pot-boiler pen aside and write
to please himself, he continued to write with an eye to a large
audience, and he enjoyed his ability to produce books that sold
"right along with the Bible." Moreover, in the one form of
property that was most important to him—literary copyright—
he showed an interest as vigorous, aggressive, and sustained
as any capitalist might show in the ownership of factory or

[35] *Letters,* I, 145; a letter of January 24, 1868, to Mrs. Jane Clemens
and Mrs. Pamela Clemens Moffett.

mine.[36] As a publisher, associated with Charles L. Webster and Company, he consistently looked for the big sale instead of the fine book. He enjoyed his absorption in the big business of publishing the *Memoirs* of General Grant;[37] he enjoyed his friendships with big business men such as Andrew Carnegie and H. H. Rogers of Standard Oil. So close was his association with Rogers, and so much was he indebted to him for help in straightening his increasingly tangled affairs, that on one occasion he felt bound in common decency to refuse the chance of a probable best seller, because of its attacks on the Standard Oil Company.[38] All these facts do not, of course, necessarily suggest any conscious or subconscious *surrender* on his part to the ways of capitalistic industrialism; but they do suggest a good deal of unconscious *adaptation,* a process that Mark Twain was able to understand well enough in others, if not in himself.[39]

And yet, in spite of all these facts, the conclusion that Mark Twain took a wholly commercial view of literature is faulty; for it fails to allow for the largeness and the variety of his nature, and for his way of suddenly dropping some interest, in which he had appeared to be absorbed, and passing on to another and perhaps even a contradictory one. His interest in publishing as a big business, for instance, lasted no longer than his prosperity in it. As early as May of 1893 he had become "terribly tired" of business;[40] and when failure finally closed his publishing career, he could even grow lyrical in writing of his escape:

When the anchor is down, then I shall say:
"Farewell—a long farewell—to business! I will never touch it again!

[36] See, in his *Letters,* II, 479, a letter of December 18, 1887, to H. C. Christiancy, and II: 831-2, a letter of June 5, 1909, to Champ Clark.
[37] Paine, *op. cit.,* pp. 799 ff.
[38] *Letters,* II, 611-3; a letter of February 15, 1894, to Mrs. Olivia Clemens.
[39] See his essay entitled "Corn-Pone Opinions," *Europe and Elsewhere,* pp. 399-400.
[40] *Letters,* II, 583; a letter of May 30, 1893, to Fred J. Hall.

"I will live in literature, I will wallow in it, revel in it, I will swim in ink!" [41]

When he did "live in literature," he no doubt sought for popularity; yet he did not deliberately hurry or cheapen his production, and he could turn down even a lucrative contract, if he felt that he would have to "run emptyings" in order to fulfill it.[42] Several books, too, he wrote from noncommercial motives: *Joan of Arc* for "love"; *What Is Man?* and *The Mysterious Stranger* for self-expression. These three titles should, by the way, suggest the need for using the utmost reserve before concluding that the commercial influence on art is necessarily bad. Few discriminating judges would prefer *The Mysterious Stranger*, a romance written to please the author, to *The Adventures of Huckleberry Finn*, a romance written to please not merely the author, but the book-buying public as well.

In regard to industry in general, Mark Twain's enthusiasm for the comforts, the materialities, the new inventions of the Machine Age is too well known to require elaboration. From his middle years onward, at least, any new mechanical gadget could awaken in him all of a small boy's reckless enthusiasm for a new toy. Indeed, more! Apparently, he had always been susceptible to the speculative fever; and in his frontier days, hectically searching out timber and mining claims, he contracted a case of it from which he never recovered. The Machine, as soon as he became engrossed in its possibilities, became simply a new area in which to speculate, a new frontier to exploit. The flighty schemes of Colonel Sellers, which he knew so well how to ridicule, were hardly more fantastic than his own. At one time or another, he invested in or gave financial backing to a steam generator, a steam pulley, a new method of marine telegraphy, a watch company, an engraving process, a carpet-pattern machine, a *Fernseher* (vague ances-

[41] *Ibid.*, II, 607; a letter of late January, 1894, to Olivia Clemens. Reprinted by permission of Harper and Brothers, publishers.

[42] *Letters*, II, 486; a letter of May 14, 1887, written to Miss Jeanette Gilder, but not sent. See also, accompanying this, the editor's quotation from a letter written him by Mark Twain on April 30, 1909.

tor of television), and a spiral hat pin, besides inventing, himself, a game of kings, a self-pasting scrap book, and an automatically adjusting vest strap.[43] Fondest of all his speculative dreams were, of course, those awakened by the Paige typesetting machine. In a typically enthusiastic mood he wrote to his brother Orion: "Telephones, telegraphs, locomotives, cotton-gins, sewing-machines, Babbage calculators, Jacquard looms, perfecting presses, all mere toys, simplicities! The Paige compositor marches alone and far in the land of human inventions."[44] Upon this machine he spent nearly $200,000—without return.

Carried away by these speculative enthusiasms, Mark Twain passed by with little concern the grave social problems evoked by the Machine. To the suggestion that the Paige typesetter would throw men out of work, his response was, simply, "The machine will not diminish the number of printers but increase composition and make it much lighter work for both body and mind"[45]—a rather cavalier way, to say the least, of disposing of technological unemployment. In regard to the speculative exploitation of the Machine, there remained still, as there had been in the old prospecting days, an amusing and very human divergence between what Mark Twain said and what he did. Not long before his indulgence in the Paige typesetter he had written, "No sound and legitimate business can be established on a basis of speculation." Not long after, he wrote, "There are two times in a man's life when he should not speculate: when he can't afford it, and when he can."[46] Now in such discrepancies between theory and practice, it would be idle, of course, to look for any hypocrisy. In dealing with his own exuberance and immense energies, Mark Twain simply failed to achieve a perfect integration. And if one part of his nature tugged against another part, he was, even in this, almost perfectly a type of his age, reflecting within himself

[43] Paine, *op. cit.*, pp. 725 ff., 756, 1098, 1151.
[44] *Ibid.*, pp. 902 ff.
[45] *Mark Twain's Notebook*, p. 187.
[46] See, respectively, *A Connecticut Yankee*, pp. 164-5; *Following the Equator*, II, 215.

its waverings between plunging and prudence, between speculative adventure and security.

If Mark Twain's published expressions on speculation ran counter to his actual practice, his attitude toward the Machine, and toward its value in the production of material comforts, remained, in both its public and its private expressions, thoroughly consistent. Even here, however, it is necessary to qualify. His chief panegyric of the Machine is, of course, the *Connecticut Yankee;* and of this Gargantuan satire it is not well to speak too simply, for it reveals all the elusive suggestiveness, all the bewildering complexity, of ultimate genius. The core-idea is, no doubt, the superiority of industrial democracy to feudalism, and of that industrial democracy the Yankee is both type and spokesman. Nevertheless, in some episodes the Yankee appears to be the butt of Mark Twain's satire, not its agent; when the Yankee can find no better work for his captive knights than high-pressure advertizing, the joke is not wholly on the knights. As Mark Twain is reported to have instructed his illustrator, "This Yankee of mine has neither the refinement nor the weakness of a college education; he is a perfect ignoramus; he is boss of a machine shop; he can build a locomotive or a Colt's revolver, he can put up and run a telegraph line, but he's an ignoramus, nevertheless." [47]

Yet, after all needful qualifications have been made, the *Yankee* remains chiefly a paean of praise for the industrial revolution and the Machine Age. To both the Yankee and his creator, the heroes of modern times are not statesmen or scientists or artists, but inventors—"the creators of this world—after God—Gutenberg, Watt, Arkwright, Whitney, Morse, Stephenson, Bell." [48] Hence the Yankee, in his social program for feudal England, is not satisfied merely with freedom and equality; he must have material comforts as well. "The telegraph, the telephone, the phonograph, the typewriter, the sewing machine, and all the thousand willing and handy servants of steam and electricity were working their way into

[47] Paine, *op. cit.,* pp. 887-8.
[48] *A Connecticut Yankee,* p. 323.

favor. We had a steamboat or two on the Thames, we had steam war-ships, and the beginnings of a steam commercial marine." [49]

All in all, Mark Twain's recurrent speculative fever; his enthusiasm (though not a permanent one) for business; his friendships with big business men such as Carnegie and Rogers; the frank commercialism of his policies as a publisher; the frequent commercialism of his policies as a writer; his reiterated celebration of the Machine and of material comforts —all these considerations might indeed, if taken alone, lead us to think of Mark Twain as a prophet of capitalistic industrialism. But they must not be taken alone. Alongside Mark Twain's enjoyment of materialism and the Machine must be placed his passion for democracy, his passion for social justice, and his application of both these ideals to some of the fundamental problems of industrialism. We shall now turn to this other side of the picture; and in observing it we shall keep in view, as before, the extent to which Mark Twain's privately expressed views appear in his published works.

V

The youthful Mark Twain took his democracy very much as a normal young man takes his health—he took it for granted. Mark Twain's development into a militant protagonist of democracy took place during the latter eighties, the time, significantly enough, of the awakening of the nation's social conscience to the problems of industrialism. In keeping with an American tradition that was at least as old as the time of Freneau, Mark Twain thought of democracy as an international movement, which would in time make its way among all the intelligent peoples of the globe—by peaceful means, if possible; by violent revolution, if that were necessary. Looking back upon the French Revolution, he realized that he himself was not a Girondin, but a "Sansculotte!—And not a pale, characterless Sansculotte, but a Marat." [50] The French Revo-

---

[49] *A Connecticut Yankee*, p. 398.

[50] *Letters*, II: 490-1; a letter of August 22, 1887, to William Dean Howells.

lution itself was to him "the noblest and the holiest thing and the most precious that ever happened in this earth. And its gracious work is not done yet—not anywhere in the remote neighborhood of it." Looking out on the progress of the democratic movement during his own time, he was delighted at the fall of the Brazilian monarchy; and he felt that not only revolution but assassination would be justifiable in overthrowing the Czar and setting up a republic in Russia.[51]

This militant democracy Mark Twain applied, in a way that was none the less genuine for being unsystematic and impulsive, to certain questions of social justice in the Machine Age. Emotionally, perhaps instinctively, he sympathized with the underdog; his heart and soul were with those who do the hard work of the world. As he was for the people as against kings, so he was for labor as against capital; and to his general loyalty to the people he added, at times, a keen awareness of the sufferings of the submerged classes.[52] He did not, however, formulate any definite social philosophy, and it was the feeling of Howells that sociological inquiry "baffled and dispirited" him. Although he was fascinated by *Looking Backward* and had Bellamy visit him, he never came to agree with Bellamy that it is an indispensable function of republican government to democratize industry as well as politics.[53] Instead, he looked, for the solution of the problem of social justice, to the organization of labor. Not long after Hay had virtually said in *The Breadwinners* that organized labor and crime are identical, Clemens praised the Knights of Labor—then the most powerful labor body—and said of the organized laborer, "He has before him the most righteous work that was ever given into the hand of man to do, and he will do it."[54] There-

[51] See, for the above quotation, *Letters*, II: 513-4; a letter of September 22, 1889, to William Dean Howells. See also *ibid.*, II, 519, a letter written during October of 1889 to Sylvester Baxter; II, 535-8, an article written by request for the periodical *Free Russia*, but not mailed.

[52] Paine, *op. cit.*, pp. 849-50; Howells, *My Mark Twain*, p. 43; *Mark Twain's Notebook*, p. 324.

[53] Howells, *My Mark Twain*, pp. 43-4, 80-1.

[54] Paine, *op. cit.*, pp. 849-50; the quotation is from the essay, "Knights of Labor," sent to Howells, but not published.

after, at least until 1900, and perhaps longer, in conversations both at home and abroad, he warmly and consistently championed the value of labor organization. According to Howells, "He would show that side with such clearness and force that you could not say anything in hopeful contradiction." [55] Evidently, to Mark Twain, the labor union meant, in economics, what the advance of democracy meant in politics.

Although Mark Twain never substantially changed his position about labor, his expressions on the subject after 1900 are not numerous. Meanwhile, another outlet for his passion for social justice had been furnished by events that followed the Spanish-American war. As to the motives behind American —and English—territorial expansion, and as to the grounds of his own opposition to both, Mark Twain was equally clear. Colonial empire, he understood, was a natural corollary of industrial expansion; but to assume control over "backward" races was, clearly, to deny them those very privileges of independence and self-government to which American democracy had been theoretically devoted. For once, therefore, Mark Twain's materialism and his democracy came into direct conflict. Victory went to the latter; and it was essentially his democracy that called forth his bitter opposition to imperialism. In speaking of England's South African war, for instance, he pronounced it sordid, criminal, shameless, excuseless. To him, moreover, the slow-paced life, the pastoral virtues of the Boers made up a better civilization than the "intellectual and other artificialities" of the English and Americans.[56] Similarly, the American conquest of the Philippines provoked in him chiefly contempt. Not professing to be moved by any Large Patriotism, he nevertheless felt distressed and troubled and befouled by his country's policy; and about that policy, if Livy would let him, he would have his say.[57]

[55] *My Mark Twain*, pp. 43-4; see also *Mark Twain's Letters*, II: 679-80; a letter of May 12, 1899, to William Dean Howells.

[56] *Letters*, II: 692-3; a letter of January 25, 1900, to Howells; II, 694; a letter of January 27, 1900, to Reverend Joseph Twichell.

[57] *Ibid.*, II: 704-6; a letter of January 29, 1901, to Reverend Joseph Twichell.

It was during these latter years, when he was well over the threshold of old age, that he appears to have had his only serious doubt of the value of material comforts—an attitude toward which he was very likely influenced by his pessimistic view of the "damned human race." In arguing against his friend Joseph Twichell's belief in progress, he wrote, after a fashion strange enough in the man who had spoken of inventors as "the creators of this world—after God":

> Well, the 19th century made progress . . . colossal progress. In what? Materialities. Prodigious acquisitions were made in things which add to the comfort of many and make life harder for as many more. But the addition to righteousness? Is that discoverable? I think not. The materialities were not invented in the name of righteousness.[58]

Now, in comparison with Mark Twain's privately expressed views on democracy, social justice, and imperialism, what were his public pronouncements? For answer, we must again turn first of all to that enormously complex satire, the *Connecticut Yankee,* and afterward to certain magazine articles and other lesser works.

To begin with, the militant democracy of the Yankee himself is a precise duplicate of that of his creator. To the Yankee, as to Mark Twain, the French Revolution is the chief event in world history; it is "the ever memorable and blessed Revolution." [59] To the Yankee, as to Mark Twain, Democracy is a militant, a violent movement; "All revolutions that will succeed must *begin* in blood, whatever may answer afterward." [60] To the Yankee, as to Mark Twain, the proper object of a citizen's loyalty is not the government, or the church, or some other institution; it is the entire nation, the democratic body as a whole.[61] With this view, the political policies of the

---

[58] *Letters,* II. 700-9; a letter of March 14, 1905, to Reverend Joseph Twichell. Reprinted by permission of Harper and Brothers, publishers.

[59] *A Connecticut Yankee,* p. 105. Cf. the *Letters,* II: 490-1; a letter of August 22, 1887, to William Dean Howells.

[60] *A Connecticut Yankee,* p. 171.

[61] *Ibid.,* p. 107. See also Mark Twain's explanation of his purpose in the *Connecticut Yankee, Mark Twain's Notebooks,* p. 199. Precisely this

Yankee, which are aimed at the final transformation of Arthur's kingdom into a republic with universal suffrage, are thoroughly consistent.

Even more than with democracy, however, the *Connecticut Yankee* is concerned with social justice,[62] or, rather, with the excoriation of social injustice. It is, as Vernon Louis Parrington has said, "not an attack on chivalry—at least not primarily; it is rather an attack on thirteen centuries of reputed Christian civilization that under pretense of serving God has enslaved and despoiled the children of God." [63] As Parrington implies, the *Yankee* is in no sense a historical novel. It is not true to, nor was it meant to be true to, the facts of any one era in history. The civilization of Arthur's court is, as Mark Twain portrays it, a composite of many generations in history, which were alike in that, in them all, the masses were ruled by the classes. Moreover, the fact that Mark Twain's illustrations of social injustice come from the past rather than from the present implies, on his part, no evasion of contemporary issues; it is simply another example of his habitual methods of work. In only one novel, *The Gilded Age,* does he deal effectively with

---

same view of loyalty, it might be observed, Mark Twain expressed in other writings; for example, in his article, "The Czar's Soliloquy," the pronouncement that "the modern patriotism, the true patriotism, the only rational patriotism, is *loyalty to the Nation,* ALL *the time,* loyalty to the government when it deserves it." "The Czar's Soliloquy," *The North American Review,* 180: 324 (March, 1905).

[62] It is, of course, hardly possible to iron out all the inconsistencies of objective involved in the *Yankee* and in Mark Twain's attitude toward the book. Besides the aims already mentioned, there was, quite evidently, another—that of rendering a *tu quoque* in reply to British criticisms of America. In refusing to have the English edition of the work cut, for example, Mark Twain wrote, "It was written for England. So many Englishmen have done their sincerest best to teach us something for our betterment that it seems to me high time that some of us should substantially recognize the good intent by trying to pry up the English nation to a little higher level of manhood in turn." (*Letters,* II: 524-5; a letter of late 1889 to Messrs. Chatto and Windus.) Although this purpose has been felt to involve an evasion of *American* problems of justice, there is no real ground for seeing in it anything but an additional feature of a very rich and complex book.

[63] *The Beginnings of Critical Realism in America,* p. 97.

contemporary life; his imagination, a dominantly romantic one, moved more easily in shaping a pliable past than in conforming to the more rigid factual restrictions of the present. Accordingly, in a manner which in fundamentals curiously resembles that of Hawthorne, Mark Twain came to use a selective, composite, romantic background, rather than a realistic one, for the illustration of social and moral ideas.

In the composite past the Yankee is forced to live in, one of his earliest discoveries is that the masses of humanity are—in a phrase which has come to label an important American political movement—in need of a "New Deal"; [64] and as he goes about Arthur's kingdom, he discovers, in episode after episode which Mark Twain handles with telling, climactic power, what sufferings the many have undergone at the hands of the few. The essay on the responsibility of priest and noble for the enslavement of the populace; the portrayal of the prisoners of Queen Morgan; the story of the experiences of the Yankee and the King as slaves; the picture of the wanton destruction of a peasant family in "The Smallpox Hut"; the dramatization of the legal murder of a young mother for a petty theft [65]—than this climactic series, there is in all American literature no more tremendous indictment of social injustice; an indictment which, beginning in the familiar style of the back-country humorous essayist, reaches at last the finality of profoundest tragic drama. It is in the last of these episodes that Mark Twain makes explicit, in the words of a humane priest, the theme of the entire series—the superiority of human rights to property rights. Although it has been urged in the young mother's behalf that she has stolen only in order to get food for her baby,

the prosecuting officer replied that whereas these things were all true, and most pitiful as well, still there was much small theft in these days, and mistimed mercy here would be a danger to prop-

[64] *A Connecticut Yankee*, p. 108. According to President Roosevelt's own statement, it was from the *Connecticut Yankee* that he got the phrase. See Cyril Clemens, *Mark Twain and Mussolini*, p. 51.

[65] The *Connecticut Yankee*, respectively, pp. 62-5, 142, 190, 282 ff., 361.

erty—oh, my God, is there no property in ruined homes, and orphaned babes, and broken hearts that British law holds precious! [66]

Without question, the democratic humanitarianism which underlies so much of our middle-class economic critique is illustrated in the *Connecticut Yankee;* is, indeed, more powerfully illustrated than in any other novel of the period. Moreover, no alert reader need have missed the bearing of the novel on the injustices of the contemporary Machine Age. According to Howells, "There are passages in which we see that the noble of Arthur's day, who fattened on the blood and sweat of his bondmen, is one in essence with the capitalist of Mr. Harrison's day who grows rich on the labor of his underpaid wagemen. . . . Our civilization of today sees itself mirrored in the cruel barbarism of the past, the same in principle and softened only in custom. With shocks of consciousness, one realizes in such episodes that the laws are still made for the few against the many, and that the preservation of things, not men, is still the ideal of legislation." [67]

But how far did Mark Twain himself intend such an application as Howells made? In the absence of any statement of his own, it is impossible to say. Some inferences may, perhaps, be drawn from the fact that in certain passages the generalized, romantic method is dropped, and modern economic issues are criticized directly. In the episodes dealing with Dowley the blacksmith, for instance, the tariff (not an Arthurian but an American tariff!) is discussed, and the high-wage argument of the American protectionists is neatly disposed of. As the Yankee says, "It isn't what sum you can get, it's how much you can buy with it, that's the important thing." [68] The characterization of Dowley himself is evidently meant as a satire on the acquisitive ideal of a *petit-bourgeois*, and on its typically American product, the Self-Made Man. "Self-made men, you know. They know how to talk. They do

[66] *Ibid.*, pp. 360-1.
[67] Howells, *My Mark Twain*, p. 147; a reprint of Howells' original review of the *Connecticut Yankee*.
[68] *A Connecticut Yankee*, p. 304.

deserve more credit than any other breed of men, yes, that is true; and they are among the very first to find it out, too." The ideal of Success is convincingly flayed when Dowley, who is inordinately proud of having meat twice a month, and white bread once a week, and of owning five stools of the "sweetest workmanship," is crushed by the Yankee's display of superior wealth.[69]

In the same series of episodes, the Yankee—that is, Mark Twain—predicts the rise of the labor union as an economic protection for the common man, and defends the union very much as Mark Twain was accustomed to do in conversation. After Dowley has explained that the "magistrate," representing the employing interests, determines the wage rate, and that the fixing of wages is solely the concern of the employer, the Yankee replies:

But I thought the other man might have some little trifle at stake in it, too; and even his wife and children, poor creatures. The masters are these: nobles, rich men, the prosperous generally. These few, who do no work, determine what pay the vast hive shall have who *do* work. You see? They're a "combine"—a trade union, to coin a new phrase—who band themselves together to force their lowly brother to take what they choose to give. Thirteen hundred years hence—so says the unwritten law—the "combine" will be the other way, and then how these fine people's posterity will fume and fret and grit their teeth over the insolent tyranny of trade-unions.[70]

Near the turn of the century, when events were so vividly proving the *liaison* between industrialism and foreign conquest, Mark Twain's public expressions on social justice turned, as did his private ones, upon the issue of imperialism. His treatment of English expansion in South Africa, while it displays some dislike of the lethargy of the Boers and of their indifference to progress, nevertheless reveals clearly that he understood the economic motives back of the struggle. His

[69] *Ibid.*, pp. 314 ff.

[70] *A Connecticut Yankee*, p. 332. Reprinted by permission of Harper and Brothers, publishers. For qualifications of Mark Twain's general approval of trade-unions, see *The American Claimant*, p. 112.

sympathies appear to have been chiefly with the natives, upon whom, he felt, the alleged cruelties of the Boers weighed less heavily than the lingering death to which they were condemned as laborers in the British industrial system.[71] When, finally, war broke out between England and the Boer republic, Mark Twain, keenly as he felt, refrained from any public utterance. Even though England was wrong, she must, he maintained, be upheld; for her defeat would endanger the European balance of power and bring on "an inundation of Russian and German political degradations which would envelop the globe and steep it in a sort of Middle-Age night and slavery which would last till Christ comes again."[72] Nevertheless, his expressions on imperialism were only delayed, not prevented or suppressed.

His complete expression on imperialism came, presently, in the two articles in the *North American Review* which were provoked by our own Philippine conquest. The latter of the two, "A Defense of General Funston,"[73] is a brilliant deflation of the achievement of the man who might have become the "hero" of the Philippine war. The former, and by far the more important, "To the Person Sitting in Darkness,"[74] is a satirical excoriation of the whole movement of Euro-American expansion into Asia, the Pacific Islands, and Africa; an attack which in fierce indignation, in blighting, shattering power is comparable only to Swift's "A Modest Proposal." Herein, Mark Twain attacks imperialism by an ironic defense, the burden of which is that the "Blessings of Civilization Trust" can do no wrong. Missionaries are attacked as being, in reality, agents of imperialism; German policy in China is denounced; the English adventure in South Africa is labeled as "purely a private raid for cash," a war manufactured out of materials "so inadequate and fanciful that they make the boxes grieve and the gallery laugh." As to the American adventure in the

[71] *Following the Equator*, II, 332 ff.
[72] *Letters*, II: 692-3; a letter of January 25, 1900, to William Dean Howells.
[73] *The North American Review*, 174: 613-24 (May, 1902).
[74] *Ibid.*, 172: 165-75 (February, 1901).

Philippines, it is "defended" in an imaginary address of an American Christian to a heathen:

There have been lies; yes, but they were told in a good cause. We have been treacherous, but that was only that real good might come out of apparent evil. True, we have crushed a deceived and confiding people; we have turned against the weak and the friendless who trusted us; we have stamped out a just and intelligent and well-ordered republic; we have stabbed an ally in the back and slapped the face of a guest; we have bought a Shadow from an enemy that hadn't it to sell; we have robbed a trusting friend of his land and his liberty; we have invited our clean young men to shoulder a discredited musket and do bandit's work under a flag which bandits have been accustomed to fear, not to follow; we have debauched America's honor and blackened her face before the world; but each detail was for the best.[75]

Finally, the ultimate questioning of the value of "materialities," which appears in Mark Twain's correspondence with Joseph Twichell, appears also in the two caustic apologues, "The Man that Corrupted Hadleyburg" (1900) and "The $30,000 Bequest" (1906). In the former story, the concealed greed and selfishness of a self-righteous village is exposed through an appeal to the motive of avarice. In the latter, the happiness of a quiet, thrifty, small-town couple is destroyed underneath the feverish expectations awakened by the prospect of sudden wealth; a prospect which, after all, turns out to have been illusory. Both stories are quite in agreement with Mark Twain's known views at the time of their writing; both are in accordance with the deep pessimism which showed him the emptiness of many commonly accepted values, without enabling him to discover others in their stead.

Summed up, Mark Twain's privately and publicly expressed views on social justice present a complete, an exact parallel. In both, the starting-point is his passion for democracy, regarded not merely as political equality, but as a scheme of essential justice to the masses. In both, democracy is looked on as an aggressive, world-wide movement whose ends are to be gained, if extreme methods prove necessary, by violent

[75] *Ibid.*, p. 174.

revolution. In both, economic exploitation is recognized as a mortal enemy of democracy, and in both, the labor union is regarded as the best practical instrument for combatting that exploitation in modern society. In both, imperialism is opposed on the ground that it exploits the weaker nations in behalf of the strong and deprives them of their chance of democratic development. And, in fine, the only significant private conviction which Mark Twain refrained from publishing was his belief that the continued assassination of Czars would be justifiable! [76]

VI

The various segments of Mark Twain's economic thought may have appeared, as we have followed them so far, sufficiently disparate. The satire of speculative exploitation in *The Gilded Age* certainly does not suggest Mark Twain's own absorption in speculative enterprise; nor does either suggest, of itself, that deep, intense humanitarianism which prompted his passionate defense of the common man. But perhaps the threads are not so dispersed as to forbid our gathering them up, finding the pattern by which to weave them together, and judging the worth of the whole. In such a process of synthesis and evaluation, several questions are pertinent. First—to dispose most quickly of a rather thankless task—what were the essential weaknesses and limitations of Mark Twain the economic critic? Again, can the diverse, even contradictory fragments of his thought be so reconciled as to make up any coher-

[76] The latter years of Mark Twain's life did not witness any *fundamental* changes in his social philosophy. The old passion for democracy, honesty, and social justice, the old habit of sporadic and unsystematic utterance, continued; and an occasional expression that points another way—such as his melancholy speculation on America's probable relapse into monarchy—only modifies and does not substantially change the course of the main current of his thought. A number of these later expressions on economics are assembled in the section entitled "The Plutocracy" in *Mark Twain in Eruption: Hitherto Unpublished Pages about Men and Events,* edited by Bernard DeVoto (New York, 1940), pp. 61-106.

ent pattern of ideas? And, if they can be so reconciled, of what worth is that pattern of ideas today?

Of weaknesses and limitations, it must be allowed, Mark Twain's genius bore an unusually heavy crop. Notwithstanding his passion for honesty and social justice, economics was with him only an occasional and secondary concern; and, as a consequence, he never came to know enough about it to produce social criticism comparable with that of the masters. Of Marx, of Morris, of Ruskin, and of all the orthodox economists, he was practically unaware; and with the social prophets of his own country, Henry George and Edward Bellamy, he was only casually acquainted. The complexities of actual economic life, likewise, he was far from comprehending; any such intricate network of business relations as that shown in, say, Dreiser's *The Titan* was beyond his scope. And as he lacked the broadest knowledge of economic fact and theory, so he lacked knowledge of the processes of critical thinking. Nowhere does he reveal any genuine understanding of scientific or philosophical method; never, in facing a problem, does he succeed in passing dispassionate judgment on the basis of systematically reviewed evidence. Moreover, most of his work bears witness to a kind of spiritual loose-jointedness, a lack of perfect integration, in his character. Not only are there downright contradictions, as when he satirized Colonel Sellers with his right hand and imitated him with his left. There is lacking —and this is far more serious—the finer sort of self-discipline which was needed to coördinate his myriad energies and employ them consistently for some worthy creative purpose. He lived and thought as he constructed most of his books—in fragments, in brilliant, picturesque, discontinuous episodes, and without the aid of that consistent firmness of purpose which would have coördinated and focused his powers, and thereby have insured a critical result worthy of his supreme energy.

And yet, when all qualifications are made, and when all of Mark Twain's uncertainties and cross-purposes are admitted, it is still possible to hold that his work is pretty much of a piece, and that that piece is of considerable value. Both his

casual comments and his apparently wayward satire follow
in reality a coherent, underlying pattern of ideas, which constitutes an informal, unsystematic philosophy of the business
life. The seeming disparities, including that supposed conflict
between the artist and the business man which has so troubled
Van Wyck Brooks, mostly disappear when we quit trying to
understand Mark Twain in the thought-categories of 1920-40,
and adopt, instead, the viewpoint of 1885 or 1890. To make
plain the essential unity of Mark Twain's ideas, it is only necessary to look at them in the climate of opinion to which they
are native, and relate them to the critical movement of which
they are a part.

During the whole of Mark Twain's literary prime, American
thought on industrialism was, as has been shown in the preceding chapter, extremely active. According to our previous
discussion, which it is pertinent to recall here, most people
agreed in accepting and welcoming the machine. But the
majority recognized, too, that the energies loosed by the
machine had so intensified some of the old antisocial tendencies of business as to require castigation in satire and sermon.
This same critical majority recognized, further, that the machine had at least temporarily accentuated some very old
social evils—insecurity, unequal distribution of wealth, and
poverty. Yet in seeking to remedy these evils, American critics
did not embrace the proletarian philosophies which were then
becoming current in Europe; instead, they sought, by a score
of different routes, the goal of insuring the fruits of industry
to the whole people, and not merely to a privileged class,
whether capitalist or proletarian. They simply adapted an old
American ideal—that of a larger life for the average man—to
the industrial era; they carried over the republican principle
from politics into economics.

To place beside Mark Twain's economic philosophy the
ideas on industrialism which were then current among American authors, is to show how nearly identical was his thought
with that of his place and time, how coherent were his opinions, and how free from any hint of deadly conflict between
the artist and the businessman or democrat within him. As a

businessman, he joined his contemporaries in glorifying the machine, fascinated with the possibilities of exploiting it and of controlling nature through it. As a satirist, he joined his contemporaries in attacking, never the machine itself, but certain economic abuses, such as speculation, which the machine, with its enormous release of energy, had made more dangerous. And as a pioneer democrat, inheritor of American liberalism, he joined his contemporaries in insisting on a wide diffusion of material comforts, and on the protection of the average man from economic, no less than from political or religious, tyranny.

Mark Twain's, then, was a comparatively simple, coherent philosophy of acquisition, control of obvious abuses, and concern for the interests of the whole people. Within him, satirist, capitalist, and democrat worked toward the same object— that of enjoying the uses of the machine, and lessening the abuses. And, whatever its defects, this attitude toward industrialism has continued to be the dominant American attitude. The great bulk of Americans are irrevocably committed to a machine culture. Yet the great bulk of Americans have avoided, and continue to avoid, the class philosophies which have arisen in other industrial nations. They have consistently sought, instead, a *via media*, more consonant with the traditions of democracy, in which the interests of the whole citizenry should be preserved. These, in brief, were the views of Mark Twain. He did not create them or even systematize them. He expressed them, dramatized them, salted them with his incomparable humor, and helped to store them up in the consciousness of millions of readers. Here, as in so many other ways, Mark Twain worked fruitfully at the very center of the American cultural tradition, nourished by its past, and nourishing, in turn, its future.

Yet one can hardly avoid, in closing, the observation that the permanence of Mark Twain's work has not been seriously affected, one way or another, by its occasional burden of social and political criticism. Men read imaginative literature for individual objects, not social; they read for psychological fulfillment, not for the acquiring of ideas about the State or the

Machine. They read that they may have life, and have it more abundantly. They read Mark Twain because he offers them, abundantly and intensely, the heightened sense of life they crave. They continue to read him because he offers that heightened sense of life not merely as a temporary excitement, but as an enduring nourishment for a thousand deepseated capacities for experience which, amid the monotony of civilized living, too easily go undernourished. By his touch are awakened potentialities stored in men's deepest nerve centers by generation after generation of experience:—the sense of broad incongruity whose voice is bluff laughter; the sensitiveness to superstition that lingers in the subrational part of all our natures; the perennial craving for some picaresque escape from responsibility; the enjoyment of those images of sky and river and wooded shoreline amid which the race has lived for countless generations. The work of Mark Twain is great and permanent work because, through it, an immensely powerful creative mind ministers to those central and enduring psychological needs of the race. The social criticism of Mark Twain is of enduring significance, not alone because it is in such close accord with our main American tradition, but also because it has been, almost as if by accident, drawn along in the current of an achievement far greater than itself.

CHAPTER FOUR

I

More systematic than the scattered deliverances of Mark Twain, and of more artistic importance than the now forgotten novels of several score journalists and reformers, is the work of Hamlin Garland. With Garland, both as man and as artist, economics and economic reform were, over a period of some ten years, a major interest. Prior to, and during, this decade, many influences converged upon Garland's maturing personality; in the course of it, he produced a unique body of work in which these forces were shaped by the creative imagination into forms more or less artistic; toward its close, he was already being diverted from this characteristic expression, and his work was beginning to reveal that indirection, that temporary frustration, even, which has so curiously baffled our American commentators.[1]

Of the backgrounds out of which Garland's work emerged, that of his youth on the middle border in Iowa is so fundamental that it calls less for elaboration than for the merest resumé. Certain scattered, idyllic memories he retained, to be sure, of a childhood passed among the coulées of Wisconsin; but it was the life on the Iowa prairie, where he lived from his tenth through his twentieth year, that furnished the real matrix of his imagination. From this source, chiefly, came the myriad concrete images that give his descriptive writing its individual color and tone and texture—sights of low, treeless horizons and the waving of ripe wheat; sounds of turning-plows thrusting through grassroots embedded in black loam; the lurch of plowhandles, the rasp of cornhusks, the bite and

[1] See below, p. 172.

weight of the prairie blizzard. Here in Iowa, too, under the Spartan regime on his father's farm, he first learned that the satisfaction of work might be outweighed by its tortures: by the man's ache of fatigue, by his irritation over the threshing of fly-lanced horses or the stench of cattle stalls; still more, by the woman's perpetual treadmill of "cooking, sewing, washing, churning, and nursing the sick."[2]

The middle border society, into which he had been so early adopted as to be virtually a native, Garland took, throughout his life, curiously for granted; he never became more than vaguely aware of such a different region as the South, or of such a different class as the urban proletariat. The Garlands and most of their neighbors were native American stock—sturdy, hard-working, moderately well-to-do, religious folk. A kind of agrarian middle class, they formed an outpost of the midwestern rural democracy of Lincoln, with a vein of backwoodsy angularity and rudeness in their collective character, and more than a vein of the restlessness of the pioneer. Living among these people, the youth Garland assumed, with no serious question, the premises common in our agrarian democracy before the Civil War. Politically, he assumed a democratic tradition, heightened by memories of a heroic struggle fought ostensibly for the cause of human freedom.[3] Socially, he took for granted the equality with which his folk mingled in sports, in the church, in neighborhood fairs, and in sociables of the Grange. Economically, he assumed the Western principle of the pre-emption and exploitation of the public lands. Indeed, at the very time when he came on the book which awakened his first serious thought on social problems, the *Progress and Poverty* of Henry George, he was himself engaged in homesteading in Dakota.[4]

Yet even while he was absorbing the viewpoints of his Iowa society, Garland was, though with no clearly defined intention, preparing his escape from it into a life less physically exacting,

[2] *A Son of the Middle Border*, pp. 42, 87, 127, 155-6.

[3] For an example of Garland's attitude toward the Civil War, observe the manner in which his father's service under Grant is treated in *Trailmakers of the Middle Border*, pp. 296-406.

[4] *A Son of the Middle Border*, pp. 313-4.

more intellectually satisfying; and here, too, the Border society provided him with his main bearings. Through the "Seminary" at Osage, it provided him at least an introduction to culture— a sense of the value of literature and of the power of the written or spoken word. The heated discussions of the townspeople over the writings of Bob Ingersoll, especially "The Mistakes of Moses," helped crystallize his religious independence and agnosticism. The reading of Eggleston's *The Hoosier Schoolmaster* in *Hearth and Home* gave him his first taste of the romanticizing of the common regional life of the West. A sermon delivered by a young Methodist minister stimulated his awareness of the value of art and beauty—a theme which recurs like a refrain in his maturer work. To his homestead in Dakota he carried copies of Taine, of Chambers' *Encyclopedia of English Literature*, and of Greene's *Short History of the English People*.[5] Altogether, if his coming to Boston in 1883 was that of a passionate pilgrim in search of a richer culture, it was also that of a pilgrim who knew with unusual clearness what things he was seeking.

II

For eight or ten years, after his removal to Boston, Garland developed with a rapidity, with an overwhelming energy, which suggests a major creative genius. Beginning in the obscurity of a cheap lodging house, reading fourteen hours a day from the shelves of the Boston public library, he presently found work as teacher in a school of oratory; formed a dozen profitable associations in literary and artistic Boston; wrote book reviews, thirty-odd short stories, two plays, three novels, and much of the material for a book of critical essays; associated himself with the reform journal, the *Arena*, and with its aid toured the West to observe the Populist movement at first hand; and, all this while, acquired and developed his views on philosophy, on literature, and on economics. In the growth of this threefold view of life—philosophical, aesthetic, and social —lies the key to this first period in Garland's career.

[5] *A Son of the Middle Border*, pp. 114, 192, 194, 361 ff.

That Garland, when he came to Boston, was already inclined to a natural rather than a supernatural view of life, is
indicated by his previous interest in Ingersoll and Taine. Now,
in Boston, it was to the nineteenth-century scientists and their
interpreters that he naturally turned—to Fiske, to Darwin, and,
most of all, to Herbert Spencer.[6] From these masters, however, Garland did not derive, for himself, a scientific method
of thought. Instead, he accepted, almost without question, the
main conclusions of Spencer. He came to look upon Spencer
as the greatest living thinker, and he accepted the authority
of the Synthetic Philosophy as that of a new and more plausible
Bible which, to him, endued the universe with a rationally
acceptable harmony and order.

Under such influences, the remnants of Garland's belief
in Christian theology, including his belief in an after-life,
sloughed quietly away; but the loss of the elder faith brought
to him no such suffering as it had brought, say, to Carlyle. For
within Spencer's Synthetic Philosophy had lingered much of
the optimism of the Enlightenment, and in the thought of
Garland, as in that of other Spencerians, the idea of the evolving of all things from the simple to the complex was fused
with an assumption of indefinite progress. The belief that the
evolutionary process extends to human society gave sanction
to Garland's radicalism and instructed him to welcome reform.
The belief that the evolutionary process extends also to the
arts—he once planned to write literary histories of the evolution of English and American ideals[7]—gave sanction to his
bold disregard of many established classics and to his attempt
to strike out a literary way of his own—Veritism. The loss of
any faith in a future life only called for a more vigorous attempt to make the present life tolerable;[8] the individualism of
Spencer, which might have stood in the way of Garland's interest in any socialistic program of economic reform, only con-
firmed him in his discipleship to Henry George; and, in short,

[6] *A Son of the Middle Border*, pp. 322-3.

[7] See, especially, *Roadside Meetings*, p. 36.

[8] In this connection, see particularly the story, "Before the Low Green
Door," *Wayside Courtships*, pp. 253-64.

the Synthetic Philosophy furnished, with Garland, a most favorable nourishment for the growth of literary and economic radicalism.

In the forming of his scheme of aesthetics, Garland drew upon sources more complex and varied than those which had contributed to his general philosophy. Of the European critics and artists, Taine attracted him by his naturalistic interpretation of literary history, Eugene Véron by his opposition to the French Academy, and Max Nordau by his savage treatment of the "Conventional Lies" of our civilization. Garland admired, too, the great dramatists and novelists of Norway and Russia, whom he regarded as being "almost at the very summit" of modern authorship.[9] Of the American authors, Whitman, whose *Leaves of Grass* he read in 1883, "changed the world" for him, taught him the "mystery of the near at hand," and let loose upon him "the spiritual significance of America." Besides the poetry of Whitman, Garland read also the *Specimen Days* and especially the vigorous *Democratic Vistas*, with its caustic romantic critique of the commercialism of the Gilded Age. Whitman himself he visited in Camden, approaching the elder poet with the respect due to "one of the very greatest literary personalities of the century." [10] Of other American authors, it was chiefly Howells who taught him to look upon fiction as a fine art.[11] Above all, however, he studied the works of the local colorists—Eggleston, Kirkland, in fact, almost every significant author of American regional fiction; [12] and it is from this literary type that his own earliest work most immediately derives.

No less curiously instructive than these influences which Garland accepted are those which he rejected; for, if there

[9] *Crumbling Idols*, pp. 3, 9, 49, 58; *Roadside Meetings*, p. 32.

[10] *A Son of the Middle Border*, pp. 323, 408-9; *Roadside Meetings*, pp. 197 ff.

[11] *Roadside Meetings*, pp. 58-60, 121, 125.

[12] Two pages of *Crumbling Idols* (34-5) contain references to Cable, Miss Murfree, Harris, Mary Wilkins Freeman, Kirkland, and Frederic. Garland also considers here the local color work of the British Kipling and Barrie. In another context, he considers the regional elements in the work of Whittier, Lowell, Harte, and Miller (*Ibid.*, p. 6).

were certain masters whom he admired, there were others against whom he was more or less consciously in revolt. The New England school he referred to as "eminent but bookish"; men like Bulwer, Scott, and Hugo he disliked because of their "aristocracy." [13] Many of the classics of the past, he felt, had by the inescapable processes of social evolution lost their validity for the present: "Shakespeare, Wordsworth, Dante, Milton, are fading away into mere names—books we should read but seldom do." [14] In this complex of rejection and assimilation, it is difficult, of course, to find any very systematic set of principles; but of one main drift we may be reasonably sure: Garland accepted and assimilated chiefly those influences he thought pertinent to the shaping of a literature which should deal powerfully, truthfully, and, if possible, beautifully, with the secular life of his contemporary America; and those influences which he felt inimical to a realistic literary treatment of our democracy, he rejected

From such materials, and from their interaction with his own personality, Garland developed his own, individual scheme of aesthetics—a fusion of insurgency, realism, and ethical earnestness. As an insurgent—that is, as a rebellious individualist—he holds first of all that the true artist must be a creator, not an imitator. Excessive bookishness hinders rather than helps the artist. He may be warped or destroyed by libraries; he is made by vital contact with life. In the task of creation, he must free himself from the dominance of literary centers; he must thrust aside all models, even living writers, and "consciously stand alone" before life and before nature. Rebellion is therefore prerequisite to creation; "the iconoclast is a necessity." [15]

Moreover, only by such independence of mind can an author arrive at that entire truthfulness for which Garland preferred a stronger name than realism—Veritism. The essence of Veritism is complete sincerity in the treatment of such

[13] *Crumbling Idols,* pp. 148-9.
[14] *Ibid.,* p. 54.
[15] *Crumbling Idols,* pp. 11, 24, 139, 145-62, 190.

phases of contemporary life as are known to the author. To the apprentice writer, Garland's counsel is,

> Write of the things of which you know most, and for which you care most. By so doing you will be true to yourself, true to your locality, and true to your time.[16]

By this basic principle of truthfulness, Garland's emphasis on the value of local color in literature is, to his own mind at least, justified. The presence of local color in a work of fiction means that the writer "spontaneously reflects the life that goes on around him"; it gives a novel "such quality of texture and background that it could not have been written in any other place or by anyone else than a native." Because of the organic union of truthfulness and local color, the latter is "demonstrably the life of fiction," and is a factor in the greatness of many of the classics both of modern and of ancient times.[17]

Veritism—fidelity to the truth—was, moreover, an ethical principle with Garland as well as an aesthetic; for the truthful portraiture of the unjust and evil necessarily suggests, by contrast, the ideally just and good. By delineating the ugliness and strife of the present, the artist aims to hasten the age of beauty and peace. The Veritist

> sees life in terms of what it might be, as well as in terms of what it is; but he writes of what is, and, at his best, suggests what is to be.[18]

Hence the artist may adopt the aim of spreading everywhere the reign of justice and yet keep his artistic interests paramount—provided only that he convey his social message not by preaching, but by exemplifying, "not by direct expression, but by placing before the reader the facts of life as they stand related to the artist." [19] Veritist and indirect propagandist are one. Seen in this light, the social bearing of fiction need in no way interfere with its aesthetic values, which are to afford the

[16] *Crumbling Idols*, p. 35.
[17] *Ibid.*, pp. 57-8, 62, 64.
[18] *Ibid.*, p. 52.
[19] *Crumbling Idols*, p. 51; *Roadside Meetings*, p. 125; *A Son of the Middle Border*, pp. 374, 472.

writer "keen creative delight" and to enrich the experience of
the reader by touching, lifting, and exalting him.[20]

On the whole, Garland's aesthetics are as individualistic as
his general philosophy of life; and the individualism of both
is of a piece with that of his sociology. While still a home-
steader, himself sharing in the disposal of the public domain,
Garland, as we have seen, read *Progress and Poverty* and accepted George's thesis that the root of social evils is monopoly
of land. Some years later, this abstract conviction was transformed into personal loyalty; George spoke in Boston, and his
impressive power, his sincere altruism, and his personal charm
combined to make of Garland a disciple. Garland joined the
Anti-Poverty society which George's visit had called into being, and attended and addressed its meetings. Later, while
living temporarily in New York, he fell into the habit of visit-
ing "the Prophet and his delightful family," and became an
observer, if not an intimate, of the circle of reformers that fore-
gathered about George.[21]

Sensitive as he was to every appeal to humanitarian feeling,[22] Garland could hardly, if he would, have escaped the
general humanitarian temper of the times, of which the work
of George was only one of many manifestations. The influences he met with in the circle of George were reinforced by
numerous others. His connection with B. O. Flower and the
Arena brought him into fellowship first with another Eastern
group of social critics, and later with the Western leaders of
Populism. The time was one in which he could awaken an
enthusiastic interest in the Single Tax in his friends the Hernes,
or argue against socialism in the company of Howells. It was,
in short, an era of "parlor-socialists, single-taxers, militant pop-
ulists, Ibsen dramas, and Tolstoyan encyclicals against greed,
lust, and caste."[23] Upon Garland, the effect of this welter of

[20] *Crumbling Idols*, pp. 34, 125.

[21] *A Son of the Middle Border*, p. 431.

[22] For examples of this trait in Garland's character, see particularly the
poems, "Altruism," "The Prairie to the City," and "Sport," in *Prairie
Songs*, pp. 74, 78, and 110 respectively. See also *Roadside Meetings*,
p. 122.

[23] *Roadside Meetings*, p. 126.

reform movements was chiefly to deepen his concern for social justice. Only one phase of the reform program provided him with intellectual meat. From his all but religious discipleship to Henry George, he was not diverted.

The sociology of Garland is, then, a simpler version of the sociology of George. Equally with George, Garland is aware, sensitively aware, of the curse of poverty and the burden of human suffering; and he is capable of an equally burning hatred of social injustice. Along with George—and, indeed, with the thinkers of the eighteenth-century Enlightenment— he assumes that the primary causes of human suffering do not lie in the beneficent scheme of Nature, but in the imperfect and unjust laws of man.[24] His particular concern is, of course, with that scheme of law which allows the speculator to monopolize the natural resources of the earth. He assumes, with George, that the destruction of monopoly and of speculative values in land is the crucial task of the economic reformer, the one stroke needful to insure the restoration of the buoyant prosperity that had accompanied the era of the open frontier.

The effect of the tax on land values is precisely like that of opening new land to settlement. It brings it out of the speculator's hands into the settler's hands. It passes out of the hands of the monopolist into the hands of the contractor and builder.[25]

More explicitly than George, Garland rejects all tendencies toward collectivism. The sufferings of the victims of society are not due, as the Socialists claim, to free competition, but to the lack of free competition—in short, to monopoly. Not the paternal care of the government, but opportunity merely, is the need of the average American citizen. Given a chance, the average man is industrious enough and frugal enough to be trusted with the management of his own affairs; and the interference of government with his business ought therefore, Jeffersonian fashion, to be diminished rather than increased.

[24] For two illustrations of this idea, which is either expressed or implied in all of Garland's economic fiction, see *Prairie Songs*, p. 78, and *A Son of the Middle Border*, p. 363.
[25] "The Single Tax in Actual Operation." *The Arena*, X, 57 (June, 1894).

Moreover, the restoration of opportunity, and the consequent abolition of poverty, are not economic aims merely; they are aesthetic as well. With William Morris, Garland believed that widespread social injustice dwarfs the growth of art. If he lacked Morris's profound understanding of the creative values of craftsmanship, he at least realized that if the arts are ever to have meaning for the populace in general, poverty must first be alleviated. The exhausted sweatshop girl or farm hand has no chance to care for beauty. Hence, "if you would raise the standard of art in America you must first raise the standard of living...." "With leisure to enjoy and means to purchase to his refining taste, the common man would be no longer a common man, and art, genuine art, with free and happy intellects before it, would no longer be the poor, begging thing that it seems now." [26]

III

The same decade that witnessed the crystallization of Garland's view of life—philosophical, aesthetic, and economic—witnessed also the completest expression of that view in fiction. As early as 1885, Garland was publishing, through the *New American Magazine*, a series of local-color articles describing Western haying, wheat-harvesting, threshing, and winter sports. [27] When Joseph Kirkland's Western novel, *Zury*, appeared, Garland reviewed it, became acquainted with the author, and, on his way home for a visit in 1887, stopped by Chicago to see him. Kirkland challenged him with the question, "Why shouldn't our prairie country have its novelists as well as England or France or Norway?"; and, knowing of Garland's local color articles, he urged him to undertake the writ-

[26] The most compact expressions of Garland's economic views are three articles which he contributed to the *Arena*: "A New Declaration of Rights," III: 157-84 (January, 1891); "The Land Question and Its Relation to Art and Literature," IX: 165-75 (January, 1894); and "The Single Tax in Actual Operation," X: 52-8 (June, 1894). The quotations are from the second article, p. 174.

[27] *Roadside Meetings*, pp. 37-9.

ing of fiction, and to portray the life of the West truthfully, leaving out no essential.[28]

Garland's experiences on the remainder of that westward journey were the final factor which precipitated his stories of the Middle Border. Day after day, studying the land, he brooded over the contrasts between the prodigal beauty of Nature and the gracelessness of human life. For the first time, he could observe the Western farmer not only with the sympathetic understanding of a native, but also with the perspective of an Easterner. The poverty of large numbers of the people, the sordidness of their lives, the ugliness of their homes, the attrition of the beauty and the freshness of youth, the hopeless treadmill of toil walked by the average farmer, and the futility of the life led by the average farm woman— all this he observed as if for the first time. Moreover, the decline of his own mother, who was beginning to break after a lifetime of toil, gave the depressing picture a final touch of poignancy. Always intensely susceptible to the most personal motives, Garland responded with a profound, smouldering indignation, with a determination to portray in fiction these stern and even repellent facts which the more idyllic storytellers had neglected.[29]

As his visits carried him to his old place in Iowa, to his father's farm on the treeless lands of Dakota, and back to his childhood home in Wisconsin, Garland observed and recorded. At least the *suggestion* for his stories usually came, as he later testified, from life; and now, from the people he observed, and from the youthful memories his visit reawakened, he got materials for the characters, situations, and incidents of the stories in the *Main-Travelled Roads* series.[30] Even before his return

[28] *Ibid.*, pp. 111-7.

[29] *A Son of the Middle Border*, pp. 356-8.

[30] Compare, for instance, the notes in *Roadside Meetings*, p. 114, with the description of the two principal characters in "Sim Burns's Wife"; also *Roadside Meetings*, p. 119, with the stories, "A Branch Road" and "Up the Coulée"; also the characterization of Mrs. Knapp, in *A Son of the Middle Border*, p. 364, with that of Mrs. Council in "Under the Lion's Paw." See, for a more detailed discussion of the beginnings of the *Main-Travelled Roads* series, Eldon Cleon Hill, *A Biographical Study of*

to Boston he had begun the writing of the stories; and once
back at his desk in the city, undisturbed, still supported by
his salary as a teacher of literature, he sat down, in an independence that he later looked back to with envy, to render
his materials into fiction with the finest art he could command,
uninfluenced by the needs of the literary market or the demands of any editor.[31] By the close of 1888 he had written most
of the thirty-three stories in the *Main-Travelled Roads* series
and the play, *Under the Wheel;*[32] under much the same impulse, he produced, first as a drama and later as a novel, *A
Member of the Third House,* and transformed *Under the
Wheel* into the novel, *Jason Edwards. A Spoil of Office* (1892)
he wrote later than the others, and, as we shall see, with a
slightly different philosophy and purpose. Fortunately for
Garland's work, his own interests so closely resembled those of
certain contemporary editors that, notwithstanding his independence, he had no unusual difficulty in publishing his
stories. B. O. Flower of the *Arena,* in particular, aided him
and encouraged him to speak his mind fully; indeed, it was at
Flower's suggestion that six of Garland's stories were brought
together in the volume, *Main-Travelled Roads* (1891). The
volumes *Prairie Folks* (1893) and *Wayside Courtships* (1895),
together with later and extended editions of *Main-Travelled
Roads,* completed the publication of the stories Garland had
written in '87 and '88.

IV

Since Garland himself has so emphasized his concern over
social injustice, one is surprised to find, on examining his
stories, that less than a third deal, even indirectly, with economic reform. One story, "Black Ephram," is vaguely humani-

---

Hamlin Garland from 1860 to 1895. A doctoral dissertation of the
Ohio State University (Columbus, 1940), pp. 78 ff.

   [31] "Limitations of Authorship in America." *The Bookman,* 59: 257-8
(May, 1924).

   [32] According to the foreword to *Main-Travelled Roads,* 1922 edition.
However, Garland's handling of dates is not always accurate.

tarian, but devoid of any bearing on the specific economic causes of suffering in Garland's own time. Two others, "A Day of Grace" and "The Test of Elder Pill," express Garland's opposition to the hell-fire evangelism and emotional excesses of much rural religion. Nine stories, such as "The Sociable at Dudley's," are regional narratives, concerned with local color and with the peculiar folkways of a remote rural community. The subjects of ten others, including "The Return of a Private," are general and miscellaneous; and among these at least one, "God's Ravens," deals with provincial life much in the idyllic manner from which Garland supposed he had broken away. By the most liberal interpretation, the need for economic reform and the influence of economic conditions are major themes in only nine stories: "A Branch Road," "Up the Coulée," "Among the Corn Rows," "Under the Lion's Paw," "A Day's Pleasure," "Sim Burns's Wife," "A Stop-Over at Tyre," "An Alien in the Pines," and "Before the Low Green Door."

The economic creed expressed in these nine stories is as simply conceived as it is powerfully driven home. That because of economic injustice rural life is now barren and intolerably painful; that such suffering must be relieved, and such barrenness enriched; and that these gains may be had by the one thoroughgoing act of destroying all monopolistic holdings in land—this is Garland's platform. All in all, it is the sufferings and the spiritual deformity of the victims of society that he renders most powerfully. Among these victims, there is the farmer Sim Burns:

The man thrust his dirty, naked feet into his huge boots, and, without washing his face or combing his hair, went out to the barn to do his chores.

He was a type of the average prairie farmer. . . .

No grace had come or ever could come into his life. Back of him were generations of men like himself, whose main business had been to work hard, live miserably, and beget children to take their places when they died.[33]

[33] *Prairie Folks* (1899 edition), pp. 89-90.

And beside the portrait of the man there is that of his wife, Lucretia, who, after a day of vexations and sufferings and quarrels, wears a pitifully tired, almost tragic, face—

long, thin, sallow, hollow-eyed. The mouth had long since lost the power to shape itself into a kiss, and had a droop at the corners, which seemed to announce a breaking down at any moment into a despairing wail. The colorless neck and sharp shoulders sagged painfully.[34]

There is power in portrayals such as these, the unforgettable power of a profound indignation which has found truthful and adequate voice. And these two are reinforced by other descriptions of equal force—that of Grant MacLane in "Up the Coulée"; those of such farm women as Mrs. Sam Markham in "A Day's Pleasure" and the dying Matilda in "Before the Low Green Door"—descriptions that say all that need be said about the futility of the lives, women's lives especially, that never escape from the imprisonment of poverty.

Besides descriptive portrayal, Garland's one other important method of economic teaching is the illustration of some economic principle or problem in a series of imagined events. In "A Stop-Over at Tyre," he suggests the economic effect of premature marriage in preventing a man from his intended career; in "A Branch Road" he suggests the problem, whether a woman should remain faithful to a marriage in which she is being wrecked by unhappiness and overwork. In "Under the Lion's Paw," the most admirably executed of all the stories, he illustrates the effect of land monopoly on the farmer Haskins, who, when he buys the place he has worked as a tenant, is compelled to pay for his own improvements and to accept terms that make of him an economic slave. The economics of "Under the Lion's Paw" is, of course, straight out of *Progress and Poverty*; Garland himself has spoken of the work as a single-tax story;[35] and, indeed, its relation to George's main thesis is precisely that of example to theorem in mathematics.

[34] *Prairie Folks* (1899 edition), pp. 83-4. The two quotations are reprinted by permission of the Hamlin Garland Literary Estate.
[35] *Roadside Meetings*, p. 125.

Not the least triumph of Garland's work is that he successfully translates the abstractions of George into such concrete, human, dramatic, and moving terms.

Description and exemplification, then, are the common fictional methods of Garland. Mindful of Howells's counsel to exemplify and not to preach, he was almost over-careful in avoiding the explicit statement of any economic views, particularly his own. Rarely, he has his characters discuss some industrial problem of the times;[36] even more rarely, he employs a chorus character to inculcate his own views. Chief of these characters is the radical, Radbourn, who, in "Sim Burns's Wife," protests against the "horrible waste of life involved in it all," who wishes to "preach discontent, a noble discontent," and whose program of practical reform involves

the abolition of all indirect taxes, the State control of all privileges the private ownership of which interfered with the equal rights of all. He would utterly destroy speculative holdings of the earth. He would have land everywhere brought to its best use, by appropriating ground rents to the use of the state.[37]

And yet, even in the stories that are definitely economic in purpose, the didactic element is not obtruded. The economic teaching is suspended, as it were, in a current of more purely fictional elements, especially of the kind common among local color stories. In characterization, for example, there is an abundance of *genre* paintings, like those of Mrs. Ripley and Uncle Ethan Ripley, or the Yohe boys in "The Sociable at Dudley's." In the talk of Garland's people, a Western rural idiom, which gives an impression of entire naturalness, abounds. The natural scene, the prairie background, while not insisted on as is the Tennessee mountain scenery in Miss Murfree's stories, is skillfully, often beautifully, employed.

Indeed, to one who came to Garland's stories without any preconceptions, their principal merit might seem to reside in the sheer craftsmanship of the writer. Stimulated by the artis-

---

[36] For example, "Up the Coulée," in *Main-Travelled Roads*, pp. 112-3, or "Sim Burns's Wife," in *Prairie Folks*, pp. 101-2.

[37] *Prairie Folks*, pp. 106-7.

tic example of his friend Howells, situated independently, at liberty to take his time and brood over his materials until he brought them to full creation, Garland, writing and rewriting,[38] wrought out his stories with the conscious artistry of the master craftsman. The result is a carefully wrought expansion of scene, a deliberate build-up and calculation of effect, and a plausibility dependent on the aesthetically consistent use of precisely the right detail, that are beyond praise. Often the movement of the story culminates in some dramatic or even melodramatic climax—the quietly intense talk of Grant and Howard MacLane in "Up the Coulée," or Haskins' narrowly averted murder of the speculator Butler in "Under the Lion's Paw." Richly suggestive, intensely human touches abound; the language, intentionally rugged, intensifies at times into restrained rhythmic beauty. Underneath the surface, unobtruded but continually felt, the force of the author's profound indignation urges the stories along. Above all, Garland knows when to close, and how to strengthen his conclusions by abandoning direct statement for impressive restraint and suggestion. When, in "Up the Coulée," the prosperous Howard MacLane learns the entire tragedy of his brother's defeat by the poverty he could have relieved, we are told only,

The two men stood there, face to face, hands clasped, the one fair-skinned, full-lipped, handsome in his neat suit; the other tragic, sombre in his softened mood, his large, long, rugged Scotch face bronzed with sun and scarred with wrinkles that had histories, like sabre-cuts on a veteran, the record of his battles.[39]

The reception of *Main-Travelled Roads* was a puzzling affair, at least to Garland. The book sold steadily, to be sure, but mostly in the East; its sale in the West remained small for many years.[40] Certain critics, unprepared for Garland's relentless truth-telling, evinced an antagonism which the author found astonishing. But he had the cordial appreciation of Flower, Mary Wilkins, Howells, and others; and although

[38] *Roadside Meetings*, p. 121.
[39] *Main-Travelled Roads* (Border Edition), p. 129.
[40] *Roadside Meetings*, pp. 178-9.

conservatives like Edward Fuller might look at him askance, he had at least become a force.

V

Besides the short stories in the *Main-Travelled Roads* series, Garland's economic fiction consists of three novels: *Jason Edwards* (1892), *A Member of the Third House* (1892), and *A Spoil of Office* (1892). The two former were originally dramas, and were made into novels by a rather awkward process of expansion and chink-filling. The third represents Garland's first attempt, except for certain unpublished writings, to create a novel directly from his Western materials.

Garland's two dramatic attempts were a natural outgrowth of his friendship with James and Katharine Hearn, both of whom he had converted to the Single Tax without, it seems, interfering with their genial and sometimes hilarious friendship. As they shared his interest in economic reform, so he shared their interest in the creation of a realistic American drama of literary merit. Of course, his plays, *Under the Wheel* and *A Member of the Third House,* were, as he himself recognized, unavailable for the commercial theater; but it does not follow by any means that they are lacking in general merit. The manuscript of *A Member of the Third House* has never been made public; but, if one may judge by the reading of *Under the Wheel* (the play which became the novel *Jason Edwards*) Garland possessed unusual dramatic force. In sheer power, none of the commercial plays of the era can be seriously compared with it; nor did Garland's generation produce, in any other literary form, a more striking treatment of the victim-of-society theme.[41]

The situations in both *Jason Edwards* and *A Member of the Third House* are, therefore, basically dramatic. In the former, Jason Edwards, an "average man," is forced out of an Eastern city by a simultaneous wage-cut and rise in rent. Having emigrated westward, he and his family find all the good land in

[41] It does not appear necessary to speak of the plot of *Under the Wheel,* since it is practically the same as that of *Jason Edwards.*

the hands of speculators, and, in order to buy, have to mortgage their new place. Visitations of interest, drouth, and hailstorm leaves Edwards penniless, homeless, and permanently broken in health. His daughter Alice, who has hitherto refused to marry the prosperous Walter Reeves until she could be free of obligations to her family, is compelled to surrender, and accept Reeves' aid for them all.

In *A Member of the Third House*, Wilson Tuttle, a young scholar and idealist in politics, is conducting an investigation of the influence of a powerful railway monopoly over a state legislature. In the absence of positive proof of bribery, the investigation temporarily stalemates. It is saved by the confession of an aged senator, and, contrary to Tuttle's expectation, comes to involve directly the "Iron Duke," Davis, president of the railway and father of Helene, with whom Tuttle is in love. The young people's dilemma is tragically resolved by Davis's suicide.

Both in ideas and in method, these two novels are a continuation of Garland's short stories. In ideas, they reconsider the question of the speculative and monopolistic holding of natural resources, and extend it so as to include the corrupting effects of monopoly on government. Here, as in *Main-Travelled Roads*, Garland employs a four-fold method of (1) the portrayal of the sufferings of the victims of society; [42] (2) the illustration, in certain dramatic conflicts, of the disastrous effects of economic injustice; (3) the discussion of the treacherous conduct of the speculative interests or the discussion of economic problems in general; [43] and (4) the occasional preachment of Garland's own ideas by means of a chorus character. [44] And not only are Garland's methods the same as in his short stories; the relative *proportion* even, is much the same. Exemplification and description are, as before, his main

---

[42] For example, *Jason Edwards*, pp. 24-5, 69-78.

[43] For example, *ibid.*, pp. 119-28; *A Member of the Third House*, pp. 16-7.

[44] For example, *Jason Edwards*, pp. 41-3; 82-3, the expressions of Walter Reeves. Reeves is not presented, however, as a believer in the Single Tax.

devices; and the proportion of direct discussion or preachment is not, in the novels, noticeably larger.

The technical resemblance of the novels to the short stories is the more noteworthy, for the reason that their aesthetic values are so much inferior. The collection of stories has retained an honorable place in our literary history as at least a minor classic; the novels have been, except by the special student, quite justly forgotten. Garland himself, always oversensitive to the charge that he was a social preacher instead of an artist, felt that in the novels he had allowed his didactic purpose to destroy his art. In preparing the 1922 edition of his works, for instance, he rejected *Jason Edwards* on the ground, in part, that it was "too sour, ... too preachy." [45] But, as we have seen, the proportion of direct inculcation in *Jason Edwards* is not noticeably larger than that in the artistically meritorious economic stories in *Main-Travelled Roads*. The cause of the aesthetic failure of the novels must, therefore, be sought elsewhere.

The most evident cause is the inferior and apparently hasty workmanship of the author in transferring the stories from drama to fiction. For, in the novel, the reader expects the author to furnish him with that fullness of background and gesture and movement, which his own imagination is trained to supply for the closet drama. But, in making his dramas into novels, Garland appears to have slighted the careful elaboration which would have made them rich and lifelike instead of spare and mechanical. Hence, although some of the power of *Under the Wheel* survives in *Jason Edwards*—such power as is inherent in the bare, naked situations themselves—the general effect of the novel is far inferior to that of the play. The characters are only pasteboard figures. Jason Edwards himself is less a man than a mere voice of protest and ineffectual complaint. His daughter Alice is a type of sterile independence; the editor Reeves, of a too facile success. In brief, when Garland spoke of the novel as being "too short, ... too drab of clothing," he was on sounder critical ground than when

[45] *My Friendly Contemporaries*, p. 395. See also *Roadside Meetings*, p. 126.

he dismissed it because of its bitter tone or its didacticism.

If the case of *Jason Edwards* is that of a novel only half emerged, that of *A Member of the Third House* is even worse. For example, Garland, in order to inform the reader that the young legislator Wilson Tuttle is tender-hearted, shows him watching an old-fashioned horse car being laboriously hauled uphill. "Tuttle," the reader is told, "gave a sigh of relief when the horses on the car reached a level and turned a corner. This sympathy for the suffering animals marked him as a man of rather keen sensibility." [46]—Surely, when an author allows himself to write such banality, to attribute his failure to didacticism is beside the point. *Jason Edwards* and *A Member of the Third House* are bad not because they are didactic, but because they are artistically incomplete. They are to genuine novels as a mere framework is to a house, or a skeleton to a complete human body.

To a similar end of essential failure in the presence of great possibilities, Garland arrived in *A Spoil of Office* (1892), his only attempt to translate his economic materials directly into a full-length novel. In this novel, the failure is, to be sure, less decisive. To begin with, Garland had whatever advantage there may be in dealing with a spontaneous, immensely popular folk-movement, a rebellion of the agrarian and debtor West against the dominance of the commercial and creditor East.

Apparently, the Western farmers had abundant grounds for rebellion. The general loss of prosperity—indeed, the widespread poverty—that had come from the decline in the prices of farm products; the corrupting influence of the railroads on Western politics, and their discrimination among shippers and shipping points; the foreclosure of mortgages which, in the single state of Kansas, caused eleven thousand farms to change hands in four years; a deflationary fiscal policy which caused the value of the dollar to appreciate three hundred per cent between 1865 and 1895, and thus made the lifting of mortgages harder [47]—all these forces, and others, contributed to the growth of widespread, intense, and bitter discontent in the

[46] *A Member of the Third House*, p. 9.
[47] John Donald Hicks, *The Populist Revolt*, pp. 56-88.

West. A milder, earlier expression of this discontent had developed during the seventies and eighties in the social and cooperative Grange. More bitter and aggressive expressions appeared in the late eighties and early nineties in the Farmers' Alliance, the aim of which was to capture the governments, state and federal, and control them in the interest of the producers; and the Populist Party, which included in its platform the demands of the farmers, freesilver men, and other rebels. The movement was spontaneous, popular, powerful; it created, in Garland's words, "mightiest enthusiasms." The movement was also native, mid-Western, folk-flavored—a movement whose spirit is summed up in Mary Ellen Lease's appeal to the Kansas farmers to raise less corn and more Hell.

As a reformer and son of the middle border, Garland must under any conditions have become interested, perhaps involved, in the Populist revolt. As it happened, it was B. O. Flower and the *Arena* that enabled him to become, himself, a part of the movement. On Flower's commission, Garland went to Washington to do an article on the Farmers' Alliance bloc in Congress,[48] and from Washington through the South and West to observe the agrarian revolt at first hand. During his tour he not only met and talked with Western farmers and Populist leaders; he spoke almost daily for six weeks under the direction of the State Central Committee for the Populist Party in Iowa.[49] Already Garland had done part of a novel dealing with the Grange; and his task for the *Arena* included that of completing this manuscript and bringing it down to date as a novel of the Farmers' Alliance and the Populist party.[50] Assuredly, no lack of opportunity, or of intimate knowledge of his materials, is responsible for the indecisive result he obtained in *A Spoil of Office*.

This curiously indecisive impression is made not only by the plot but by the ideas illustrated in the novel—partly, no doubt, because the obstacles in the way of reform are as powerfully realized by the author as is the need for reform itself. Although

[48] Published in the *Arena*, V: 447-58 (March, 1892).
[49] *A Son of the Middle Border*, p. 427.
[50] *Roadside Meetings*, pp. 180-1.

Garland occasionally takes up other issues, such as the economic bearing of feminism,[51] the major premise of his economic philosophy remains, in this novel as before, the thesis of Henry George—that economic suffering is traceable mainly to the effects of monopoly, and that therefore, if poverty is to be abolished, monopoly must first be destroyed. The class alignment, the economic struggle he contemplates is that between the productive and the exploitive interests. "There is no war between the town and the country. The war is between the people and the monopolist wherever he is." The cause of the people, the cause of the productive interests, is the same everywhere.[52] Consequently, the logical means of securing social reform is "union among the poor of every class." [53]

But neither Garland nor his characters have any illusions about the difficulty of uniting the poor; even Ida Wilbur, the most courageous and consistent reformer in the story, acknowledges, for instance, that the decline of the Grange is a result of the farmers' inability to learn the lesson of coöperation.[54] And, with even more emphasis, Garland insists upon the danger that popularly elected legislators will forget that public office is a public trust, will allow the lust of office to grow upon them, will succumb to the easy-going corruption common in American politics, and will become mere tools of the speculative interests. The jovial vice, the duplicity, the hypocrisy of a large proportion of legislators, both in the smaller circle of the state legislature and in the larger circle of the national Congress, are so disheartening to Garland's hero, Bradley Talcott, that, until he is stimulated by the more buoyant spirit of Ida Wilbur, he comes to despair of remedying suffering.[55] If the victims of injustice are unable to combine, and if, combined, they cannot depend on the integrity of their political agents, then (we conclude, after a fashion

[51] *A Spoil of Office*, pp. 143-4; the speech of the lecturer Ida Wilbur.
[52] *Ibid.*, pp. 121-2, 192; ideas expressed in the speeches of Garland's hero, Bradley Talcott.
[53] *Ibid.*, p. 362.
[54] *Ibid.*, pp. 150-2.
[55] *Ibid.*, pp. 238, 253, 255 ff., 263, 284 ff., 316-7, 348, 352.

that Garland probably did not intend) the outlook for economic reform must be dark indeed.

The plot of *A Spoil of Office* is quite as curiously indecisive as is the philosophy. Within the novel are included, as we have seen, an earlier story of the Grange, and a later story of the Farmers' Alliance and the Populist Party; and the two portions are most imperfectly fused. The earlier story, which apparently survives in the first third or half of the book, describes Bradley Talcott's development from a farmer's hired hand into a student, lawyer, and state legislator; the latter story relates his growing disillusion with politics and politicians, his partial surrender to the temptation to become a "political pensioner," parasitical rather than productive, and his rescue from moral enervation by Ida Wilbur and the crusading spirit of the Farmers' Alliance. The theme of the former story is that of self-realization, of the latter, service; the temper of the former is individualistic, of the latter, altruistic; the former might be called the "rise" of Bradley Talcott, the latter, his decline. Naturally, the presence of two such conflicting themes, while it would in no way damage a book devoted to the realistic study of a vacillating personality, seriously harms the value of one presumably meant as a coherent illustration of certain political and economic forces.

The reading of *A Spoil of Office* leads one to suspect that, as early as 1892, the author's mind was more divided than he himself understood. Later, with his usual over-sensitiveness to the charge of didacticism, Garland dismissed the novel as a "partisan plea for a stertorous People's Party,"[56] but it is nothing so clear-cut as that. As is the case with *Jason Edwards* and *A Member of the Third House*, its weakness does not lie in its didacticism, even though it contains more direct preachment than does any other work of Garland's. That weakness

---

[56] *Roadside Meetings*, pp. 186-7. For corroboration of the statement that Garland's recession from the extreme left began as early as 1892, see Eldon C. Hill, *op. cit.*, especially the section entitled, "The Reformer's Ardor Cools," pp. 151 ff. Mr. Hill includes in his discussion certain evidence from the Garland manuscripts. See also the related evidence presented by Mr. Hill on pages 183-4, 193-4, and 204.

lies in faulty execution. As the former novels lack elaboration, so *A Spoil of Office* lacks a sufficiently clear-cut thesis, lacks a story sufficiently dramatic to create suspense while illustrating that thesis, and lacks characters sufficiently interesting to hold the reader's interest in their own right. It is, consequently, a *melange* of ill-assimilated elements, which are all of them promising in themselves, but which are not fused by the author's imagination into an artistically effective whole. If the work retains any besides a documentary value, that worth resides in the individual scenes: in the impressive pictures of the picnics and processionals of the Grange and the Alliance; in the absolutely authentic account, partly autobiographical, of Bradley Talcott's work as a hired hand, his schooling, and his breaking-away from the farm.

VI

With the completion of *A Spoil of Office*, we are brought to the verge of that break in Garland's career—that disintegration, so far as his social aims are concerned—which has so piqued the curiosity of our historians and critics. The fact of the break was not, for some years, apparent to Garland's contemporaries; nor, indeed, would a mere array of Garland's titles show that it occurred so early. However, *Prairie Folks* (1893) and *Wayside Courtships* (1895) are mostly made up of stories that were written before 1890. Even *Crumbling Idols* (1894) represents a viewpoint which Garland had matured four or five years previously. *Rose of Dutcher's Coolly* (1895) does indeed vary sharply from Garland's earlier prairie stories in that its object is not the rendering of local color or the illustration of social injustice, but the portrayal of the escape of a gifted individual from the drab, narrow life of the farm. Nevertheless, the naturalistic descriptions of life on the prairie, unusually frank for the time, might well leave with the reader the impression that the main drift of Garland's work had suffered no change.

After *Rose*, however, came *Ulysses S. Grant, His Life and Character* (1898), a biography which advances the rather surprising thesis that Grant's administrations were "right upon all vital questions," and that they failed "only upon matters which are now seen to be of minor importance"; [57] next, *Boy Life on the Prairie* (1899); then the light extravaganza, *Her Mountain Lover* (1901) and, in a series of romances of the far West and the Rockies, *The Eagle's Heart* (1900), *The Captain of the Gray Horse Troop* (1902), and *Hesper* (1903). By the early nineteen hundreds, no intelligent observer could have failed to see that Garland was entering on an entirely new period; that, at the very time when he was mastering the technique of the novel, he had abandoned the serious artistic and social aims of his youth, and, except for a lingering vein of humanitarianism, had become simply another popular entertainer.

Interpretations of Garland's change of policy are as numerous as the historians and critics who have attacked the problem. To Russell Blankenship, Garland was a realist who allowed his passion for social justice to overcome his art, who declined from realism to propaganda, and who then, because he could no longer bear to treat his prairie material realistically, sought an escape in superficial romances of the Wild West.[58] To Carl Van Doren, Garland was a local colorist who felt, after exhausting the thin soil of regional peculiarities, that it was necessary for him to seek new materials—a new local color—elsewhere.[59] To Granville Hicks, Garland was a traitor to the cause of the workingman, a renegade who abandoned his true career in order to secure comfort and respectability.[60] To Vernon Louis Parrington, he was a son of the older agrarian, individualistic America, who, when the last wave of Populist revolt had died down, had already outlived his day.[61]

Of the four interpretations of Garland's change, the first appears, when considered in the light of all the evidence at

[57] *Ulysses S. Grant, His Life and Character*, p. 449.
[58] Russell Blankenship, *American Literature as an Expression of the National Mind*, pp. 495-7.
[59] Carl Van Doren, *Contemporary American Novelists*, pp. 43-4.
[60] Granville Hicks, *The Great Tradition*, pp. 146-7.
[61] Vernon Louis Parrington, *The Beginnings of Critical Realism in America*, pp. 299-300.

hand, to be the least tenable. For the three earliest novels of Garland, as we have seen, are not noticeably more didactic than are his short stories, and the weakness of them must be attributed less to didacticism than to lack of sound craftsmanship or clearly conceived purpose. The other three interpretations are not, of course, mutually exclusive; abundant support may be found for any one or all three of them, and, indeed, for the consideration of certain other factors as well. The basic, the original factor, however, appears to have been, as Parrington suggests, the decline of the middle-class protest against industrialism—or, more exactly, the diversion of that protest from its agrarian and romantic expression into other forms.

Although there is some reason for believing that the middle-class drive for social justice was already losing force as early as 1892, the definite outward symptom of that decline, and one of the decisive turning-points in American history, was the defeat of William Jennings Bryan and of the Populist-Democratic fusion in 1896. Thenceforward, Populism was no longer a national power, and the force of events directed the liberal elements in the Democratic party toward other issues. The inflation for which the free-silver men had for years ineffectually struggled, followed naturally upon the discovery of new gold fields and an enormous increase in the world-supply of gold;[62] the trough of a world-wide economic depression was passed; once more America, the middle border included, knew prosperity; and the quest for social justice lost the tragically dynamic motive power of unusual and widespread suffering. The Spanish-American and Philippine wars tended, likewise, to divert popular attention from domestic reforms; so that, when Bryan undertook his second campaign for the presidency, he found it expedient to crystallize the democratic and humanitarian sentiment of the country about the issue of imperialism instead of economic reform. The middle-class opposition to the plutocracy was carried on for a while only by isolated groups of single-taxers, nationalists, and others, and by the occasional novel of some critic or humanitarian. When,

[62] John Donald Hicks, *The Populist Revolt*, pp. 387-9; Mark Sullivan, *Our Times*, I, 298.

presently, that protest again received a national hearing—in the work of the muckrakers and in the progressive movement led by Theodore Roosevelt—it was under the leadership of other men, and under the influence of another time-spirit, than that which had given it focus in the Gilded Age.

Without a single important exception, the men who had directed and popularized the middle-class *critique* were being thrust from the national stage, by death, or by the diversion of their energies into other channels, or simply by the rapid shift of national interest elsewhere. Henry George, leading his 1896 campaign for the mayoralty of New York after his health was permanently broken, apparently chose to die in harness. Edward Bellamy, after spinning out the last delicate filaments of his socio-democratic scheme in *Equality* (1897), yielded to tuberculosis and died in 1898. The eloquence of Mary Ellen Lease, the wit of Jerry Simpson, the sensational parables of Ignatius Donnelly, the financial instruction of Coin Harvey— all these were rapidly becoming only memories instead of forces. As constructive spokesmen for the American middle class, these people had, properly speaking, no successors. In the popular consciousness, they were replaced by military figures like Roosevelt and Hobson and Dewey.

In a direction whose main drift at least is clear, the literary current of the times was drawn along with the social and economic. From active interest in reform toward indifference— the counter-swing of the pendulum had definitely begun. Whether by conscious choice or by unconscious response to their environment, the leaders of our literature turned from the consideration of social justice toward other themes. From the powerful social parables in the *Connecticut Yankee*, Mark Twain turned to an indecisive, milk-and-water estimate of democracy in *The American Claimant* (1892), thence to the melodrama of *Pudd'nhead Wilson* (1894), and thence to the journalism of *Following the Equator* (1897) and the high romance of *Joan of Arc* (1896). William Dean Howells, than whom no shrewder journalist was then at work in America, laid aside his unfinished Utopia, *Through the Eye of the Needle*, kept it by him for thirteen or fourteen years, and finally completed and published it in 1907, when a revival of such economic speculations significantly coincided with another period of economic stress. Meanwhile, he returned to the solid, old-fashioned study of character in *The Landlord at Lion's Head* (1897) and to deft bourgeois comedy in *The Kentons* (1902). The young Stephen Crane turned from the slum backgrounds of *Maggie* (1892) to a Civil War story in *The Red Badge of Courage* (1896), and thence to war-reporting and miscellaneous literary work.

Meanwhile new, or perhaps only dormant, species and subspecies of literature sprang up like mushrooms—the vagabondia songs of Carman and Hovey; the rowdy, romantic, primitivistic stories of Norris and London; above all, the crop of belated Waverley romances which flourished at the turn of the century. In the field of economic fiction, while the novel of protest was still written, its relative importance declined as that of another type advanced—the romance of economic struggle. Samuel Merwin and H. K. Webster in *The Short Line War* (1899) and *Calumet K* (1901), Charles K. Lush in *The Autocrats* (1901), Frank Norris in *The Octopus* (1901), and still more in *The Pit* (1903), were only discovering in a modern industrial environment the values of conflict and adventure which infused the contemporary historical romances. It is, of course, with these romances of economic struggle, rather than with his own earlier tales of the middle border, that Garland's story of the Colorado miners' war in *Hesper* is to be associated.

In brief, the middle nineties, whether considered from the viewpoint of factual history, or that of the leadership of public opinion, or that of *belles-lettres,* were a time when certain powerful forces, which had come to focus within the two preceding decades, were rapidly disintegrating. The culture of antebellum, agrarian America, its protagonists now grown old, its way of life fast becoming only a memory, its forces spent in the effort to transform or control the Machine Age, had lived its active life and was ready for whatever doubtful immortality might belong to an influence and a heritage.

In the middle nineties, therefore, Garland held the unenviable position of a spokesman for a disintegrating movement, of a survivor of a fast disappearing culture. The social, the cultural foundation on which he had hitherto stood was dissolving, and it behooved him either to find another stance, or to retire from literature as a vocation. Moreover, if he were to marry, to create a home, to realize himself completely in a normal human life, he must find a stance that promised economic security. His fundamental problem (although he himself never stated it in just these terms) was simply a problem of literary survival in a rapidly changing *milieu*. Stated in another way, his was the problem of discovering, as journalist and free lance writer, materials and methods interesting enough to the public to command an adequate income, an income by which he might realize his aims, not as a member of society but as an individual, not as a social prophet, but simply as a man. These materials he was already finding in the local color, the romance, of the Rocky Mountain West.

VII

During all this while, Garland's personal relationships were such as to strengthen the general influence of the times. His personal contact with the distress of the middle border was severed when, at his insistence, his father and mother removed from their Dakota ranch to the retirement of their old village in Wisconsin. Nor did his Georgian economics seriously interfere with his pleasure when his father's purchase of real estate in West Salem insured the elder couple a dignified and confident old age.[63] Presently, too, his own marriage made at least a moderate financial success imperative, and automatically diverted much of his energy from social ends to personal. Intensely occupied with providing for his family, industriously keeping a safe distance ahead of the wolf, he necessarily turned to subjects that would please and not antagonize his readers. Having given hostages to fortune in a capitalistic society, he counted his days of controversial writing at an end.[64] Formerly careless about commercial success, he now worked with an

[63] *A Daughter of the Middle Border*, p. 170.
[64] *Companions on the Trail*, pp. 3, 207.

eye to the main chance, pleased when, after a number of vicissitudes, he formed a connection with a strong and reliable publisher; pleased when *The Eagle's Heart,* in serial, discernibly raised the circulation of the *Saturday Evening Post;* pleased when *The Captain of the Gray Horse Troop* sold over 100,000 copies and *Hesper* over 50,000.[65] In all this, to be sure, Garland was never sympathetic with the journalism that is exclusively commercial; that, unconcerned with either art or ethics, strives merely to "embody the greatest common denominator." He felt that he resisted, more or less heroically, certain demands of the editor and publisher; but in the end he was compelled to conform. We Americans, having no backing, no secure footing, are, he explained, of necessity wage-earners even in our art.[66]

Garland's novels of entertainment, while never phenomenally popular, enabled him to move gradually from an economic position among the Have-Nots to one among the Haves. He came to own a rather unprofitable Mexican mine, purchased a home in the Woodlawn district of Chicago, purchased a thousand acres of Oklahoma ranch land, purchased several small homes in his native village, and, having sold them, bought bonds and enjoyed the security and regularity of the steady income they afforded.[67] Naturally enough, his personal friendships meanwhile carried him farther and farther away from the defeated farmers of the Middle Border; more and more completely among people whose lives were passed in moderate comfort, if not in wealth. Notwithstanding the grimness of his earlier writing, Garland had always been a warm-hearted, socially disposed, agreeable person; he had always possessed an unusual talent for friendship. Sooner or later, therefore, he contrived at least a passing acquaintance with almost every American literary figure of the times: with

[65] *Roadside Meetings,* pp. 102, 111, 397-9; *Companions on the Trail,* p. 13.

[66] "Limitations of Authorship in America," *The Bookman,* 59: 257-62 (May, 1924); also *My Friendly Contemporaries,* p. 97.

[67] *A Daughter of the Middle Border,* pp. 69, 247-50; *Back-Trailers from the Middle Border,* pp. 171-2; *Companions on the Trail,* pp. 225-8, 515.

Howells, of course, and Clemens, and, besides these, Crane, Miller, Riley, Walter Hines Page, Gilder, Stedman, Bacheller, Tarkington, James Lane Allen, and Henry Adams. For several years, he was associated in Chicago with Henry Blake Fuller, Brand Whitlock, Will Payne, George Ade, Harriet Monroe, and the publisher Herbert Stone. Of the English authors, he knew Kipling, Hardy, Shaw, and, particularly, Israel Zangwill, who helped him purchase his first evening outfit for a dinner of the authors' society.[68] Several of these men—Bacheller and Tarkington, for instance—had made small fortunes, owned handsome houses, and lived "as authors should, surrounded by books and pictures";[69] and their success established a standard which Garland, in a more modest way, naturally strove to emulate. Friendships, social gatherings, the physical decencies and comforts, the recognition of those who had "arrived," the enrichments and amenities of civilized life— these things, never matters of indifference to Garland, came to occupy an increasingly large place in his standard of values. Instead of the thrill of the solitary discovery of Whitman and Taine and Spencer and Henry George, he now had the thrill of being a guest of Theodore Roosevelt when Paderewski played at the White House:

For a few hours Zulime and I enjoyed the white light which beat upon two of the great personalities of that day—one the world's greatest piano player, the other the most powerful and the most popular man in all America—and when we retired to the obscurity of our hotel we were silent with satisfaction. For the moment it seemed that fortune was about to empty her golden horn at my feet. I was happily married, my latest book was a hit, and I had the friendship and the favor of the President.[70]

It had been in 1891, in the course of his trip for the *Arena*, that Garland had discovered the *locale* he now employed in his noncontroversial novels of entertainment, the Rocky

[68] Most of these associations, as well as numerous others, are recorded in *Roadside Meetings*.

[69] *My Friendly Contemporaries*, p. 125.

[70] *A Daughter of the Middle Border*, p. 246. Reprinted by permission of the Macmillan Company, publishers.

Mountain West. The freedom of movement, the healthful activity to be had there, as well as the wild, impressive natural beauty of the region, had appealed to a man who remembered having seen, during an active pioneer boyhood, the last bands of wild horses disappear from the low, grassy swells of the Iowa prairie; and this first experience in the mountains was to influence his work for two decades. As the persistent antagonism to his prairie stories continued, he retired in imagination, as repeatedly in fact, to the silver-and-purple summits of the high country—an area in which all his associations were pleasant, and where his concern over injustice was correspondingly less keen.[71] Always possessed of a latent vein of romanticism, always rather stiff, rather unplastic in imagination, he came to portray the life of the high trails somewhat after the conventional themes of Waverley romance—flight and pursuit, courage and chivalric love, daring deeds of knights and other adventurers costumed as cowboys and ranchmen and soldiers and Indians. Occasionally, some economic or humanitarian or "progressive" theme is illustrated in these romances—the government's responsibility for the Indian in *The Captain of the Gray Horse Troop*, the plight of the independent miner in *Hesper*, and the problem of conservation in *Cavanagh, Forest Ranger*; but the issues that occupy Garland's interest are so scattered, the treatment often so casual, that one can hardly feel that the romances have any serious and consistent social value. Their tone and temper is that of decent general entertainment, midway between the banalities of popular subliterature and the fine artistic maturity of his own earlier short stories.

To about the proportion in which Garland became absorbed in these other interests, his concern over the Single Tax and the plight of the Western farmers underwent a gradual atrophy. Although his conviction about the rightness of the Single Tax did not immediately change, the emotional drive that had made that conviction a creative force died gradually away. With the passing of the years, the popular mind did not be-

[71] *A Daughter of the Middle Border*, pp. 20-9; 31; 35; *Roadside Meetings*, pp. 183-5.

come discernibly more receptive to the gospel concerning land tenure; the arrival of the millennium appeared to be indefinitely delayed. Meanwhile, the service-worn phrases of anti-poverty propaganda were becoming wearisome to Garland. His proselyting zeal was gone; from the Pentecost at Jerusalem he had journeyed to Laodicea.[72] And as his ardor in the Single Tax crusade gradually cooled, the gulf between him and his prairie materials, at least as seen in their former light, steadily widened. In the *Main-Travelled Roads* series he had said all that he had to say about that particular area of Western life. What he had written he had written; and as the record was, so it must remain. When, about 1902, some of his friendly critics suggested that he do more stories of the Middle Border, he could only conclude that any attempt to recapture the spirit of his youth would be not merely a failure but a bore.[73]

These prairie materials, from which Garland was so irrecoverably growing away, had been significant, and in many of his stories they had been admirably rendered. If, now, he were to retain his place as an important literary artist, it was essential that he find other materials equally significant, and render them equally well. But this, in his series of Western romances, is precisely what he failed to do. Intellectually, aesthetically, artistically, the romances occupy a plane which may be designated, with no attempt at sarcasm or depreciation, as a respectable mediocrity. They render no really significant experience, for the reason that Garland had no added experience —none, that is, of national or enduring value—to render. The growth of his creative personality, unusually rapid and powerful for a while, had been arrested at an unusually early period of life. By the middle nineties, at the latest, Garland ceased to learn rapidly and vitally; the mental horizons that had once expanded so swiftly became stationary or actually constricted. After that date, Garland's voluminous autobiographies and reminiscences disclose no assimilation of any important new idea, convey no further thrill of intellectual discovery. So far as he remained interested in ideas, Whitman and Taine, Spen-

[72] *Companions on the Trail*, pp. 128-9, 266.
[73] *A Daughter of the Middle Border*, pp. 257-8.

cer and Henry George, continued to suffice him. Consequently, when the work of *Main-Travelled Roads* was done, he was ill prepared to find other work of equal or even comparable value.

This closing-in of his mind, combined with his inability to outgrow his agrarian conditioning and prejudices, shut Garland off from the more radical modern forms of economic protest, and contributed to his development away from the economic left toward the extreme right. A child of the Western democracy of Lincoln, he could feel little sympathy with the twentieth-century *hoi polloi*, with the drab anonymous multitude that pressed upon him unpleasantly in elevated and subway. Abstractly, he could grant their right to life, liberty, and the pursuit of happiness; concretely, he did not trust them, and they were a problem.[74] If, occasionally, the squalor of slum or tenement were borne in upon him, and if he marvelled at the patience of the unrebelling poor, he yet recoiled, with the fear of one belonging to an alien and unsympathetic race, from the thought of a proletarian dictatorship. "To give these folk power would unchain strange beasts."[75] In the arts, what good could come from the portrayal of people of this class? Was it not better to turn aside from the work of the artist Higgins, a powerful and savage delineator of the submerged tenth, and, instead, enjoy going to "Mrs. Charles Worthington's beautiful new flat in the 'Wyoming,' meeting Saranoff again, and George Hamlin the tenor, and others quite as eminent and interesting"?[76] From the classes, not the masses, are to be expected the beauties and the enrichments of life; democratic art is poor art; and if he, Garland, were to devise a Utopia, he would create not the dullness of communism, which would prove an intolerable bore, but a Utopia of such variety and color as would rival the splendors of medieval chivalry.[77]

[74] *My Friendly Contemporaries*, p. 123.
[75] *Ibid.*, p. 365; also, *Back-Trailers from the Middle Border*, p. 257.
[76] *Companions on the Trail*, p. 344.
[77] *Ibid.*, p. 122; also, *Back-Trailers from the Middle Border*, pp. 228-30.

Moreover, the wealthy, as he was coming to know them, revealed few of the marks of the beast which his radical youth had been led to expect. Wealth had its kindly side; in many people, it developed the nobler, rather than the baser, qualities, and made of itself a "justifying, civilizing agent." [78] Consequently, the creator of wealth, the great original businessman like Henry Ford, is a person of far greater importance than the artist. While the men of the pen and the brush must content themselves with being merely historians, the businessman, a poet and philosopher combined, more highly imaginative than they, serves in vital ways.[79] And if still there were times when the awareness of some less fortunate social class was borne in upon Garland—times when at night, from the windows of a train, he watched, gliding by, the lonely lights of invisible farmhouses dotting the wide dim prairie, and thought upon how little improvement the last forty years of invention had wrought in the lot of these rural folk—why, it was best merely to hope that such lives had remained unaware of their own futility.[80] Advancing age was bringing, if not indifference, at least resignation; his struggle in behalf of the common people was over; and the latter years might yield him, instead of other struggles, the quiet of his home in Southern California, and the pleasant companionship of his afternoon neighbors.

It is this resignation, this acceptance of finality, which Garland had evidently reached in some measure by his early fifties, that chiefly distinguishes A Son of the Middle Border from his earlier portrayals of the rebellious West, and which supplies that distinguished autobiography with its undertone of profound sadness. Immense energy the book has, immense richness in American life, absolute authenticity, and the mellow tone that comes of long perspective. Its place in our national literary history is secure. Increasingly, however, the reader is aware of the author's assumption that he is writing of issues that have long been dead, of struggles that have

[78] Back-Trailers from the Middle Border, p. 123.
[79] Afternoon Neighbors, pp. 498-511.
[80] Ibid., p. 126.

passed out of the national consciousness as completely as a
thousand nameless battles of the Civil War. Therefore the
sadness of finality, if not of futility, everywhere permeates a
book which in reality records the decline, the last stand, and
the fall of our antebellum agrarian democracy. When the advancing frontier had been halted, when the high tide of Populist fervor had begun to recede, the rural America of elder
times was condemned to rapid attrition. The era, the way of
life which had produced a Howells, a Clemens, a Lincoln, had
reached its dusk; and it is Garland's chief distinction that he
was able to record, adequately, the darkening of this latter
twilight of the gods.

I

Upon certain basic assumptions, it must have become increasingly plain, our middle-class critics of industrialism were in pretty thorough agreement. With negligible exceptions, they agreed that the Machine had come to stay, and that thenceforward the process of production would be largely a machine process. They agreed in the desire for an equable, not equal, distribution of the machine product, and, accordingly, in a desire for the social dominance of a comfortable, not wealthy, middle class. They mostly agreed in their exposure of the evils of industrialism—the immoral practices of business, the exploitation of the laboring class, and the destruction of human values among both the very rich and the very poor. In the advocacy of such miscellaneous projects as profit-sharing, slum clearance, and the purification of politics, they agreed at least on the retention of an individualistic society. Of the more important authors, Mark Twain shared this same general outlook, though his expressions on economics are scattered and fragmentary. George and Garland, on the other hand, although their critical work is consistent and powerful, advocated a reconstructive program that was essentially nostalgic and unrealistic—nostalgic in that they sought to recreate artificially the lost opportunities and the lost glamor of the era of free land; unrealistic in that their individualism afforded no means of controlling that huge collective force, the Machine.

Did intellectual leadership among the middle class, then, afford no recognition whatever of the new interdependence, of the all but irresistible drive toward consolidation, which the Machine had brought forth? To this question, the answer is

to be found first of all in the single classic produced by that
solitary genius, Edward Bellamy, and next in the series of
economic problem novels written by the professional man of
letters, William Dean Howells.

In any other era, the temperament, the family influences,
and the childhood experiences that entered into the character
of Edward Bellamy would hardly have produced a critic of
the conduct of business. A native of Chicopee Falls, Massachusetts, he became by birth, and remained throughout his
life, essentially a villager in his outlook and sympathies. The
son of a Baptist minister, he grew up under the influence of a
religious denomination whose membership has traditionally
come from the Have-Nots instead of the Haves, and whose
system of church government is traditionally democratic.
Without retaining the formal theology of his church, the maturing Bellamy kept with little change its plebeian social
sympathies, its humanitarianism, and, by no means least, its
assumption that the final goal of living is the acquirement of
inward instead of outward riches. As a boy, he appears to have
been, in a mystical, introspective way, intensely religious.
Alongside unusual sensitiveness, unusual intelligence, there
developed in his character a certain passivity, a certain lack of
entire robustness and gusto. His temperament was, in the
Elizabethan sense of the word, mildly melancholic; but behind
its reserve and apparent inertia lay the incalculability of
genius.[1]

Of the growth of this unusual mind, the scant materials of
Bellamy biography afford only occasional and half-satisfying
glimpses. A year at Union College appears to have resulted
chiefly in deepening Bellamy's previous dislike of formal instruction. A year in Europe, during which he was impressed
by the gulf fixed between the hovel of the peasant and the
castle of the nobleman, appears to have first awakened him

[1] Such, at least, are the impressions made on the writer during the
reading of some fragments of a projected autobiography of Bellamy's.
These readings are available in the excellent thesis of Dr. Robert L.
Shurter, *The Utopian Novel in America, 1865-1900*, Western Reserve
University, 1936. See especially pp. 99 ff. for a treatment of Bellamy's
early life.

to the extent and gravity of social injustice. At home once more, in Chicopee Falls, he studied law, without ever being able to force himself to the practice of that (to him) uncongenial profession. Meanwhile, after the romantic manner of the youthful Longfellow, he evidently nourished an ambition for a literary career; a certain Miltonic sense of being, in some way, a dedicated spirit coexisted in his personality with a curiously non-Miltonic passiveness and dearth of vital fire.[2]

The earlier novels of Bellamy are, like his personality, strangely provocative and strangely unsatisfying. Before or about 1880 he wrote, in *The Duke of Stockbridge,* a romance of Shays' Rebellion in which the reader's sympathies are held throughout on the side of the defeated villagers and back-country farmers rather than on the side of the victorious forces of law and order—a curious example both of Bellamy's life-long sympathy with the common folk and of his grasp of the interrelation of economic and political forces. For reasons that have never been satisfactorily explained, *The Duke of Stockbridge* remained unpublished until after the death of its author. Instead, two quaint romances, along with a few lesser works, made Bellamy known to a limited circle of readers. *Dr. Heidenhof's Process* (1880) deals with the theme of dissolving out of the mind the memory of a past shame. *Miss Ludington's Sister* (1884), a romance with as little savor of actuality as its predecessor, deals with the fancy of a separate immortality for each of one's outgrown selves.

The action of these stories takes place—insofar as they can be said to have an action and a place—in an environment resembling in tone and quality that of an antebellum, pietistic village. "I have been interested," Howells later wrote of their author, in recurring to his earlier work, "to note how almost entirely the action passes in an American village atmosphere";[3] and yet the village of Bellamy's imagination is no actual village, but an ideal one, visualized, as if illumined with a certain dull lambency, through the dreamy haze of nineteenth-cen-

[2] *Ibid.,* pp. 109-10.

[3] William Dean Howells, "Edward Bellamy." *The Atlantic Monthly,* 82: 253-6 (August, 1898).

tury sentimentalism. At first view, the two stories appear to be no more than belated mid-century parlor romances. On closer examination, they reveal constantly that fineness of texture which distinguishes the work of an artist from that of an entertainer; and they reveal also, occasionally, a haunting power, the product of an imagination that has been aware, to an unusual degree, of feelings of solemnity, exaltation, depression, and cosmic fear. Instead of the *weltschmerz* of German romanticism, a kind of cosmic dread gives tone to Bellamy's imagination—a passive, a largely unconscious dread of the impersonal, subrational life-forces that lie beyond the control of man's conscious will.—Nevertheless, and in spite of all that can be said for the earlier work of Bellamy, there is no doubt that he would be remembered, if at all, only as an unimportant minor romancer except for one book, *Looking Backward*, the first important Utopia which both illustrates and humanizes the huge potentialities of the Machine, and one of the three or four genuinely great books produced in the course of the middle-class *critique* of economics.

II

The story of the development of this obscure village romancer into the author of *Looking Backward* cannot yet be told in full. From the rather sparse biographical materials that have so far been made public, it appears that, notwithstanding his previous sympathy with the common people, and notwithstanding the obvious economic bearing of *The Duke of Stockbridge*, Bellamy's concern over modern industrialism awakened suddenly and because of the most personal motives. According to his friend, William Dean Howells,

he told me that he had come to think of our hopeless conditions suddenly, one day, in looking at his own children, and reflecting that he could not place them beyond the chance of want by any industry or forecast or providence; and that the status meant the same impossibility for others which it meant for him.[4]

[4] Howells, *op cit.*, p. 256.

Once awakened to the question, Bellamy began reading widely on economics and government,[5] and the interest that was at first merely personal rapidly became general. Conceivably, too, even in the first awakening of his interest Bellamy was more influenced than he supposed by contemporary currents of thought. Significantly enough, the time of his change was about 1886 or '87—the very time when the thought of our middle classes was first becoming vividly aware of economic problems, the time when the same humanitarian concern was moving in the propaganda of George, the middle border sketches of Garland, and the Tolstoyan studies of Howells.

Were Bellamy's own statements about the genesis of *Looking Backward* as complete as they are doubtless authentic, the origin of that book would be quite easily explained. Already Bellamy had observed and admired the efficiency of military conscription and of the use of a standing army for national defence. Presently, in the course of his economic studies, he stumbled upon the idea of organizing an army not for military purposes but for the conduct of industry; and from the elaboration of this germ-idea, we are told, there developed his entire vision of the completely socialized state.[6] Already he had had in mind the plan of a romantic Utopia, a mere "fairy-tale of social felicity," the time of which was to be the year 3000. Now, as the idea of the industrial army elaborated itself in his mind, and as he came to realize the potency of this instrument, he came presently to believe that his cloud-palace for an ideal humanity could actually be realized, and in the not-too-distant future. Instead of the year 3000 he adopted 2000 as the date for his Utopian scheme; instead of an unreal, unattainable paradise, he evolved a scheme of society which he thought the rapid progress of mankind would make entirely practical and attainable.[7]

[5] Shurter, *op. cit.*, p. 120.

[6] "How I came to Write *Looking Backward*." *The Nationalist*, I: 2-3 (May, 1889).

[7] See, in this connection, besides the references already given, Shurter, *op. cit.*, pp. 121 ff.; also Nicholas T. Gilman, "Nationalism in the United States." *The Quarterly Journal of Economics*, IV: 50-76 (October, 1889).

Bellamy's own testimony about *Looking Backward* would therefore make it appear that he worked out the details of the book deductively, by imagining the various applications of his germ-idea of an industrial army. Such a task was, to be sure, of the precise kind best suited to his imagination, which delighted, Hawthorne-like, in the elaboration of moral cause and effect in an idealized and highly selective world of fancy. But Bellamy's explanation, while no doubt a truthful one, by no means tells the whole story. Before writing *Looking Backward,* Bellamy, as we have seen, read extensively in economics and government; consequently, before we examine the Utopia itself, we shall find it in point to examine some of the sources from which Bellamy's thought derived.

For *Looking Backward,* though it practically created the vogue of Utopian fiction, was not absolutely the first American book of its kind. In 1880 there had appeared, in *The Diothas,* by John Macnie, one of the very few really significant works among the now-forgotten romances of the Gilded Age. In *The Diothas,* a young man is translated from the present into a Utopian future by the same type of mesmerics which Bellamy employs in *Looking Backward;* he falls in love with a descendant of his nineteenth-century sweetheart, both of whom, as in *Looking Backward,* are named Edith; and he learns about the new society in much the same way as does Bellamy's hero. Furthermore, the treatment of the Utopian society into which he is oriented resembles that of *Looking Backward* in such respects as the anticipation of the radio, the advocacy of communal cooking, and the proposal of an industrial army. *The Diothas,* though it enjoyed no such popularity as *Looking Backward,* was at least moderately well known in the eighties; and while it has not been proved that Bellamy read from Macnie, it is in the highest degree improbable that so many similarities could develop without some connection—at the very least an indirect one—between the two minds.[8]—Nevertheless, interesting as is the question of Bellamy's possible indebtedness to this elder American Utopia, the actual formulation of his ideas appears to have been an outcome not of his

[8] For a discussion of these similarities, see Shurter, *op. cit.,* pp. 172-6.

reading in Utopian romance but of his acquaintance with contemporary socialistic thought.

In 1884 there had appeared the first widely known American treatment of modern socialism, Laurence Gronlund's *The Coöperative Commonwealth,* a book whose reception by men like Bellamy and Howells affords a most suggestive study in cultural importation and adaptation. For, while the socialism of Bellamy and Howells is a thing quite fully Americanized, the socialism of Laurence Gronlund is chiefly foreign; it is, in essentials, the socialism of Karl Marx. Gronlund claimed, to be sure, that he had become a socialist independently, and had later found his system elaborated in (vague phrase) "German" books.[9] He does, however, disclose an acquaintance with the work of Marx,[10] and in all fundamentals his socialism is Marxian. His is the Marxian assumption that economic forces are anterior to political, and that the political forms of a given age and people are largely the instrumentalities of the economic system. His is, likewise, the Marxian belief that the independent middle class is doomed to absorption in the capitalist and proletarian classes, and that a proletarian revolution, military or elective as the needs of the individual country may require, will finally overthrow the capitalists and set up the socialistic state, the Coöperative Commonwealth.[11] But Gronlund, notwithstanding his general acceptance of Marxian ideas, did not look on Marxian socialism as an altogether authoritarian gospel. To him, it was merely a significant, though doubtless fallible, system of human thought. In his writings, the ideas of Marx are constantly held in perspective by, and understood in reference to, his awareness of other thinkers such as George, Spencer, Ruskin, Robert Owen, and Carlyle.[12] Already, in the mind of Gronlund, Marxian socialism was undergoing some change—some adaptation, that is, to the backgrounds and the social habits of English-speaking peoples.

[9] Laurence Gronlund, *The Coöperative Commonwealth,* pp. 7, 101.
[10] *Ibid.,* p. 50.
[11] Gronlund, *op. cit.,* pp. 40, 70, 73-4, 97, 160-9, 263-74.
[12] See, for examples, *ibid.,* pp. 58-9, 77, 107, 131.

It was to undergo still more changes, immensely more, in the mind of Edward Bellamy. On the one hand, it is clear that the social system of *Looking Backward* derives, more than from any other source, from *The Coöperative Commonwealth*. It is known that Bellamy read *The Coöperative Commonwealth,* and his indebtedness to Gronlund has been demonstrated not only by the general similarity of the two works, but by the assembly of an overwhelmingly convincing array of specific parallels.[13] On the other hand, it is equally clear that the outcome of Bellamy's thought is, in certain important respects, utterly different from the Marxian socialism he had found in Gronlund. It is, instead, a kind of socialism that might naturally have originated in America (though it apparently did not) out of the impact of the new problems of the Machine Age upon our tradition of middle-class democracy.

It is now pertinent to examine the system of ideas into which Bellamy's thought finally crystallized. In this consideration, we shall have in mind first of all his expression of these ideas in *Looking Backward,* inasmuch as practically all of them are, either by explicit statement or by assumption, present in that one book; but occasionally it will be in point to refer to Bellamy's various articles or to *Equality,* in which he

[13] Shurter, *op. cit.,* pp. 176 ff. Quotations from *The Coöperative Commonwealth* and *Looking Backward* show both intellectual and verbal parallels in the treatment of sixteen subjects, such as the future of the trusts, planned production, woman's place in the new society, the elimination of crime from the socialistic state, etc. On the other hand, Bellamy himself claimed that he did not know *The Coöperative Commonwealth* when he wrote *Looking Backward.* See G. W. Arms, "Further Inquiry into Howells' Socialism," *Science and Society,* III, 245-8 (Spring, 1939), an article in which the author cites a letter of Bellamy's to William Dean Howells, June 17, 1888. See also G. W. Arms, *The Social Criticism of William Dean Howells.* A doctoral dissertation of New York University (1939), p. 210. Notwithstanding Bellamy's statement, Dr. Shurter may be said to have proved *some* causal relationship between *The Coöperative Commonwealth* and *Looking Backward,* as the parallels between the two cannot possibly be accidental. Conceivably, the problem may sometime be cleared up by the discovery of an intermediary between Gronlund's work and Bellamy's, or by the relating of both books to a common antecedent. See also Shurter, *op. cit.,* pp. 190 ff., in regard to Bellamy's possible indebtedness to August Bebel's *Frau.*

sometimes elaborates in detail ideas that are merely touched
on in his masterpiece.

III

The Utopian future of *Looking Backward* is distinguished
from the America of 1887 chiefly by a single thoroughgoing,
causative change, the abolition of poverty and the creation
of what has come to be called, in our day, an economics of
abundance. In the new society there is no consideration of
money or of wages; an adequate income, based on the credit
of the nation, is made available, equally, to all. In the absence
of money, the heaping-up of wealth and the consequent enjoyment of unhealthful luxury are impossible, and, on the
other hand, thrift is not encouraged—a policy which insures,
within rational limits, the secure possession of private property.[14] The new society is thus founded on a solid basis of
physical security and of tangible, material comfort. This
security, this comfort has been achieved by certain simple, but
profound, far-reaching, fundamental changes in the American economic system.

Of the two principal changes, the less important consists
in a considerable expansion of the use of mechanical power.
Unlike Samuel Butler, Bellamy expressed no fear or dislike
of the Machine; unlike William Morris, he suffered no nostalgia for the vanishing era of the handicraftsman. Accordingly, in *Looking Backward*, he accepts the advance of
technology, welcomes it, and attempts to build it into a complete system of human values. Bellamy's Utopian society owns,
therefore, devices which are the equivalent of the radio and
television; it tills its farms with power-drawn plows; and it
manufactures its goods in gigantic mills which, unlike the
factories of the nineteenth century, are as thoroughly habitable as they are powerful—airy, cheerful, and all but noiseless.

More important than technological advance, however, are
the immense economies in the use of human energy that have
come with the establishment of socialism and the elimination

[14] *Looking Backward,* pp. 88-9; *Equality,* p. 117.

of the wastes of the competitive system. Under the new regime, production is accurately adjusted to consumption; the distribution of goods is enormously simplified; and many tasks, particularly the household drudgeries of laundering and cooking, are handled communally and thereby lightened.[15] Above all, the entire population between the ages of twenty-one and forty-five are marshaled into an industrial army, the organization of which both eliminates any exploitive or parasitic class, and allows the maximum latitude possible in the adjustment of the individual talent to its appropriate task.[16] In short, Bellamy's ideal humanity is, by the mechanical conquest of nature, by the equal distribution of goods, and by the wise economy of human effort, forever placed beyond the reach of insecurity and want.

Of Bellamy's emphasis on the economic and material foundations of the Utopian state there can be no question; with him, economic security, material comfort are primary, are essential. Yet these material things are by no means his sole concern, and those who, like William Morris, have deplored his emphasis on the comforts and minor luxuries of life have, it is quite possible, allowed themselves to become preoccupied with only one of the several facets of his mind. For with Bellamy, after all, material comfort is rather the foundation than the finished structure, is oftener a beginning than a conclusion. His system of economics is not just that alone, but is also a portion of a more general, a more far-reaching system of ideas —political, social, and philosophical—which is most closely and carefully articulated with the traditions of the American middle classes, and which occupies a quite clearly defined place in the general pattern of nineteenth-century thought.

For example, the economic theory of Bellamy demands, necessarily, an accompanying political theory; and in the interrelations between the two, which he appears to have worked out with considerable care, Bellamy radically changes the Marxian socialistic program and adapts it to his own American tradition. The socialistic revolution to which he looks

[15] *Looking Backward*, pp. 106, 183.
[16] *Ibid.*, p. 62.

forward is not to be a class struggle, but a natural outcome of the advance of democracy. Just as, in former times, the American citizenry had assumed control of their political affairs, so, in the future, they would assume control of their economic affairs. In this change, the Jeffersonian ideal of the minimized government will, to be sure, have to be surrendered, but the new function to be assumed by the state—the creation of economic security—is the only means by which the true aims of democracy can be realized, is the "only adequate pledge of these three birthrights—life, liberty, and the pursuit of happiness."[17] The protection of economic liberty is quite as important as the protection of civil liberty;[18] the protection of a people from "hunger, cold, and nakedness" is as essential as the protection of them from foreign enemies.[19] The gist of Bellamy's proposal is, then, simply to expand the functions of democratic government.

Nationalism ... [that is, the socialism of *Looking Backward*] is the doctrine of those who hold that the principle of popular government by the equal voice of all for the equal benefit of all, which in advanced nations, is already recognized as the law of the political organization, should be extended to the economical organization as well.[20]

In this logical and persuasive manner, then, Marxian socialism is adapted to the democratic tradition of America.

Moreover, just as Bellamy's economics is woven into his system of political thought, so it is woven, likewise, into his system of ethics. Here, too, Bellamy's treatment is such as to adapt his socialism to his American audience and background; for most of the ethical views within which his economics is enveloped are such as were already accepted by, or would be easy of acceptance to, the ordinary American citizen. This is true, in part, of Bellamy's ethical justification of socialism. It

[17] *Equality*, p. 17; see also, in this connection, *Looking Backward*, pp. 56-7.
[18] *Equality*, p. 79.
[19] *Looking Backward*, p. 59.
[20] "The Progress of Nationalism in the United States." *The North American Review*, 154: 742-3 (June, 1892).

is true, in even larger degree, of his treatment of the ethical effects of socialism in his Utopia, and of the relation of his entire scheme of ethics to nineteenth-century thought.

From one side, the justice of Bellamy's Utopian communism is buttressed by a curious reinterpretation of an old, familiar Whig principle, the right of property; or, more specifically, the right of the laborer to the product of his labor. But—so Bellamy continues from this premise—the labor of individual, isolated man, the labor of man in a state of nature, is so ineffective as hardly to keep soul and body together, whereas the labor of collective man, the labor of modern man employing the resources of the machine, is far more productive, and, with proper economy in management, can be made enormously more productive yet. The difference between the two—between, say, the productivity of the cave man on the one hand and of the skilled artisan on the other—is properly the creation, not of the individual, but of Society. That difference is the outcome, first, of that entire human heritage of arts and crafts and skills in which all men theoretically share as equals, and, second, of those advantages in coöperation and specialization which are afforded by a complex, highly integrated society. Human society as a whole, then, and not the individual man, is the great creator, and thereby rightfully the owner, of wealth; and, consequently, every man is entitled to a share therein equal to that of every other member of society. The mere fact of a person's humanity, the mere fact of his membership in the collective social body, is sufficient to entitle him to support by the State.[21]

Equally important with this theory of socially created value is the ethical sanction for socialism which Bellamy discovered in Christianity. Himself a liberal Christian, aware of the extent of the influence of Christianity among his middle-class audience, he could hardly have avoided founding his social plans upon a basis of religion, as well as of abstract justice. Even

[21] For Bellamy's development of these ideas, see *Looking Backward*, pp. 93, 136, and *Equality*, pp. 87-91. Compare with these passages Henry George's treatment of the socially created value of land, as discussed above, p. 49.

upon purely economic grounds, the Christian principle of coöperation would be found, he thought, more efficient, more productive than the naturalistic principle of uncontrolled competition; [22] and the conduct of men's daily business affairs in accordance with the spirit of Christianity would, in turn, be prerequisite to the full and entire growth of religion.[23] Socialism is, moreover, the only adequate means of putting into practice the Christian ethics of loving one's neighbor as one's self. Socialism contemplates "nothing less than a literal fulfillment, on a complete social scale, of Christ's inculcation that all should feel the same solicitude and make the same effort for the welfare of others as for their own." [24]

Bellamy's concern over the ethical sanctions of his scheme is of a piece with his concern over its ethical effects. By no means the least of these effects would be, he felt, the virtual abolition of crime, along with all the social and moral economies which that tremendous achievement would bring about. In the present, the capitalistic, state, the overwhelming majority of crimes are crimes against property; and of the remainder, many are chargeable to the frightful slum environment to which so many children are condemned by the inequalities of capitalistic industrialism. To make income both adequate and equal would therefore, at one blow, destroy most of the present incentives to crime; and to improve the living conditions and the education of the common people would destroy the miasmatic environment responsible for the remainder. In a society both communistic and prosperous, crime would dwindle to a negligible amount.[25]

But the elimination of crime, however important, would be only a negative thing. More important would be the achieving, through the bearing of economic security on the forces of heredity and environment alike, of a superior human type In a capitalistic society—so Bellamy maintains, in a passage of vigorous criticism suggestive rather of a Godwin or a Shel-

[22] *Equality*, p. 194.
[23] *Ibid.*, p. 269.
[24] *Ibid.*, p. 340.
[25] *Looking Backward*, pp. 200-1.

ley than of a genteel American romancer—conventional marriage does not operate to preserve and develop the finer
qualities of the race. In such a marriage, property, not personality, is a paramount interest. To obtain a dubious economic security in an insecure world, a woman must often
forego the personally fine and complete man, and accept as
a husband the merely acquisitive man. The man of property,
however unfit personally for marriage, may have children; the
man without property, however personally fit, may not.

But in the Utopia of the future, where the specter of insecurity will exist no longer, where men and women will be
wholly free and independent in their mating, the human being of superior personal attainment, not merely of superior
wealth, will be chosen. In a passage which now, in a less optimistic era, appears somewhat naïve, Bellamy predicts the
growth, among women especially, of the highest sense of responsibility in the choosing of mates. Hence the unlovely in
human nature will be gradually eliminated, while "gifts of
person, mind, and disposition; beauty, wit, eloquence, kindness, generosity, geniality, courage" will be perpetuated. For
the first time in human history, "the principle of sexual selection, with its tendency to preserve and transmit the better
types of the race, and let the inferior types drop out," will
have unhindered operation. And therefore each generation,
strained through a finer mesh than its predecessor, will advance farther in the creation of a superior humanity.[26]

However great the possibilities of this superior humanity,
the environment of the new state will be such as to develop
them to the fullest. The Utopian youth are to live in a world
permeated by fresh thought, and are to be prepared to respond to it. Education is to be universal, not only at the elementary level, but at the university level also; from six years
of age to twenty-one, all young people attend school.[27] During
the citizen's maturity, a broad margin of leisure is to be main-

[26] For Bellamy's consideration of economics and marriage, see, especially, *Looking Backward*, pp. 266 ff., and *Equality*, pp. 142 ff.

[27] *Looking Backward*, pp. 222-3. It is observable that Bellamy is as
careful to provide for physical as for mental education.

tained, and his retirement from the industrial army is to come at a comparatively early age—conditions which will still further encourage intellectual pursuits. Finally, the achievement of the social revolution, with its disclosure of enormous new possibilities for human nature, may be expected to lead to an outburst of mental activity, of which the intellectual energy of the Renaissance was but a faint foreshadowing.[28]

Far from being preoccupied with the enjoyment of material luxuries, then, Bellamy was almost over-careful about the ethical and intellectual bearing of his Utopia. He took care to link his economics with the average American's ethics of property-ownership; he took care to harmonize it with the social message of Christianity. He took care to point out its probable consequences for love and mating, and for the personal inheritance and the educational environment of the young. He took abundant care, in short, to make clear that his chief concern was not the enjoyment of luxury but the experiencing of personal and racial growth. *Looking Backward* is therefore not only a social document, but also, sometimes by explicit statement, sometimes by implication, an expression of a complete scheme of values. As such, it is a natural result of the fusion, and the reinterpretation within Bellamy's personality, of several strains of nineteenth-century thought.

Like Henry George, like Garland, like many another thinker of the latter nineteenth century, Bellamy was, in larger measure than he himself realized, an intellectual child of the Enlightenment. Just as the eighteenth-century belief in the natural goodness of man had nourished the political expectations of a Paine or a Shelley, so, continuing, it nourished the economic and social expectations of Bellamy. To him, as to them, the source of evil lay in the conditions of human life, and not in any essential core of human character; and hence the felicity of the Utopian state is to require no deep-seated changes in humankind, but only changes in the conditions of human life and in the motives called forth by the human environment.[29] Human nature in the midst of a selfishly indi-

[28] *Looking Backward,* p. 161.
[29] *Ibid.,* pp. 60-1.

vidualistic society is like a stunted rosebud struggling for life in the darkness of a fetid swamp. For abundant growth and bloom, no change in the rosebud is needed, but only an environment of sweet, warm earth, of sunshine and the upper air. Correspondingly, in the more favorable environment of the Utopian state, it will be found "that human nature in its essential qualities is good, not bad, that men by their natural intention and structure are generous, not selfish, pitiful, not cruel, sympathetic, not arrogant, godlike in aspirations, instinct with divinest impulses of tenderness and self-sacrifice, images of God indeed." [30]

For this hopeful view of human nature, Bellamy found fresh sanction in certain ideas that had been popularized by Victorian scientific thought. He everywhere assumes, though he seldom puts the matter explicitly, an evolutionary view of life. His faith in social progress is supported by the Spencerian concept of the state as an organism, an *evolving* organism.[31] This concept of evolution he combined, in a manner strikingly like that of Tennyson in *In Memoriam*, with an informal Victorian humanism and with the idea of progress. Human evolution, to Bellamy, *is* progress; and it is progress, furthermore, in the distinctively human and "higher" qualities of human nature—in qualities ethical, intellectual, and spiritual. Out of the fusion of such elements of thought—Bellamy's trust in human nature, his humanism, his faith in evolution as progress, above all, his grasp of the new possibilities opened up to mankind by the Machine—out of all these there developed, finally, a new and singularly persuasive version of the old dream of human perfectibility; for the achievement of the Coöperative State was to mean, not merely the setting up of a just economy, but "the rise of the race to a new plane of existence with an illimitable vista of progress." [32] And con-

[30] *Ibid.*, pp. 287-8.
[31] Edward Bellamy, *"Looking Backward* Again." *The North American Review*, 150: 351-63. See especially p. 360. It has not yet been shown that Bellamy read Spencer, but this particular Spencerian idea was available in Gronlund's *The Coöperative Commonwealth*, pp. 77 ff.
[32] *Looking Backward*, p. 161.

sequently, out of the confusions, the crossed purposes, the manifold sufferings of the Industrial Revolution, one person, at least, was able to emerge with a vision of potential human achievement as radiant as any prophecy of Condorcet:

Do you ask what we look for when unnumbered generations shall have passed away? I answer, the way stretches far before us, but the end is lost in light. For twofold is the return of man to God "who is our home," the return of the individual by the way of death, and the return of the race by the fulfillment of the evolution, when the divine secret hidden in the germ shall be perfectly unfolded. With a tear for the dark past, turn we then to the dazzling future, and, veiling our eyes, press forward. The long and weary winter of the race is ended. Its summer has begun. Humanity has burst the chrysalis. The heavens are above it.[33]

IV

But the literary Utopia has been, ordinarily, more than merely a vision of the ideal; it has been likewise a criticism of the actual. From the perspective afforded by his imagined commonwealth, an author may reveal the more clearly the failures and limitations of his own actual age and place; the brilliant phase of the ideal implies constantly the dark obverse of the real. Accordingly, alongside Bellamy's bright vision of the Utopian future, lies everywhere his case against the American present, its darker features accented by contrast with the radiant dream with which they are intermingled.

In his case against capitalistic industrialism, precisely as in his vision of Utopia, Bellamy is concerned first with the purely economic arrangements of society, and afterwards, in increasing importance, with that society's general conditions of living and its fruitfulness in creating human value. As to the mere economics of capitalism, it must have been with the enjoyment of a sardonic humor that Bellamy directed his main attack at precisely the point at which the system was supposed to be

[33] *Looking Backward*, p. 292. Reprinted by permission of Houghton Mifflin Company, publishers. The quotation is from a sermon of Bellamy's character, the Reverend Mr. Barton, who, like the physician Dr. Leete, is a spokesman of the author's.

strongest—efficiency in production. Capitalism, for all its claims of efficiency, involves, according to Bellamy, four important wastes, any one of which might alone mean all the difference between national poverty and wealth: "first, the waste by mistaken undertakings; second, the waste from the competition and mutual hostility of those engaged in industry; third, the waste by periodical gluts and crises, with the consequent interruptions of industry; fourth, the waste from idle capital and labor, at all times." [34] In other words, Bellamy is aware of the extent and formidable proportions of technological unemployment; [35] of the fact that capitalism, because of its costly vested interests, may nevertheless actually resist technological advance; [36] and of the fact that, within an unregulated profit system, periodical depressions, with all the widespread and intense suffering they entail, are unavoidable.[37] Furthermore, Bellamy continues, no effective system of regulation has yet been put into practice. No true science of political economy, to which one may look for sound principles of social control, has yet come into being. Instead, there are only those orthodox descriptions and defences of the status quo which, to Bellamy's mind, might properly be entitled, "Studies into the Natural Course of Economic Affairs when left to Anarchy by the Lack of any Regulation in the General Interest." [38]

Plainly, in a polity so void of direction and intelligent control, any permanent security is out of the question—not only for the submerged tenth, not only for the two hundred thousand laborers who each year suffer in industrial accidents, but even for the wealthy:

Do your work never so well . . . rise early and toil till late, rob cunningly or serve faithfully, you shall never know security. Rich you may be now and still come to poverty at last. Leave never so much wealth to your children, you cannot buy the assurance that

[34] *Looking Backward*, pp. 226 ff.
[35] *Ibid.*, p. 240.
[36] *Equality*, pp. 223 ff.
[37] *Ibid.*, pp. 158-69.
[38] *Equality*, p. 190.

your son may not be the servant of your servant, or that your daughter will not have to sell herself for bread.[39]

In a society where all men are haunted by the specter of fear, universal exploitation is hardly avoidable. In a struggle for survival as ruthless as any within a tropical jungle, the economically strong make use of the weak, and, so far as is possible, thrust upon the weak the toil and pain of living. Hence, in a famous illustration, Bellamy compares society to a coach, upon which a few ride in idleness and comfort, while their fellows, through dust and mud, laboriously drag vehicle and riders along.[40] Coach, riders, and human beasts of burden are, of course, only a symbol of the unjust distribution of the rewards of society, and of the selfish dominance of the high-propertied class. In the words of Julian West, "the rule of the rich, the supremacy of capital and its interests, as against those of the people at large, was the central principle of our system." [41]

A society thus organized, Bellamy maintains, allows the finer human qualities to come only rarely to flower, and even involves a continuous and ruthless destruction of value. For the qualities necessary for success are not intelligence or culture, but rather a lifelong habit of taking advantage of others, ruthlessness, intellectual dishonesty, absorption in a narrow self-interest.[42] Even among the successful, therefore, fineness develops rather in spite of our society than because of it. As to the unsuccessful, Bellamy can only say, after presenting, in a portrait as grotesque as it is powerful, a picture of an evening in the slums among the underprivileged, "On each brutal brow was plainly written the *hic jacet* of a soul dead within." [43]

Summed up, Bellamy's case against the established order appears equally powerful and simple. Inefficiency in produc-

---

[39] *Looking Backward*, p. 321. Reprinted by permission of Houghton Mifflin Company, publishers.
[40] *Looking Backward*, pp. 10-11.
[41] *Equality*, p. 13.
[42] *Ibid.*, p. 397.
[43] *Looking Backward*, p. 324.

tion, even in the midst of an appearance of efficiency; failure
in intelligent, scientifically directed social control; universal
insecurity; universal exploitation; the destruction of value, to
some degree among the rich, universally among the poor:—
these are the charges which he brings against capitalistic industrialism. The charges are trenchant, they are central, they
are profound; and yet the influence they wielded over Bellamy's contemporaries probably owed less to their trenchancy
and centrality and depth than to other factors: to Bellamy's
unusual power of presentation, and to the climate of opinion
into which his Utopia was born. We may now examine these
other factors, considering first how Bellamy dramatized his
charges and invested them with emotional appeal, and, later,
what response his beautiful, persuasive dream awakened in
the popular imagination.

V

The story which Bellamy employs as a carrier for his social
criticism would, in any era, have its appeal; in our Gilded Age,
a period illumined as it were with a quiet afterglow of romanticism, it was one calculated indeed to hold children from
play and old men from the chimney corner. The hero, Julian
West, a type of the well-to-do, genteel, intelligent Bostonian,
owns an underground vault to which he retires for quiet, and
in which he sometimes has himself placed in a mesmeric sleep
as a relief from insomnia. As he is sleeping, hypnotized, his
house burns, and he is supposed to have perished. Instead,
after a trance of a hundred and thirteen years he is awakened
into the coöperative Boston of the year 2000, and, after the
first stunning revelation is over, sets about orienting himself
in this brave new world.

His education in Utopian socialism is disposed about a love
story, genteel and sentimental indeed, and yet quaintly and
movingly beautiful. Prior to his awakening, Edith Leete, the
daughter of his host, has come to love him; but, following the
customs of his own nineteenth century, she conceals her love.
His utter aloneness in the new world, his brooding fear, his

occasional feelings of inferiority and depression—all these cast him into a position of emotional dependence on her, and her exquisite tenderness for him, fully as much as her personal charm, awakens his love in return. Such a range of feeling, so closely resembling that of Bellamy's earlier romances, was one peculiarly suited to his brooding, Hawthornesque imagination; and one, consequently, which he succeeded in unusual degree in bringing alive.

On broader lines, the story of *Looking Backward* is that of Julian West's introduction into the new, coöperative way of life. The "conflict" in the plot is the conflict (an unequal one, it must be admitted) between the modes of life of the nineteenth and those of the twenty-first century, between capitalistic industrialism and socialism; the development of the hero lies in his gradual passage from an individualistic point of view to a collectivist. Arid as such a story might be elsewhere, it acquires, in *Looking Backward,* a piquancy, a freshness, and a set of emotional overtones that are owing, no doubt, to the love interest with which it is intermingled. Moreover, there develops, from chapter to chapter, even a kind of heightening of the philosophical conflict, akin to the *nouement* which takes place in an old-fashioned drama of intrigue. The climax—a series of scenes in which the artistic illusion is as completely achieved as anywhere in American literature—is the return of the hero to nineteenth-century Boston, his new and terrible perception of the waste, the squalor, the deformity, the repulsiveness of a competitive society; his realization, presently, that his return is, after all, only an unutterably hideous nightmare; his awakening; and his final escape into the relief, the freedom, the glad high loveliness of the new coöperative world.

To the persuasiveness and the dramatic power of its story, then, *Looking Backward* owed much of its immense popular appeal; but it owed even more, no doubt, to its all but perfect adaptation to the time-spirit of Bellamy's America. As Bellamy himself pointed out, "A book of propaganda like *Looking Backward* produces an effect precisely in proportion as it is a bare anticipation in expression of what everybody was thinking and about to say." [44] It was "the present unprecedented ferment in the minds of men" which had alone "given the book its circulation and the movement its emphasis." [45] This "unprecedented ferment" it had been not only Bellamy's peculiar good fortune to express in a single book, but his peculiar gift as well. He spoke not merely *to* his readers, but *for* them. "Somehow,"—so his friend Howells interpreted his talent—"Somehow, whether he *knew* or not, he unerringly felt how the average man would feel." [46]

Looking Backward was from the beginning a best seller. By January of 1891, some 371,000 copies altogether had been sold.[47] By 1897, some 400,000 copies had been sold in the United States alone; the book had been translated into the language of every civilized country; 250,000 copies had recently been issued in a low-priced edition in England; and the total sale had risen to a point almost beyond computation.[48] Among the American *intelligentsia*, while no reputable economist would express any belief in the practicability of the Nationalist program, such authors and reformers as Edward Everett Hale, Frances E. Willard, Thomas Wentworth Higginson, and William Dean Howells were in general sympathy with Bellamy. Within six months, in 1890, nonpropagandist magazines of national importance carried seven articles on nationalism; [49] and lesser novels and Utopias by the score added to the treatment of the subject. Typical in its expression of the warm admiration, even adulation, which was awakened by Bellamy is a passage in Lynn Boyd Porter's preface to the

[44] "The Progress of Nationalism in the United States," *The North American Review*, 154: 742-52 (June, 1892).

[45] "*Looking Backward* Again," *The North American Review*, 150: 351-3 (March, 1890).

[46] William Dean Howells, "Edward Bellamy," *The Atlantic Monthly*, 82: 253-6 (August, 1898).

[47] Shurter, *op. cit.*, p. 138.

[48] According to the publishers, D. Appleton & Co., in an announcement of *Equality*, printed in their 1897 edition of Garland's *A Spoil of Office*.

[49] For a fuller treatment of the popular response to Bellamy, see Shurter, *op. cit.*, pp. 150 ff.

popular sociological romance, *Speaking of Ellen* (1890). Having illustrated the plight of modern laborers by painting an imaginary picture of a group of men hopelessly chained in a dungeon, the author continues:

As I stood there, lost in pity for the unfortunates, a sudden gleam shot across the darkness. A ray of the blessed sun penetrated the noisome depths. The confined ones struggled to their feet and took deep breaths of joy! A heroic soul had scaled the outer wall and forced aside a heavy stone. I did not see the man, but someone said his name was BELLAMY.

I could not have made that bold ascent, but by the new light I saw many things. I learned that the prison had doors whose bolts, though rusted in their sockets, were not immovable.

Among other peculiar literary phenomena for which *Looking Backward* was chiefly responsible was the extraordinary vogue of Utopian fiction from 1888 until after the turn of the century. Not less than fifteen replies, continuations, and counter-replies employed a Utopian framework—often Bellamy's own— as a carrier for discussions of nationalism. Opposed to nationalism were such works as Arthur Dudley Vinton's *Looking Further Backward* (1890), Richard Michaelis's *Looking Forward* (1890), and Mary H. Safford's translation of Conrad Wilbrandt's *Mr. East's Experiences in Mr. Bellamy's World* (1891); in favor, were such works as Ludwig Geissler's *Looking Beyond* (1891) and Solomon Schindler's *Young West* (1894). Between 1888 and 1900 there appeared altogether over sixty Utopias—an average of five a year—which deal specifically with the abuses and possible reform of society. In kind, these works range from pieces of highly competent literary workmanship like Howells' *A Traveller from Altruria* (1894) to short, crudely written pamphlets, the sincerity of which is attested by the fact that they were often published by the authors themselves, or at least at the authors' expense. In the pointing out of such abuses as the hostility of capital and labor, the trend toward monopoly, and the unequal distribution of wealth, the authors of Utopian fiction were mostly agreed. In the advocacy of reforms, they varied from complete acceptance of Bellamy's nationalism to the outlining of innocuous schemes for humanitarian reform or the purification of politics.

Naturally, a thought-movement of such general interest took on also, almost from the first, a political, pragmatic, and organized character. In September, 1888, a Bellamy club was formed in Boston; others followed; and by June of 1892 about 150 Bellamy or nationalist clubs had come into existence. These clubs made up what has sometimes been called the Nationalist Party, although there appears to have been among them no real party organization, or, indeed, any central organization at all. Two periodicals, *The Nationalist* and *The New Nation*, served as the principal organs of nationalist propaganda, and some ten or eleven other periodicals gave the movement active support or, at the very least, favorable attention.[50]

The enthusiastic reception accorded to *Looking Backward*, together with the pragmatic and propagandist turn taken by the nationalist movement, determined the course which the remainder of Bellamy's life was to follow. A deeply conscientious man, he came to feel that it was his duty to renounce *belles lettres* and give himself chiefly to the cause of nationalism—a feeling whose sincerity is proved by his resolute refusal to commercialize his fame. From the Hawthornesque romancer, he developed into the nationally known lecturer and publicist, and, in his work with *The New Nation* from January, 1891, through 1893, into the editor of a propagandist journal. As the leader, now, of a definite, tangible movement looking toward feasible ends, he found it necessary to outline a practical program, and to designate specifically the first steps to be taken toward the final goal of nationalism.

In his survey of the route to the nationalized state, Bellamy characteristically rejected any way—any name, even—that

---

[50] In regard to the propagandist phase of nationalism, see Shurter, *op. cit.*, pp. 159-63; also Edward Bellamy, "The Progress of Nationalism in the United States," *The North American Review*, 154: 742-52 (June, 1892); also, for a somewhat deprecatory and even hostile treatment, Nicholas T. Gilman, "Nationalism in the United States," *The Quarterly Journal of Economics*, IV: 50-76 (October, 1889).

might be offensive to the democratic middle class of whom he was, in so many ways, a spokesman. Already, in *Looking Backward*, he had dismissed the radical way offered by the followers of the "red flag." According to the satirical theory advanced there by his spokesman Dr. Leete, the Reds had actually been subsidized by the former capitalists with the purpose of hindering the creation of the new order. They hindered it "very effectively while they lasted, for their talk so disgusted people as to deprive the best considered projects for social reform of a hearing."[51] It is not out of such class hatred and class warfare that economic reform is to come, but rather out of the natural extension of our middle-class democracy from the field of politics into that of economics:

From the period at which the democratic idea gained ascendancy it could be a question of but a short time before the obvious interests of the majority of the people should lead to the democratizing of the national economic system to accord with the political system.[52]

The nationalizing of industry would, Bellamy felt, be a gradual process. To be sure, a more rapid change *might* possibly be contemplated, "subject to the leading of events"; but Bellamy's real expectation was that the socialistic revolution would come as a development, not as an abrupt overturn.[53] The most immediate objective of the Nationalists might well be, then, the improving of the public schools, with a view to the preparation of a citizenry of an industrialized state. Next might come municipal and state ownership of natural monopolies—lighting, traction systems, telephones, telegraphs, the express, and railroads—under a civil service administration so designed as to eliminate the spoils system. Afterward, the government might gradually assume control of other businesses of national scope, until, finally, the entire economic

[51] *Looking Backward*, pp. 251-2.
[52] "The Progress of Nationalism in the United States," *The North American Review*, 154: 742-3 (June, 1892). See also *Equality*, p. 98.
[53] "*Looking Backward* Again," *The North American Review*, 150: 362 (March, 1890).

machinery of the country should have become completely nationalized.[54]

The closing years of Bellamy's life were spent in this earnest effort to translate the dream of *Looking Backward* into the realities of an American reform program. During this time, alongside his work as lecturer and editor, Bellamy must have cherished, also, the ambition to complete his case for nationalism—to make it intellectually, as well as emotionally, conclusive. To this end he evidently continued his economic studies; his acquaintance with the Fabian program of the Webbs and Shaw appears, for instance, to belong to this time.[55] The results of such studies he laboriously, conscientiously included in the immensely detailed *Equality* (1897), an acute, intelligent, and systematic treatment in which the author's elaborate marshalling of economic detail is, after all, no adequate compensation for his loss of freshness and emotional power.

Like Henry George, Bellamy was fortunate in the time of his death. Already, the middle class protest of which he had become one of the two foremost spokesmen was losing integration. The reforming energies of the public were near exhaustion; the economic distress which had lent the movement a peculiar poignancy during the early 1890's was passing; and in the Spanish war the nation was about to be flung off upon a parabola which the humanitarian of 1890 could not possibly have foreseen. After 1898, the Coöperative Commonwealth, far from steadily approaching with each year of human progress, was to recede into the future so far as to be hardly discernible. From the disillusion of knowing these things, Bellamy was mercifully spared. The conviction that the work of his hands might be established upon him in the creation of a glad new world could still be his. At the time of his death, the cloud-palace of Utopia still hovered discernibly upon the horizon of the future, lovely, and not quite unattainable.

[54] *Ibid.*, pp. 362-3.
[55] See his Introduction to the American Edition of *Socialism: The Fabian Essays*, edited by G. Bernard Shaw. Boston, 1894.

VI

Seen through the perspective of fifty years of history, the historical significance of Bellamy's work—a matter about which his friendly and his hostile contemporaries were equally confused—appears sufficiently clear. Bellamy was not the Moses of a new order; he was not a well-meaning but impractical reformer; he was not an earnest but self-deluded charlatan. He was, instead, an extraordinarily gifted author and thinker, who, in many ways, gave completest voice to the American middle-class protest against plutocracy. Like many of his middle-class contemporaries, he brought to bear on the social problems of our Gilded Age, the culture of our Golden Day. Like most of his contemporaries, he assumed the rightness of democracy, opportunity for the personal growth of the individual, and progress; and when these values were threatened by corrupt business practices and the rule of the rich, he rebelled. Like the average American citizen, he desired economic security, abundance, and the personal development to which a moderate prosperity is almost prerequisite. In his emphasis on a collective rather than on an individualistic solution of the economic problem, Bellamy was, to be sure, among the minority. Nevertheless, and in spite of this important variation from majority opinion, his chief work as a social critic was to grasp the principal aims and ideas of the middle-class protest, to systematize them, voice them, and persuasively dramatize them.

When we turn from an historical to a judicial estimate of Bellamy, when we cease to think of him as the voice of a movement and begin to weigh his intellectual leadership in the scales of permanent value, certain limitations suggest themselves. His weaknesses are the ones inherent—we might almost say, inevitable—in his tradition. For Bellamy's view of life is not, in essentials, a novel one; it is, simply, a belated corollary of the eighteenth-century concept of man as a rational being, naturally good, and capable of continued growth toward perfection. *Looking Backward* is, after all, only

the twilight glow of that brilliant day of optimism which had
been illumined by Condorcet's *History of the Progress of the
Human Spirit,* Godwin's *Political Justice,* and Shelley's *Prometheus Unbound.* With Bellamy, as with his predecessors, once
the premises of man's rationality, natural goodness, and perfectibility are granted, the remainder of his scheme of human
development unfolds with the inevitability of mathematical
proof. It was simply Bellamy's misfortune, in contrast with
the happier lot of Shelley, that his work lay so much nearer
in time to the era when psychology, piercing into the hitherto
unsuspected realm of man's subconsciousness, was to discover
materials for a picture of human nature more complex, more
menacing, more nearly incalculable than had been dreamed
of by the thinkers of the Enlightenment, and thus to make
immeasurably harder the acceptance of the premise on which
their hopeful schemes for the advancement of humanity were
founded. With the rise of behavioristic and Freudian psychology, with the outbreak of the vast disintegrative social and
military forces of the twentieth century, Bellamy's roseate
view of life, matured by nineteenth-century liberalism in an
old-fashioned New England village, appears a thing increasingly faint, increasingly far-off from reality.

Yet, in other respects, Bellamy has strong claims to a place
among the most realistic social thinkers of his time; and nowhere is his realism more apparent than in his frank recognition of the Machine—its permanence, its possibilities, the
profound social changes it must entail. Confronted with the
same phenomena, George and Garland had both avoided
rather than considered them; they had both sought refuge,
instead, in what was really a nostalgic return to the frontier—
their attempt to recover, by artificial means, the vanishing era
of individualism and large personal opportunity. Confronted
with similar phenomena in England, Ruskin, and, to some
extent, even so robust a figure as William Morris, had sought
to turn back the clock, to arrest the march of the Machine,
and by so doing to preserve the humane satisfactions and fulfillments afforded by the handicrafts. In contrast with the

romantic programs of these men, how sanely realistic is Bellamy's frank recognition that the Machine has come to stay; that it possesses enormous potentialities for extending man's control over nature and thereby improving life; and that only by some form of collective control can these possibilities be made to serve the general good. The rapid advance of collectivism in the twentieth century—whether in the form of Communism, or Fascism, or the economic program of a liberal democracy like that of Sweden, or certain portions even of the New Deal—has demonstrated, on nearly a world-wide scale, the principal thesis of *Looking Backward*.

Moreover, it is pertinent to remember, in the summing-up of Bellamy's work, that, in his search for some way to make the Machine contribute to the general good, he was far from being concerned with materialities alone. The constant drift of his thought is not merely toward economic achievement, but also toward the translation of economic achievement into humane value. To him, the final goal of economic reform is (in a phrase which in spite of its triteness is too significant to abandon) the more abundant life. Beyond the enjoyment of material comforts lies always, to Bellamy, the larger enjoyment that comes from the full exercise of the best in one's person and personality—the hearty physical enjoyment of outdoor sports; the enjoyment of the plastic arts and of music and literature; of love and mating; of advancement in knowledge; of the growth of all those intangible attributes which may be called spiritual; of the realization, in short, of a fine and complete human personality.

From the standpoint of aesthetic value, as distinguished from that of his service as a spokesman or the quality of his intellectual leadership, Bellamy must stand or fall by one book —*Looking Backward;* and against few great books can more serious limitations be charged. May a work of fiction justly be called a classic when it contains no memorable characters, no purple passages of imaginative splendor, no finally just discrimination or subtle dialectic such as challenge the reader of Plato's *Republic;* when, above all, it fails to give convincing evidence of the intangible force, the gusto, the sense of life, the high seriousness possessed by the masters? In the case of *Looking Backward,* the answer is, in all human probability, "Yes." Of the voluminous economic writings of our American Gilded Age, it is one of the four or five whose values are most assuredly large and lasting.

The case for *Looking Backward,* a twofold one, rests upon its significance and its artistry. To have recaptured again the elusive immortal dream of a human Golden Age; to have wrought into and fused with the ancient Utopian tradition the most fundamental problems of a democracy confronted with the new, bewildering intricacies of the Machine—all this is surely, in the historical growth of our American culture, no insignificant thing. And equally important is Bellamy's success in dramatizing, artfully, beautifully, powerfully, the contrast between two ways of life—the individual as opposed to the collective, the present as opposed to the future. From the very opening chapters of *Looking Backward,* the conflict between the two is discernible. Throughout the body of the book, owing to Bellamy's skillful, classically symmetrical disposal of his scenes, it recurrently intensifies and heightens. Toward the close, in Julian West's dream of his return to nineteenth-century Boston, it reaches its overwhelming climax, wherein one sees, as if in some ultimate panorama, in the foreground the sordid ugliness of the present, darkly misshapen as the figures in some Dantean purgatory, and beyond, the lucent, the clear, the Godlike loveliness of the future, suspended, like some radiant cloud-castled sunset, beyond the distorted shapes of grotesque, forbidding mountains.

I

William Dean Howells, the most important literary figure among the friends of Edward Bellamy, has been less generally fortunate in his later interpreters than in his earlier. Delmar Gross Cooke and Oscar W. Firkins, who wrote of Howells shortly after his death, were possessed not only of acumen and intelligence, but of an understanding of the democratic and equalitarian sources of Howells' thought. Vernon Louis Parrington, however, familiar as he must have been with Howells' middle-class background, failed to allow for it in designating Howells as a *Marxian* socialist;[1] and after Parrington critical error swiftly lapsed into eccentricity. Hartley Grattan, writing in 1930, announced the astonishing conclusion that Howells' view of America was "scarcely distinguishable from Andrew Carnegie's, whose attitude was that of the triumphant bourgeoisie."[2] Not long afterward, Matthew Josephson explained that Howells "wrote from no depth of conviction; he celebrated or attacked no institution with a fixed moral passion"; and his realism "consisted merely of an avoidance of arbitrary or improbable episode, of a duplication of the exact length, propriety, and dullness of middle-class American conversation."[3] And in 1933 Granville Hicks explained that Howells' socialism was vague, that he had no

[1] *The Beginnings of Critical Realism in America*, pp. 244 ff.

[2] Hartley Grattan, "Howells: Ten Years After," *The American Mercury*, XX, 46 (May, 1930).

[3] Matthew Josephson, *Portrait of the Artist as American*, pp. 163-5.

understanding of economic forces, and that, consequently, "the issues in his book are never clear." [4]

Confusion of this sort illustrates the fallacies of a criticism that either has a partisan axe to grind, or lacks the corrective of a sound historical method, or both. In identifying Howells' view of American life with Carnegie's, Mr. Grattan has seen—perhaps has chosen to see—only one side of a many-sided nature, and has neglected to point out that Howells differed from Carnegie in more ways than he agreed with him. Mr. Josephson, in assuming that Howells held the same view of life as the bourgeois characters in his fiction, has fallen into the threadbare fallacy of identifying an author with his materials—a process which, if carried to its logical conclusion, would have committed the author of *Oliver Twist* to jail and the author of *King Lear* to a hospital for mental diseases. And Mr. Hicks, in concluding that the issues in Howells' books are never clear, has applied to Howells the thought-categories of our own day instead of his—of 1920-40 instead of 1880-1900. Seen through the lenses of contemporary Marxian criticism, the issues in Howells' books do indeed appear confused. Seen in the light of the time-spirit of Howells' own day, studied with an eye to his middle-class, democratic, and humanitarian background, they appear eminently clear-cut and precise.

Criticism like that of Messrs. Grattan, Josephson, and Hicks, whatever its eccentricities, has at least the merit of provocation. It poses for us, anew, the questions of just what forces contributed to form the mind of Howells, just what opinions he expressed, how he expressed them, and what is the relation of all these things to the climate of opinion in which he did his work. And in answer to the first of these questions, in search of the original roots of Howells' thinking, we must go, as with George and Mark Twain and Garland and Bellamy, back into the middle class, democratic culture that flourished during the generation just before the Civil War.

[4] Granville Hicks, *The Great Tradition*, pp. 98-9. Critical pronouncements of the past decade, however, have not been wholly adverse to Howells. For a more favorable estimate, see Arthur Hobson Quinn, *American Fiction: an Historical and Critical Survey*, pp. 257-78.

II

A youth, in the Ohio of Howells' boyhood, learned democracy by living it. He assumed, with little or no conscious questioning, the naturalness of a society where great wealth and undeserved poverty were equally rare, and where political democracy was the natural expression of a general equality in economic condition. Economically, the Howells family occupied there about an average status. The father, a village printer, had a yearly income of about a thousand dollars; the mother did with her own hands most of the household work. Naturally the boy William Dean Howells did his full share of everyday labor. For a while he clerked in a drug store; and one year, in the course of his father's abortive effort to found a communal settlement, he helped on the farm in clearing timber, breaking ground, and planting crops. But, above all, he served as an apprentice in his father's print shop; in his early teens he worked until ten or eleven o'clock on winter nights with the telegraphic dispatches, and was up before daybreak to deliver papers the following mornings.[5] From such necessities of daily work, from the norm of limited comfort which the Howells family exemplified, none of the villagers were far removed. Theirs was a neighborly equality of condition, where men fraternized easily, free from all embarrassments of caste. Theirs was, as Howells recalled it, a pleasant and morally healthful society, where dishonesty was uncommon, because there was neither wealth nor poverty, and "all had enough and few too much." [6]

When, as a young man, Howells went up to the state capital at Columbus, he found there only an enlargement of the friendly, congenial society he had already known. That

[5] For accounts of Howells' experience with everyday labor and western democracy, see his Years of My Youth, especially pp. 10-2, 28-30, 41-4; also My Year in a Log Cabin, and the fictionized version of this experience in New Leaf Mills; also A Boy's Town entire; also William Cooper Howells, Recollections of Life in Ohio from 1813 to 1840, especially pp. 122-6.

[6] A Boy's Town, p. 214.

a ten-dollar-a-week reporter should be as welcome as another at the home of the governor of the state—this and other evidences of democracy came to him with no surprise; and the society of the youth at Columbus—a gay and largely innocent camaraderie, as he recalled it—afforded him the most pleasant set of associations, except one, that he was ever to have. Moreover, a reporter's intimate knowledge of the workings of the state government appears to have given him no grounds for any cyncism in regard to popular rule.[7]

In short, democracy became to Howells an enduring reality, a scheme of life that was genuinely creative of the fine values of self-reliance, integrity, and friendship; and so deeply were these convictions, this attitude ingrained within him that to the very close of his life they conditioned his entire social thinking. As late as his fifty-fourth year, for example, his conviction of the rightness of democracy was to lead him to give aid to the Russian revolutionist Stepniak.[8] As late as his eighty-second year, this same conviction was to lead him to refuse a decoration from the King of Belgium, on the ground that an acceptance would be unbecoming to a citizen of a republic.[9] Meanwhile, when in the prosecution of his art, he had come to imagine a Utopia, he had been able to conceive of no social arrangement more desirable than an equality patterned almost exactly upon the equality he had known in antebellum Ohio.[10]

Democracy, social equality—the antebellum West made such ideas fundamental in Howells' theory of life; and in many another way it exercised an influence only less important than this one. A certain excess of gentility, for instance, a certain chariness in dealing with the more violent, sub-rational phases of human nature, which everyone observes in Howells, and which is usually attributed to the influence of his later en-

[7] *Years of My Youth*, especially pp. 130 ff., 173 ff.

[8] *The Life in Letters of William Dean Howells*, edited by Mildred Howells, II, 12-13; a letter of January 11, 1891, to William Cooper Howells; also of January 27, 1891, to J. B. Pond of Chicago.

[9] *Ibid.*, II, 386; a letter of July 7, 1919, to Hon. C. Symon, secretary of the Belgian legation.

[10] For Howells' own emphasis on this similarity, see *Through the Eye of the Needle*, p. 154.

vironment in New England, was fully developed in his character before he ever left the West, and was encouraged by his Ohio associates. As a youth there, he disliked nothing more than the police-court reporting which he did for the Cincinnati *Gazette*. With a repulsion he was never to forget, he listened to the ravings of a drunken woman in court; and at some time during these youthful experiences he reached, however intangibly and wordlessly, the conclusion that the realm of the violent and the ugly held, for him, no permanent abiding place. Even then, his longing was for the "cleanly respectabilities." Over-sensitive perhaps, excessively tender-minded,[11] he was racked by the thought of evils and sufferings that more callous spirits overlooked; and, unable to relieve them, he fled from them. Moreover, he was encouraged, in the avoidance of the vulgar and the crudely evil, by the *mores* of his Ohio society; the gentilities flourished in Columbus no less than in Boston. "Never,"—so his chief Henry D. Cooke of the *Ohio State Journal* advised him—"*never* write anything you would be ashamed to read to a woman."[12]

More profoundly also—upon the plane of fundamental religious attitudes rather than on that of personal taste or the observance of the proprieties—the antebellum West formed the mind of Howells. To be sure, the mature Howells, like Carlyle, like Emerson, grew away from the theology of his fathers, but many of the attitudes fostered by that theology remained. A descendant of three generations of Quakers—his own father had professed that faith before becoming a Swedenborgian—Howells owned a religious heritage that reenforced his democratic tastes, that lent an occasional tinge of mysticism to his prevailing rationality, that, above all, joined with other forces in awakening Howells' mind to the

[11] Examples of this trait in Howells are numerous. For a typical instance, see the *Life in Letters*, II, 147; a letter of September 29, 1901, in which he speaks of the general callousness in the administration of "justice," and of the mob spirit that followed the assassination of McKinley.

[12] For the story of Howells' training in gentility, see his *Years of My Youth*, especially pp. 142 ff.

issues of humanitarianism and social justice.[13] Slavery was then the major concern of humanitarian feeling; the Quakers, alone of the important religious groups in America, had succeeded in eliminating slave-owning from their membership and in maintaining a consistent opposition to slavery; and Howells' great-grandfather, grandfather, and father, all reared as Quakers, had all been anti-slavery men. His mother's people, the Deans, were likewise abolitionists; and as a child Howells is said to have been present at one of their meetings when an objector hurled a stone through a window.

Besides the abolition of slavery, other means for attaining social justice were being talked of, tried, and presently abandoned in Howells' West. The coöperative colony, Owenite or Fourierist, appealed to many generous minds as the most promising means of achieving a better ethical and economic organization of society. The elder Howells, together with three brothers, evolved a plan for building just such a community about a milling privilege they had purchased; and while the community itself never came into being, while, indeed, the only result for Howells was a year of manual labor on the farm, the planning and the talk of the family must have helped expand the mental horizons of an impressionable boy.[14] Moreover, an uncle of Elinor Mead Howells, John Humphrey Noyes, had been among the founders of the Oneida Community in New York; [15] and there is every reason to believe that Howells knew, either as a youth or not greatly later, of the communal life of the Shakers, of Robert Owen's community at New Harmony, Indiana, and of other experiments in coöperative living.[16] All in all, the society that shaped Howells' youthful thinking was one in which social and economic experiment might be accepted as a normal phase of human life.

[13] For Howells' religious background, see the *Life in Letters* I, 3 ff.; also *A Boy's Town*, pp. 10-1.

[14] See the account in *Years of My Youth*, pp. 44 ff.; also the more extensive and only slightly fictionized version in *New Leaf Mills*.

[15] For a reference by Howells to Noyes, see *The Life in Letters*, I, 11.

[16] *Ibid.*, I: 166-7, 208-9. See also the references in the "Editor's Study," *Harper's Magazine*, 76, 803 (April, 1888).

Such being the background of Howells, it was only natural that, upon the eve of the Civil War, he should have been found on the humanitarian side. He, no more than many an elder and wiser man, knew what tragedy was impending; and so, along with the other gay young blades on the staff of the *Ohio State Journal,* he could join lightly enough in the sport of "firing the Southern heart." The raid of John Brown, however, brought to him an intenser excitement, a deeper seriousness, and the man's "martyrdom" aroused him to enthusiasm.[17] The campaign life of Lincoln which he wrote the next year was more than a clever stroke of journalism; it indicated Howells' sincere attachment to the only candidate who appeared likely to achieve any practical gains toward the goal of social justice.

A generation later, Howells was to marvel that this youthful interest in social justice had been so entirely confined to the issue of chattel slavery, and had so entirely overlooked the comparable evils of America's nascent industrialism. As a youth, he visited, to be sure, the great mills at Lowell, and knew "the bewildering sight and sound of all their mechanism," all of which was later to appear to him as "the death of the joy that ought to come from work, if not the captivity of those who tended them." In this spectacle, however, the youthful Howells discerned no tragedy.[18] Many years were to pass before the social problems raised by the machine took on vitality for him.

Moreover, just as Howells' main social and political attitudes were formed in early Ohio, so, in many respects, was his attitude toward literature; so was his attitude toward philosophy, if we may use the word informally and with reference to Howells' general outlook on life. As Midwestern America equipped him with a political philosophy, so it gave him direction toward an ample *general* culture. In the shop of the older Howells there lingered something of the old tradition which made of the printshop an intellectual center as well as a place of business, and its owner an apostle of culture no less than

[17] *Years of My Youth,* pp. 187 ff.
[18] *Literary Friends and Acquaintance,* p. 48.

of trade. Books were always available to the Howells family; Thomson and Scott and Dickens were read aloud among them; and in at least one locality the interests of the family were typical of the community at large. Of the village folk of Jefferson, Ohio, it was Howells' impression that

they were, in a degree which I still think extraordinary, literary. Old and young, they read and talked about books, and better books than people read and talk about now, as it seems to me, possibly because there were not so many bad ones; the English serials pirated into our magazines were followed and discussed, and any American author who made an effect in the East became promptly known in that small village of the Western Reserve.[19]

In the abundant reading which Howells did as a youth, his preference was chiefly for the polished expressions of English neoclassicism. His earliest poems were imitations of Pope, and the prose style which he gradually developed took on the lucidity, the restraint, the smoothness, even the quality in tone and rhythm which one might expect of a neoclassic essayist. To be sure, Howells knew other influences, innumerable others, influences as diverse as those of Heine and Henry James; but his basic assumptions about literature, and in considerable measure about life, remained the ones that had their widest currency during the neoclassic period. The principal gifts of his mind remained the gifts that the neoclassicist prized most highly—gifts of restraint, balance, orderliness, urbanity, dependence on reason and common sense. With Howells, as with many another from Addison through Holmes, the neoclassic outlook tended to produce high qualities of clarity, intelligence, and, in the finest sense of the word, of civilization. It tended also toward a weakness by no means confined to neoclassicism—the weakness of oversimplifying, of assuming too easily that the natural tendency of life is toward order instead of disorder, that the silken reins of reason are strong enough to control a largely unreasoning race, and that the most complex problems may be solved

[19] *Years of My Youth,* pp. 106-107. Copyright 1916 by Harper and Brothers. Reprinted by permission of Miss Mildred Howells.

simply by thinking about them in an honest and somewhat legalistic way.[20] But whatever their strength, whatever their weakness, the literary and philosophical ideals of neoclassicism remained, in large measure, those of Howells. Of his own early writings, for instance, he has said,

In the spirit of my endeavor there was no variableness; always I strove for grace, for distinctness, for light; and my soul detests obscurity still.[21]

In short, the character of Howells was largely a product of rural and village Ohio in the two decades before the Civil War. In the youth who left the West in 1861 to accept the consulate at Venice, there was present every important trait of the mature Howells: his dominant interest in humane culture, especially in literature; his active though not dominant interest in political and social equality; his preference for the decent and decorous; his philosophical attitude of neoclassic orderliness and reason. With him, as with George and Clemens and Garland and Bellamy, the social critic of the Gilded Age was a product and a representative of the culture of the Golden Day.

III

Between Howells' departure from the West and his first productive interest in sociological and economic fiction, twenty-five years intervened. During these years, and especially from 1878 to 1886, Howells' most distinctive and widely known work was done; and in any *general* consideration of that work, the heart of the problem, the core of the critical study, would no doubt be found here. Within these time-limits are comprehended the major developments in Howells' art—the transformation of the graceful familiar essayist and travel writer into the mature novelist, the growth of a dis-

[20] See, for an example of this kind of reasoning, Howells' pronouncement against the popular election of senators. The "Editor's Study," *Harper's Magazine*, 86, 968 (May, 1893)
[21] *Years of My Youth*, p. 118.

tinctive theory and practice of realism, and the flowering of his concept of the novel as primarily an art form, designed mainly for aesthetic ends, and dependent for much of its efficacy on competent craftsmanship. But since our concern here is merely with Howells the social critic, and since Howells' social expressions during this time are of relatively small importance, we must speak only cursorily of this important quarter-century, attempting to follow the growth of those concepts of life, and those theories of art, that later affected his sociological fiction. Even this limited task—so rich was his general experience, and so late was his entrance into the field of social criticism—is in reality most complex. In the case of Howells, the complete story of the "gathering of the forces" would require a volume in itself, so that we must be content, here, with singling out only a few of the major threads in his rich web of thought.

During this quarter-century, the matrix of Howells' character suffered few or no important changes; his personality only exercised itself upon a larger fund of experience, within a wider circle of life. While in Venice, he added to his mental stores another language, rich in literature and stores of tradition, and came to know at first hand the rich, the dim, the dark Old World of Henry James. Here, too, he had his first contact with social codes that were sharply at variance with his own—that of the native Italians, and that of the decorous bourgeoisie who were comprised in various circles of American tourists and expatriates. His attitude toward the latter code, it is too seldom observed, remained as detached as toward the former. Far from becoming the slave of the bourgeois proprieties, he was to remain primarily the amused observer of them, and was to turn upon them, in such comedies as *The Lady of the Aroostook,* the examination of a deft and brilliant ridicule.

Important as the Venetian experience was in maturing and broadening Howells, it was not until he returned to America that he discovered a social environment with which he was really congenial. That environment—the one which, of all he ever knew, most fully satisfied him—he found in Cambridge in the late sixtics and early seventies. Here was a society which, with the added charm afforded by a mellow literary tradition, reinforced the influence of the West of Howells' youth; for the elder authors of New England were, even more than himself, survivals of that agrarian republic whose doom, unknown to them, had been sealed already by the Civil War. Cambridge had not yet lost its quiet village atmosphere; life there was as genial, as unpretentious as in the Western villages of his earlier youth. Men moved there, Howells felt, in precisely that civilized equality which he prized; the effect even of Longfellow, the wealthiest of the group, was of an "entire democracy." [22] The social and ethical interests of his companions were just such as he had known before the Civil War, and if these interests were already becoming anachronistic, that was a fact that some of his elders were never to know, and that he himself was to wait many years to realize. Longfellow revealed to him a genuine if gentle humanitarianism; Lowell's name, because of his part in the anti-slavery struggle, was a synonym for the love of freedom and the hope of justice. And if either of these two had been insufficient, there remained to him his acquaintance with that gentle near-by spirit, Whittier, who honored him by asking him to write his biography.[23] Later, Howells was to remark, with apparent though unadmitted surprise, how few of the antebellum reformers took the logical step of extending their concern over chattel slavery to the equally immediate and pressing issue of industrial slavery.[24]

Among the Cambridge *literati*, more nearly than in any other circle, Howells saw realized his ideal of a society which, basically democratic and equalitarian, was enriched with all the resources of the arts and of a tradition of civilized living. In this environment, the middle-class ideals of culture which

[22] *Literary Friends and Acquaintance*, p. 207.
[23] In regard to these and other ethical and social influences on Howells, see *Literary Friends and Acquaintance*, pp. 11, 24, 108-11, 135-6, 202-7, 218. See also *The Life in Letters* I: 380-1; letters of Whittier to Howells, March 18 and 23, 1886.
[24] *Literary Friends and Acquaintance*, pp. 58-9.

he had developed in the West appeared to have come to maturity. The effect was to be that, while Howells' materials were bourgeois in one sense, his outlook on life was bourgeois —or, more accurately, middle-class—in quite another. Howells' materials, both in character and in situation, are taken quite often from the life of the commercial bourgeoisie of our Victorian age; but with this wing of the bourgeoisie Howells himself had, as we shall see, so little sympathy that he more than once confessed boredom with it, and sometimes ridiculed it. His own personal sympathies were with the more moderately prosperous *intelligentsia* who coupled plain living with, if not *high* thinking, at least some pursuit of inward riches; an *intelligentsia* who were diffused throughout New England, and whose spokesmen and finest expression had been the literary groups of Concord and Cambridge. In one of the *obiter dicta* which, contrary to his own principles of fiction, he sometimes allowed himself, he explains that

The people who can afford to pay ten dollars a week for summer board, and not much more, are often the best of the American people, or, at least, of the New England people. They may not know it, and those who are richer may not imagine it. They are apt to be middle-aged maiden ladies from university towns, living upon carefully guarded investments; young married ladies with a scant child or two, and needing rest and change of air; college professors with nothing but their modest salaries; literary men or women in the beginning of their tempered success; clergymen and their wives away from their churches in the larger country towns or in the smaller suburbs of the cities; here and there an agreeable bachelor in middle life, fond of literature and nature; hosts of young and pretty girls with distinct tastes in art, and devoted to the clever young painter who leads them to the sources of inspiration in the fields and woods. Such people are refined, humane, appreciative, sympathetic . . .[25]

It was toward making possible a society in which people might be "refined, humane, appreciative, sympathetic," that

[25] *The Landlord at Lion's Head*, p. 64. Copyright, 1897, by Harper and Brothers; 1924, by Mildred Howells and John Mead Howells. Reprinted by permission of Miss Mildred Howells.

much of Howells' social thinking and social effort was to be directed.

In the purely literary and critical field, the forces which Howells assimilated were both too many and too intangible in their effects to be entirely catalogued here. So numerous were his "literary passions," and so fully has he himself put them on record, that the task of the historian becomes one of selection and proportion merely. Apparently it was with the fiction of social comedy that his own temperament was most congenial, and no doubt it was for this cause, as well as on account of the fineness of her art, that he chose Jane Austen as his favorite of the English novelists, and often employed, in handling his American materials, a method that so closely resembles hers. The thread of social comedy is among the most evident and continuous in Howells' work; it extends from his early travel writings such as *Their Wedding Journey* down through his last published novel, *The Vacation of the Kelwyns,* again and again expressing itself in some such sparkling comedy of manners as *The Lady of the Aroostook, Indian Summer,* and *The Kentons.* Of Howells' economic novels specifically, it may be said that it is this intelligent, this sprightly, this perennially recurring sense of comedy that, as much as any one factor, distinguishes them from other novels of their kind. In a literary type that is on the whole distressingly solemn, one comes with profound relief upon such an epigram as "We ought to think twice before doing a good action," upon such an exuberant character as Fulkerson in *A Hazard of New Fortunes,* upon such clever, provocative satire as is scattered from cover to cover of *A Traveller from Altruria.*

But if there is much in Howells' art of fiction that reminds one of the social comedy of Jane Austen, there is even more that suggests what may loosely be called the problem novel, or, more accurately, the fiction of moral cause and effect. The study of moral cause and effect had been, indeed, almost a preoccupation of one of the New England school whose mantle had been assumed by Howells—only, with Hawthorne, the progress of moral causation is illustrated in a highly selective and therefore romanticized setting, where the factors of life can be shifted about at the artist's pleasure, where the lights and shadows of the picture may be heightened or deepened at will. Closer in method to Howells' work, however, are the ethical novels of George Eliot, where moral causation is studied in an imagined setting which at least appears actual, in which personalities can be made to develop or retrograde as they do in actual life—a setting, finally, where it would not seem inappropriate to have various opinions and problems discussed by opposing spokesmen.

Now this type of novel came to be, fully as much as the comedy of manners, the characteristic expression of Howells. In *A Modern Instance*, the "problem" is that of unhappy marriage and divorce, the story is moved chiefly by the natural and inner compulsions of the characters of Marcia Gaylord and Bartley Hubbard, and the principal spokesmen in the debate on divorce are, pro and con, Ben Halleck and the Athertons. In this kind of novel, Howells had at hand a technique that could be adapted to the problems of society at large almost as easily as to the moral problems of individuals; and it is to this *genre*, accordingly, that his economic novels belong.

But the conscious concern of Howells was devoted less to these matters than to his chief guiding principles of fiction—realism and "objectivity." These principles, these qualities in his art owe more than perhaps any others to the natural unfolding of his own personality. The sensible, the delicate, the penetrating observation disclosed in his travel books developed, with no serious lapses, into the broader and profounder observation disclosed in his ethical and economic studies. Familiar as he was with French and Russian fiction, he was, in his own words, "authorized rather than inspired"[26] by the example of Balzac and Flaubert. But from certain of the Russians, he derived authorization, if not influence, of a more specific kind. It was in Turgenev, for instance, that he found a method that created the impression of entire objectivity:

[26] Quoted in Arthur Hobson Quinn, *American Fiction, an Historical and Critical Survey*, p. 258.

"Here was a master who was apparently not trying to work out a plot, who was not even trying to work out a character, but was standing aside from the whole affair, and letting the characters work the plot out." [27] And it was in Tolstoy that he found a method which—as he tells us in one of his most questionable pronouncements—not only seemed free from artifice, but was so.

It would be too much to claim for Howells that his realistic theory of fiction deals, after the manner of the great critics, with the really fundamental problems of criticism—problems of essential value, of the function of aesthetics, of imaginative quality and force, of the building-up of artistic illusion. The importance of Howells' critical theories is rather historical and individual—historical in the sense that some such criticism was needful in its time to explain and sanction the correction of the excesses of romanticism; individual in that a knowledge of it is essential to the understanding of his own fiction, which possesses a larger intrinsic value than his criticism. In his economic novels, no less than in his others, Howells tried to achieve his professed aims of simplicity, naturalness, honesty, truthfulness, ethical balance, and sane Americanism. Here, as elsewhere, he attempted to withhold the personality of the author from any undue prominence.[28] Here, as elsewhere, he tended toward, without ever quite reaching, a goal which he had set in one of his earlier critical dicta: "The novelist's main business is to possess his reader with a due conception of his characters and the situations in which they find themselves. If he does more or less than this he equally fails." [29]

But how, one might ask, could a novel written in accordance with such theories be adapted to economic discussion? How could a realism apparently so impersonal be made to serve that most personal thing, a didactic purpose? The an-

[27] *My Literary Passions*, p. 230.
[28] For Howells' own expression of these principles, see *Criticism and Fiction*, pp. 3, 14, 33-6, 95, 138-40.
[29] "Henry James, Jr." *The Century Illustrated Magazine*, XXV: 25-9. (November, 1882).

swer is, no doubt, that even after an author has surrendered both the conventional plot and the privilege of addressing the audience in his own person, the basic requisites of didactic literature remain. Nothing in Howells' theory, for instance, prevented him from so disposing his story as to illustrate his own standard of values—a personal equation which not even the most "objective" realist has ever yet quite escaped. Nothing in Howells' theory prevented him from having his characters discuss, pro and con, the problem he wished to pose. Above all, nothing prevented his choosing his materials from those phases of life in which the play of economic forces might be discerned. Accordingly, after the year 1886, his choice reveals a rapidly growing awareness of the effect of the general social organization upon the lives of individual men. This new interest, these new materials were characteristically well-balanced. Avoiding any pseudo-humanitarian concern over the poor exclusively, he maintained that truth would not discover the victims of society among them alone, but also "among the rich, cursed with the aimlessness, the satiety, the despair of wealth, wasting their lives in a fool's paradise of shows and semblances, with nothing real but the misery that comes of insincerity and selfishness." [30]

And, in fine, from among those forces that affected Howells prior to his awakening of interest in economics, two other factors, at the least, are of enough importance to require explicit mention. Of these two, one is Howells' entire awareness of the fact that, under the conditions that obtained in America, the production of literature was a business as well as an art, and was subject, like any other business, to the conditions of the market and the fluctuations of popular taste.[31] The other (and quite unrelated) consideration is the steadily widening range of Howells' knowledge of character, especially of American character, and the fineness and delicacy of his art in enabling his readers to realize his characters almost three-dimensionally, as individuals and not merely as

[30] *Criticism and Fiction,* p. 186.
[31] See especially, in this connection, his essay, "The Man of Letters as a Man of Business," *Literature and Life,* pp. 1-36.

types, from the pages of his fiction. To the creator of Mrs. Farrell, of Squire Gaylord, of Silas Lapham, it was only natural that his work in economic fiction should take, as a major direction, the study of *character* in its relation to modern industrialism.

IV

The economic novels of Howells, it should be quite evident by now, represent no radical break in his development. By the middle eighties, his understanding of ethics and government had long been mature, his literary method had become firmly crystallized; and in his economic novels these ethical and political interests are only extended into a new field, this familiar literary method only applied to the new materials he discovered there. Yet such a broadening of interest is itself sufficiently uncommon in an author fifty years of age; and in Howells' own case it could hardly have come about but for the impact, upon his mind, of fresh forces of considerable strength. Those influences were both strong and numerous, and often mutually interrelated. For our convenience solely, and not because Howells himself ever seemed to feel any essential difference in the two classes, we may regard them as, first, foreign, and second, American. And with regard to both classes we shall bear in mind that Howells' response was highly selective. Only such forces as could be adapted into his civilized and rational personality, only such as could be harmonized with his Western equalitarian tradition, were acceptable to him; others, he rejected. This selectivity, this critical mingling of acceptance and rejection, is characteristic of his attitude toward his chief foreign master, Tolstoy.

It was probably during the year 1885 that Howells opened Tolstoy's *The Cossacks*, a volume which had for some time lain unnoticed about his study. Impressed by the unpretentious truthfulness and power of Tolstoy's work, he proceeded, apparently, to *Anna Karenina*, which he pronounced a "wonderful book; ... the subtlety of the observation in it is astounding, simply." [32] Before April, 1886, he had read *My Religion* and before July of the next year Tolstoy's autobiographical treatment of ethics and economics in *Que Faire*.[33] And within three or four years more, he had read sufficiently in Tolstoy to canvass virtually the entire range of the Russian's thought and art,[34] with the result that his own view of life had been, he felt, permanently changed.

Tolstoy's principal gift to Howells was, no doubt, an intangible one; it was the general intensifying of personality, the general broadening and deepening in the awareness of life, with which a sympathetic reader responds to a great creative mind. Long past the age when he could consciously or unconsciously imitate a master, Howells felt that he had been quickened and enlarged by a greatness which he himself could never emulate. "As much as one merely human being can help another"—so runs the familiar tribute in *My Literary Passions*—"I believe that he has helped me; he has not influenced me in aesthetics only, but in ethics, too, so that

[32] *My Literary Passions*, p. 253; *The Life in Letters*, I: 372-3, a letter of October 30, 1885, to Thomas S. Perry. The text of this letter shows that Howells' statement that he had "turned the corner" of his fiftieth year when he came to know Tolstoy (*My Literary Passions*, p. 258) is inexact, unless it is to be applied to his reading of the social and religious treatises instead of the fiction of Tolstoy.

[33] The French title is commonly used by Howells instead of the English *What Is to Be Done? My Religion* is reviewed in Howells' "Editor's Study" for April, 1886, *Que Faire* in the "Study" for July, 1887. *Harper's Magazine*, 72: 808 ff., 75: 316 ff., respectively.

[34] Besides the works already mentioned, Howells refers in one place or another to the following titles from Tolstoy: *War and Peace; Scenes at the Siege of Sebastopol; Childhood, Boyhood, and Youth; Katia; Poulikouchka; My Confession; Master and Man; The Death of Ivan Ilyitch; The Power of Darkness;* and *The Kreutzer Sonata.* He mentions separately, also, Tolstoy's essay on Money, "The Kingdom of God," "What is Art?" "What is Religion?" and "Life." For additional notations on Howells' reading in Tolstoy see G. W. Arms, *The Social Criticism of William Dean Howells.* A doctoral dissertation of New York University (1939), pp. 231-3. See also, in regard to the general question of Tolstoy's influence on Howells, J. Allan Smith, *Tolstoy's Fiction in England and America.* A doctoral dissertation of the University of Illinois (Urbana, 1939), pp. 101-19.

I can never again see life in the way I saw it before I knew him." "He has been to me that final consciousness, which he speaks of so wisely in his essay on Life." [35]—Except for this spiritual awakening which he had from Tolstoy, Howells would not, in all likelihood, have responded so vigorously to those compelling *American* forces of 1887-8, which appear to have been more immediately responsible for his economic novels.

The more specific effects of Tolstoy on Howells are, on the whole, less than the force of his general influence would suggest. In Tolstoy's aesthetics, Howells found an additional sanction for his artistic ideals of simplicity, honesty, and "truth, which is the highest beauty"; [36] but the aesthetics of Tolstoy, while Howells pronounced them perfect except in certain didactic writings, were of less importance to him than the ethics. A mystical Christianity, the Christianity of Quaker and Swedenborgian, had been among the earliest forces to enter Howells' life; and now, in his middle age, he discovered anew in Tolstoy the ethical spirit of that religion, stripped of any crust of creed, and intensified by a powerful imagination. The Christian principle of renunciation, in the sense of seeing life not as a pursuit of personal happiness but as a field of endeavor toward the happiness of the whole human race, and the kindred Christian ideal of the brotherhood of man—this, primarily, was what the ethics of Tolstoy meant to Howells. Except the life of Christ, "there is no other example, no other ideal, and the chief use of Tolstoy is to enforce this fact in our own age, after nineteen centuries of hopeless endeavor to substitute ceremony for character, and the creed for the life." [37]

In *Que Faire*, Howells read the story of how Tolstoy attempted to practice this system of Christian ethics—how he tried, as a wealthy man, to do good among the poor in Moscow and failed, although the poor succeeded in kindnesses

[35] *My Literary Passions*, especially pp. 250, 257, 258.
[36] *Ibid.*, p. 252.
[37] *Ibid.*, 251, 257. See also Howells' introduction to Tolstoy's *Master and Man*, xiv-xv.

to each other; how he discovered an impassable social gulf between the rich and the poor; and how, finally, he resolved to give up the advantages of unearned wealth, which had become horrible to him, and to lead the life of a common laborer.[38] Several of these issues and experiences—the inadequacy of charity, the social cleavage between the rich and the poor, and the concept of leading a life of Christlike simplicity among the laboring classes—entered almost immediately into Howells' fiction in that most Tolstoyan of his novels, *Annie Kilburn;* and while other forces, such as the work of the anti-poverty societies, might possibly have suggested these subjects to him, it is far more reasonable to ascribe Howells' treatment of them to the influence of Tolstoy.[39] However, it is only in the person of the minister, Mr. Peck, in *Annie Kilburn,* that Howells' treats sympathetically the ideal of a life of renunciation lived among the poor. In later writings his attitude toward the same ideal ranges from sympathetic detachment to opposition.

In the characters of Matt Hilary, in *The Quality of Mercy,* and the publisher Chapley, in *The World of Chance,* Howells embodied, much more definitely than in *Annie Kilburn,* the problem of renouncing the middle-class comforts and luxuries in favor of a life of Christlike simplicity. In both cases, and especially the latter, his humorous perception of the probable impact of the idea of Tolstoyan renunciation on a bourgeois American family appears to have got the better of him, with the result that neither treatment discloses his serious and final view. It is in the words of the reformer David Hughes in *The World of Chance*—a character who ordinarily serves as his author's mouthpiece—that Howells definitely breaks with

[38] See Howells' review of *Que Faire,* in the "Editor's Study," *Harper's Magazine,* 75: 316-7 (July, 1887).

[39] Since we know that Howells was sufficiently interested in *Que Faire* to publish a review of it in July of 1887; since we know that he was at work on *Annie Kilburn* in the autumn of that year, and since he mentions Tolstoy's "heart-searching books" in the very letter in which he first mentions the novel (*The Life in Letters,* I: 403-5; a letter of November 18, 1887, to his sister, Mrs. Achille Fréchette) it would appear probable that the themes treated in the book were suggested by Tolstoy.

Tolstoy. Condemning Tolstoy's "utter impracticality," Hughes maintains, "In quitting the scene of the moral struggle, and in simplifying himself into a mere peasant, he begs the question as completely as if he had gone into a monastery." [40] Later, Howells, speaking in his own person, objected with equal force to what he sometimes spoke of as Tolstoy's "eremitism"; "Solitude enfeebles and palsies, and it is as comrades and brothers that men must save the world from itself, rather than themselves from the world." [41]

Evidently Howells was an independent, even a critical disciple; and his independence was shown in other ways than in his reaction against Tolstoy's extreme individualism. The profound gloom of *The Power of Darkness,* for instance, he felt to be only partly applicable to the American scene; America, while far enough from social justice, was yet immeasurably nearer than Russia. Our civilization had not the misdeeds of theirs and need not have their remorse and despair.[42] Miscellaneous *dicta* of Tolstoy's also—on music, for instance, and on marriage—Howells sometimes objected to.[43] Even the literary method of Tolstoy, which at its best Howells designated as perfect, had to his thinking numerous lapses from its highest level, and declined too often to the merely didactic and hortatory, to the production of "pale fables" instead of dramatically conceived illustrations of life.[44]

Tolstoy, in brief, gave to Howells first of all a stimulus which the latter felt to have intensified and enlarged his sense of life. He also suggested to Howells certain problems about charity, social stratification, and the bearing of Christian ethics on modern society, which Howells considered seriously and illustrated in his fiction. He suggested, finally, certain other policies and points of view—retreat from the world, and a profoundly pessimistic view of modern conditions of life—

[40] *The World of Chance,* pp. 90-1.
[41] *My Literary Passions,* 252.
[42] The "Editor's Study," *Harper's Magazine,* 75: 478 (August, 1887).
[43] *Ibid.,* 81: 802 (October, 1890).
[44] For such pronouncements, see the "Editor's Study," *Harper's Magazine,* 76: 642 (March, 1888) and *My Literary Passions,* pp. 256-7.

which Howells, as an independent thinker and an American, found it necessary to modify or oppose.

Of the other foreign influences that are definitely marked in Howells' economic thinking—those of Ruskin, of Morris, and of the Marxian socialists [45]—only the last has any claim, and that a doubtful one, to be included among the forces that awakened his interest in economics. Their effect was rather to contribute some idea or ideas to a current of thought that had already been set in motion. Howells' first genuinely sympathetic references to Ruskin and Morris, for instance, appear in the "Editor's Study" for December, 1888, [46] two and a half years after his review of Tolstoy's *My Religion,* and seventeen months after his review of *Que Faire.* Later, Howells evidently kept in mind Ruskin's economic experiments and his examination of the evils of industrialism, [47] but it was of the work of Morris that he made the larger use. His emphasis on craftsmanship, and on the joy of voluntary, happy work, [48] ideas rare enough in American economic criticism, is owing, apparently, to his sympathetic reading of Morris; and, in conceiving the Utopian country of Altruria, he went with Morris rather than with his friend Bellamy in preferring the simple to the materially abundant life.

Even the influence of Marxian socialism may have contributed less to the initiation than to the growth of Howells' economic philosophy. Marx himself Howells appears never to have read. Such Marxian socialism as he knew he had indirectly, in the modified forms disseminated by Laurence Gronlund and Edward Bellamy; and in Howells' mind it underwent still further modification. Conceivably, Howells had been interested in socialism in 1886 and '7—there are vaguely collectivistic dicta in *The Minister's Charge* and much more

[45] In the separation of Morris from the Marxians in general, it is not implied that Morris differed seriously from Marx in any fundamental ideas, but rather that the non-Marxian elements in his thought are those that chiefly influenced Howells.

[46] *Harper's Magazine,* 78: 159-60.

[47] Observe, for example, the allusions in *A Hazard of New Fortunes,* II: 143, and *Through the Eye of the Needle,* pp. 208, 213.

[48] See the discussion below, pp. 262-3.

definite ones in *Annie Kilburn;* but the first conclusive evidences of his concern with socialism belong to early 1888; and of these the most striking is his favorable discussion, in the "Editor's Study," of Gronlund's *Coöperative Commonwealth.*[49] Howells presents Gronlund's program tactfully but with substantial accuracy, and criticizes it only on the ground of a certain vagueness as to the first practical steps to be taken toward the socialistic goal.

But Howells' assimilation of Marxian socialism was as discriminating as his assimilation of Tolstoy, and in the one case, as in the other, he proved impervious to ideas that could not be made to harmonize with his personality and tradition. On the one hand, he was in complete sympathy with the Marxian assumption that politics and political history are secondary to the primary force, economics. His definition of a plutocracy, for instance, as "not so much ... the rule of the money-making class as ... the political embodiment of the money-making ideal"[50] is one which tallies precisely with the Marxian conception of government as being chiefly an instrument for the expression of economic needs and forces. On the other hand, the Marxian doctrine of class conflict, with its corollaries of the destruction of Howells' own middle class and of political or military revolution, a doctrine which Gronlund proclaimed uncompromisingly,[51] Howells rejected in favor of the hope that the democratic institutions of America might evolve naturally and peacefully into agencies of collectivism. Evidently, pure Marxian socialism held no such dominant place in Howells' economics as was supposed by Parrington. Much modified, critically assimilated, it was at most only one influence among many.[52]

[49] *Harper's Magazine,* 76: 801-5 (April, 1888).

[50] "Are We a Plutocracy?" *The North American Review,* 158: 185-96 (February, 1894).

[51] *The Coöperative Commonwealth,* pp. 73-4, 97, 263.

[52] It is in point to observe here that Howells was in agreement with the Marxian socialist Lawrence Gronlund in opposing the "eremitism" of Tolstoy (see Gronlund's *Coöperative Commonwealth,* p. 107), and also in opposing George's land-tenure program on the ground that to begin the socializing process with land would be inexpedient. (*The*

V

But the agitation of Marxian socialism, the teaching of Ruskin and Morris, and even the influence of Tolstoy, could hardly have touched Howells deeply had not his own, American environment been such as to cause him not only to understand, but to realize emotionally, to the very depth of his being, the importance of the problem those men were attacking. The entire Gilded Age was, as we have seen, a period of numerous and often bitter economic conflicts, and the years that saw the beginning of Howells' acquaintance with Tolstoy saw likewise an intensification of struggles that were already keen. The contest between the pretentious Knights of Labor and the newly formed American Federation of Labor was still before the public mind.[53] Moreover, in 1886, over ten thousand manufacturing and commercial establishments were involved in strikes, and the average number from that year through 1894 was nearly six thousand.[54] In view of the epidemic of strikes in 1886, President Cleveland sent Congress a special message on labor, the first on this subject since the foundation of the government, advocating the establishment of a federal board of arbitration. Although Congress delayed until 1888 and then limited its enactment to railway employees, four states—Kansas, Iowa, Massachusetts, and New York—took action in 1886 and '7.[55] In every case, arbitration was made a voluntary process entirely.

During these years, and for a long time thereafter, Howells followed such public affairs with close and intelligent attention. Struggles such as the C. B. and Q. strike of 1888 and

---

Coöperative Commonwealth, p. 123; *The Life in Letters*, I: 107-8, a letter of January 15, 1888, to Hamlin Garland.)

[53] Frank Tracy Carlton, *The History and Problems of Organized Labor*, pp. 72-82.

[54] See the table in Frank J. Sullivan's chapter, "Twenty Years of Strikes and Lockouts," in *The Making of America*, edited by Robert Marion LaFollette. (Chicago, 1906) VIII: 148-51.

[55] Davis Rich Dewey, *National Problems*, p. 48.

the Homestead Strike of 1892 awakened his concern over the apparent splitting-up of a democratic people into hostile factions: an aristocratic oligarchy of wealth on the one hand, and an underprivileged proletariat, ready to resort to violence, on the other.[56] Moreover, Howells had first-hand experience of at least one sample of the warfare between labor and capital. In 1886, in the very year in which he moved to New York, and just prior to the enactment of the state arbitration law, the city experienced a serious traction strike, which lasted for months and was accompanied by violence; no car was driven without a police guard.[57] This strike and the difficulties of voluntary arbitration both figure in *A Hazard of New Fortunes*[58]—two out of a number of instances in which Howells not only disclosed a knowledge of the contemporary scene, but drew his materials directly from it. Evidently, with the shift of Howells' writing from problems of individual to problems of social ethics, the general stress, the intensification of the conflict between capital and labor had much to do.

The native intellectual *milieu* in which he moved during those years had even more. The middle-class concern over economics, which had been growing since the labor troubles of the seventies, and which had been stimulated by the controversies awakened by George and Hay, reached its climax in 1886 and the years immediately following. In the absence of explicit references on Howells' part, it must remain conjectural how much he knew of the voluminous minor fiction produced by the movement. His wider reading was, apparently, rather in its economic treatises than in its fiction; and such diverse materials as Richard T. Ely's *Social Aspects of Christianity* and *Land, Labor, and Taxation*, William M. Salter's *Ethical Religion*, and even newspaper articles on the

[56] See, in *The Life in Letters*, the following: I: 419, October 28, 1888, to Edward Everett Hale; I: 429, December 29, 1889, to Samuel L. Clemens; II: 26, June 24, 1892, to William Cooper Howells.

[57] Dewey, *op. cit.*, pp. 44-5.

[58] For evidence that Howells had this particular strike in mind, see the preface to the 1909 edition.

condition of house servants, sewing girls, and miners, all went into the synthesis of his economic views.[59] Moreover, with the two main currents of this agitation, those stemming from George and Bellamy, Howells had more than an observer's familiarity.

It was chiefly through Hamlin Garland that Howells was subjected to the pressure of Georgian Single-Tax propaganda. In 1887, Garland was no less a literary disciple of Howells than he was a social disciple of George; and in his ardor for industrial reform he could hardly have avoided trying to convert Howells to his land-tenure program. "How I must have bored that sweet and gracious soul!" Garland wrote, later. "If he moved to Belmont I pursued him. If he went to Nahant or Magnolia or Kittery I spent my money like water in order to follow him up and bother him about my work, or worry him into a public acceptance of the single tax." [60] To be sure, Howells was never able, either in 1887, or later, when he knew George personally,[61] to accept the adoption of the Single Tax as an immediate goal; to his mind, the nationalization of land would probably be, for reasons of expediency, one of the final steps in a program of economic security which could more practically begin with the socializing of natural monopolies.[62] But there can be no question of his interest in the Single-Tax movement, of his sympathy with its ultimate goals, and of the part played by the Single-Tax agitation in focussing his attention on economic reform.

But it was with Bellamy rather than with George, with the collectivist wing of middle-class criticism rather than the individualistic, that Howells came to be chiefly in sympathy. It is possible that he knew *Looking Backward* immediately upon its publication, and it is certain that he was familiar with the

[59] These are referred to in various "Editor's Study" papers in *Harper's Magazine* as follows: 76: 802-3 (April, 1888); 78: 160 (December, 1888); 79: 479 (August, 1889); 80: 484 (February, 1890).

[60] *A Son of the Middle Border* (Modern Readers Series Edition), p. 389.

[61] In regard to his acquaintance with George, see *The Life in Letters*, II: 21, a letter of January 20, 1892, to William Cooper Howells.

[62] *Ibid.*, I: 407-8; a letter of January 15, 1888, to Hamlin Garland.

book before June of 1888, as his review in the Editor's Study appeared at that time.[63] In the review, Howells points out the similarities between *Looking Backward* and Gronlund's *Coöperative Commonwealth,* and deals adequately with the force of Bellamy's strictures on modern civilization. Of the popularity of *Looking Backward* he adds, humorously, "Here is a book which in the sugar-coated form of a dream has exhibited a dose of undiluted socialism, and which has been gulped by some of the most vigilant opponents of that theory without a suspicion of the poison they were taking into their systems"—a comment that was to become equally true of his own *A Traveller from Altruria.*

In the partisan agitation to which the publication of *Looking Backward* gave rise, Howells had no share. In any formal sense, he was never a Nationalist. Yet Edward Bellamy and Edward Bellamy's work affected him deeply. Of the man, whom he came to know personally, he spoke affectionately as one rich in a romantic imagination second only to Hawthorne's, as one who knew, more than anyone else, how to move the American reading public, as one whose imagination had revived throughout Christendom the hope of a millennium.[64] In the opinions which he finally came to hold on economics, and on the relation of economics to human values in general, he was closer to Bellamy than to any other thinker; and years later, when he could look back upon the middle-class agitation of the late eighties as a thing already long overpassed, he designated Bellamy, along with Henry George, as one of the creators of the *milieu* that had shaped his own writings. In speaking of the writing of *A Hazard of New Fortunes,* he explained:

We had passed through a period of strong emotioning in the direction of the humaner economics, if I may phrase it so, the rich seemed not so much to despise the poor, the poor did not so hopelessly repine. The solution of the riddle of the painful

[63] *Harper's Magazine,* 77: 154-5.
[64] See, for Howells' estimate of Bellamy, the article, "Edward Bellamy," *The Atlantic Monthly,* 82: 253-6 (August, 1898).

earth through the dreams of Henry George, through the dreams of Edward Bellamy, through the dreams of all the generous visionaries of the past, seemed not impossibly far off.[65]

These powerful forces that Howells was subjected to—the influence of Tolstoy and Ruskin and Morris, the impact of Marxian socialism, the widespread spectacle of class warfare, the awakening of the middle class to the problems of industrialism, the dreams of George and Bellamy—these forces would, of themselves, no doubt have changed the temper of Howells' work. It so happened, however, that one event, or rather, series of events, dramatized for Howells the whole economic *impasse* and drove it home to his mind with the force and fervor of a religious experience.

It is unnecessary, now, to review the painful story of the Haymarket disorders at Chicago, of the wave of hysteria and the public demand for retribution that ensued, and of the conviction of eight men and the execution of four for a crime they were not shown to have committed. That Howells had been following the anarchist trials with more than ordinary interest is shown by his letter of September 25, 1887, to the anarchists' counsel, Judge Roger A. Pryor. "I am glad," Howells wrote, "you have taken the case of the Chicago anarchists, and that you see some hope for them before the Supreme court, for I have never believed them guilty of murder, or of anything but their opinions, and I do not think they were justly convicted. I have no warrant in writing to you except my very strong feeling in the matter." [66]

Judge Pryor's reply requested Howells to issue a "temperate claim" to the public on behalf of the anarchists—namely, that there was grave doubt whether, in the whirlwind of local passion, they had had a fair trial.[67] Evidently Howells declined the task, being unwilling to challenge public obloquy

[65] Preface to the 1909 edition of *A Hazard of New Fortunes;* quoted in C H A L., III: 82. Original copyright, 1889, by Harper and Brothers. Copyright, 1916, by Mildred Howells and John Mead Howells. Reprinted by permission of Miss Mildred Howells.

[66] *The Life in Letters,* I: 393.

[67] *Ibid.,* I: 394-5.

to no effect.[68] But when the Supreme Court affirmed the legality of the forms of the Chicago trial, Judge Pryor urged Howells to appeal for executive clemency. After first attempting to get Whittier and George William Curtis to undertake the task,[69] Howells himself wrote to the Governor of Illinois, and through *The New York Tribune* appealed to others to take the same course. Addressing this letter to the editor, Howells wrote:

I have petitioned the Governor of Illinois to commute the death-penalty of the Anarchists to imprisonment and have also personally written to him in their behalf; and I now ask your leave to express here the hope that those who are inclined to do either will not lose faith in themselves because the Supreme Court has denied the condemned a writ of error. That court simply affirmed the legality of the forms under which the Chicago court proceeded; it did not affirm the propriety of trying for murder men fairly indictable for conspiracy alone; and it by no means approved the principle of punishing them because of their frantic opinions, for a crime which they were not shown to have committed. . . .

But the worst is still for a very few days reparable; the men sentenced to death are still alive, and their lives may be finally saved through the clemency of the Governor, whose prerogative is now the supreme law in their case. I conjure all those who believe that it would be either injustice or impolicy to put them to death, to join in urging him by petition, by letter, through the press, and from the pulpit and the platform, to use his power, in the only direction where power can never be misused, for the mitigation of their punishment.[70]

There can thus be no doubt that the same Howells who has been so often accused of timidity did for once definitely and courageously challenge public opinion. Accounts of the anar-

---

[68] *Ibid.*, I: 397; a letter of November 1, 1887, from Judge Pryor to Howells.

[69] According to the testimony of Brand Whitlock in *Forty Years of It*, quoted, *ibid.*, I: 399-401.

[70] *The Life in Letters*, I: 398-9. Copyright, 1928, by Doubleday, Doran and Company. Reprinted by permission of Miss Mildred Howells.

chist episode are generally agreed as to the violence of public feeling regarding the condemned men. Furthermore, Howells himself mentioned at least on two occasions the abuse heaped on him by certain journals because of his intervention. "Some of the papers abused me as heartily as if I had proclaimed myself a dynamiter." [71] The depth of the feeling that prompted such a challenge can be gauged by other utterances in Howells' correspondence. His usual mildness forgotten, he denounced the execution as "forever damnable before God and abominable to civilized men," and summed up the matter in the dictum, "The historical perspective is that this free republic has killed five men for their opinions." [72]

By January of 1888, Howells had progressed in his economic thinking far enough to attempt an estimate of his own development. "You will easily believe," he wrote to Hamlin Garland, "that I did not bring myself to the point of openly befriending those men who were civically murdered in Chicago without thinking and feeling much, and my horizons have been infinitely widened by the process." [73]

VI

To examine the concentration of forces that led to the writing of Howells' economic fiction has taken quite a long time. These influences once in mind, however, one may speak, with a much closer approach to exactness, of the nature and purpose of each of Howells' economic novels, of the general economic philosophy which he expressed in them, of the reasons for his abandonment of the economic field, and of the general qualities and values of his work.

The Minister's Charge (1887) is the first novel affected by Howells' shift of interest from individual to social ethics. In

[71] *Ibid.*, I: 413; a letter of April 14, 1888, to Thomas S. Perry; also p. 402, a letter of November 13, 1887, to William Cooper Howells.

[72] *Ibid.*, I: 401-2; a letter of November 11, 1887, to Francis A. Browne; also a letter of November 13 to William Cooper Howells. The five victims mentioned by Howells are the four prisoners who were executed and one who committed suicide.

[73] *Ibid.*, I: 407-8; a letter of January 15, 1888, to Hamlin Garland.

the main plot—that of the minister Sewell and his mistaken kindness to the country boy Lemuel Barker—Howells is still in the realm of individual ethical relationships. In certain lesser episodes, however, he has advanced to general and social considerations. Such are the passages where tho ineffectiveness of charity is ridiculed, and those where the social doctrine of "Complicity"—a precursor of Howells' later collectivism—is discussed.[74] Moreover, in describing Lemuel Barker's experiences in the park and police station and "Wayfarer's Lodge," Howells produced his most extensive picture of the submerged classes; and in the deliciously comical characterizations of 'Manda Grier and Statira Dudley, his only convincing figures from the proletariat.

Annie Kilburn (1889), the first of the definitely economic novels, illustrates, in the setting of a New England mill town, the widening social cleavage between the rich and the poor; the pettiness of a civic leadership furnished by the merely acquisitive wing of the bourgeoisie; and, still more important, the failure of charity to counterbalance the lack of equality and justice. The central character of the story is the minister Peck, who attempts to live the life [75] rather than the doctrine of Christ. Through the minister as a spokesman, Howells voices his own speculation on the socialistic drift of the labor unions and the trusts, on the need for Christian Brotherhood, and on the possible evolution of society toward the achievement of justice.

In *A Hazard of New Fortunes*, Howells illustrates, on a more extensive scale than he attempts anywhere else, the effects of industrialism on the formation and development and expression of character. Portrayed largely in terms of their reaction to industrialism, and especially to a traction strike, are the most diverse personalities: Colonel Woodburn, of "Charlottesburg," Virginia, who argues that the condition of the laborers would be improved by the reëstablishment of a system of "responsible slavery"; Lindau, a radical socialist

[74] *The Minister's Charge*, pp. 29, 240.
[75] *The Life in Letters*, I: 403-5; a letter of November 18, 1887, to Mrs. Achille Frichette.

whose bitter enmity toward capitalism leads him finally to violence and death; Margaret Vance and Conrad Dryfoos, settlement workers moved by a Christian compassion for the poor; Angus Beaton, a temperamental artist who wants the strikers hanged because they inconvenience him; Fulkerson, a "pure advertising essence," a more intelligent and better domesticated Babbitt, who is perhaps the most immensely exuberant character that Howells ever produced; Basil March, a New England gentleman, humorous, poised, philosophical, and finally courageous; above all, the elder Dryfoos, a victim of quick wealth, who declines from the finer ideal of constructive citizenship to the coarser ideal of mere acquisition. Among the passages of dialectic, in the speeches of Basil March, are some of Howells' strongest denunciations of the insecurity wrought by chance and by destructive individualism.

The Quality of Mercy (1892), although it is principally a story of the consequences of crime, belongs among the economic novels chiefly because of its illustration of the close interdependence of all the cogs in the modern social machine. Society itself is made quite as responsible for the crime of embezzlement as the unfortunate teller, Northwick, who commits it; and, as the effects of Northwick's crime react on character after character in an ever-widening circle, society at large comes gradually to suffer the consequences.

In *The World of Chance* (1893), Howells wrote his most thorough consideration of a problem he had discussed in *A Hazard of New Fortunes*—the insecurity of life in the modern industrial state. That problem is illustrated first in the light, even humorous story of Shelley Ray's attempt to bring out his first novel, the moral being that publishing is only a type of all business in that the controlling factor is chance. It is illustrated more seriously in the story of the introduction of the seer David Hughes and his family, fresh from the protection of a socialistic community, to the struggle for life in the hurly-burly of a competitive metropolis. Hughes himself proclaims, more completely and definitely than any other character of Howells, the coming development of the capitalistic state into the coöperative commonwealth described by Gronlund and Bellamy.

A Traveller from Altruria (1894), while nominally a Utopian romance, is in reality a satirical examination, conducted with a wit no less caustic than delicate, of the conditions of life in industrial America. Less illustrative, and more controversial, than any other work of Howells, the book employs the graceful style of the eighteenth-century essay through page after page of brilliant though undramatic dialogue. A group of Americans, provoked into at least a temporary frankness by the presence of Mr. Homos of Altruria, discuss the closing of the frontier and other causes of economic distress, the increasing pressure of inequality and insecurity, the incompetence of business leadership, and the general lack of social planning in an individualistic society. Finally, in a public speech, the Altrurian traveller describes the social felicity of his country, where, under the influence of the Christian ideal of brotherhood, the coöperative commonwealth has been realized.

Through the Eye of the Needle (1907) is a sequel to *A Traveller from Altruria,* much of which, notwithstanding the lateness of its publication, appears to have been written at about the same time as the earlier work. In the first portion of the book, in connection with the love story of the Altrurian and Eveleth Strange, Howells illustrates again the futility of mere acquisition and satirizes still further the barrenness of a life conducted by merely commercial standards of value. In the latter portion, he shifts the scene to Altruria, where, as he portrays it, the hideous industrial metropolises of the capitalistic era have given way to airy cities and a park-like countryside; where a happy, intelligent people live by means of a moderate day labor, equally shared, in a state of pleasant equality; and where the eventlessness of a perfected life is compensated by the riches of natural gaiety and of art.[76]

[76] Besides the novels and Utopias just described, other expressions of the economic and social ideas of Howells are to be found in the articles listed in the bibliography (below, pp. 362-3) and in occasional comments in novels that are mainly non-economic.

VII

In these seven works, from *The Minister's Charge* through the two Utopias, the intellectual core is a system of economic thought at once more complex, more systematic, and better integrated than that of any of Howells' fellow-novelists except Bellamy. The system is, indeed, strikingly like Bellamy's in that the author's basic political assumptions are democratic, and that Howells, like Bellamy, would have democracy, through collective action, insure an economic state in which the individual life might come most fully to flower. In the examination of Howells' economic thought, it will be necessary to consider (1) his premises and controlling ideas; (2) his destructive criticism, or, more exactly, his indictment of capitalistic industrialism; and (3) his reconstructive criticism, with reference both to his immediate program and to his concept of an ultimate Utopia.

Underlying the entire social philosophy of Howells there must have been always (though he himself rather assumed these things than formulated them explicitly) certain methods of thought, and certain ideas, which had survived from the era of the Enlightenment. Notwithstanding his Quaker and Swedenborgian upbringing, and his occasional indulgence of a mystical strain in his own mature work, he thought habitually after the fashion of a typical intellectual of the Age of Reason. A belated rationalist, like his friend Mark Twain, he sought to lay out the patterns of life by a kind of heightened common sense; and it was by this method of reasoning, primarily, that he wrought out his philosophy of economics.

The possibility that a rational method might be a dangerously erroneous one—the possibility that man might be largely an irrational or subrational being—appears never to have entered Howells' mind. And, correspondingly, the idea of searching for a sound economics by any scientific process—by a study of the basic needs and emotional drives of human nature as these are revealed by economic science itself, by psychology, and by anthropology; and by an adjustment of the economic framework to the scientifically determined needs of humanity—this, too, is as foreign to Howells' thought as to that of most of his contemporaries. On the contrary, his unvarying assumption is that man is a rational being, and that human nature will be satisfied with a rationally devised, even though *a priori,* system of economics. Like Fourier, like Bellamy, though in a subtler way than either, he thus became the architect of an ideal economics the very perfection of which is, conceivably, its principal shortcoming.

Underlying Howells' social philosophy there must have been also, along with his rational method of thought, something of the old deistic concept of the universe as a scheme of benevolent order, whose norm of perfect harmoniousness is slowly to be approximated by human society. Correspondingly, human nature appeared to Howells, if actually confused and corrupt, as potentially rational and good and fine. His view of mankind is such as Condorcet and Godwin might have held, if, in addition to the ideas current in their own age, they could have become aware of Victorian humanism and Victorian thought on evolution. To such a thinker, the best goal of human effort might seem to be the realization of a scheme of order as beautifully complete and systematic as that of the Newtonian cosmos—the realization, in short, of the "ideal world" of which Howells speaks in his criticism of Dickens.[77] Yet Howells never assumes, with the naturalist, that the fundamental "order" of human life is the same as that of nonhuman nature. The humane order he conceives of, potential rather than actual, is one that cannot be created by nature but only by the conscious exercise of the will and the reason of man, who "in the midst of nature is above it."[78] Hence, in a manner and to a degree that has become increasingly difficult in our own century, he assumes that the natural tendency of mankind is toward a condition of entire orderliness, toward a state in which all the individual and all

[77] *My Literary Passions,* 98.
[78] "Who Are Our Brethren?" *The Century,* n. s., 29: 932-6 (April 1896).

the social forces that make for complete living shall be perfectly integrated.

Like more than one thinker of the Enlightenment, therefore, Howells felt that human nature is essentially good, and that its manifest evils arise out of environment instead of heredity, out of unfavorable circumstances rather than out of fundamental character; and that through the creation of more favorable circumstances the race might advance, in a kind of evolutionary progress, toward the realization of its finest possibilities. Already, and amid hostile circumstances, man had developed much that was good. The Russian peasant, under conditions that might well have degraded him entirely, remained a man. The American businessman, under conditions where survival itself depended on ruthless selfishness, was often capable of a fine courtesy and altruism.[79] Actual goodness, developed under conditions so adverse, was proof of far greater potential goodness:

I am a great friend of human nature, and I like it all the better because it has had to suffer so much unjust reproach. It seems to me that we are always mistaking our conditions for our natures, and saying that human nature is greedy and mean and false and cruel, when only its conditions are so. . . . It has always been better than its conditions, and ready for new and fitter conditions.[80]

Once the conditions of life are so adjusted as to allow mankind a natural and gradual development, the evils and distortions of the racial character will gradually be outgrown, and by a levelling-up of the lower classes, the ideal equality of the perfect state will be realized. In comparison with this ideal equality,

[79] *Through the Eye of the Needle,* pp. 3, 24, 96.
[80] "Equality as the Basis of Good Society," *The Century Magazine,* n. s., 29: 63-7 (November, 1895). See also, for other expressions of Howells' faith in human nature, *A Hazard of New Fortunes,* II: 36; *The World of Chance,* p. 220. See, on the force of environment in moulding character, *The Quality of Mercy,* p. 474. In these three instances, as frequently elsewhere, the characters March, Hughes, and Putney express the opinions of Howells himself.

none other is worth having. There must be no rudeness, no unkindness; that must be left to the savage world which will still admire force, violence, the expressions of inequality. The level, when we reach it, will be the highest yet attained by the exceptional few. The purest ideals of the philosophers and the saints are not too fine to be realized in the civility which shall be the life of the whole people.[81]

As to the important question of what conditions are most favorable to this growth toward perfection, Howells' answer is simple:—economic liberty, equality, fraternity; and, above all, economic security; four conditions which may for convenience be thought of separately, but which in actual practice (as Howells felt) blend inseparably together. In his youth he had been, as a Western democrat, much concerned with personal and political liberty and equality. Now, in his fifties, he had come, by a course of thought which he felt an inevitable one for those who profoundly sympathize with the people, to an extension of his political philosophy into the field of economics.[82] Political liberty, political equality, he felt, valuable as they are in themselves, may be reduced to mere shells in the absence of economic liberty and economic equality. The hireling, though guaranteed the right of suffrage by the constitution itself, cannot manfully use that right if his employer can take away his means of livelihood for doing so. Liberty, therefore, is only for those who have the means of livelihood; and economic equality is the mother of all the rest of the equalities.[83]

Hence, in his concern for liberty, Howells reveals little if any of Mill's interest in the restraint of government from any

[81] "Equality as the Basis of Good Society." *The Century*, n. s., 29: 66-7 (November, 1895)

[82] See, for indications of Howells' awareness of the relation of political and economic democracy, the "Editor's Study," *Harper's Magazine*, 78: 491 ff. (February, 1889), in regard to Bjornson; also *The Life in Letters*, I: 429; a letter of December 29, 1889, to Samuel L. Clemens.

[83] "The Nature of Liberty," *The Forum*, 20: 401-9, especially 405, 407, 409 (December, 1895); also "Equality as the Basis of Good Society," *The Century*, n. s., 29: 63-7 (November, 1895).

tyrannous interference in the life of the individual. Such liberty he felt to be assured by democratic forms of government. All things considered, political liberty, political equality are only means, not ends in themselves; [84] are in effect only stepping stones to the farther goal of economic security. Indeed, for the securing of this greater goal, mankind might surrender much in the way of individual privilege; the first use of a smaller liberty might be to renounce it in favor of a larger; [85] the first use of individual rights might be to subordinate them in some collective action by which the state might confer upon every citizen the fundamental liberty insured by a safe and adequate livelihood. By so doing, men might create a polity the outcome of which would be no temporizing "greatest good to the greatest number," but, rather, nothing less than the "greatest good to the whole number." [86] Through the collective action of democratic people, under the forms and by the methods of popular government, are to be created the security and therefore the economic freedom in which the completest development of the individual may be achieved.

VIII

It is from this vantage-point of collectivism, and in the light of his view of the function of the ideal state, that Howells examines the economics of capitalistic industrialism, and points out those evils that operate to dwarf and distort man's natural goodness and to bar his path toward perfection. And yet the purely economic part of his examination is the least; he has no flair at all for the formal, rigorous theorizing of George, and very little of that informed and penetrating analysis of purely economic forces that is so characteristic of Bellamy. While he does not wholly neglect these matters, his larger gift is the translation of economics into more immedi-

[84] *A Traveller from Altruria*, p. 55.
[85] "The Nature of Liberty," *The Forum*, 20: 401-9, especially 403-5 (December, 1895).
[86] *Ibid.*, p. 404.

ately dramatic and human terms. From the sphere of pure economics his criticism broadens to include, in increasing complexity, the political, social, and ethical consequences of economics, and, finally, the bearing of economics on the entire question of humane value.

Of the causes for the increasing economic pressure in America, Howells speaks with keen discernment though not at great length. Although he mentions speculation as a cause of economic ills,[87] he is more concerned with other factors such as the exhaustion of the public domain and the drive of technology. To an understanding of the effect of land speculation and the mortgage system on the Western farmer, Howells adds a perception of the increased pressure of industrial forces, of the narrowing of the scope of individual choice, that had come to the United States with the shutting of the safety valve of free land.[88] More dramatically, however, and more originally, he shows the pressure exerted upon the laboring man by another force—technological unemployment. Adopting a device of proved usefulness—that of dramatizing the impression made by some evil upon a fresh and uncalloused observer—he brings two characters, his Altrurian traveller and the lithographer Denton in *The World of Chance*, into contact with the plight of men thrown out of work by machinery. The former is horrified to find that no agency whatever, either the employer or the state, is obligated to care for the victims of invention;[89] the latter, obsessed with the idea of the suffering that will be caused by an invention of his own, goes insane.[90] And finally, more important than either the closed frontier or technological unemployment, is the destructive effect of an uncontrolled and often savage individualism—a concept which it will be necessary to speak of later, and from another viewpoint.

As a result of these causes, the American laborer has, in Howells' opinion, already lost his once fortunate position, and

[87] *The Quality of Mercy*, p. 362.
[88] *A Traveller from Altruria*, pp. 140-3, 212.
[89] *Ibid.*, p. 196.
[90] *The World of Chance*, pp. 194, 244, *et al.*

will, in time, sink to the economic level of the European peasant or proletarian.[91] And yet, clearly as Howells presents this tendency, he is not *principally* concerned with the status of labor, still less with the status of the submerged tenth, or with the lurid tragedies occasionally engendered by poverty. He is aware, to be sure, of the slum, and of the evils that flourish in the competitive metropolis, and of the destruction of all human dignity and value that goes on in the lowest levels of society; but what impresses him more is the blunting of perception which is engendered by only a little experience of poverty, and the passiveness of the poor in New York under conditions which would soon make anarchists of the best people in the city.[92] Ordinarily, however, when he turns from the causes to the conditions of American industrial life, his criticism is aimed less at the suffering of the poor than at their exclusion from the logical privileges of democratic citizenship—leisure and personal independence. In a country where chattel slavery has been abolished, the anomaly of industrial slavery persists; the restraints of poverty, and the power of the employer over the employee's means of livelihood, restrict men's freedom of action only less than the power of master over slave, and are all but equally out of place in a nation theoretically devoted to liberty, equality, and fraternity.[93] And if, in the middle and upper classes, the pressures of want and of industrial slavery are less immediately felt, even here men are constantly menaced and restricted by the danger of insecurity. Business is, in both a light and a serious sense of the word, a "perfect lottery"; the industrial world is, even for the prosperous middle class, essentially a World of Chance, where values that might thrive in a securer social climate are stunted and starved. In the words of one of Howells' chief spokesmen, Basil March,

[91] *A Traveller from Altruria*, pp. 56-7.

[92] See the descriptions and comments in *A Hazard of New Fortunes*, I: 79-88; also "An East Side Ramble" in *Impressions and Experiences*, pp. 130-45; also *A Traveller from Altruria*, p. 176.

[93] *A Traveller from Altruria*, pp. 41-2; 52, 88, 173-8; *Through the Eye of the Needle*, p. 144.

What I object to is this economic chance-world in which we live, and which we men seem to have created. It ought to be law as inflexible in human affairs as the order of day and night in the physical world, that if a man will work he shall both rest and eat, and shall not be harassed with any question as to how his repose and his provision shall come. Nothing less ideal than this satisfies the reason. But in our state of affairs no one is sure of this. No one is sure of finding work; no one is sure of not losing it. I may have my work taken away from me at any moment by the caprice, the mood, the indigestion of a man who has not the qualification for knowing whether I do it well or ill.[94]

In this modern world of insecurity, the social ideals of the older, agrarian, democratic America are, Howells suggests, already seriously endangered, and are threatened with total destruction. Increasingly, political and social equality are being nullified, not by any original evil in human nature, but by a social system that has not dealt effectively with the basic fact of economic inequality.[95] Of all the phenomena of our economic life, it is the social inequality that is the outcome of economic inequality—it is, in other words, the widening cleavage between the rich and the poor—that Howells dramatizes in the most varied and striking situations. The story of the country-born Lemuel Barker in bourgeois and proletarian Boston, the story of the abortive effort of Mrs. Munger to compel a social union of the middle-class folk and proletarians;[96] the brilliant portrayal, in *The Landlord at Lion's Head* and *The Vacation of the Kelwyns,* of the impact of inequality upon the older equalitarian folkways—all these, and other passages as well, are the outgrowth of Howells' love of the older democratic equalities and his interest in preserving them even in the midst of a hostile industrialism.

[94] *A Hazard of New Fortunes,* II, 358-9. Copyright 1889, by Harper and Brothers; 1916, by Mildred Howells and John Mead Howells. Reprinted by permission of Miss Mildred Howells.

[95] In regard to Howells' view that the social system, not human nature, is responsible for inequalities, observe the assumptions underlying the passage on poverty in *Impressions and Experiences,* p. 275.

[96] See, respectively, *The Minister's Charge,* especially pp. 228 ff., and *Annie Kilburn,* especially pp. 190-6.

Notwithstanding Howells' sympathy with the underdog, his portrayal of inequality is mainly occupied with its effect on the more prosperous classes, a thing to be expected, no doubt, in a novelist of his background and environment. To the heart-burnings of the proletarian, if any, he accords scant notice. His concern is rather with the ferment of liberal and humanitarian ideas among the bourgeoisie, with the willingness of certain of the bourgeoisie to dodge the fundamental issue by adopting some palliative such as charity, with the moral deterioration he observes in their callousness toward the sufferings and the wounded pride of others.[97] Again and again, in dealing with issues such as these, he illustrates and dramatizes the observation of his Altrurian traveller: "Am I right in supposing that the effect of your economy is to establish insuperable inequalities among you, and to forbid the hope of the brotherhood which your polity proclaims?"[98]

Along with the decline of democratic equality has come a different, though kindred, social change which Howells regards as equally undesirable—the transfer of social leadership from the professional to the commercial class. For her older personal ideal of the statesman, or the lawyer, or the writer, industrial America has substituted that of the millionaire; the contemporary professional man or scholar is likely to be merely a satellite or agent of the commercial system.[99] And along with the rise of the new plutocratic nobility, a leadership of which it is difficult to be proud, has come a decline of that social and intellectual life which had flourished in the older-type American community.

For his condemnation of inequality, Howells had, moreover, reasons profounder, if not weightier, than that of his adherence to the democratic ideal. To him, inequality is, after all, only the natural product of competitive individualism; in other words, of the biological struggle for survival

[97] For examples, see *Annie Kilburn*, p. 164; *Through the Eye of the Needle*, pp. 48, 81.

[98] *A Traveller from Altruria*, p. 98.

[99] *Ibid.*, p. 209. Observe also Howells' general portrayal of the professor, the writer, and the minister in this book.

translated into the midst of the immense powers and complexities of industrialism. As such, it is necessarily objectionable to one whose ethical principles are humane, not naturalistic. It is in this light—that of the humanist's reluctance to admit the struggle for survival as a final law of life—that he condemns the life of the industrial metropolis as a "squalid struggle," [100] as a "fierce struggle for survival, with the stronger life persisting over the deformity, the mutilation, the decay of the weaker," as a thing "lawless, godless," and without "intelligent, comprehensive purpose." [101] It is in the same light that he refers to a strike as a "private war," [102] and that he presents, as the strongest possible condemnation of the competitive system, his character Dryfoos's admission that a capital-labor war is a matter of "dog eat dog, anyway." [103] To human beings, at least, mere survival is only a means, not an end; the end is the creation of personality, the creation of value; and the qualities developed by the environment of uncontrolled business struggle are seldom such as to achieve this goal. Instead, the conditions of competitive life are more likely to engender dishonesty, suspicion, callousness, selfishness, discord, [104] and actually to penalize the far different actions and motives that contribute most to human worth. "In conditions which oblige every man to look out for himself, a man cannot be a Christian without remorse; he cannot do a generous action without self-reproach; he cannot be nobly unselfish without the fear of being a fool." [105] The conduct of industrialism as a struggle for survival is, in short, destructive to man's best values and therefore basically wrong. [106]

[100] *Through the Eye of the Needle,* p. 11.

[101] *A Hazard of New Fortunes,* I, 244.

[102] *Ibid.,* II: 212-3.

[103] *A Hazard of New Fortunes,* II, 266. See, for similar opinions, *A Traveller from Altruria,* pp. 76-7, 205, and *Impressions and Experiences,* pp. 259-65.

[104] *A Hazard of New Fortunes,* II:3; also *The Quality of Mercy,* pp. 86, 157-8; also *The World of Chance,* p. 297.

[105] *Through the Eye of the Needle,* p. 4.

[106] No doubt it was some such line of reasoning as this that led Howells to reject the common ideal of "rising in life." Such an ideal ap-

What then of the people whom the struggle for survival has brought to the crest of American society—the prosperous upper bourgeoisie and plutocracy? In the understanding of Howells, the question of his attitude toward these people is of importance, for the reason that he is so often thought of as a timid conformist who, in Mr. Hartley Grattan's words, judges "all problems, trivial and profound, in terms of the Boston *mores*." [107] But to believe this of Howells is to lapse once more into the old fallacy of identifying an author with his materials. Howells does indeed treat of the Boston *mores;* but, far from judging all things by them, he continually judges them, and the bourgeois way of life they vaguely express, in terms of his own larger standards of humane value, and he continually reveals their shortcomings through the medium of intelligent ridicule.

Specious optimism, an absurd fear of any "paternalistic" policies of government, the acceptance of material luxury as a final value, the setting-up of work as a fetish—ideas and qualities, all of them, which are constantly associated with the bourgeoisie—are all attacked and exposed in Howells' pages, in a satire that ranges from delicate raillery to virtual castigation. [108] The general dullness of bourgeois life, as it appeared to Howells, is attacked in sarcastic comments about "the vast, prosperous commercial class, with unlimited money, and no ideals that money could not realize," and about "the culture that furnishes, showily, that decorates, and that tells." [109] Confidence in business leadership, a main pillar of bourgeois ideology, is treated as a kind of national myth. Business men, the hierarchy of the faith, "are supposed to have

peared to him as only the glorification, under a veneer of civilized usage, of the savagery of the struggle for survival. For a representative treatment of this subject, see *A Traveller from Altruria*, p. 64.

[107] Hartley Grattan, "Howells: Ten Years After," *The American Mercury*, 20: 44 (May, 1930).

[108] For examples of Howells' gentler manner in satire, see *A Traveller from Altruria*, pp. 26-8, 41, 106; for his severer style, see *Impressions and Experiences*, pp. 273-4, and *Through the Eye of the Needle*, pp. 57-8.

[109] *A Hazard of New Fortunes*, II: 70.

long heads; but it appears that ninety-five times in a hundred they haven't. They are supposed to be very reliable; but it is invariably a business man, of some sort, who gets out to Canada while the state examiner is balancing his books, and it is usually the longest-headed business men who get plundered by him." [110]

The characters produced among the commercial bourgeoisie, especially as they are dominated by the fetishes of respectability, social advancement, and Success, are likewise the objects of Howells' satire. From this general area of experience he drew, indeed, materials for a number of his most successful, his most delicately individualized portraits. Among the men, there is that genial, dapper young Philistine, the publisher Brandreth, who feels it necessary to defend his senior partner's vote for George in '86 on the ground that "a good many of the nicest people went the same way at that time." [111] Or there is the small-bore owner of a small-town mercantile establishment, Gerrish, a self-made Success who feels himself quite as capable of settling the labor problem as Lincoln was of settling the problem of slavery—"You've got to put your foot down, as Mr. Lincoln said; and as I say, you've got to keep it down." [112] Or there is that good-humored bounder, Jeff Durgin, whose achievement of worldly success does not release him from the fundamental failure of being himself. [113] Or there is the wealthy banker and embezzler Northwick, too ignorant to converse with the priest Pére Etienne and the Canadian villagers, a "figment of commercial civilization" in whom a grave repose of manner masks "a complete ignorance of the things that interest cultivated people." [114] And, alongside the portrayal of such men as these, should be placed Howells' merciless etchings of a certain type of bourgeois woman, the spoiled, parasitical, shallow-pated,

[110] *A Traveller from Altruria*, p. 215.
[111] *The World of Chance*, p. 140. For other amusing strokes in the portrait of Brandreth, see pp. 138, 260-2, 278.
[112] *Annie Kilburn*, p. 83. See also pp. 79, 85-7, 98, 220 ff.
[113] *The Landlord at Lion's Head*, entire. See also the apt comment of Delmar Gross Cooke in *William Dean Howells: a Critical Study*, p. 251.
[114] *The Quality of Mercy*, pp. 253 ff.

scheming "leader" such as Mrs. Munger in *Annie Kilburn* or Mrs. Makely in *A Traveller from Altruria.* It is of the latter that Howells, abandoning for once his satirical poise, says directly, "As a cultivated American woman, she was necessarily quite ignorant of her own country, geographically, politically, and historically." [115]—In brief, and when the entire range of Howells' satirical portraits is considered, it is hard to avoid the conclusion that, of all our novelists prior to Robert Herrick, he most extensively and intelligently illustrated the limitations of the ideal of individual worldly success, and the frequent failure of the commercial bourgeoisie to produce truly fine personalities.

At times, indeed, Howells goes farther even than this; he illustrates not merely how the acquisitive ideal may fail to produce character, but also how it may become an active agent in the deterioration of character and in the destruction of values. Where great wealth enters the door, he implies, contentment flies out the window. In *Through the Eye of the Needle,* great wealth is treated as a positive burden and source of suffering, which the possessors, once assured security, are overjoyed to be rid of. [116] More realistically, in one of his most closely-knit sequences of ethical cause and consequence, he traces, in *A Hazard of New Fortunes,* the disintegrating effects of suddenly gained riches. The elder Dryfoos, formerly a substantial farmer and conservative good citizen, has become a millionaire through the discovery of natural gas on his farm. After suffering intensely from idleness for a while after his removal to New York, he plunges successfully into speculation. But what he gains in money, he loses in satisfactions; he narrows; in all except the art of money-making, he weakens, and, except in this one sphere, he is unable to cope with life; his son is killed in a labor riot; and his wife and daughters, now *deracinés,* fail to gain a stance in New York society. His money has, as he confesses, bought

[115] *A Traveller from Altruria,* p. 135.

[116] *Through the Eye of the Needle,* 93-6; 203. With these views compare those which Howells had expressed much earlier, in a letter of December 18, 1875, to John Hay; *The Life in Letters,* I: 214.

little but trouble. And when, at the close of the story, Howells shows Dryfoos and his wife and daughters looking forward to the escape of a trip to Europe, the author leaves us
convinced that nothing will bring them any escape from
themselves or from the general futility of their lives.[117] Here,
surely, Howells touches for once the level of genuine tragedy,
the more so, even, because of his deliberate substitution, in
the place of the tragedy of violence, of the deeper tragedy
that comes from the loss of essential human disciplines and
from the slow deterioration of character.

Howells' destructive criticism of industrialism is, in short,
the most thoroughgoing by far that appeared in our literature
before 1900, ranging as it does from the treatment of undiluted economics to the most extensive evaluation of the
effects of the industrial way of life on everyday living and the
creation of values. His conclusions, insofar as they concern
competitive capitalism merely as a system, are hostile indeed.
He never forgets, however, his premise that men themselves
are better than their conditions. Man's natural goodness, in
despite of a savage competitive system that stunts and thwarts
it, continually ameliorates life with touches of unselfishness,
of fine discrimination, of the knowledge of beauty and of
grace; and it is to this natural goodness that men may look
with confidence for the gradual elimination of suffering and
the gradual shaping of the race toward perfection.

IX

The social ideal of Howells, it is well to remind ourselves at
this point, remained essentially a middle-class ideal. It looked
toward the development of some such society as existed
among the Cambridge *literati*, a society of people who, possessed of moderate means and comforts but of no great wealth,
should be "refined, humane, appreciative, sympathetic." Accordingly, Howells' positive economic program—his recon-

[117] *A Hazard of New Fortunes.* For the crucial points in Howells'
exposition of the character of Dryfoos, see I: 110 ff., 202 ff., 294-310;
II: 12-7, 121-30, 225-7, 265 ff.

structic criticism, as it might be called, is concerned, first, with the question, "By what economic conditions is this kind of civilized democracy to be produced?" and, second, with the more immediately practical question, "By what changes are the ideal economics of the future to be realized out of the injustices of the present?" What is Howells' economic goal, and what the means by which that goal is to be attained?

In speaking of the former question, we shall be unusually liable to error, or at least to the limitations of only a partial view of the truth. For, unlike his examination of the present, Howells' view of the economics of the future is available to us chiefly in romantic terms, in his picture of the felicity of the Utopian commonwealth of Altruria; and this picture has the vagueness of outline, the remoteness in beauty, and, in short, the unreal, visionary quality which Howells himself felt to be characteristic of all Utopias.[118] As a consequence, we shall hardly know to what degree Howells felt his world of art to be translatable into the world of actual life, or just how much or just what portions of Altruria he expected to see realized in the United States.

But that the ideal commonwealth of Altruria was intended to have *some* bearing on the future of America, we may not doubt. The felicity of the Altrurians was not, to Howells' thinking, a dream or a gift of chance, but an outcome of intelligently controlled social evolution, the earlier stages of which correspond precisely to those in the history of the modern industrial democracies. Like the Euro-American peoples, the Altrurians had their Dark Ages, their Feudal period, their democracy, and presently the development of their Accumulation, or money-power, before entering the more advanced stage of a coöperative commonwealth;[119] and Howells himself takes pains to point out the parallel between this development and that of America. Evidently, therefore, Howells meant the economy of Altruria to serve (with such changes as are necessary in the translation of art into life) as a goal for American progress. Only here, as in his critically hostile

[118] *Through the Eye of the Needle,* Introduction, p. xiii.
[119] *A Traveller from Altruria,* pp. 255-64.

treatment of American industrialism, economics is with Howells merely a starting point. His thought involves also, and in increasing complexity, the relation of economics to men's general conditions of living—physical, social, political, and ethical—and, finally, to the entire question of their prevailing standards of value.

The economy of the Altrurians can be more briefly described for the reason that it tends everywhere to simplification.[120] The Altrurians use no money, but share equally in an adequate supply of goods. Chance is thus eliminated, and complete economic security is made possible. Because the wants of the people are moderate, and their life a simple one, their hours of labor are relatively short. More discriminating than the Americans in their use of machines, they have retained the machine process only partly, in uses where it is obviously superior to the handicrafts, and does not spoil the pleasures of individual creation. For instance, all transportation is done by means of electricity, the Altrurian capitals being linked by electrical expresses that run at a hundred and fifty miles per hour. But most of the "labor-saving" devices of the capitalistic era, the Altrurians have disused, because the doing of work, together with the achieving of the creative values to be found in work, is one of their ideals; and their pleasure in work is the larger for the reason that, released from the pressures of the competitive system, they are able to do honest work instead of dishonest, and to make, unhurriedly, beautiful things instead of ugly things.[121]

But, in speaking of the pleasure of the Altrurians in their work, we have already passed from the consideration of their economics to that of their general conditions of living. Of these, the one which most impresses Howells' American visitor to Altruria, Eveleth Strange, is the entire freedom from the crowding, the noise, the unwholesome struggles and con

[120] *Through the Eye of the Needle,* pp. 157-8.
[121] See, in regard to most of these matters, *A Traveller from Altruria,* pp. 275-7, 284-7, 293. As to Howells' interest in craftsmanship, see also *Impressions and Experiences,* p. 34, and some of the speeches given to Matt Hilary in *The Quality of Mercy,* especially p. 80.

tentions of the American competitive metropolis. Large cities do, indeed, exist, but the policy of the Altrurians is to make them smaller; in fact, the Altrurians are as gratified when a city shrinks as are the Americans when one grows oversize. Village life is, instead, preferred among them, as rural life is preferred in England; and, in both city and village, families are kept comparatively small, with the result that there is no undue pressure of population on the means of subsistence.[122] Consequently, the Altrurians, both men and women, are possessed of unusual beauty and strength, and of the gaiety that comes of good health and buoyant spirits.[123] They live, of course, in a condition of perfect social equality. Because they have abolished want, they have no professional criminal class, and, indeed, little crime of any sort whatever.[124]

The economic system of the Altrurians is a natural outcome of their ethics, and, indeed, of their general scheme of values. Their ethics, unlike those of the capitalistic era, are the ethics of humanism and not of naturalism. As the scientist may control for human good the operation of other natural laws, so the Altrurians control that of the struggle for survival. Their main principle of ethics is that of Christian altruism; in passing from a competitive to a socialistic system, they passed from "a civility in which the people lived *upon* each other to one in which they lived *for* each other." Their communism therefore resembles that advocated by the Marxian socialists far less than that practiced by the early Christians. Indeed, Howells might have had the Altrurian say of his countrymen's economics what he says of their attitude toward war: "In this, as in all other things, we believe ourselves the true followers of Christ, whose doctrine we seek to make our life, as He made it His." [125] And as counterpoise to the benefits of Christian communism, the Altrurians insist upon an entire fulfillment of its obligations; in return for security, they de-

[122] *Through the Eye of the Needle,* pp. 160, 179-80.

[123] *Ibid.,* 134.

[124] *A Traveller from Altruria,* 305-6; *Through the Eye of the Needle,* 179-80.

[125] See, in regard to the discussion in this paragraph, *A Traveller from Altruria,* 160-1, 272, 299-300.

mand honest labor, and with all their kindness they are quite capable of enforcing discipline by applying St. Paul's rule that the man who will not work shall not eat.[126] In this secure, kindly, workaday world the Altrurians live eventlessly and happily, in the enjoyment of homely labor conducted close to a beloved earth; of innocent friendship and domestic love; of those spontaneous amusements in which a large proportion of the people can take part, moved by a natural spirit of gaiety; and of the amenities of a set of manners like those of the artist—"free, friendly, easy, with a dash of humor in everything, and a wonderful willingness to laugh and make laugh." To the Altrurians, indeed, the ideal human type is the artist; that is, someone "who works gladly, and plays as gladly as he works." [127]

In the absence of any statement from Howells himself, we can hardly know with just what degree of seriousness to take this Utopian picture of an idyllic, refined rusticity. If it be taken as prophecy, as Howells' serious effort to render the shape of things to come, there is surely an anticlimax in his having the struggles of the ages eventuate into this innocent, childlike, beautiful, and unexciting world, where the pleasantness of entire security affords such small recompense for the loss of the sense of human greatness. But the imagining of Altruria, it is well to keep in mind, was of a different sort from the imagining of, say, the New York of *A Hazard of New Fortunes*. It is the imagining of romance rather than of reality; and such economic principles as operate in Altruria, operate in a *milieu* as highly selective, as intensely idealized, as that of the romances of Hawthorne. Returning from Howells' tenuous, shimmering landscape of Utopia to his dicta on an actual, practical social program for the here and now, is like stepping from some fairylike cloud-palace back into the welcome shock and strain of reality.

For Howells did possess, and did voice in his economic works, a definite, tangible program for the reform of capitalistic industrialism—a program which involved a definite

[126] *Through the Eye of the Needle*, p. 151.
[127] *Ibid.*, 141, 161-2, 172.

rejection of certain methods of reform and a definite advo-cacy of others. Believing as he did that a thoroughgoing revision of the whole economic system was necessary, he could have only a limited sympathy with those limited re-forms which in doctoring the symptoms of economic disease left the fundamental malady untouched. For example, he dismisses with only the briefest reflection the creation of so-cialistic communities such as those at New Harmony and Brook Farm, on the grounds that this type of community has everywhere signally failed, that a community is, after all, only an aggrandized individual, and that any attempt to realize the altruistic man in the midst of conditions that remain essentially individualistic and competitive must fail of necessity.[128] The single-tax proposal of Henry George, al-though he considers it more seriously, he rejects on the grounds of the injustice of confiscation, and the inexpediency of beginning economic reform with a policy which would alienate from the reform movement the sympathies of the entire land-owning class.[129] But more important to him than either the socialistic community or the single tax—and far more extensively illustrated in his fiction—is the Tolstoyan problem of charity, and of the effects of charity on the giver, the receiver, and the entire system of society.

In extensive portions of *The Minister's Charge* and *Annie Kilburn*, Howells illustrates and satirizes the shortcomings of charitable enterprise. In the former novel occurs the satirical story of the eccentric maiden lady Sybil Vane and her flower mission among the "deserving poor." In the words of Miss Vane's niece, "Hundreds of bouquets are distributed every day. They prevent crime." The moral is summed up, appar-ently, in the aphorism of the minister Sewell, "We ought to

[128] *New Leaf Mills,* p. 154; *The World of Chance,* p. 121. In referring to Howells' novels for evidence regarding his personal views, the author is, as hitherto, using only those occasional passages in which he speaks to the reader directly and in his own person, and the speeches of those characters whose views can be shown to correspond with those of Howells himself.

[129] *The Life in Letters,* I: 407-8; a letter of January 15, 1888, to Hamlin Garland.

think twice before doing a good action." [130] In the latter novel occurs the equally satirical story of Mrs. Munger and her "social union," a project begun ostensibly to help the poor, but employed presently as a mere social plaything and as a cloak for the exercise of petty jeolousies and a petty love of display.[131] In the more serious and more sympathetically told story of Annie Kilburn herself, Howells illustrates the enormous difficulty of doing good rather than harm to the recipients of charity, and the futility which is the probable outcome of charitable deeds.[132] In the unreformed industrial society, charity is, as another of Howells' characters puts it, about as effective as the use of a blotter to soak up the drops of a rainstorm.[133] For the moment, however, and until the essential evils of industrialism are reformed, charity is the only available alleviation for much suffering, and, as such, it is to be used for whatever limited value it possesses. The real and constant aim of economic reform must be justice; but, in the meantime, "charity is far better than nothing; and it would be abominable not to do all we can because we cannot at once do everything. Let us have the expedients, the ameliorations, the compromises, even, *en attendant* the millennium.[134]

Moreover, insofar as economic reform was concerned, no political party, no group of reformers enlisted the entire sympathy of Howells. Toward the issues raised by Republicans and Democrats, he was admittedly indifferent; [135] and, while he was sympathetic with the program of Bellamy, he

[130] See, in *The Minister's Charge*, especially pp. 29, 35, 445.

[131] *Annie Kilburn*, especially pp. 43-6, 105, 193-9.

[132] See, especially, pp. 47, 159-64, 169, 179, 321. Compare with the imaginary experiences in *Annie Kilburn* Howells' own experiences in the doing of charity, and his reflections on them, as he relates them in the essay, "Tribulations of a Cheerful Giver," *Impressions and Experiences*, pp. 150-88.

[133] *Through the Eye of the Needle*, pp. 87-8.

[134] "The Editor's Easy Chair," *Harper's Magazine*, 102: 153 (December, 1900). For similar expressions in Howells' fiction, see Annie Kilburn, pp. 240, 261.

[135] *The Life in Letters*, I: 413-4; a letter of April 14, 1888, to Thomas S. Perry.

took no active part in the attempt to create a Nationalist party. Apparently, nationalization meant to him no immediate effort to propagandize an unprepared public, but a gradual social evolution in the direction of the collective control of industrialism. On the one basic principle of collectivism, however, Howells, once having accepted it, never wavered. From *The Minister's Charge,* with its hesitant references to the doctrine of "complicity," through *Annie Kilburn,* with its clear pronouncement that the goal of justice is to be achieved by the elimination of competitive strife, to the final portrayal of a communistic Utopia in *Through the Eye of the Needle,* he iterates and reiterates the collective principle.[136] For any really effective economic reform, the one indispensable change was, to Howells, the elimination of competitive individualism and the substitution therefor of some form of collective control of industry.

This collectivism—the collectivism he desired for America—is not to be the child of violent revolution, or even of any violence or injustice at all. An inheritor of three generations of Quaker quietism, a man by nature exceptionally sensitive and tender-minded, Howells could not agree to the use of wrong means even for the securing of a right end. For instance, while he reveals an unvarying sympathy with the ends and purposes of organized labor, he always decries the use of violence. "I come back to my old conviction, that every drop of blood shed for a good cause helps to make a bad cause." [137] Nor will Howells tolerate the use of other than physical force, or the doing of any injustice under the forms

---

[136] For some among his numerous pronouncements on collectivism, see *Annie Kilburn,* pp. 240 ff.; *The World of Chance,* pp. 118-20; and *Impressions and Experiences,* pp. 137-8. As to Howells' faith in some "grand and absolute change" in our economic life, see *The Life in Letters,* II: 9; a letter of November 9, 1890, to William Cooper Howells.

[137] *The Life in Letters,* II, 25; a letter of July 10, 1892, to William Cooper Howells, in reference to the conduct of labor in the Homestead Strike. See also *ibid.,* II, 26, a letter of July 24, 1892, to William Cooper Howells, about the same question. With these letters compare the talk of Basil March and his son in *A Hazard of New Fortunes,* II, 272, in regard to the wrong done by the socialist Lindau in opposing capitalism by violence.

of law, or the carrying on, even by peaceful, political methods, of class conflict, with the hatreds and general evils it necessarily entails. "Our cause should recognize no class as enemies," one of his spokesmen pronounces; [138] and he himself, in opposing the confiscation involved in the single tax program, insists, "The new commonwealth must be founded in justice even to the unjust, in generosity to the unjust rather than anything less than justice." [139]

The collective state is not, then, to be the result of class conflict or of abrupt revolution, either political or military. Its coming is to be a gradual thing, its achievement a work of social evolution. Just as, in the course of an evolutionary progress, chattel slavery had disappeared, so, in time the inequalities of competitive industrialism will disappear likewise—though not, it was Howells' hope, through the same violent means. Toward the achievement of the coöperative commonwealth, the first step to take, as Howells constantly preaches, is the nationalization of natural monoplies; and that step he was ready to take at once. Such is the opinion he expressed to his friends; [140] such is the course advocated by his spokesman David Hughes in *The World of Chance;* [141] and such, finally, is the step by which he imagines the Altrurians to have begun the achievement of their ideal state.[142] The next step (although Howells' statements on this point are not so extensive or positive as on the first) is apparently to be the nationalization of mines and of all large industries in general operated by stock companies—a procedure which will automatically destroy the evils of speculation in stocks.[143] Thenceforward, nationalization will proceed as far as is necessary to insure complete economic security. The entire procedure can, Howells felt, be kept a peaceable one; the former capi-

[138] David Hughes, in *The World of Chance*, p. 119.
[139] *The Life in Letters,* 1: 407-8; a letter of January 15, 1888, to Hamlin Garland.
[140] See the letter to Hamlin Garland, quoted immediately above.
[141] P. 120.
[142] *A Traveller from Altruria,* p. 270.
[143] *Ibid.,* 307. Compare, though, the slightly different statement, *ibid.,* 270-1.

talists, even, may in time become reconciled to the coöperative commonwealth because essential security and comfort will be provided for them as for others, and because they will be released from the burdensome responsibilities that accompany the ownership of great wealth.[144]

But the drive of social evolution alone will not be sufficient to bring forth the collective state. That state must be given shape also by the deliberate and intelligent choices of its citizens, must be built by means of the deliberate and intelligent use of the various tools of democracy, particularly the ballot. The laboring classes, owning the overwhelming majority of the votes in America, will have only themselves to blame if they do not compel such legislation as will insure them justice and economic security.[145] The really fruitful policy for formally organized laborers will be to quit striking and fighting and direct their efforts toward gaining control of the government.[146] "The way to have the Golden Age," says Howells' spokesman Hughes, "is to elect it by the Australian ballot. The people must vote themselves into possession of their own business, and entrust their economic affairs to the same faculty that makes war and peace, that frames laws, and that does justice."[147] Finally, "we must have the true America in the true American way, by reasons, by votes, by laws, and not otherwise."[148]

X

The diversion of Howells' attention from economics presents no such complicated problem of personal development as does that, say, of Hamlin Garland. The publication of *A Traveller from Altruria* in 1894 marks, definitely, the close of the period in which economic interests were foremost in his work. To be sure, occasional articles of his on economic

[144] *Ibid.*, p. 272.
[145] *Through the Eye of the Needle*, pp. 220-1.
[146] Of Howells' numerous statements to this effect, see especially *A Traveller from Altruria*, pp. 223-5, 270-1, and *Annie Kilburn*, p. 94.
[147] *The World of Chance*, p. 91.
[148] *Ibid.*, 125.

subjects still appeared, and a slight bearing on economics is to be discerned in such books as *The Landlord at Lion's Head* (1897); but for the most part it is accurate to say that Howells' production of economic fiction lapsed from 1894 until its brief revival in the publication of *Through the Eye of the Needle* (1907), and then closed entirely. Now there is no evidence that, during these and later years, Howells' economic attitude suffered any such change as Garland's. But the expression of that attitude in fiction ceased, and Howells returned to his familiar fictional types of social comedy, studies of character, and studies of ethical relationships among individuals.

In the understanding of Howells' abandonment of the economic field, it is well to remember, first, that his economic fiction as it stands constitutes a complete achievement, and that beyond this achievement he probably could not have gone if he had tried. The subjects which he had slighted—such as the more violent and disruptive forms of class warfare—were, quite obviously, outside his range; and those subjects which he genuinely was qualified to treat—the ethical bearing of competitive industrialism on the lives of the middle classes, the ferment of ideas and projects for reform among the liberal and humanitarian bourgeoisie, and the illustration of the workings of human nature in an ideal, noncompetitive society—all these he had treated with a comprehensiveness, with an intelligence which none of his contemporaries had even approached. He could reasonably have felt, therefore, that in this particular field he had done all that was possible for him, and that to keep on doing the same things over and over again would be pointless.

In some measure, too, Howells' attention, like that of other leaders of the middle-class critique, was being diverted to other than strictly economic issues, and especially to the issue of imperialism. Only, Howells, consistently anti-militarist in his convictions, and more intelligent than most of his fellow-novelists, foresaw clearly the effect of war on the drive for domestic economic reform, and consequently was opposed not merely to the conquest of the Philippines but to the Spanish war itself. Of the latter, for instance, he wrote,

Of course we are deafened by war-talk here. I hope you will not be surprised to hear that I think we are wickedly wrong. . . . At the very best we propose to do evil that good may come. . . . After the war will come the piling up of big fortunes again; the craze for wealth will fill all brains, and every good cause will be set back. We shall have an era of blood-bought prosperity, and the chains of capitalism will be welded on the nation more firmly than ever.[149]

Such utterances as this of Howells suggest again the whole complex problem of the disintegration of the middle-class literary critique of capitalistic industrialism, of the diffusion of an intellectual current which, as we have seen, reached its fullest flow between 1886 and 1896, and thereafter either lapsed or sought other channels.[150] To this broad and complex change of national interest, it was essential that Howells, as a practical journalist and writer for the commercial market, adjust himself. Whatever he personally may have desired, the literary market of 1898 was not that of a decade earlier. While his opinions remained the same,[151] the *milieu* in which he might express them in published fiction had changed.

That Howells recognized the new situation, and deliberately adjusted his literary policies in order to meet it, is indicated by his handling of the manuscript of *Through the Eye of the Needle*. This Utopia was evidently begun in 1893, along with, or immediately after, his work on the manuscript of its predecessor, *A Traveller from Altruria*.[152] The first portion of *Through the Eye of the Needle*, which consists of letters written by the Altrurian traveller about America, was completed and was stereotyped by Joseph A. Howells not later than about 1895, but was not published. The second portion,

---

[149] *The Life in Letters*, II, 90; a letter of April 3, 1898, to Aurelia Howells. Copyright, 1928, by Doubleday, Doran and Company. Reprinted by permission of Miss Mildred Howells.

[150] See above, pp. 173 ff.

[151] See, in this connection, G. W. Arms, *op. cit.*, pp. 241-2. Mr. Arms's conclusion is that Howells' "decline from militant socialism" was a "decline in enthusiasm rather than a sharp change in principles."

[152] *The Life in Letters*, II, 40; a letter of October 29, 1893, to Howard Pyle.

which consists of letters written by Eveleth Strange in Altruria to a friend in America, was written early in 1907. In explaining the renewal of this twelve-year-old project, Howells wrote, "There is now a revival of interest in such speculations, and the publishers think the book, with an interesting sequel, giving an account of life in Altruria, will succeed." [153] Evidently, conditions of publication, and the publishers' estimate of popular taste, had much to do with the stoppage of Howells' economic criticism, as well as with its temporary revival.

XI

Looking backward over the entire scope of Howells' economic criticism, and studying it with some historical perspective, we should have little difficulty in estimating the purely historical bearings of that work. But as our historical estimate merges into an evaluation of the worth of that work in the function of cultural leadership, and in the realm of creative art, we shall need to move more cautiously, well aware that no final and assured standard of values, political or economic or aesthetic, has yet been arrived at by the mind of man; and we shall need, furthermore, to know with considerable precision just when we pass from historical generalization into the more dubious realm of opinion and critical hypothesis.

In the historical development of American ideas, Howells' work, it should be now evident, tended in precisely the same direction as Bellamy's—namely, the illustration, in literature, of an extension of democratic political theory so as to include and justify a collective economics. Or, looked at from another angle, the intellectual work of both may be looked upon as the modification of a foreign economic program—Marxian socialism—so as to adapt it to the American democratic and middle-class tradition. Because of the influence of his early environment in Ohio and his later environment in Cambridge Howells had become, himself, a part of that tradition. He himself had come of the western middle class; and, along

[153] The quotation, together with evidence supporting the statements immediately preceding, is to be found in *The Life in Letters*, II: 234; a letter of February 24, 1907, to Joseph A. Howells.

with others of that class, he shared in its agrarian background, its Christian humanitarianism, its concept of social equality, and its faith in the efficacy of democracy and the value of the suffrage. And he shared likewise, as a belated rationalist, in a body of ideas that had been associated with and had appeared to sanction the founding of democracy in America—in the deistic concept of harmonious order as the natural state of life, in the romantic assumption of human rationality, potential goodness, and perfectibility.

In adapting this democratic ideology to the exigencies of life in an industrialized society, Howells found it necessary to give up only one important principle, the Jeffersonian ideal of the minimized state. Conceiving of government as a servant and not as a possible oppressor, and conceiving of economic insecurity as the main threat to true liberty and equality, Howells felt that sound democratic policy called not for the curtailing of governmental service, but for the extension of it, not for less government, but for more. In other words, he would use the government as an agency to insure collective economic security, the only possible soil for the nurture of true liberty and equality; and he would achieve this end by methods fully in accordance with our middle-class tradition —the peaceful, the democratic use of the ballot. The collective socialism of Howells is, in other words, only another of the many channels through which the main current of American democracy has taken its course.

In this program of economic democracy, certain grave weaknesses have, with the passage of a generation, and notwithstanding the enduring charm of Howells' millennial vision, become increasingly plain; and if literature is to be judged in part by its worth for cultural leadership, this fact must weigh heavily against Howells. Of these weaknesses, the most serious, though one in which Howells shares the company of such distinguished thinkers as Condorcet and Godwin and Shelley, has its roots in a limited, a partial, an over-flattering view of human nature. A long-belated rationalist, a perfectibilist whose premises were still those of the eighteenth-century Enlightenment, he erred in assuming that man is primarily rather than secondarily rational, and in underestimating the power of the more disruptive, violent, and sub-intelligent phases of human nature. As a consequence, he erred also in the assumption—an assumption almost essential for his scheme of reform—that American voters at the polls can normally be trusted to make an intelligent choice of economic policies. If the evidences of history up until our own time are to be trusted, Thoreau, for all his crabbedness, was nearer to the truth when he wrote, apropos of another issue than industrialism, "There is but little virtue in the action of masses of men. When the majority shall at length vote for the abolition of slavery, it will be because they are indifferent to slavery, or because there is but little slavery left to be abolished by their vote."

The chaotic disintegration of standards of value in our modern world, the reassertion on an unprecedented scale of the primitive code of conquest and compulsion, the instruction offered by modern psychology in regard to the devious workings of the instinctive and subrational—all these and other forces have compelled a revision of those roseate views of human nature which were given currency by the eighteenth-century Enlightenment. To be sure, no final grounds for an absolutely opposite and pessimistic view have as yet been established; but it may quite safely be said that the holding of an optimistic faith in human progress demands, in our day, a tougher hide and a tenderer brain than it did in that of Howells. Prejudices, jealousies, hatreds, the profound and powerful selfishness of firmly established vested interests, these forces are hardly to be held in leash by the silken threads of eighteenth-century sanity, order, and reason. If mankind are perfectible at all, they are perfectible with far less rapidity, with far less ease, than Howells supposed; and, consequently, the intelligent popular choice of a democratic economics must wait, if not indefinitely, at least upon a slower, more difficult, and more painful growth than he anticipated.

Nevertheless, and when all possible objections have been brought against Howells' program, certain substantial, important facts remain. Among these is the fact that, insofar as there has been any discernible tendency in the social handling of American industrialism, that tendency has been in the general direction which Howells pointed out. Our industrial system is, to be sure, still competitive and capitalistic, and even the moderate changes which have been wrought in it have been accomplished by stresses and strains the severity of which the gentle Howells could hardly have imagined. Yet, if the administrations of Presidents Hoover and Roosevelt have meant anything at all, they have meant that the national government has now assumed responsibility for the maintaining of at least a minimum of economic security. For the achievement of this end, an enormous extension of governmental activity has been necessary; and this extension has been carried out, so far, by democratic and not autocratic means, as a process of peaceful evolution and not of violent revolution. And throughout these changes, the cultural ideals of the nation have remained overwhelmingly those of the middle class.

Apparently the social program of Howells is, in spite of its serious limitations, the most realistic of those presented by American authors of the Gilded Age. Along with Bellamy, Howells faces squarely and realistically the inescapable need for collective action in the control of a complex, interdependent, and collective industrial system. Avoiding the use of such foreign formulas as that of Marxian socialism, he successfully harmonizes his collective theories with the democratic traditions of our dominant middle class. Avoiding the immediate millennial expectations of George, he allows for that slow and orderly development, that faculty for compromise, that flair for gradual social evolution which have been so characteristic of the political talent of English-speaking peoples. No other program allows so fully for all these factors; no other offers so much of final hope. For Howells' economic proposals reduce themselves, finally, to the bed-rock procedure of controlling the human and natural order not by force or according to a haphazard play of impulse, but by human intelligence and according to a sound human sense of justice. So to control society is, no doubt, difficult indeed;

but if men are to be the overlords of life instead of its victims, the task is inescapable.

And yet the entire concept of cultural leadership as a function of literature is, seen in the long perspective of literary history, a thing essentially modern, and of brief descent indeed when compared with the more ancient acceptance of literature as simply a means to the immediate enrichment of life. The modern novelist is, conceivably, descended less from the primitive sage and prophet than from the primitive scop and gleeman. For his is still, after the ancient fashion of the artist, the function of creating for the human imagination, in some realm above and beyond the actual, a home that shall be richer in experience, more significant in its scale of values, more intense and infused with a more powerful consciousness than the home it inhabits in everyday life. To what degree does the economic fiction of Howells achieve this end? What is its intrinsic value as aesthetics, as distinguished from its value for cultural leadership?

Other things being equal, that art which comprehends the broadest range of experience, that art which conveys the largest amount of life, is, it is evident, the best. In the case of Howells' economic fiction, the sheer amount, variety, and range of the experience conveyed to the reader are, it is not too much to say, enormous. The abstract ideas of Howells alone range—to take just a few of many possible examples—from the deistic concepts of the harmonious order of nature and the perfectibility of man, through such political ideals as those of democracy and equality, through such ethical concepts as humanism and Christian altruism, through such scientific hypotheses as evolutionary progress and the struggle for survival, to the purely economic ideas involved in technological unemployment and the effects of the closing of the frontier. Nor is this wealth of thought simply a miscellany. Because the mind of Howells was one of such orderliness, his ideas exist in a symmetry, in a delicate articulation and mutual adjustment, in an all but perfect integration which presents the strongest possible contrast with the roily intellectual confusion of such an author as, say, Jack London.

Or if one measures Howells' range of experience by the number of fresh and significant situations in his novels, the result is no less impressive. He does, indeed, employ the conventional theme of boy-meeting-girl, but his treatment of even this perennial formula is often, as in *The Quality of Mercy* and *The World of Chance*, fresh and unhackneyed. Morever, such narratives as those of the quest of Annie Kilburn for social usefulness, the reaction of the Hughes family to the stresses of competitive industrialism, the steadily broadening and often unexpected effects of Northwyck's crime against the capitalistic order, the degeneration of the Dryfooses after their transplantation to New York—all these and other stories give rise to situations which have a freshness, an originality, and often a significance which are not even approached in any other body of American economic fiction of the period. To compare the situations in Howells' novels with those in the run-of-the-mine fiction of his contemporaries, is to dispel any lingering doubt in regard to his radical originality.

And yet it is in Howells' comprehension of human nature—or, more technically, in his presentation of character—that the immense scope of his artistically usable experience is most convincingly shown. Within so small an amount of writing as his economic novels, the presence of such a sheer number of individualized portraits is surprising (*A Hazard of New Fortunes* contains, in the familiar metaphor, an entire picture-gallery in itself), and the relations of these characters both with one another and with the general social system are handled with a lifelikeness and subtlety that are simply amazing. In variety and range, moreover, they include such widely differing people as the New England country boy Lemuel Barker—one of Howells' most delicately executed studies—the piquantly disingenuous Mrs. Makely, the insane lithographer Denton, and the temperamental girl Christine Dryfoos. Consistently, these people come alive in Howells' pages not as types but as individuals, each distinguished by his own individual turns of thought, of speech, of gesture, and of action. Occasionally, one of them is developed with a gusto that approaches, though it never quite equals, that of Howells' friend Mark Twain. Of these latter, the juiciest figure is perhaps that of the promoter Fulkerson, at the time of his enthusiasm for his new magazine, *Every Other Week*:—"Sometimes we're going to have [for a cover] a delicate little landscape like this, and sometimes we're going to have an indelicate little figure, or as much so as the law will allow."—"It's the talk of the clubs and the dinner-tables; children cry for it; it's the Castoria of literature, and the Pearline of art, the Won't-be-happy-till-he-gets-it of every enlightened man, woman, and child in this vast city." [154]

Of Howells' technical skill in rendering these abundant materials, little need be said except that his practice is far superior to his rather inadequate theory. No doubt he himself assumed that his claims as an artist rested chiefly upon his realism, upon his faculty for being simple, natural, and honest. Instead, it is quite likely that his true excellence will be found to lie in the fullness of appropriate, concrete detail with which his imagination realized an artistically self-consistent world. His special competence is that of the master craftsman, and that competence can safely be taken for granted now, as it has usually been taken for granted hitherto. And of his scale of values—of that concept of life which everywhere controls, disposes, and orders his world of fancy—it need only be said that his dual standard of harmonious order and humane enrichment was sufficient to give his art symmetry, significance, and elevation. Conceivably, this standard, for the very reason that it was too limited to suffice for shaping the multitudinous actual world in which Howells lived, shaped his imaginative world the more perfectly.

In short, it is only when we come to one of the ultimate tests of art—its possession of some intangible force, some high seriousness, some final power of imagination which we associate with a Goethe or a Shakespeare—that the economic fiction of Howells begins to disclose any serious weakness. Many people have sensed a lack of some final adequacy in Howells, and not a few, disappointed perhaps by his failure,

[154] *A Hazard of New Fortunes*, I: 183, 292-3.

after meeting every other test, to meet the supreme one, have been tempted to speak over-hastily of the possible cause for their legitimate discontent. As a consequence, Howells is blamed for being timid, or for allowing the issues in his problem novels to become confused. But the only American author to intervene publicly in behalf of the Chicago anarchists was not timid, and the man who possessed the perfectly integrated body of ideas which we have just analyzed was not confused. To explain how Howells came to miss, by ever so slight a margin, the level of the greatest creative art, we must come upon some cause more fundamental than these.

Is it possible that Howells' lack of the supreme and final touch is due to his slighting of the instinctive and emotional in human nature? That he dealt too cursorily with the entire area of the subrational can hardly be questioned; and, as a consequence, he appears never to have understood how large a proportion of literature fulfills the human need for psychic release. That, through the medium of literature, we enjoy doing and feeling those things which our long racial experience has fitted our nerves and consciousness to do and feel, but which, among the artificialities of civilized life, we are unable to come at—all this seems never to have entered the mind of Howells. The archetypal images and feelings are not ordinarily evoked by his art, and the reader is denied the psychical completion which their presence might afford.

In plain, simple emotional power, likewise, the novels of Howells are seriously deficient. Perhaps the novelist, disliking the excessive sentimentality which was then still prevalent, allowed himself to swing to the opposite extreme. Perhaps his own acute sensitiveness led him to underestimate the emotional shock required by the average reader, so that, in building scenes which would be sufficient to awaken his own feelings, he built scenes which leave unawakened even the reader who is culturally prepared for his art. In any case, the emotional drive which alone can cause a reader to live not merely in his perceptions and understanding but in every fiber of his being, is lacking in Howells; his situations, when they are absorbed from the printed page, are often less impressive than when they are later revolved in the mind of the reader. And whatever of merely intellectual stimulus Howells may gain by such a method, he loses, of necessity, the pungency, the force, the finality of the greatest art.

Whatever the cause, the effect of Howells' fiction is that of various, abundant, and important materials which have been shaped into flawless form by perfect craftsmanship and a significant standard of values, but which are suspended in an imaginative medium a bit too fine, too mild, too tenuous to fuse them into any such impressive finality as that of, say, Hardy's *Tess of the D'Urbervilles*.[155] Possessed of materials that all but cry aloud for the dynamic fusing power of an imagination basically powerful and dramatic, he could illumine them only with an imagination like that of some Queen Anne essayist—an imagination that tended toward clear intellectual perception without force, and whose outcome is the lucidity of an Addison rather than the high seriousness of a Hardy.

And yet such critical definition, indispensable as it is to the judgment of our cultural past, is hardly a task to delight in. For even at the moment of our clearest recognition that Howells reached no Shakespearean heights or depths, it is salutary to remember that hardly once in a century is a people offered the gift of even one imagination whose creative surges wash both Heaven and Hell. The very fact that it is pertinent to point out, in the criticism of Howells, that he failed of ultimate greatness, is in itself testimony enough to the fineness and the value which he retains in spite of, or perhaps even because of, his limitations. In admitting his inferiority to the cosmic geniuses, we must not forget how enormously richer and more valuable is his achievement than that of many an author whose place in English literary history has long appeared secure. We would not willingly lose from our American tradition an imaginative world as

---

[155] For Howells' own recognition of some such limitation in himself, see his admission that his democracy is "incomparably less powerfully imagined" than Tolstoy's. "The Editor's Easy Chair." *Harper's Magazine*, 106: 327 (January, 1903).

large and habitable as that which he created:—a world endowed with the fruits of extensive knowledge, entire clarity of intellect, an exquisite flair for the gracious and the civilized, an admirable sense of artistic restraint and symmetry; an imaginative world, in short, where national experience of immense scope has been assembled, synthesized, and artistically disposed by the action of a great creative, order-producing personality.

I

Frank Norris, although his life came to a close eighteen years before that of Howells, belongs in many respects to a later generation. For Howells—and, indeed, Henry George, Clemens, Bellamy, and even Garland—had all been born into a society earlier than that of the Gilded Age. They were all middle-class democrats, who applied to the time of Carnegie an ideology derived from the time of Lincoln. Norris, on the other hand, was a child of the Gilded Age itself, and was as thoroughly at home there as any Chicago newsboy in the jungles of the Loop. In the Chicago of the eighteen-seventies, the rural democracy of Lincoln must have begun to seem, already, somewhat faint and far away; and its influence certainly never penetrated, in any effective degree, into the life of the boy who dwelt in the well-appointed house at Michigan Avenue and Park Row.

Norris was, in fact, a child of the wealthy upper bourgeoisie —a class whose way of life much more closely approximated that of the plutocracy than that of the masses. His father, a wealthy merchant, first of Chicago and later of San Francisco, and in the latter city a neighbor of the railway magnate C. P. Huntington, provided for the family in at least a moderately luxurious manner, and accumulated an estate of close to a million dollars. [1] With this prosperous pattern of life, Norris's early sociological ideas were quite in keeping. Untouched by the old American dream of a larger existence for the common man, he was, simply, a moneyed youth, fond of express-

---

[1] Franklin Walker, *Frank Norris, a Biography*, pp. 13-18, 87.

ing his contempt for the mob and his desire to see all radicals "drowned on one raft." Presently, to be sure, the divorce of his parents, and the loss of his expectations of an inherited fortune, undermined his complacency and awakened within him a larger sympathy—but such democratic leanings were not among his earliest, or deepest, impressions.[2] On the whole, Norris's early environment inclined him to accept, for whatever it might be worth, the commercial struggle amid which he was born and reared. It bent the prospective novelist away from an interest in reform and toward an interest in the romance of economic struggle. It constrained him away from the radical economic Left represented by Howells, and from the liberal Left-Center represented by Mark Twain, and turned him toward that conservative Right-Center of which he was to become, himself, the principal representative.

If Norris was born with a silver spoon in his mouth, he was also born with, or at least developed early, the temperament and emotional endowment of a novelist. In an abounding zest for life, a craving for adventure, a flair for the dramatic, and a fondness for storytelling, the child Frank Norris was father to the man. His mother, formerly an actress, read to the children from Scott and Dickens;[3] and as boys he and his brother Charles joined in concocting "certain lamentable tales of the round (dining-room) table heroes, of the epic of the pewter platoons, and the romance cycle of 'Gaston le Fox.'"[4] And for Norris, as he grew up, this world of imagined adventure was to remain a living world. He was to come to define a true novelist as one in whom the child's instinct for storytelling has not died out, but has grown up and come to dominate him.[5] And in his own reading he was to be most attracted by the tellers of stirring tales—by those who still kept alive, in the midst of a somewhat over-refined literature, the tonic of vigorous action and the thrill of marvellous adventure.

[2] *Ibid.*, p. 88.
[3] *Ibid.*, p. 13.
[4] Dedication of *The Pit*.
[5] *The Responsibilities of the Novelist*, pp. 30-2.

Norris's literary life was thus to resolve itself, in large degree, simply into a quest for adventure; his most clearly discerned objective was to be the discovery of romance amid the realities of modern life. Toward that goal were directed most of his explorations of experience, whether in his reading or in his own writings. Norris's reading was not, of course, wholly confined to the literature of adventure. He also read much elsewhere; his frame of reference, while not absolutely a large one, still included the writings of Tolstoy, Howells, Eliot, Balzac, and many others.[6] Notwithstanding these more general influences, however, Norris's chief interest remained with the creators of the adventurous, the thrilling, the strange. If he respected Howells, he was far more congenial in temperament with Kipling, sympathizing as he did with Kipling's themes of imperialism and Anglo-Saxon supremacy, and with his fondness for swiftly moving action.[7]

But of all the novelists he read from, Norris's favorite, and the one who most nourished and formed his imagination, was Émile Zola. Even within Zola, however, Norris's choices and rejections were determined mostly by his own romantic tastes. The quasi-scientific side of Zola's mind did not, apparently, much appeal to him. That Norris cared much for the ideals of scientific validity in fiction set up in "Le Roman Experimental," there is no reason to believe; nor did he ever put those ideals in practice, except as he made it a point to study his subjects thoroughly and to handle them honestly according to his impression of the Truth. That in Zola which really appealed to Norris was, rather, the man's vitality, his

[6] Norris's biographer, Franklin Walker, mentions his reading in such continental authors as Flaubert, Hugo, De Maupassant, the Goncourt brothers, Daudet, Balzac, and Tolstoy; in Shakespeare and the Bible; and, among recent or contemporary writers in English, in Browning, Stevenson, Conrad, Eliot, Howells, James, Mark Twain, Harold Frederic, Crane, Garland, Dreiser, and Herrick (*Op. Cit.*, pp. 283-4). Allusions in Norris's work show some familiarity also with Fenimore Cooper, Irving, Holmes, Harte, Cable, Eggleston, Joel Chandler Harris, Richard Harding Davis, Thomson-Seton, Maeterlinck, and Paul Bourget (*The Responsibilities of the Novelist*, pp. 37-45, 61, 87, 97, 106, 137, 141).

[7] Walker, *op. cit.*, p. 67.

bigness, his command of the crude, the strange, the violent, the grotesque, and the terrible. What Norris found in Zola's pages was, in short, Romance. "Everything—" so he wrote of Zola, with youthful enthusiasm—"Everything is extraordinary, imaginative, grotesque, even, with a vague note of terror quivering throughout.... Naturalism is a form of romanticism, not an inner circle of realism." [8] While realism was to become in Norris's thinking "the kind of fiction that confines itself to the type of normal life," romance, immensely more fascinating, was to become "the kind of fiction that takes cognizance of variations from the type of normal life." It was to become the literature of the unusual, the adventurous, the thrilling; and Zola was accordingly to remain fixed in his thinking as "the very head of the Romanticists." [9]

And just as Norris's passion for the discovery of romance formed his tastes in reading, so it dominated his search for literary materials of his own. His quest for stories-to-tell reduces itself to a quest for adventure. But where—he must have asked himself—where, in the midst of the luxuries and humdrum securities of modern America, are to be found materials for any tales as big and thrilling as those of Zola? Where might a young author come upon exciting, plausible, and modern adventure? Much of Norris's biography is the history of his efforts to answer those questions—efforts that presently led him, through refusals and failures and partial successes, to his principal work in *The Octopus* and *The Pit*.

II

In the course of his search, Norris apparently concluded that one area of adventure, which had formed an unfailing resource for some of the elder romanticists, was closed to him. He did not choose to romanticize war. As a correspondent in South Africa and in Cuba, he had seen little enough romance in the business. At first, it is true, he had been ready enough

[8] *Ibid.*, pp. 82-3. Mr. Walker quotes from an editorial in the *Wave*, June 21, 1896, unsigned, but evidently by Norris.
[9] *The Responsibilities of the Novelist*, p. 164.

for the war with Spain; and even at the close of the Santiago campaign he could thrill to the solemnity of the raising of the American flag.[10] But on the whole he had to conclude that "there is precious little glory in war," and that in the end one remembered only the hardships and horrors, and nothing of the finer side. War was, in part, courage in battle. It was, in much larger part, swarms of refugee children who had to be fed; it was wounded men who lay out beside the Division hospital, shelterless and unattended, for forty-eight hours; it was the body, first discovered by Norris himself, of the young girl who had been raped and then knifed to death just before a battle.[11] Wherever the genuine thrill of romance might still be found, it was not to be found—so Norris apparently concluded—in war.

Meanwhile, however, Norris had already discovered, with Zola's aid, another and to him a far more interesting source of adventure. That source was what Norris called the "Brute" in man—individual man, and not the collective man of modern war. It was that entire drive of primitive instinct and passion —fear and anger and lust—which is at best but precariously held in check even among civilized human beings. Adventure—the thrill of intense feeling or daring action—was to be found in the release of these primal energies, whether in heroic enterprise in some remote corner of the earth whither civilization had not yet penetrated, or in the occasional violent outbreaks in which even presumably civilized men throw off the chains of civilized restraint. It is the former theme— the excitement of heroic physical adventure—which is dominant in *Moran of the Lady Letty* (1898) and *A Man's Woman* (1900). In *Moran of the Lady Letty,* the chief adventurer is the Amazon Moran herself, bossing her gang of cutthroats about the Pacific, going berserk and attacking her lover, and finally surrendering, cave-woman fashion, to his superior strength. In *A Man's Woman,* the adventurer is the explorer Bennett, whether forging undefeatably through the hardships

[10] *Works,* Complete Edition, X, 276.

[11] *Ibid.,* X: 282-3; Walker, *op. cit.,* pp. 201-2. Mr. Walker quotes from a letter of Norris to Ernest Peixotto, August, 1898.

of his Arctic march, or killing a runaway horse with a single convincing blow of a hammer.

On the other hand, it is the latter theme—the outbreak of destructive passion even within the pale of civilized society—that is dominant in *Vandover and the Brute* (posthumously published, 1914) and *McTeague* (1899). *Vandover* is in effect a series of nightmare-pictures that give form to many an instinctive, hidden, half-suppressed fear of youth— the fear of venereal disease; the fear of the sheer cruelties of life, like the cruelty of the frenzied passengers beating off from the lifeboat the hands of the drowning Jew; the fear of the strange foulness of death and decay; the fear of the inward beast that in this story comes to dominate the man.[12] *McTeague* is a more mature, more credible, more coherent, and more powerful *Vandover,* in which the degeneration of the main character—that is, his gradual loss of control over the brute within—is convincingly motivated by relentless economic pressure and by his growing hatred of his avaricious wife. Here, too, the thrill afforded by the book is the thrill of surrender to primitive, destructive passion, the passion which eventuates in the murder of Trina and the unspeakable horror of the final scene in the desert.

Stories like *Vandover, Moran, A Man's Woman,* and *McTeague* show forth clearly enough the main drift of Norris's literary exploration.[13] His search was constantly for thrills, for excitement; and those he found either in "red-blooded" action or in some release of the primal forces of anger and fear. Such writing reduces at last to a kind of naturalistic primitivism, although the return to the elemental is stripped therein of any illusion of natural beauty and goodness. To man—a material being functioning as part of a harsh, material nature —the main value of life lies in the thrill of successful struggle for survival, or at least in the release of those fears and angers and other energies that might make him victorious over forest and ocean, over hostile tribesman and wild beast.

In evoking the stuff of good fiction from the thrill of ad-

[12] See, especially, pp. 118-20, 189, 213.
[13] The charming *Blix* (1899) is of course an exception.

venture, Norris's earlier works are not, on the whole, successful. *Vandover, Moran,* and *A Man's Woman* all fail, quite
simply, in credibility. Norris's technique could not yet insure
an adequate building-up of scene and a steady maintaining of illusion; nor was the imaginative texture of his work
yet sufficiently rich and strong to make the raw horrors of
those books convincing. With *McTeague* the case is different.
Of the earlier novels it is the only one that is adequately
imagined. A consistently powerful treatment of legitimate,
though unpleasant, materials, it remains in some ways Norris's
most impressive achievement. Nevertheless, it is doubtful
whether Norris succeeded, in *McTeague,* in solving a problem
only less important than that of artistic credibility—the problem, that is, of creating out of the actually unpleasant the
fine product of aesthetic pleasure. *McTeague* is more admirable than enjoyable.

Before Norris could go beyond the imperfections of these
earlier stories and arrive at his best work, it was necessary
for him to do two things: first, to find what were, for his
own unique imagination, more usable sources of adventure;
and, second, to grow into a larger maturity in both his social
and his aesthetic views. What, then, we may ask, were Norris's
maturing opinions about the art of fiction? About the management of society? What were, in short, the views which he
held during the writing of *The Octopus* and *The Pit,* and in
accordance with which those two novels are to be understood?

III

In his quest for adventure, Norris came on materials that
were both valuable in themselves, and genuinely suited to his
talents, only when he made the discovery that the great modern adventures were to be had in Business."[14] Business—
modern, competitive Business—was to modern people what
warfare had been to people of former times; the competitive
spirit, so deplored by ethicists like Bellamy and Howells, was
to Norris a main source of interest. Within modern Americans,

[14] See, in this connection, Walker, *op. cit.,* pp. 239, 244.

he concluded, ran the blood of the old Frisian marsh people, carrying along with it the same aggressive instincts, the same fighting impulses, as of old; only, in a changed time, in which the "whole scheme of modern civilization" works in favor of the businessman,[15] those instincts must now discover their outlet not in War but in Trade. Yet the change from war to trade is not really as great as it seems; Business, after all, *is* Battle. The American commercial expansion to the Orient can be spoken of only in military terms. "It is a commercial 'invasion,' a trade 'war,' a 'threatened attack' on the part of America; business is 'captured,' opportunites are 'seized,' certain industries are 'killed,' certain former monopolies are 'wrested away'...."[16] Accordingly, the modern man of action, true counterpart of the medieval adventurer, is the businessman. Richard the Lion-Hearted, living at the close of the nineteenth century, would be a leading representative of Amalgamated Steel; Andrew Carnegie, living in the middle ages, would have been the most efficient organizer among the crusaders. The great financier is motivated in his ventures not by the love of money, but, like the warrior, by his love of the excitement of battle.[17] In short, for the modern writer, working in and for a commercial society, the most fruitful source of convincing adventure lies in economic struggle.[18]

Now between this view of economics as a sporting contest, and the views professed by the great majority of sociological novelists, there is indeed a great gulf fixed. Novelists of the middle class Left and Left-Center were mostly interested in economic security; Norris was interested in adventure. They

[15] *The Responsibilities of the Novelist*, p. 99.

[16] *Ibid.*, pp. 56-7.

[17] Walker, *op. cit.*, pp. 281, 293.

[18] It is highly probable that Norris, as a journalist and publisher's reader, was acquainted with some of the stories of economic struggle that preceded his own. Such things as Will Payne's *The Money Captain* (1898) or Merwin and Webster's *The Short Line War* (1899) might quite naturally have come his way. The similarities between these books and both Norris's theory and his practice of fiction are sufficiently striking; but pending the discovery of external evidence linking the two, any relationship between them must remain a matter of hypothesis only.

were overwhelmingly moral; Norris was frequently amoral and at times deterministic. Nevertheless, Norris was often more closely akin to that majority than might, *a priori*, seem possible. For, across the major current of his buoyant interest in business as adventure, there ran a divergent and even contradictory stream of moralism, even of humanitarian sympathy for the underdog. Following the divorce of his parents and the loss of his prospective fortune, Norris had become more nearly one of the people; he had learned compassion for those who, unlike himself, knew actual poverty.[19] Faced with obvious social evils, he could sometimes turn away from the moral irresponsibility of the adventurer and speak with the intensity of a Hebrew prophet. Of the terrible degradation which as a reporter he had found in a certain type of Pennsylvania mining community, he wrote,

Look long enough at Melonsville and you will wonder why its miners were content merely with striking, and you will wonder how the statesmen and lawyers and governors of the next fifty years are to prune and trim the tree whose seed is sprouting in just such "culm-banks" and ash dumps all over these United States. For the tree bears a red flower, and its sap is heady and strong and its fruit distils a poison which is as swift to act as it is sure to stay.[20]

Norris's economic philosophy was, therefore, never wholly consistent. His was no systematic, coherent, and well-ordered personality, like that of Howells, but rather a zestful, exuberant, unsystematic one like that of Mark Twain. His uncritical enthusiasms might shift easily enough from a zestful enjoyment of business adventure to an equally zestful exposure of social injustice.

Equally variant strands of thought make up the curiously mixed texture of Norris's theory of fiction. Alongside a major interest in the telling of a good, big, thrilling story, Norris maintained a lesser but still important interest in the use of

[19] Walker, *op. cit.*, p. 88.
[20] "Life in the Mining Region." *Everybody's*, 7:241-8 (September, 1902).

the novel for popular instruction. Always, of course, Norris emphasized first of all the function of the novelist as a teller of tales, as one dominated by an instinct for storytelling which has survived from childhood.[21] The best stories, so he felt, are those which reawaken in their readers a child's fascinated delight in something marvellous and strange. They are not products of the new Realism, which, preoccupied as it is with ordinary life, is likely to be a piddling, humdrum, superficial thing; nor are they products of the false Romance which hides the truths of life behind a veil of specious glamour. The best stories are, rather, products of genuine Romance, of adventurous variations from the norm of everyday experience, of those exceptional conflicts and crises during which the life-currents run large, powerful, and free. Not to Realism, then, but to Romance, belong "the wide world for range, and the unplumbed depths of the human heart, and the mystery of sex, and the problems of life, and the black, unsearched penetralia of the soul of man."[22] Far from having passed away with the age of chivalry, romance is still intensely alive; Michigan Avenue and King Arthur's Court are equally romantic and realistic; and the novelist's difficult and challenging task is to get at the romance immediately around him.[23] Within the area of romantic fiction, the best stories are the "big" ones, that require elaboration by all the structural mechanics of the "big" novel. Such a novel develops through a leisurely approach to the theme, through carefully wrought exposition, preparation, disclosure of characters, heightening of action, and speeding-up of the narrative pace until the pivotal event, gradually and perfectly prepared for, "fairly leaps from its pages with a rush of action that leaves you stunned, breathless, and overwhelmed with the sheer power of its presentation."[24]

But if Norris was concerned first of all with the business of telling a rousing, vital story, he was concerned next, and

[21] *The Responsibilities of the Novelist,* pp. 30-2.
[22] *Ibid.,* pp. 167-8.
[23] *Ibid.,* p. 16.
[24] *The Responsibilities of the Novelist,* pp. 114-5.

quite seriously, with the function of the novel as a means of popular enlightenment. Since the novel has become the "great expression of modern life," [25] since more than any other art form it is produced of, by, and for the whole People,[26] the task of the novelist is a responsible one. The novelist must resist the temptation to be just an entertainer and nothing more; he must resist even more stoutly the temptation to exploit and deceive his readers with false views of life. The People "have a right to the Truth as they have a right to life, liberty, and the pursuit of happiness." [27] The best kind of novel is, therefore, the novel of "Purpose." It is a novel in which the writer, always keeping his story paramount, never preaching, remaining always within the concrete, illustrates from the broadest areas of life some significant truth.[28] Such a novel "proves something, draws conclusions from a whole congeries of forces, social tendencies, race impulses, devotes itself not to the study of men but of man"; and therefore it may be, along with the church and the university, a great force for good, fearlessly showing "that power is abused, that the strong grind the faces of the weak, that an evil tree is still growing in the midst of the garden," and that the course of empire and of great popular movements in history is not yet finished.[29]

What, then, is Truth? Faced with Pilate's inescapable question, Norris could only admit that ultimate truth is no more attainable by the novelist than by anyone else. Nevertheless, the novelist can at least refuse the role of a mere entertainer, and can insist on the larger task of presenting the tragedies that arise out of injustice, crime, and inequality.[30] If his America is too various to be truthfully treated in any one novel,

[25] *Ibid.*, pp. 4-5.
[26] In regard to Norris's respect for the People as readers, his trust in their potential good taste, and his view of their relation to literary art, see *The Responsibilities of the Novelist*, pp. 6, 80, 158, 196, 199-200.
[27] *Ibid.*, pp. 7-9.
[28] *The Responsibilities of the Novelist*, pp. 21-4.
[29] *Ibid.*, pp. 21-2, 26.
[30] *Ibid.*, p. 25.

he may at least be true to the life of some one locale.[31] Furthermore, he may, and should, thoroughly study up his subjects, acquainting himself as fully as possible with the area of life he proposes to treat.[32] He can, finally, be honest; he can "convey a credible impression of the truth as he sees it."[33] For such thoroughly honest work, there may be no great financial return; the proper reward of the novelist is not wealth, but the pride of personal integrity and sound workmanship.[34]

By the spring of 1899, Norris had developed the main outlines of a plan for a series of novels, in which these ideals of fiction might be realized. His plan called for the writing of a trilogy about the one subject of Wheat: "First, a story of California (the producer), second, a story of Chicago (the distributor), third, a story of Europe (the consumer)." Such a series, with its "huge Niagara of wheat rolling from West to East," would be modern, distinctively American, and epic in scope.[35] It would involve the telling of big, interesting stories dealing with the adventure of modern economic struggle and illustrating the truths to be found in modern life. The first novel of the series would be, specifically, "all about the San Joaquin wheat raisers and the Southern Pacific." It would be a long, a serious, an immensely detailed, and perhaps a very terrible story. It would be, moreover, an exhaustive treatment of an exhaustively studied subject, a treatment which would "say the last word on the R. R. question in California."[36]

These plans were realized, insofar as Norris lived to execute

[31] *Ibid.,* p. 66.

[32] For an interesting sidelight on Norris's own early methods of study, see Willard E. Martin, "Frank Norris's Reading at Harvard College." *American Literature,* 7:203-4 (May, 1935).

[33] *The Responsibilities of the Novelist,* pp. 173-4.

[34] *Ibid.,* pp. 17-8.

[35] Walker, *op. cit.,* p. 239. Mr. Walker quotes from *The Life in Letters of William Dean Howells,* II:102-3, a letter of Norris to Howells, written in March, 1899.

[36] Walker, *op. cit.,* p. 244. Mr. Walker quotes from a letter of Norris's to Harry Wright, April 5, 1899.

them, in *The Octopus* (1901) and *The Pit* (1903). The very presence of these two books within the same series is, however, a possible source of confusion about each of them. For, whereas the novels of a trilogy are quite naturally taken to be similar, *The Octopus* and *The Pit* differ widely, and, indeed, derive from different facets of Norris's personality. On the one hand, *The Octopus,* a huge, wide-ranging story, derives from Norris's understanding of the mechanics of the "big" novel, his love of strong, sensational themes, and his sympathy with the novel of purpose. On the other hand, *The Pit,* a more limited fiction, derives more immediately from Norris's romanticizing of the businessman and of business adventure. To what extent, then, did Norris, in each of these two novels, reach the specific goals which he had set for himself? And, while carrying out his own specific aims, to what extent did he succeed in creating the general values of good fiction?

IV

The Octopus, outgrowth as it is of Norris's admiration for the "big" novel, really puts on record in vigorous narrative an entire regional society; economic conflict is only the dominant one among its several themes. The principal story is, of course, that of the struggle between the ranchers and the railroad for the possession of the fertile wheat lands of the San Joaquin valley. It is in itself a multiple story, including as its main thread of interest the tragedy of the leader of the ranchers, Magnus Derrick, and as minor threads the bearing of the railroad-rancher struggle on the lives of a dozen sharply conceived though technically subordinate characters. Associated with this major story, tied in with it by a hundred interlinking threads, are at least three fully developed minor plots: the contest between the railroad and the discharged engineer, Dyke; the love story of Hilma Tree and the rancher Annixter; and the idyl of Vanamee and the two Angéles. And besides all these, even, the immense network of narrative encloses and bears along a number of subsidiary episodes, like the sketches of Father Sarria and of the fate of the

Hooven family, which are associated with some one of the several plots, though not essential to it.

The characters of *The Octopus,* like its immensely complex narrative, cover virtually the entire range of an entire social order. Chief among them, the focal and typical figure of the story, is, of course, Magnus Derrick, owner of the great Los Muertos Ranch, leader of the ranchers in their resistance to the railroad, a Prominent Man by virtue of a certain natural largeness of character, a frontier adventurer on the grand scale,[37] yet a man so rigidly honest and at the core so tender-minded that he is unable to stand up to the shock of the corrupt practices into which he is forced. Magnus's compromise with conscience, and the resulting slow disintegration of his personality, make up the most carefully elaborated character-study in the book; but at least a score of other characters are sufficiently developed to take on sharp individuality. Among the ranchers and their associates are Osterman, Broderson, Annixter, and Dabney, amusingly variant types of the eccentric; Hilma Tree, Norris's version of the *ewige weibliche;* and the poet Presley, from whose point of view much of the story is told. More remotely associated with the ranchers are the shepherd and mystic, Vanamee, and those persons, particularly Father Sarria of the Mission, who link the modern San Joaquin with the romance of the Spanish past. Widely varying proletarian types appear in the Hooven family, the saloon-keeper Caraher, and the engineer Dyke. At the opposite end of the economic scale, the wealthy upper bourgeoisie are represented by the Cedarquists of San Francisco; the plutocracy, by the arresting and too little developed

---

[37] See, in regard to Norris's intention in presenting Magnus Derrick as a gambler by disposition, Willard E. Martin, "Two Uncollected Essays by Frank Norris." *American Literature,* 8:190-8 (May, 1936). In the first of the two essays, "The Literature of the West," Norris explains that it is the business of the writer to present characters typical of their places and times, and that the characteristic Western type has always been the adventurer. The Western adventurer, moreover, need not be of the red-shirt-and-revolver type. He may indeed be sober, decorous, and outwardly conventional; nevertheless, "scratch the surface ever so little and behold—there is the Forty-niner" (p. 193).

figure of the railway president, Shelgrim. Associated with the interests of the railroad are, finally, the divertingly assorted rascals Delaney, Ruggles, Genslinger, Lyman Derrick, and S. Behrman.

And as these numerous and varied characters comprise virtually an entire Folk, so the various scenes and episodes of *The Octopus* comprise what might be called—no doubt inexactly—the Folk-experience of their region, which was in considerable measure the folk-experience of late-nineteenth-century America. Superficially, this typical quality of the book appears in Norris's portrayal of Western usages and folkways and customs: the rabbit drive, the gigantic plowing at Los Muertos, the dance at Annixter's barn. More fundamentally, it appears in his truly remarkable grasp of the most significant and central *economic* experiences of his generation. Whether deliberately so intended or not, the struggle between the ranchers and the railway monopoly typifies the most far-reaching and important class conflict of that age in America, the conflict between the middle classes and the plutocracy; and the main issue between ranchers and railroad —the disposal of the public lands[38]—has been from the very beginnings of America one of those half dozen absolutely primary factors that have shaped the entire course of our economic history. Equally central in the experience of the Gilded Age is the struggle of the two opposed groups for political control, together with the resulting corruption of all branches of government by the influence of victorious Big Business.[39] And besides these more significant and typical economic problems, *The Octopus* treats still others: problems of speculative business, such as stock-watering; problems of labor, such as unemployment, labor insecurity, and the blacklist; problems of railway control, such as those growing out of obstructive shipping regulations and the practice of charging all the traffic will bear.[40] In its industrial bearings alone,

[38] For this phase of the story, see especially Vol. I, pp. 264 ff.

[39] For examples of the treatment of this subject in *The Octopus*, see I: 102-13, II: 6, 154 ff., *et al.*

[40] See, for examples, *The Octopus*, I: 15, 63-6.

it appears, *The Octopus* comes very near summing up the American experience of economics from the Civil War to 1900; and in the largeness and the multiplicity of its total materials—story, characters, subject-matter, ideas—it can be compared only with those Hugoesque, Tolstoyesque leviathans of fiction that Norris was emulating.

The Octopus is as admirably organized as it is big. The structural mechanics of the book—in exposition, preparation, interweaving of plots, and handling of climaxes—are both sound and ingenious enough to challege comparison with those of that masterpiece of structure, *Tom Jones;* and the net effect is just that deliberate beginning, that steady acceleration of movement, and that final onrush of overwhelming power which in other novels Norris had so much admired. Moreover, once the book gets under way, it is, as Norris intended, a thrilling, hair-lifting story, a story almost too crowded with adventurous incident. Here, as in his earlier stories, Norris discovers excitement chiefly in the resurgence into civilized life of primitive passions and the primitive struggle for survival; he all but over-insists on the presentation of man as a fighting animal. The fury of the ranchers, at the meeting where they learn of the railroad's ruinous prices on land, becomes to him "the hideous squealing of the tormented brute, its back to the wall, defending its lair"; [41] the excitement of the posse trailing the fugitive Dyke is that of "the trackers exulting on the trail of the pursued." [42] In Norris's earlier writing, such episodes had frequently failed to "come off"; in *The Octopus*, supported by the whole texture of story and by the force of a maturer imagination, they become natural, credible, and powerful.

If, then, Norris succeeded so completely in the writing of a big, thrilling, intricately organized naturalistic story, what of his other and almost equally emphasized aim, the aim of telling the People that Truth to which he contends they have an inalienable right? Insofar as Truth is synonymous with the use of fact, he may very well have claimed success in this

[41] *The Octopus,* I, 265.
[42] *Ibid.,* II, 185.

endeavor too. For, in his preparation for writing *The Octopus,* Norris had studied his material with characteristic thoroughness. He had gone back to California especially for that purpose, had lived on a California ranch, had studied materials in the Mechanics Library in San Francisco, and had consulted the files of the San Francisco *Chronicle* about the railroad-rancher affair. The climax of the book—the shooting at the irrigating ditch—is based on the actual fight between farmers and deputies at Mussel Slough; the central situation, as to the leasing and price-grading of the lands, is historically accurate, even to the prices; the minor story of the engineer Dyke is derived from the actual train-robberies of Chris Evans and John Sontag. In the handling of all these and other materials,[43] Norris practiced a degree of fidelity to fact beyond which, it might well be claimed, a novelist could not afford to go.

What is more, the materials of *The Octopus* are as significant as they are authentic. The character of Magnus Derrick, for example, is significant not only in itself, but as a type of personality which Norris felt to be, in peculiar measure, the product of the West—the adventurer; and the economic experience summed up in the story lies, as we have seen, at the very core of American economic history during the latter nineteenth century. Yet, notwithstanding the centrality of these experiences, there runs through much of Norris's picture a certain disproportion. The very People of whom he theoretically made so much—the great mass of laborers and tenants on the Los Muertos ranch, for example—appear for the most part as only shadowy figures in the background of the story. The real conflict in the story is not the conflict of a free folk against aggressive tyranny, as Norris's poet Presley thinks.[44] It is rather the conflict of one big enterpriser—the collective ranchers—with another and larger enterpriser—the railroad.

[43] See, for a fuller discussion of Norris's preparation for *The Octopus,* with references to Norris's original source-material, Walker, *op. cit.,* pp. 243-61. Of especial interest is the passage (p. 261) about the adaptation of the story of Presley's poem, "The Toilers," from the historical story of Edwin Markham's "The Man with the Hoe."

[44] *The Octopus,* II, 249.

What interests Norris is not the struggling of average humanity, but the warfare of Titan against Olympian.

But facts alone, even facts discerningly chosen, are not
enough. When a novelist speaks largely of Truth in fiction,
we may reasonably expect of him, at the least, that he relate
these facts to ideas that are significant in themselves, and
that are sufficiently in agreement with one another to make
up a coherent view of life. Now it is in just this matter of
philosophical consistency that Norris, in *The Octopus,* falls
short. For, on the one hand, he interprets his story at times
by a philosophy of free will, according to which life is a moral
experience, and man a being of importance; and, on the other
hand, he interprets his story at other times by an optimistic
determinism, according to which life is an amoral experience,
and the individual man of no importance in comparison with
the total life-scheme. It is the moral viewpoint which controls
the story of Annixter's development in character under the
influence of Hilma Tree,[45] which gives tragic meaning to the
story of Magnus Derrick's decline,[46] and which motivates
throughout most of the story Presley's fierce indignation
against the railroad.[47] It is the amoral, deterministic viewpoint
which evokes Shelgrim's advice to Presley, "Blame conditions,
not men"; which finds voice in Vanamee's optimistic fatalism,
and which leaves with Presley, at last, the consolation of faith
in the cosmic Force that, although indifferent to the individual, works irresistibly toward the total good.[48] But the
reader, who has received so much of the story through the
medium of Presley's earlier, moral point of view, is nowhere
prepared for this sudden change of front, so that the large
optimism of the concluding pages, instead of serving its
apparent purpose of closing the terrible story upon a level
of serene reconciliation, has rather the disconcerting effect
of a verdict given against the evidence. The reader feels (to

---

[45] *The Octopus,* pp. 118, 148.
[46] *Ibid.,* II: 113. Observe also the moral implications of such a
phrase as "the anguish of compromise with conscience" (II, 171).
[47] For example, *ibid.,* II, 23.
[48] *Ibid.,* II, 285, 344-5, 359-61, respectively.

speak impressionistically) that he has been witnessing a flurry of hectic action without meaning, a spectacle sufficiently dramatic and thrilling, but of doubtful significance, or none at all. And therefore *The Octopus*, fine achievement that it is, is still not so fine as it might well have been could Norris have equalled in orderly thinking his excellence in keen perception and dramatic force.[49]

V

The Pit, although a story of some complexity itself, covers no such encyclopedic range as its predecessor. It is not a "big" novel, not a portrayal of an entire social order, nor, except incidentally, a novel of Purpose. Primarily, it is a romance of business struggle. It is a product of the same facet of Norris's mind that led him to proclaim, in *The Responsibilities of the Novelist*, that the true adventure of modern times is to be found in business, and that the businessman is the true descendant of the heroic man of action of the past. Like many a previous romancer, however, Norris was evidently unwilling to rest the whole interest of his story on adventurous enterprise; the adventure story must be a love story too. *The Pit* is, accordingly, made up of two distinguishable though clearly interlinked plots. The first is the story of the corner in wheat, in which the speculator Curtis Jadwin successfully fights his opponents, the Crookes gang, only to be faced with the larger obstacle of the sheer mass and weight of the Wheat itself. The second is the love story of Laura Dearborn, Curtis Jadwin, and Jadwin's rival, the artist Corthell. Subsidiary to the

---

[49] See, for a detailed and thoughtful study of the problem of Norris's philosophical inconsistency, Charles Child Walcutt, *Naturalism in the American Novel. A doctoral dissertation of the University of Michigan* (Ann Arbor, 1937), pp. 247-351. For a contrary opinion—namely, that Norris was philosophically consistent—see H. Willard Reninger, "Norris explains *The Octopus:* a Correlation of His Theory and Practice," *American Literature*, XII: 218-27 (May, 1940); and for a rejoinder, pointing out certain errors in Reninger's treatment, Charles Child Walcutt, "Frank Norris on Realism and Naturalism," *American Literature*, XIII: 61-3 (March, 1941).

first story are such episodes as the financial rehabilitation of the broken speculator Hargus, and the tragedy of Charles Cressler; subsidiary to the second are the episodes of Landry Court's infatuation with Laura Dearborn, and his later successful courtship of Laura's younger sister, Page.

But in the creation of a romantic story of love and adventure, Norris did not by any means forget his convictions about fiction and Truth. In its substructure of fact, for example, *The Pit* is to Chicago what *The Octopus* is to California, although, of course, on a much more limited scale. Norris's knack of abundant and precise observation is at its best in the brilliant opening scenes at the opera, and again in Laura Dearborn's perception of the mingled romance and formidable power of Chicago itself—the great gray city which, brooking no rival, "imposed its dominion upon a reach of country larger than many a kingdom of the Old World." [50] Norris did not, however, depend upon general observation alone, but, according to his custom, thoroughly studied up his subject. With the help of George Gibbs, he studied the operation of the Wheat Pit at the Chicago Board of Trade; and later, during the actual writing of *The Pit*, he sought the advice of the young broker George Moulson. For a central core of story he chose, as in *The Octopus*, an actual event—in this case the corner in wheat engineered by Joseph Leiter in 1897. [51] And, having chosen his story, he developed it with an evident view to complete plausibility, so that the account of Jadwin's first important venture on the market, of his intricate maneuverings, of his clash with the Crookes gang, of the increasing burden of keeping track of his immense holdings, of his gradual exhaustion in strength and judgment, and of the final collapse of his Corner, unfolds with such entire naturalness as to appear inevitable. The effect of the story is to convey to the reader a complete realization of the Pit, both in its outer and dramatic aspects, as seen in the picture of a typical day's trading, and in its remoter and more involved economic results, as Jadwin's corner reacts in wider and wider causation on pro-

[50] *The Pit*, pp. 55-8.
[51] Walker, *op. cit.*, pp. 275-8.

ducers and consumers throughout the world.[52] And in the interpretation of these abundant factual details Norris employs, with more consistency though far less emphasis than in *The Octopus*, the idea of determinism. Natural forces, it appears, dominate men. As Jadwin puts the matter, "The Corner made itself. I happened to stand between two sets of circumstances, and they made me do what I've done." [53]

The characters of *The Pit*, although they are limited in number, and although only one is essential to Norris's aim of evoking the romance of business, reveal once more his eye for amusing eccentricities and his knack of individualizing his people. Among the vividly drawn grotesques and humors of the novel are the wrecked financier Hargus, the wealthy blackguard Scanlon, the plaintive Jewish trader Grossman, the placid Aunt Wes,' and the *malapropos* Isabel Gretry. More elaborately drawn are the apparently substantial merchant, Charles Cressler, the keen young businessman, Landry Court, and the beautiful and quaintly solemn Page Dearborn. Of the three major figures, Corthell is vividly but somewhat too perfectly the gentleman turned artist; Laura Dearborn, a piquant combination of zest for life, delicately statuesque beauty, imperiousness, and temperament; Curtis Jadwin, by far and away the principal figure of the novel, the embodiment of Norris's ideas of the romance of business.

Looked at in the light of his portrayal of Curtis Jadwin, the outcome of Norris's attempt to romanticize business appears curiously indecisive. Within Norris's Jadwin, to be sure, the romantic motive of love of excitement has superseded the less interesting motives of rapacity and greed frequently attributed to the financier. Jadwin plays the wheat market for "the fun of the game," and, when once habituated to speculation, finds it too fascinating to give up.[54] The game is, of course, warfare without quarter; throughout the story Norris insists on the idea of business as battle. To Laura Dearborn, for ex-

[52] See particularly pp. 84 ff., the trading-day in summary, and pp. 318 ff., the most extensive account of the economic effects of the corner.

[53] *The Pit*, p. 270.

[54] *The Pit*, pp. 80, 180-1, 220, 247-50.

ample, Jadwin is a hero of the Battle of the Street, that ruthless struggle into which only the strong and the brave may venture. He piques her curiosity as a type of the "fighter, unknown and unknowable to women...; hard, rigorous, panoplied in the harness of the warrior, who strove among the trumpets, and who, in the brunt of conflict, conspicuous, formidable, set the battle in a rage around him, and exulted like a champion in the shoutings of the captains." [55] All this is, no doubt, too grandiose; but that Norris made of Jadwin's commercial warfare a gripping and stirring drama, which the reader follows with the same taut intensity with which he might observe a brilliantly fought-out football game, no one is likely to deny.

Nevertheless, whether or not by Norris's deliberate intention, his portrayal of Jadwin is constantly slipping over from the plane of romance into that of realism, almost of satire. His theoretically heroic Jadwin gradually takes form, almost as if in spite of the author, as no romantic hero at all, but as a very human, good-natured fumbler who, in the absence of much inward resource or discipline, picks up first this and then the other toy to amuse himself with, wears off its freshness, and thrusts it aside. The Jadwin who sets out to make of his Mission enterprise the "biggest Sunday School in Chicago," a veritable "Sunday School Trust," and then abandons it; the Jadwin who professes Christian good will *a la* Moody and Sankey and then enjoys conducting his corner on the principle of *vae victis;* the Jadwin who pursues Laura Dearborn aggressively until she is formally listed among his assets, and then neglects her; the Jadwin whose determinism occurs to him only when, small-boy like, he needs a means of evading moral responsibility [56]—this Jadwin is indeed a most affectionately drawn, interesting, and convincing character; but he is not a romantic hero. Whether because Norris's knack of realistic observation got the better of him, or because his ideas of romance were inadequate, he

[55] *Ibid.,* p. 60.

[56] See, in regard to these aspects of Jadwin's character, *The Pit,* pp. 67-8, 116, 215 ff., 270, 310 ff.

certainly created in Curtis Jadwin neither a belated antique fighter nor a modern financial genius, but rather a big, overgrown boy blundering through situations that call for a mature, self-controlling man. Jadwin is, in short, less the descendant of Scott's Ivanhoe than the ancestor of Sinclair Lewis's Babbitt.[57]

VI

Both *The Octopus* and *The Pit*, understood in the light of Norris's literary theories, show how tenuous were his ties with traditional American democracy, and how little he shared the concern of the authors of the Left-Center over the extension of the democratic principle into economics. The agrarian democracy which had helped form the minds of Clemens and Howells had had too little chance to reach him; and although some of his contemporaries might still be destined to carry on that tradition, he himself had been born under a different star. Conditioned from childhood into the business materialism of the Gilded Age, and equipped by temperament as a novelist of adventure, he accepted readily enough the sternness of the business struggle, and found within it the stuff of adventures he felt to be as exciting as those of the feudal heroes of the past. Gifted as he was, he was therefore able to take up a type of fiction—the romance of economic conflict—that was being produced competently but with no great brilliance by a sizeable minority of novelists, and, having made it his own, to lift it from the subliterary to the literary level. In so doing, he went far toward interpreting his stories by a philosophy peculiarly appropriate to them—a naturalistic determinism which sets up as the principal human value the thrill of successful struggle for survival. But in that interpretation he did not go the whole way; and the survival in his work of moral themes and attitudes, the mingling of deterministic and undeterministic strains of

[57] Jadwin acts with something like romantic heroism in only one instance—in the very closing scene of the book, where he and Laura accept the loss of their fortune calmly, almost indifferently, and set out together to make their way again.

thought, shows to what extent the contradictory leadings of two widely divergent views of life left him confused.

In any discriminating judgment of Norris's worth, this confusion of mind must necessarily be remembered to his detriment. Philosophical consistency, philosophical unity, is not, of course, the *most* important requisite in the art of fiction. But neither is it negligible; and the author who neglects it denies to himself (in another sense than that in which Poe meant the phrase) the immense force derivable from totality. More serious than Norris's confusion of ideas, however, is a certain dearth within him of the very finest imaginative quality, a limitation more easily felt than defined, and not at all similar to Howells' easily discernible lack of force. Force Norris had preëminently, along with immense fecundity, immense exuberance. But he did not have, in the highest degree, a certain "fusing" quality of imagination—the power, that is, of causing the most diverse elements in a story to appear, not as if they had been put together by formal handiwork, but as if they had grown together naturally and of themselves. Norris's imagination recombines rather than recreates; and its artistic product sometimes appears, in consequence, artificial and synthetic rather than natural and organic.

This falling-short of Norris's imagination, or perhaps his impetuous, uncritical temperament, is reflected in his vigorous but imperfect style. His speech is, to be sure, always forceful, often powerful, and sometimes admirably sensitive and transparent; but, on the other hand, it is frequently turgid, confused, and merely voluble. Like an inexperienced wood-chopper, he does with a half-dozen haphazard blows the thing a skillful workman would do with a single clean stroke. His words are a miscellaneous shower of projectiles hurled in the general direction of the target. It is not by any finality of diction, surely, but by mere abundance and brute force that Norris suggests the symbolism of the speeding locomotive in *The Octopus*:—"The galloping monster, the terror of steam and steel, with its single eye, Cyclopean, red, shooting from horizon to horizon; ... symbol of a vast power, huge, terrible, flinging the echo of its thunder over all the reaches of the valley, leaving blood and destruction in its path; the leviathan, with tentacles of steel clutching into the soil, the soulless Force, the iron-hearted Power, the monster, the Colossus, the Octopus." [58]

Nevertheless, when all the legitimate criticisms of Norris have been made, they do not appear, when weighed against the solid worth of his writing, of major importance. The very need for pointing out that his imagination fell short of finality indicates that that imagination was a superior one indeed; and Norris's failures in philosophical consistency and in economy of style are failures in certain useful accessories of fiction, not in its absolute essentials. In those essentials, Norris is strong indeed. When all objections have been urged against him, certain conclusions about the solidity of his achievement remain unchanged. Those conclusions are (to speak summarily) as follows:—The aims Norris set up for himself are on the whole legitimate aims, to whose worth the history of fiction affords more than sufficient testimony. He had an uncanny knack of finding, recognizing, and telling good stories; and he equipped his stories with an abundance of characters, many of them curiously interesting, some of them racy and picturesque, most of them sharply individualized. Both his stories and his people he rendered through a medium of rich and vivid perception, the wide range of which includes the homeliest commonplace, the harshest ugliness, the most richly colored beauty, and an elusive mysticism. In fine, Norris succeeded abundantly in the proper work of the novelist—the creation of a large, credible, interesting, and significant imaginative world.

[58] *The Octopus,* p. 48.

CHAPTER EIGHT

SUMMARY AND CONCLUSIONS

I

So far, we have looked at the economic novel chiefly from the viewpoint of its service in social leadership. We have seen how, in its portrayal of virtually all phases of industrial life, it provided all necessary means whereby the society of the newly born Machine Age might be made known to itself. We have seen by what ideologies it sought to interpret that society and to point the way to its improvement. Yet these critical and didactic functions of the novel, however great their importance, do not include—as the majority of readers will doubtless agree—the novel's main and primary function. The main and primary function of the novel is to give pleasure. In the more ephemeral, journalistic sorts of fiction, the novelist offers at least the minimum pleasure of passing entertainment; in novels of more stamina, he offers also the larger, completer, and more meaningful pleasure afforded by the fine arts. The economic novelist is under precisely the same obligation as any other novelist to give pleasure; and in the giving of pleasure he must depend, like any other novelist, on his resources of technique, his repertoire of interesting stories and interesting people, and his intangible creative power.

Accordingly, before we review in final summary the social message of the economic novel, we shall pause for a while, and perhaps even digress, in order to look at the economic novel not as an agency in cultural leadership, but simply as fiction. We shall inquire (1) in what ways the forces

of society entered into the purely fictional qualities of
the novel—the authors' typical methods, their stories, their
characters; and (2) what degree of artistic success the economic novelists achieved. In answering the first question, it
will be possible to speak with considerable exactness, although
we shall not escape subjective judgments altogether. In answering the second, it will be necessary to depend very largely
on subjective evaluation and opinion.

But into many of the art-qualities of the economic novel—
it should be made clear immediately—the immediate social
background hardly enters at all; and this is especially true
of all that pertains to the authors' methods of fiction, as distinguished from their materials. It is true of their choice of
approach, their technique, their style. If there exists any
organic relation between materials and form, the American
economic novel fails to disclose it. Nothing is clearer than
that the typical procedure of a novelist was not to develop
some fictional form peculiarly suited to his materials, but to
shape his materials into whatever form he had found suited
to his own talents. Into the writing of economic fiction
Clemens carried his previously developed knack of racy
anecdote, pungent satire, and telling apologue; Howells, his
previously developed skill in the ethical problem-novel and
the realistic presentation of character; Bellamy, his strange
gift for unworldly fantasy. All three, along with other novelists, taught their social lessons by means of the usual devices
of didactic fiction. That is, they illustrated the lesson in a
series of imagined events, or they had their characters talk
about it, or they preached it directly. In the economic novels
of all three, as well as of other writers, the proportioning of
realism and romanticism varies through about the same
gamut as in the general fiction of the time.

Likewise, the style of the economic novel insofar as a
composite style may be observed among the numerous individual variations—is simply the general prose style of the
period. That style observes, practically without exceptions,
the proprieties which that period inherited from the latter
eighteenth and early nineteenth centuries. It observes, that

is, the restraints laid upon it by the Genteel Tradition. Nevertheless, in the treatment of the unpleasant and the immoral, authors were very little hampered in saying what they meant. The conventions of the age permitted the *ethical* treatment of the unpleasant and the immoral; and therefore, although the obscenities characteristic of recent proletarian fiction nowhere appear in its published work, the literary exposure of social degradation stands forth in stark, astonishing completeness—in such completeness, in fact, that the writings of an additional generation have not added a single major charge to that indictment.[1]

Quite evidently, the style and method of the economic novel are, in all matters except those immediately dependent on the author's personality, simply the outcome of contemporary usage. In their origin, these usages themselves may, of course, relate to certain social forces; but no such relationship is discoverable within the time-limits of the so-called Gilded Age. It is not, then, in the methods of fictional art, but rather in the materials, that the effects of contemporary social forces are most clearly visible; for, in all that concerns the choice of stories, of characters, of scenes, and even of ideas and interests, the coming of industrialism wrought, even within a single generation, immense changes.

This is not to say that industrial life gave novelists many stories that were absolutely new. The established stories of fiction, based as they are on a few central, permanent human relationships, have a way of perpetuating themselves from age to age, changing of course in incidents and scenes and social backgrounds, but remaining basically the same. Now the stories in economic fiction are mostly just these old, tried, established plots, their ancient outlines refurbished with in-

---

[1] However, on a quite different ground from that of the observance of the Victorian proprieties, a strong case might be made out against the stylistic conventions of the Gilded Age. The most serious fault appears to be the frequent toleration of the vague, the general, the *cliché*. Expressions like Henry Francis Keenan's "the most alarming threats were openly uttered," or Merwin and Webster's "five minutes later the legal luminary stepped out of the telephone box" reveal these shortcomings so patently as to make comment unnecessary.

cidents from modern industrial life. Originality in plot, it would seem, consists mostly in putting new wine into old bottles, and making both look as if they belonged together. This blending of new incidents and ancient formulas reveals all degrees of craftsmanship, and achieves all degrees (except the absolute highest) of artistic success. In the poorer stories, the cleavage between some quaint, fantastic story and its modern industrial message is absurdly patent. In the better, the fusion is so nicely managed that the basic situation about which the plot is built is likely to *look* original, although actually it is not.

No story-type is, for instance, more permanently useful than that in which love is made to triumph over obstacles. The plot-formula itself, at least as recently outlined by a popular dramatist, is sufficiently simple:—Boy meets Girl, Boy loses Girl, Boy gets Girl. But it allows of any amount of variation. The obstacle to be overcome may be parental hostility, as in the *Midsummer Night's Dream;* or a series of misunderstandings, as in *Pride and Prejudice;* or class differences, as in *The Squire of Low Degree;* or any one of a thousand other things. Now, in the management of plot, nothing could be simpler than so to adapt this ancient formula as to allow the obstacle to true love to grow out of industrial conflict; and such an adaptation actually occurs in a number of economic novels. In Lynn Boyd Porter's *Speaking of Ellen,* Ellen Eastland, a gifted labor leader, supposedly of illegitimate birth, and Philip Westland, the legal agent of a corporation against which she directs a strike, are attracted to each other, but are held apart, for a while, by their conflicting class-interests and points of view. The obstacles between them are overcome, finally, by the discovery of Ellen's legitimacy and inherited wealth, and their finding a common social ground in interest in philanthropic work and profit-sharing. In this story, the adaptation of an old formula to a new background is sufficiently crude; the plot-machinery audibly creaks. The difficulty, moreover, is not merely that portions of the story are incredible. More fundamental than that, it lies simply in the absence of a creative imagination powerful enough to fuse old formula and new incident into a convincing artistic unity.

A much superior adaptation of the same ancient plot occurs, however, in Mary Wilkins Freeman's *The Portion of Labor*. Ellen Brewster, daughter of a respectable but unsuccessful New England family, has been the schoolmate and youthful friend of Robert Lloyd, son of the local mill-owner. Reverses suffered by her family compel her to go to work in the mill; and when Robert, inheriting the property, finds it necessary to reduce wages, she leads out the factory girls on strike. After several weeks, during which the mill people are brought to the edge of starvation, the strike collapses. The later reunion of Robert and Ellen, following their bitter struggle; the quiet resurgence of their sense of companionship, their reconciliation and unspoken forgiveness, are the theme of one of the most finely imagined passages in the economic novel. The superiority of this sort of writing to anything in *Speaking of Ellen* inheres largely in the immensely finer articulation of the old story-pattern with the life of the latter nineteenth century; and this, in turn, is a natural product of the superior imaginative quality of the author's mind.

Another kind of story, less ancient, perhaps, but still of quite respectable age, is that in which some sensitive individual falls victim to the unjust institutions of society; and this story-pattern, too, could be adapted easily to the uses of the economic novel. As Mrs. Stowe had painted the sufferings of victims of slavery in *Uncle Tom's Cabin,* so a Garland or a Howells could paint the sufferings of victims of capitalism in *Jason Edwards* or *A Hazard of New Fortunes.* As Mrs. Stowe's Uncle Tom is destroyed by slavery, Garland's Jason Edwards is destroyed by the capitalistic combination of low wages and land-monopoly. Garland, however, did not bring his story to the fullness of imaginative realization which Mrs. Stowe had reached, or which he himself had reached in his short stories, with the result that *Jason Edwards*, in spite of its sturdiness and occasional power, fails of artistic authority. Moreover, just as Mrs. Stowe's St. Clare is, notwithstanding his wealth, as truly a victim of slavery as is Uncle Tom, so are

Howells' Dryfoos family in A *Hazard of New Fortunes* victims of the capitalistic craze for money, as they uncomprehendingly suffer their tragedy of deracination, aimlessness, and loss of the deeper human satisfactions. In this story, as in Mary Wilkins Freeman's *The Portion of Labor*, the author's imagination has been fine and strong enough to elaborate the old story-outline perfectly with convincing modern incident, with the result that the *Hazard*, understood in the light of Howells' purpose and of its contemporary climate of opinion, achieves precisely that complete aesthetic authority which is absent from Garland's *Jason Edwards*.

Besides these two stories—that of lovers overcoming obstacles and that of some victim of society—many others long familiar to readers of fiction proved adaptable to an industrial background. The story of the effort of an idealist (remote kinsman of Shakespeare's Brutus) to right some great wrong in the state appears in such a novel as Florence Converse's *The Burden of Christopher*, in which Christopher Kenyon fails in his effort to ameliorate the lot of the poor through profit-sharing. The story of a young man's growth through error toward mature self-realization, employed by Goethe in *Wilhelm Meister's Apprenticeship*, appears in Robert Herrick's *The Web of Life*, in which the physician Sommers grows into self-mastery in the midst of Philistine Chicago and the violence of the Pullman strike. The story of the deterioration of a character, employed by George Eliot in *Romola*, appears in Charles K. Lush's *The Federal Judge*, in which the decline of the central character, Judge Dunn, follows his unconscious adaptation to social and economic pressures. The story of the solution of a crime, a commonplace in fiction since the time of Poe, appears in John Hay's *The Breadwinners*, in which the criminal is at the same time a leader of organized labor. Above all, the story of the struggle between men for mastery, comparable to Scott's *Ivanhoe*, appears in the stories of economic conflict written by Will Payne and Frank Norris.

Apparently, the finest narratives in economic fiction are those (qualities of keen suspense and general value being assumed) in which the new materials afforded by industrial society are most perfectly integrated with the established story-patterns of the race. The very considerable originality of the economic novelists is expressed, not in the development of new story-frameworks, but in the discovery and use of new and convincing materials with which to elaborate the old.

This wealth of new incidents almost necessarily brought with it into the novel a number of new character-types. Naturally, the new population of the novel were also a product of industrial life; or, rather, a product of the impression which industrial life made upon the middle-class mind. Significantly, the new characterizations include relatively few figures from the proletariat; the Poor—primary object of middle-class solicitude—come into focus only as a class, not as individuals. The one sharply limned character-type drawn from the proletariat is the walking delegate, who is usually conventionalized as a type of unreliability, of parasitism. Beside him appears sometimes, in contrast, the "sound" labor leader, as the workman-leader Tom Keating in Leroy Scott's *The Walking Delegate* is contrasted with the rascally organizer Buck Foley. Somewhat more nebulous than these two typical figures is that of the slum-girl-driven-to-prostitution—Fawcett's Cora Strang or Crane's Maggie; and more nebulous still—indeed, hardly discernible at all—are the figures of the ordinary, everyday working man and working girl.[2]

But the majority of the characters that throng the pages of the economic novel came either from the middle classes directly, or from the members of the plutocracy in which the middle class had some primary interest. These characters include the old-fashioned, "solid" middle-class businessman, like the elder Hilary in Howells' *The Quality of Mercy;* the business adventurer, like Bidwell in Lush's *The Autocrats;* the capitalist's tool or henchman, like Hilliard in Keenan's *The Money-Makers;* the corrupt politician, like Senator Dilworthy in *The Gilded Age;* the wealthy dilettante, like Fred Lawrence in *Hope Mills;* the social climber, like Selma White

---

[2] One or two exceptions to these rather sweeping generalizations suggest themselves—most notably, Norris's engineer, Dyke, in *The Octopus.*

in Grant's *Unleavened Bread;* the reformer, like Murvale
Eastman in Tourgée's novel of that name; the settlement-
worker, whether a man, like Boyesen's Philip Warburton, or
a woman, like Howells' Margaret Vance; the idealistic young
capitalist, like Kenyon in *The Burden of Christophor;* and,
probably most important, the modern capitalist and organizer
of large-scale corporate business.

Crowded as is this gallery of human figures, it is almost
wholly devoid of characters of real fictional greatness. The
raciness, the rich humanity of a Huck Finn or a Nigger Jim
simply do not exist there; and, indeed, it is only in the hands
of a preëminently skilled craftsman like Howells that these
people so much as take on individuality. One character-type
among them did, however, receive more attention than the
others, and in repeated handlings did come to give promise of
a significance, for the industrial era, which Cooper's Leatherstocking had had for a former time. That type was the great
capitalist.

In earlier novels, the great capitalist is presented in much
the same way as the walking delegate; that is, he is studied
always from a hostile viewpoint, and his character is simplified into the handful of malevolent traits which appeared
most appropriate to a business pirate. For instance, the magnate Belcher in J. G. Holland's *Sevenoaks,* Henderson in
Warner's *A Little Journey in the World,* and Kishu in Tourgée's *Murvale Eastman,* all have in common the repellent
traits of greed, thirst for power, mysterious control over business, utter lack of scruple, and utter disregard of the public
interest. Decided variations from this conventional norm,
however, were already appearing:—Howells' Dryfoos, pathet-
ically confused in the midst of a highly complex world where
he understands only the getting of money; presently, Charles
K. Lush's Gardwell in *The Federal Judge,* persuasive, amica-
ble, magnetic, "as soft-spoken a man as ever . . . scuttled a corporation in a sea of watered stock"; [3] and, still later, Norris's
Shelgrim in *The Octopus,* dominating the indecisive Presley
and comforting him for the deaths of his friends with a cheer-

[3] Charles K. Lush, *The Federal Judge,* p. 178.

fully callous fatalism. Among these less conventional studies, two characters, at least, achieve not only individuality but some qualities of greatness. Dexter, the "Duke of Gas" in Will Payne's *The Money Captain,* leaves a unique impression of immense, quiet power, considerably humanized by the contrast between his anti-social business methods and his personal consideration for others. Quite as individual as Dexter, quite as powerful, and much more fully aware of the code, at once unscrupulous and creative, by which he lives, is the capitalist Harrington in Robert Herrick's *Memoirs of an American Citizen.*

Beginning his career in the eighties as a young man in Chicago, Harrington resolutely sets for himself the one goal which society there offers him—Success. Observing the impotence of the middle-class ideal of civic righteousness as it is practiced by his employer Dround, he discards it in favor of a Nietzschean philosophy of power:—"The strong must rule. . . . Yes, life was for the strong, all there was in it! I saw it so then, and I have lived it so all my life." [4] To Harrington, the assertion of strength often requires the use of illegal methods, never of wholly irresponsible ones. He will not sell dishonest goods, nor abandon a group of unprotected stockholders; but he will, without scruple, secure rebates, secretly break secret agreements, indirectly bribe a judge, and directly buy a legislature. Illegalities, after all, matter less than the doing of creative work. Thinking over these things, and rebelling against the rigidly conventional scale in which his former sweetheart, now alienated, continues to weigh him, Harrington reflects:

These were my plants, my car line, my railroads, my elevators, my lands—all good tools in the infinite work of the world. Conceived for good or for ill, brought into being by fraud or daring —what man could judge of *their* worth. There they were, a part of God's great world. They were done; and mine was the hand. Let another, more perfect, turn them to a larger use; nevertheless, on my labor, on me, he must build.

Involuntarily my eyes rose from the ground and looked straight

[4] Herrick, Robert, *Memoirs of an American Citizen,* p. 94.

before me, to the vista of time. Surely there was another scale, a grander one, and by this I should not be found wholly wanting.[5]

From such a characterization, transcending as it does the limitations of the class struggle and the class philosophy that made it possible, the road leads straight to Theodore Dreiser's epochal study of Frank Cowperwood in *The Financier* and *The Titan*.

Besides incidents and characters, many scenes and physical backgrounds—the composite stage on which the action of the economic novel transpires—are also shaped out of materials furnished by contemporary industrial life. The millionaire's palace, the noisome slum, the sweatshop, the humming factory, the business office, the crowded street—all these are as integral a part of economic fiction as the dark forests, the gray skies, and the gray seacoasts of New England are a part of the stories of Hawthorne. And all of these things enter, necessarily, into what might be called the sensuous texture of the novel, its satisfactions for eye and ear and sensitive touch.

Moreover, there is a sense in which the principal ideas and interests of any age are themselves materials of its fiction, while at the same time they are factors in the interpretation and disposal of other materials. Of the former—the ideas employed in our fiction—we shall speak again, in a concluding summary. Of the latter, it may be remarked that the Gilded Age witnessed often the old phenomenon of the evoking or diverting of literary effort by some shift in the events that caught the public mind. The capital-labor conflicts of the latter seventies and early eighties were significantly followed by the fictional controversy in which Aldrich and Hay and others attacked organized labor, and Keenan and Clemens and others defended it. Likewise, during the latter nineties, the diversion of the national interest from economic reform to the return of prosperity, to war, and to imperialism, was significantly accompanied by a relative decline in humanitarian fiction, and an increase in the writing of romances of economic struggle. Evidently, the idea-and-interest content

---

[5] *Ibid.*, p. 346. Reprinted by permission of The Macmillan Company, publishers.

of the public mind—at least the public mind as interpreted by writers and publishers—determined what fictional methods and materials were more acceptable, what less; what kinds of novels were frowned on, what kinds encouraged.

Even so brief a survey of the introduction into the novel of materials from industrial life should serve to give a new concreteness and freshness to the time-worn platitude that literature is an outgrowth of society, a product not merely of individual minds but of the total culture of a given place and time. Evidently there is involved, in the making of even a commonplace novel, a confluence of many social forces. Evidently, in the work of a major author, literary creation involves an exceedingly complex fusion of social and personal factors, in which are intermingled the influence of the society known to the author's youth, the influence of the society known to his maturity, his own individual temperament, his personal experiences and relationships, his knowledge of literary tradition and technique, and the conditions of publication in the midst of which he wrote. Extensive knowledge in regard to all these things—the kind of knowledge preëminently which is afforded by historical investigation—undoubtedly contributes much to our understanding of an author's *total* intention and *total* achievement in any given work. Without knowledge of this sort, we are liable to such elementary errors as, for example, the view that Howells' *A Hazard of New Fortunes* is to be interpreted as a study of class conflict in the Marxian sense; and our critical judgments, however sound the taste that prescribes them, will necessarily go awry because they are premised on actual error or on insufficient fact. But once equipped with such knowledge, we own at least one indispensable group of the tools needful in that most difficult and challenging task, the conquest of all the resources of some great creative mind.

Nevertheless, when historical, genetic study has done its entire and important work, it still leaves unaccounted for some of the very mainsprings of literary art. For a genuine literary creation is always more than the sum of the materials and the tangible forces that enter into it. The intangible factor of creative power mingles tone with tone and makes, not a chord, but a star; adds two and two and makes, not four, but infinity. And therefore the status of the economic novel as art cannot be wholly gauged from a study of materials and forces alone. It must be approached also from another point of view—that of the value of the finished and total aesthetic product; and to that subject, accordingly, as a conclusion, it will now be necessary to turn.

II

Now judgments of the value of fiction are necessarily subjective, if for no other reason than that they must often pass beyond matters of execution and form into the larger matter of human values. Any answer to the question, "How valuable is the human experience offered by this novel?" turns inescapably upon the critic's answer to the larger question, "What human experiences are of most worth, after all?" and upon this final question it is plain that even the wisest human beings may not agree. The objectivity of value, however the philosophically minded may theorize about it, is still only a theory; we still value simply what we intuitively feel to be valuable, and we do not all feel alike. Until this condition becomes otherwise—until men are agreed on values as they are agreed on the principles of physics—there can be no "objective," precise, and fully dependable aesthetics; and judgments of art will continue to vary in accordance with the varying personal standards of the critics.

All this, however, need not justify critical eccentricity, or excuse the vagaries of an undisciplined impressionism. For, although we have no *absolute* science of aesthetic values, we nevertheless own some exceedingly useful—indeed, indispensable—criteria for *relative* judgments. The race, in its long experience with literature, observing, choosing, preserving, discarding, has gradually developed a body of collective judgments, by reference to which individual vagaries of taste may be chastened, and also a body of "classic" writings, according to which the merits of other writings may be gauged. Even the novel, which as literary types go is still quite young, possesses, in the writings of a Fielding, an Austen, a Tolstoy, a Hardy, a group of classics sustained by this sort of permanent collective approval. In some rough measure, therefore, the artistic worth of a Hay, an Aldrich, or a Howells can be gauged by mentally placing his work alongside the acknowledged classics of fiction, and estimating, in comparison, the quality and range of the total aesthetic pleasure he affords.

"Total aesthetic pleasure" comprehends, of course, far more than the pleasure sought by most readers of fiction—that of entertainment. Entertainment—the pleasure of somewhat passively watching the story-spectacle float before the fancy— is furnished by most of the competent journalistic storytellers, by the artistically poor as well as by the good. It is furnished likewise by most writers of the economic novel. Those writers excluded whose aims clearly reached no farther than the production of tracts, it may be safely claimed that the typical economic novelist understood and practiced the novelist's basic craft of getting a story started and keeping it going; he knew how both to awaken and to maintain suspense. But the pleasure on which aesthetic judgment must turn is a larger pleasure than this. It is no less than the pleasure of complete living, inasmuch as the objective of literary art is, after all, a certain heightening, intensifying, and refining of experience, to the end that the reader may live not a barren life but an abundant one, not an incomplete life but a complete one, not one life alone, but, in imagination, many. The finest literary art is, in short, that which offers in largest measure the whole experience of enlarged, intensified, and more significant living, and in so doing creates a spiritual home adequate for the needs of the race. To the degree in which the economic novelists succeed in that sort of creative task, as its scope and possibilities are revealed in the admitted classics of fiction—to that degree we may be sure that the economic novel is good art.

A priori, we might, according to our point of view, expect the economic novel to be either better or worse than the novel in general. On the one hand, the American economic novelist carried out quite thoroughly a program whose value had been drilled into the minds of our creative authors for generations—

the program of abandoning foreign themes and of using, instead, "vital" American materials; and if that program were sound, the novel should have profited accordingly. On the other hand, the novelist faced a very great difficulty in what we might call the task of "humanizing" his industrial materials. The Machine was—and is—too new in human development to have become much interwoven with the rich resources of human experience stored in the racial memory; too new to satisfy the thousand inborn nervous capacities for perceiving and doing which have grown up throughout centuries of delicate interplay between the human organism and a non-mechanical environment. A shoe factory obviously calls forth no such train of aesthetically valuable associations as a ruinous well-sweep or grove-sheltered cottage; and therefore the novelist, if he would make aesthetic use of that factory, has need of much skill in overcoming the handicap of its barrenness in connotation.

Nevertheless, and in spite of any apparent advantages or disadvantages of the fiction of industrialism, the plain, simple fact is (if the impressions of one observer may be trusted) that the specialized subject-matter of the economic novels has neither helped nor harmed them as art, and that they are no whit better or worse than are novels in general. In the economic novel, as in any other fiction, the scale from the best writing to the poorest is a wide one indeed, and the overwhelming majority of novels find their inescapable place on the inferior side. Such inferior novels do not, now, appreciably enlarge, intensify, or in any way nourish the imaginative life. Casual parlor entertainment and instruction at their earliest and best, they are now become only documents; so that in preserving them the bibliographer, who appears to have taken as his motto the dictum that none of these little ones should perish, can be said to have done no favor to the general reader, but only to the historian. Competence, intelligence, and occasionally real charm speak from their yellowing pages, but still without bringing forth one significant thought or feeling that is not duplicated, or improved on, in the fine minorities of superior art. No neglected Melville, we may rest assured, will ever rise from these ashes. Except as the exacting muse of history may have need of them, we may safely leave them to a repose appropriate to the quiet dead.

To pass from these commonplace writings into the work of some author of classic or near-classic quality is to pass from some dull half-drowse into wakefulness. It is to exchange a world of drab, limited, and shallow experience for one in which the life-currents flow large, intense, and deep. Now among the novels of industrialism, as among novels in general, a minority do awaken this sense of multitudinous, finely perceived life. None, perhaps, enrich and awaken as do the half-dozen final masterpieces of the race—the *Hamlets* and *Fausts*—but several own a life sufficiently broad, strong, and significant to place them among or near the enduring classics of our literature. To attempt a ranking of a few of these novels in the order of their aesthetic worth might well be suggestive and valuable, although any such procedure must of course be highly arbitrary, highly subjective.

Among these few superior writings, the supreme work appears to be Mark Twain's *A Connecticut Yankee in King Arthur's Court*. Faults that book has in abundance, as Andrew Lang and others have sufficiently pointed out; but its faults are negligible when weighed against its immense vitality. For, more than any other among the economic novels, it realizes through sheer creative force the one supreme end of literary art—that the reader may, in the completest and finest sense, have life, and have it more abundantly. Beyond any other, it comprehends within itself the specific qualities of greatness. It has bigness, exuberance, zest, intensity, emotional power. It has humor—overflowing, pungent, irresistible humor. It has, unlike some of Mark Twain's writings, artistic unity. It has an uncanny aptness to the bent of our national mind, with its somewhat strangely mingled trends of materialism, humanitarian feeling, and frontier independence. It has that tremendously important quality which we must call, for lack of a better term, archetypal appeal—the ability to awaken the deepest, oldest human capacities for aesthetic perception and experience. It has, above all, the final elusiveness, resourcefulness, and challenging incalculability of genius.

Second to the *Connecticut Yankee* in artistic worth, we might place, with more questionable justice, Bellamy's *Looking Backward*, partly because of its artistry, but chiefly because of its immense significance in the democratizing and humanizing of the Machine. For the third position we might reasonably choose Howells' *A Hazard of New Fortunes*, which in perfect workmanship, in broad, acute observation, and in mellow wisdom rises superior to the *Yankee*, but in some indispensable quality of dynamic force falls far below it. For fourth place, we might choose Garland's finely wrought *Main-Travelled Roads* series; for fifth, Norris's *The Octopus*, big, but lacking in some final authority; and for sixth, Mark Twain's and Warner's exuberant but inchoate satire, *The Gilded Age.* These six books, together with a few others of nearly equal value, add up at most to only a small minority of our economic novels; but that minority is nevertheless as large a proportion and of as genuine a quality of excellence as we might reasonably expect. Indeed, it would be difficult to find in the problem-fiction of any one generation, anywhere, a half-dozen volumes offering values more fine and abundant than do these.

Yet these novels, which in their final effect appear so rich and significant and powerful, stemmed from precisely the same environment which nurtured literally hundreds of small barren shoots of fiction that withered in a day, and that neither should, or can, ever be revived. The same historical background, the same social forces, the same climate of opinion that produced Mark Twain's *Connecticut Yankee* produced also Lynn Boyd Porter's ephemeral romance, *Speaking of Ellen.* Both these books were wrought out in the course of the struggle of an older middle-class democratic culture to control the powerful forces loosed by the Machine; both represent, on the whole, the viewpoint of the liberal Left-Center. Nevertheless, for all their similarities in ideology, their differences from each other are immense, their divergence in aesthetic worth incalculable. They differ as the mind of a well-

intentioned and reasonably competent journalist—Porter—
differs from the mind of one of the great geniuses of the race—
Mark Twain. If then one effect of historical investigation is
to make plain the exact and full accomplishment of a major
author, another effect is, by designating sharply all those
environmental factors which the major creative artist owns
in common with his inferiors, to bring into sharp focus the one
factor in which he is absolutely distinct—largeness of creative
personality. And therefore the final outcome of our survey of
the aesthetics of sociological fiction might well be the re-
inforcing of a very old, fundamental concept of criticism—that
of the importance, the greatness, and the enduring mystery of
the creative imagination.

III

In surveying the fiction of our latter-nineteenth-century
critique of economics, we have so far considered the environment in which that movement developed, the work of its lesser
novelists in general, the work of five major figures in particular, and the fictional methods and artistic quality of the
economic novel as a literary type. With our factual survey
now complete, we are ready for a summary of the social *critique* produced by the economic novelists—a summary which
can now be composed not of guesswork, or theories, or even
hypotheses, but of historically valid generalizations.

Among those generalizations—it must now be abundantly
clear—the Brooksian thesis of the complacency of the Gilded
Age cannot be included. The idea that American authorship,
faced with the grave industrial evils of that time, remained
complacent; the idea that the literary fraternity were joined
solidly in league with the financial fraternity is simply not supported by the facts; it is, indeed, perilously close to the quality
of pure myth. Like many myths, it contains its germ of truth;
certain authors, at certain times, *were* rather smugly unaware
of the evils they lived among. But to condemn an entire literary generation because of the blindness of these few is to
fall into the sophomoric fallacy of judging a whole by certain

fragmentary and nonrepresentative parts, and in the course of that error to degrade and cheapen a great national past, of whose entire riches we shall continue to have most pressing need.

On the other hand, if economic criticism was by no means absent from our fiction, neither was it dominant; the critical function of literature was far from absorbing, or even overshadowing, the numerous other functions. Nothing is clearer, from a scanning of the ten thousand and one book reviews that bourgeoned into ephemeral life on the pages of nineteenth-century magazines, than that the great body of popular fiction of the Gilded Age was written, like that of any other age, first of all for entertainment, and only secondarily for critical or aesthetic value. Economic problem-novels were then, as now, considerably outnumbered by light genteel romances on the perennial theme of boy-meets-girl. What the evidence actually reveals, therefore—a condition equally far from two mythical extremes—is the existence of a considerable number of novels in which fiction appears to be at once an outgrowth of economic forces, and a means of criticizing and attempting to control them.

This body of critical fiction, while relatively in the minority, is in the aggregate large, and is of evident importance in the work of a half-dozen authors of major or near-major rank. It is an outgrowth of the bewilderingly rapid economic changes that followed the Civil War, of the numerous class conflicts and social cross-currents that stemmed from these changes, and in particular of the clash between the formerly dominant middle classes and the new plutocracy. Among these novels, not a few are conservative in that they give either explicit or implied support to the interests of the propertied classes, especially that prosperous class of upper bourgeoisie whose economic dominance the authors regarded as a *status quo*. Some novels offer this support by an idealization of the old-fashioned middle-class businessman; others, by an attack on the rising threat of organized labor; and still others, by the avoidance of any social philosophy whatever and the presentation of only the romantic thrill of economic conflict. But the great majority of American economic novels, while remaining well within the middle-class intellectual pale, adopt points of view that range from liberal to radical, from the Left-Center to Left.

The writers of all these economic novels, and particularly of the liberal and radical majority, put on record, with surprising completeness, the economic experience of their generation. They put on record—indeed, with virtual unanimity they put on *favorable* record—the coming of the Machine. Seldom if ever do they make the Machine *per se* the object of critical attack. American fiction offers nothing comparable to Samuel Butler's ingenious questioning of the Machine process itself, nothing comparable to Ruskin's bitter hostility toward the factory system entire, and little that parallels William Morris's deep concern over the preservation of the values of craftsmanship. In America, in the course of the conquest of the immense distances, the immense resources of a continent, the usefulness of the Machine was a thing difficult indeed to call in question; and, whether because of a tacit understanding of that difficulty, or because of some other causative factor, American novelists practically never did so. Instead, they mostly agreed with Mark Twain in welcoming the Machine, seeing in mechanical power, properly controlled, simply a means of realizing the old democratic dream of universal material well-being.

What our novelists put on *un*favorable record, what they subjected to telling exposure and criticism, was not the Machine itself but the misuse of the Machine by Society; not industrialism *per se,* but the workings of an industrial order administered by a *laissez-faire* capitalism. The corrupt practices of this capitalistic order—particularly all forms of speculation and all forms of corrupt influence on government—make up an important part of that fictional indictment. Practices such as rebating and stock-market gambling, although not different in kind from the age-old knaveries of commerce, now that they were conducted on the immense scale of American Big Business, were felt to be dangerous to the general welfare, and were condemned as violations of the well-known though unwritten middle-class code of productive work, thrift, and fair competition.

THE ECONOMIC NOVEL

But business piracy, however fully exposed, is not the main object of attack in the economic novel. Unquestionably the central charge brought against capitalistic industrialism is its destructiveness to our democratic, middle-class pattern of life. That destructiveness inheres—so runs the indictment—in the heightening of the conflict between capital and labor, with all such undesirable symptoms as bitter feeling, strikes, and outbreaks of violence; it inheres, still more, in the widening of the gulf between the rich and the poor, with the result that both classes are shut away from the finest human values. Than the exposure of the life of the urban poor, no part of our economic *critique* is done with more voluminous illustration, with more frankness, with more honesty and courage in the facing of an inescapably unpleasant subject. The suffering wrought by bad working conditions, by killing work-hours, by starvation wages; the spiritual enervation of the submerged classes; the squalor and the social destructiveness of the slum—all these things come to life on a thousand pages as grim and unsparing as anything in Gorky. And almost equally thoroughgoing is the fictional indictment of excessive wealth:—the decrying of "Success" as merely a phase of the blind naturalistic struggle for survival; the portrayal of the emptiness of a life directed toward the one goal of acquisition; the analysis of the ill effects of wealth in the fostering of subservience and the undermining of professional integrity; the inculcation of the idea that great wealth is rather a hindrance than a help to superior living.

But some deeper, underlying economic forces receive, except in certain Leftist writings, less attention than their importance might well have justified. One of the very basic factors in our social development, the exhaustion of the frontier, is considered only by a handful of writers. The powerful force of technological unemployment is intelligently handled only by Bellamy, Howells, and a few of their socialistic imitators; the nationwide drive toward consolidation in business is considerably scanted in treatment; and the entire problem of craftsmanship is, except by Howells, virtually overlooked. Evidently, the social observation of our novelists suffered from some serious blind spots; but such limitations are by no means sufficient to invalidate what is on the whole a substantial and intelligent *exposé*.

The social observation of our novelists was, in recognizable measure, enlarged and given direction by foreign influences; and this is particularly true, as might be expected, of the more important writers. Ideas in their fiction refer now to the Utopian socialism of Fourier or Robert Owen; now to Carlyle, Ruskin, or Morris; now to Marx, Tolstoy, or Zola. Naturally, American economic novels resemble in many ways the Victorian *"roman social"* of Disraeli and Mrs. Gaskell and Dickens, although particular cases of imitation or direct derivation would be extremely hard to prove. But these foreign influences, while they enlarged the intellectual pale of our critical fiction, were by no means strong enough to have called that fiction forth, or even to have determined its main trends. Instead, they were invariably adapted into our American scheme of culture; they were invariably assimilated into the powerful current of our own social and political tradition.

The principal factors in the making of our economic fiction were, then, native factors. The American economic novel, like the larger, general *critique* of industrialism of which it forms a portion, arose out of the conflict between a native cultural tradition and the new, threatening forces of capitalistic industry. In part, that cultural tradition had expressed itself, before the Civil War, as a way of life which our people grew into naturally amid the everyday world of village or farm. That world was on the whole a friendly, easygoing, and moderately prosperous one; a world where rapid changes from hard, lawless frontier to comfortable agrarian commonwealth made progress appear the most natural order of life; a world where, under the influence of Protestant Christianity, material well-being might co-exist quite naturally with motives of humanitarian kindness, and might as naturally be accepted as a needful foundation for immaterial and presumably "higher" interests. To this antebellum world, men like George and Clemens and Bellamy and Howells had become acclimated in their youth; and we may be sure that it was no mere nostalgia that caused them so often, and often so involuntarily, to establish it in their thinking as a norm of general social welfare.

And, in part, that cultural tradition expressed itself also as an ideology, distinctly American (although many of its remoter sources were European), well integrated, admirably adapted to the mode of life to which it gave interpretative sanction. Within that ideology, the very heart and inmost core was the theory of democracy—a theory which, far from being limited to politics alone, was rapidly becoming an educational, a social, an economic ideal as well; a theory which looked ultimately to no less generous a goal than the enlargement and enrichment of the whole life of the common man. Seen in its relation to this climate of opinion, the major critical trend in our economic novels was that of continuing, on a broader scale and with reference to later issues, that extension of democracy from politics to economics which earlier thinkers had begun.[6]

The democratic theory of economics was, like other forms of democracy, the especial property of the middle classes; and the economic novel which gave it voice was, accordingly, a product of middle-class culture. That theory included, and that species of novel expressed, certain ideas which appear to have sprung directly out of the middle-class experience of life—ideas of the value of productive work, of the value of thrift, of the value of fair dealing, of the need for security in one's possessions; ideas which were, in short, also *standards* which automatically condemned the speculative plunging

[6] It is not claimed here that the economic novelists were all believers in a democratic philosophy, or that all of those who *were* democratically inclined were fully aware of the cultural forces to which they were responding. The lesser minds among them, especially, appear to have reacted readily from the observation of some social evil to the prescription of some rule-of-thumb remedy, quite unaware of the broader philosophical implications of either. Yet even among these lesser writers, who seem to have paid so little conscious attention to any systematic scheme of ideas, the influence of an American and democratic ideology is conspicuous. By the abler writers—Howells, for example—democratic theory was more systematically understood, and was more deliberately applied to economics.

and business piracy of the Reconstruction era. The economic goal to which middle-class thought looked forward was a norm of moderate comfort, equally removed from luxury and pauperism, and attainable by the masses as well as the classes. This condition of moderate physical comfort, in which mankind was removed from want, but not from work, was looked upon as the one in which the finer human qualities were most likely to come to flower.

In its more formally philosophical bearings, the ideology back of the economic novel derives, like so many other branches of nineteenth-century liberalism, from eighteenth-century origins. The method of critical thought ordinarily employed by the novelist is identical with that of the eighteenth-century Enlightenment; it is, in other words, a rational, pragmatic, reflective method; a kind of heightened good sense, unsupported by scientific investigation, or intuition, or institutional authority. To Clemens and Howells, the Reason was as completely the key to reliable knowledge as it had been to Freneau and Paine. Likewise, the framework of ideas presupposed in the economic novel is in large measure an eighteenth-century creation, although reinforced by certain supporting ideas of more recent birth. The foundation-idea is, no doubt, the old deistic optimism which assumes that the universe is favorable rather than indifferent to the best qualities of mankind, and that its ultimate forces tend toward order rather than toward disorder. Such optimism implies, of course, faith in human nature; faith in progress; faith, even, in human perfectibility; and this faith is reinforced by the early Victorian concept of evolution as an advance toward man's higher possibilities. Consequently, a Bellamy or Howells could feel that in his labors for the improvement of society he was at one with the deepest forces of the universe, and that his most earnest effort at reform would therefore prove abundantly justified.

The remarkable coherence to be found in the ideology of the economic novel, as well as in its *exposé* and diagnosis of industrial evils, does not extend to its program—or rather, programs—of constructive reform. Therein, the novelists reach substantial agreement on only one major group of ideas —the avoidance of any philosophy justifying class conflict; the avoidance, insofar as possible, of any use of force whatever; the employment, rather, of methods of peaceful negotiation, enlightenment, and fair dealing. With this one, this characteristically American plank, agreement on any platform of remedial action ceases.

For several novelists of Right-Center inclinations—the romancers of economic struggle—gave no evidence of feeling that any reform whatever was necessary; economic conflict, with its accompanying thrill of combat, was both inevitable and sufficient. And still other conservatives indicated that all might be well if only the leadership of the old-fashioned middle-class businessman were more respected, or if the criminal activities of organized labor were suppressed. Meanwhile, on the Left, the middle-class radicals formed two widely divergent factions. While an individualistic group, headed by Henry George, sought by means of the Single Tax to reopen opportunity and to establish fair competition, a collectivist group, headed by Edward Bellamy, sought to abolish competition altogether and to bring all industry under the only authority belonging to the whole people—the State.

Within the Left-Center—the largest and more characteristic group of novelists—the multiplicity of reform programs approached a veritable Babel. Some liberal novelists went little farther than the bestowing of their blessing on the organization of labor. Others emphasized the responsibility of the wealthy for leadership in lifting society out of its impasse, and suggested many a method by which the wealthy might help alleviate suffering. They advised charity as a temporary expedient, slum clearance, model-tenement building, settlement work among the poor, and liberal factory-administration devices such as profit-sharing. And still other novelists, probing deeper, sought the gradual refining of human motives through the influence of Christianity or of humane culture.—There existed, in short, no general agreement about how to correct the ills of industrialism. The economic novelists were in the position of a group of medical doctors who, after agreeing in diagnosis, prescribe a dozen divergent and mutually contradictory remedies.

IV

When the social leadership afforded by our literature is thus historically reviewed, certain broad, general concepts become fixed with the certainty of scientific generalization. It becomes evident that that literary work was one of cultural assimilation; precisely, it was an effort to control the disruptive forces of capitalistic industrialism and to adapt them into the existing American scheme of humane culture.[7] Within that body of work, it becomes equally plain, the observing and recording of an industrial way of life is remarkably thorough, and the social analysis is at least intelligent. So that, if it is well to be broadly aware of life, if it is well to have a cultural tradition at all, these achievements of our literature must, independently of any subjective opinion, be adjudged good.

But in other judgments we cannot possibly stand on such firm ground. To judge the cultural leadership afforded by a literature, we must at the last judge the truth and value of the ideas upon which that literature is built; and so far we human beings possess no final, no assuredly objective standards of either truth or value. We may say, roughly, that ideas are true if they "work," or if they are consistent with other ideas that work; yet even so we cannot be certain that our entire frame of reference is not relative rather than absolute. And therefore, in judgments on these profounder matters, we cannot wholly escape the personal, the subjective. No matter how carefully we may make use of the known disciplines provided by historical experience, our conclusions will be based on grounds short of proof; they will be not generalizations, but opinions.

Yet a belief that grave weaknesses exist in our industrial *critique* is hardly a matter of opinion alone. These weaknesses

[7] It seems pertinent to repeat here, as an aside, that the critical work of George and Bellamy and Howells and others is the American counterpart of the work of the great Victorian critics from Carlyle through William Morris, differing from the English as species differs from species within the same genus.

are shown in the failure of our writers, even those of similar philosophy and class interests, to agree on any program of constructive reform; they are shown in that a *critique* which is impressively powerful in its destructive analyses simply disintegrates when confronted with the Tolstoyan question, "What is to be done?" Now this confusion is, in measure, simply the natural condition of human thought when the race is confronted with some new and difficult situation. Industrialism on any socially predominant scale was new to latter-nineteenth-century America—newer to the United States in 1880, say, than to Carlyle's England in 1840. Moreover, our *laissez-faire* economics, our Jeffersonian theory of a minimized state, and our long experience of the princely *largesse* of the frontier left us peculiarly unprepared to grapple with the novel social pressures of the Machine Age.

Nevertheless, to a degree that seems uncalled for by the natural confusion of the times, our novelists failed to grasp the complexity or even the sheer power of the new forces. Already within the portals of one of the most difficult eras of human experience, they too often took intellectual haven in a certain quaint illusion of millennial simplicity. Social evils, they too often assume, are attributable altogether to some one cause—competition, according to the diagnosis of Bellamy; land-monopoly, according to the diagnosis of George. Correspondingly, the cure must consist of a single social formula, the Nationalized State or the Single Tax. The golden hall of social justice, it appears, may be entered through a single door, opening to a single key—strange echo, within that later time, of the Utopian fantasies of early-nineteenth-century reformers. From the immediate practical application of such fatally simple programs, the good sense of the American people did well to shy away, even though that popular aloofness was founded on no clear recognition of the flaw of false simplicity, but rather on an intuitive grasp of the important truth that the reasonable is not always the sensible.

For the misleading simplicity arrived at by thinkers like Bellamy and George, much blame must be charged against the ways of thought of nineteenth-century liberalism, within whose general limitations and fallacies the particular weak-nesses of our liberal economic criticism are included. And one such limitation, fundamental and far-reaching, was the tardi-ness of the liberal mind in conceiving of any genuinely scien-tific approach to social problems. The classical economy, the body of thought which most nearly constituted a social science, was at best only half-way scientific, and could be bent at the economist's will into the service of a *laissez-faire* capi-talism or an assault on monopoly in land; and even this im-perfect instrument was for the most part blandly disregarded by the fraternity of storytellers. No American novelist, it ap-pears, had yet arrived at any concept of the inductive de-termination of human needs, or the inductive discovery of how society might be so engineered as to fulfill those needs. The tacit assumption underlying our economic fiction is pre-cisely that of the Age of Reason—the assumption, namely, that the right design for society may be laid out by reflecting on it reasonably and seriously. The social design of a Godwin, the social design of a Fourier, has in common with the social design of a Bellamy or a George, however they all may differ otherwise, this common quality of the neglect of science in favor of an *a priori* rationalism.

But much more serious than this negative error of over-looking the possibilities of social science, is the positive error of trusting too fully in the natural forces for order in the uni-verse, or—what amounts at last to the same thing—the natural goodness of man.[8] Again and again our novelists renew the naïve romantic expectation that some favorable change in man's intellectual environment will of itself release in human nature some instinctive drive toward the best values. This primitivistic fallacy, potentially dangerous in any case, was of course terribly serious in the fluid times of the nineteenth century, when the ideas tossed up by a dynamic romanticism were likely to be hurried into the most extensive applications in government, in education, in economics. And it was only the more dangerous for the fact that it came to birth twinned

[8] "Order" and "goodness" are necessarily used here, of course, in their usual relative and human sense.

with a profound truth—the truth of the importance of the subrational; the truth that the instinctive motivations, the instinctive satisfactions, are fundamental in successful human living. The rediscovery of that truth was the great achievement of romantic primitivism; its continued influence, the joint effect of the romantic spirit and psychological science; the net result already, an immense enrichment of the storehouses of value possessed by our West-European and American culture.

The fallacy of primitivism, on the other hand, lies in the assumption that, given some favorable "break" in the social environment, natural factors and motives will of themselves effect the improvement of human life. Good conditions make good character; the natural man needs only a chance. Once given that chance, once started upon the path of perfectibility, he can look to Nature not only for impulse but for law, not only for force but for control. Now this Wordsworthian, Rousseauistic doctrine rests at bottom on the premise that natural and human values are identical; that Nature, left to her own automatic processes, will produce through mankind the world-order which mankind will find most desirable. Nevertheless, to overwhelming degree, the goal of human effort through thousands of years uncounted has been to substitute what we may call a human order for a natural one; to make Man the master of Nature instead of the servant; and, to the end of superior living, to subject Nature's enormous energies to the control of human intelligence—a process which extends from the first rude savage observations of cloud and starlight and sunlight through the complexities of twentieth-century engineering. And this deliberate control of life—precisely the objective of nineteenth-century liberalism—has not yet been effected by any naïve and childlike surrender to natural forces, but only and always by intelligent, disciplined direction of them. This vigorous, steadily maintained, and intelligent human effort, which is a *sine qua non* in the disciplined control of life, is taken almost fatally for granted by the economic novelists, whose characteristic error lies in proposing reforms in the social machinery, without also proposing that conscious fostering of disciplined character, individual and social, which alone might make those reforms genuinely effective.

To point out even such wide *lacunae* as this forgetfulness of discipline is not, of course, to dismiss nineteenth-century liberalism as a failure. Much, it must be admitted, could be urged in support of that pessimistic view, for the liberal attitude is open to attack not only on the ground of grave theoretical omissions, but also on the ground of a dearth of practical achievement. The great cloud of discussion raised by the Single-Taxers, the Nationalists, and the What-Nots precipitated, during their own and even the following generation, the merest sprinkle of actual reform;[9] and even the social gains of the nineteen-thirty decade, while very impressive in the aggregate, are less impressive when weighed in balance with the increasing pressures of the Machine Age. Nevertheless, the past decade has witnessed, without the sacrifice of any essential of a democratic state, one tremendous advance in conscious social management—the acceptance by the national government of the responsibility for insuring at least a minimum of economic security. And this substantial advance has been wrought out, moreover, precisely along the Left-Centrist direction so frequently pointed out in the economic novel; that is, it involves not revolutionary but moderate changes, not the destruction of capitalism but the control of capitalism in the interest of the general welfare.

To have anticipated the modern drive for economic security, to have nourished and given voice to the tradition that shaped that immense effort, is no slight achievement. But much more than this can be claimed for the writers of economic fiction. The composite program they outlined appears, when studied in its fundamentals rather than in its superficies, to be the only one which offers to our particular people, under our American conditions, any final hope of superior living.

[9] The liberal achievement of the latter-nineteenth and early twentieth centuries looks much larger when the immense volume of private humanitarian work is considered, in addition to the rather ineffective social efforts of government. See, however, in regard to the weaknesses of liberalism, Mr. John Chamberlain's trenchant analyses in *Farewell to Reform* (New York, 1932).

In the long view, the thousand and one dubious social devices included in that program appear immaterial. What really counts is that the program is founded solidly upon every one of the few major, indispensable pillars of a permanently livable society. It is founded upon the principles that (1) the national economy must be brought under *intelligent* control; (2) that control must be exercised in behalf of the security and welfare of the *whole* people; and (3) the ultimate authority over the economic system must remain with the people themselves. No program which violates the first of these principles can possibly cope with the complexities of the Machine Age; no program which violates the second or third will, it is safe to say, finally satisfy the American people.

Indeed, now that the romantic ideal of *laissez-faire* has grown untenable, there exists only one alternative to the policy of a democratically controlled economics. That alternative is the totalitarian state, so curiously anticipated by Carlyle, in which the decisive rule of the capable few theoretically assures the welfare of the entire state. This is not the place, of course, to dwell on the merits or demerits of totalitarianism —matters which, in any case, work themselves out in large disregard of theoretical debate. It must suffice to say that, whatever values dictatorship may have elsewhere, among people of a different tradition, and whatever temporary gains in security dictatorship may give, it offers no more *final* hope than did the old system of absolute monarchy, which, in accordance with the varying character of the monarch, might run the entire gamut from supreme effectiveness to impotence. The totalitarian state offers, moreover, no assurance at all that the general interest will be served along with the special interest of the ruling clique; it offers no training by which its citizenry may develop through experience toward political maturity; and, in encouraging that citizenry to rest the burden of rulership wholly upon other shoulders than their own, it fosters what would be, for us, a plain evasion of responsibility.

For the people of the United States, then, the only conceivable choice is that of following the social program outlined in the literature of our first industrial era, preserving that in it which is wise and strong, replacing that which is foolish and weak. Our necessary, our unavoidably necessary course of action is to retain the large heritage of liberty, of hope, of concern for the common welfare bequeathed us by nineteenth-century liberalism; and, having retained these ideals, to implement them with the knowledge and the discipline which alone can make them practically effective. Much of this implementation will no doubt be found in the further development of the physical and social sciences; in the further removal of the social studies, particularly, from the area of theory and rationalization to the area of genuine science, where knowledge is based on comprehensive observation, sound method, and a tacit recognition of the complexities of life.

For the most part, however, the further realization of the great social objectives of nineteenth-century liberalism appears to depend less on scientific knowledge than, in the broadest sense of the word, on self-discipline, both individual and social. The democratic administration of a just and intelligent economic policy will most certainly require the extension, into a much larger proportion of the electorate than now possess them, of certain basic intellectual and moral qualities. For example, a sufficient number of citizens must certainly know how, within the limits required by their everyday needs, to distinguish truth from error, and to come to decisions by means of intelligence instead of prejudice. A sufficient number must, moreover, be able both to give and to exact just dealing. A sufficient number must, above all, be able to recognize and to follow able leadership; for by no other means than the choice of a wise and strong leadership may a self-governing people hope to preserve the necessary and yet most delicate balance between liberty and authority.

It is no longer possible to hope, with Condorcet and Shelley, that these indispensable qualities of mind and spirit will be generally developed in the race by any natural means, or by the shifting-about of a few cogs in man's social environment. While we may still legitimately believe, with the nineteenth-century liberal, that mankind is capable of progress, we must recognize, as he too often failed to recognize, that progress is not a natural condition but an artificial one, and that it comes only by means of slow, steadily maintained, immense, and calculated effort. Within the individual, progress toward inward self-discipline is normally the outcome of a long habituation, begun in infancy and continued well into mature life. Within a self-governing nation, a disciplined direction of life is achieved only by the building-up of a sufficiently large number of disciplined individuals. With this discipline accomplished on a sufficiently broad scale, institutions, reforms, and social devices will be taken care of as a natural consequence. Without it, no economic or political techniques, however perfect, will avail to preserve from the blind chancework of an indifferent nonhuman universe the untrained hands that wield them.

Important, even crucial, as is the problem of self-disciplined character, it has so far had no adequate treatment in our sociological fiction. The literature of our early twentieth century, which its creators felt to be so revolutionary, is in this as in many other vital respects only a continuation of the literature of the nineteenth. Indeed, the emphasis on self-discipline has, within the past two generations, actually declined. Although Bellamy and his contemporaries neglected that subject, they did so in the expectation that Nature herself, operating through the natural tendencies of mankind, would produce values of beauty and order as well as of power. On the other hand, the representative author of the nineteen-thirties —a Hemingway, a Caldwell, a Steinbeck—has abandoned this expectation; and in its absence the value of his naturalistic fiction reduces itself, quite simply, to the value of psychic release. The pleasure we find in the reading of *Tobacco Road* or *Grapes of Wrath* is the pleasure of having released for us, in the readiest and most direct manner possible, all those subrational impulses of lust, and hatred, and disgust, and fear, which in our everyday living the severe demands of civilization require us to inhibit. Discipline, constructiveness manifestly have no place in such fiction; for its very objective is escape from discipline, and its keenest intensity often awakens in the inevitably destructive moment when the individual life clashes in predetermined struggle with natural law. Now if we take this sort of fiction imaginatively, distinguishing sharply between the imagined and the actual world, then indeed we may find in it both satisfaction and value; for necessarily we rebel at times against the heavy burden of keeping order in our actual world, and welcome even a brief and fanciful escape from that responsibility—an escape in which we may, without consequent disaster, enjoy the thrill of watching

the frame of things disjoint, both the worlds suffer.

But if we take this sort of novel as serious critical literature, we can hardly avoid the harsh judgment that it fails decisively —far more decisively than does even the blandly optimistic fiction of nineteenth-century liberalism—to give any adequate treatment of the crucial problem of self-discipline.

The value of the critical leadership afforded by the nineteenth-century economic novel is then, in summary, the value of an important but unfinished work. It is the value inherent in a literature which presents a social objective of marvellous worth, but which overlooks the personal and social disciplines by which alone the human army may hope to attain that objective. Consequently, the logical work of twentieth-century liberalism is that of completing the still incomplete task of its predecessor. It is the work of offering a persuasive and powerful leadership in the building-up of those disciplines which are necessary to the successful working of a democratic society. Simple, even platitudinous as that policy sounds, the actual execution of it would call for revolutionary changes in our national thinking. That execution would require, for example, a thorough revamping of our pseudo-liberal public school system, in which a theory of self-expression lapses in actual practice too often into mere self-indulgence. It would require, likewise, an equally thorough revamping of our over-organized, confused, and ethically half-efficient religious groups—not to speak of many other equally thoroughgoing changes.

Of course, nothing so strenuous as all this is likely to be done, except during times of grave national emergency; nothing requiring such general, steady use of intelligence and self-control is likely to be completely done at all; nor, in any case, would it probably be well for our literary leadership to embrace anything so misleadingly simple as a cause. But it *does* seem clear that, within relative human and practical limits, our contemporary authors could, if they would, find in the general field of personal and social self-discipline a new source of significance, a new source of value. In exploring that field, they would be carrying on toward completion the great but incomplete task of nineteenth-century liberalism. In making that contribution to the final end of a larger life for the *entire* people, they would be continuing what is in reality the Great Tradition of American literature.

BIBLIOGRAPHY

The following bibliography is intended solely as a list of sources. Exhaustive bibliographical information about the significant writers treated in this study is either available elsewhere, or is being accumulated through the efforts of the American Literature Group of the Modern Language Association; and there seems to be no point in duplicating that work.

The works in the following list, then, have contributed as sources in some specific way to this study. Material which has only a general pertinence to the subject has been excluded.

I. NON-FICTION

Adams, James Truslow, *The Epic of America.* Boston, 1931.

Addams, Jane, *Twenty Years at Hull House.* New York, 1910.

American Catalogue, The (1876 ——). Founded in 1876 by Frederick Leypoldt and continued under the direction of R. R. Bowker, Miss I. A. Appleton, and others. New York, 1885 ——.

American Literature, A Journal of Literary History, Criticism, and Bibliography, edited by Jay B. Hubbell and others. Durham, North Carolina, 1929 ——.

Annual American Catalogue, The (1886 ——). Compiled under the direction of R. R. Bowker. New York, 1887 ——.

Appleton's Cyclopedia of American Biography, edited by James Grant Wilson and John Fiske. Volumes I-VI. New York, 1887-9.

Baldwin, Joseph Glover, *Flush Times in Alabama and Mississippi.* New York, 1853.

Beard, Charles, and Mary Beard, *The Rise of American Civilization.* New York, 1927.

Bennett, Mary Angela, *Elizabeth Stuart Phelps—A Critical Biography.* Philadelphia, 1938.

Björkman, Edwin, *Voices of Tomorrow.* New York, 1913.

Blankenship, Russell, *American Literature as an Expression of the National Mind.* New York, 1931.

Bogart, Ernest Ludlow, *An Economic History of the United States.* New York, 1907. Fourth Edition, 1924.

Boyeson, Hjalmar IIjorth, "Immigration." New York, 1888.

———, *Literary and Social Silhouettes.* New York, 1894.

Brooks, Van Wyck, *America's Coming-of-Age.* New York, 1915.

———, *Letters and Leadership.* New York, 1918.

———, *New England: Indian Summer.* New York, 1940.

———, *Sketches in Criticism.* New York, 1932.

Browne, Charles Farrar, *The Complete Works of Artemus Ward.* New York, 1868.

Buck, Solon J., *The Agrarian Crusade.* New Haven, 1920.

Calverton, Victor Francis, *The Liberation of American Literature.* New York, 1932.

Cambridge History of American Literature, The, Edited by W. P. Trent, John Erskine, Stuart P. Sherman, and Carl Van Doren. New York, 1917-21.

Campbell, Mrs. Helen, *Darkness and Daylight,* or *Lights and Shadows of New York Life.* Hartford, 1891.

———, *The Problem of the Poor, a Record of Quiet Work in Unquiet Places.* New York, 1882.

Carnegie, Andrew, *The Autobiography of Andrew Carnegie.* Boston, 1920.

———, *Triumphant Democracy.* New York, 1885.

Cassady, Edward E., *The Business Man in the American Novel, 1865-1900.* A doctoral dissertation of the University of California. Berkeley, 1939.

Cazamian, Louis, *Le Roman Social en Angleterre.* Paris, 1904.

Chamberlain, John, *Farewell to Reform.* New York, 1932.

Commons, John Rogers, and others, *A History of Labor in the United States.* New York, 1918.

Cooper, Frederic Taber, *Some American Story Tellers.* New York, 1911.

Coöperative Index to Periodicals, 1885-91, The. Edited by W. J. Fletcher. New York, 1885-97. Continued as *The Annual Literary Index,* 1892-1905, edited by W. J. Fletcher and R. R. Bowker, New York, 1893-1906, and *The Annual Literary Index,* 1905-10, edited by W. J. Fletcher and H. E. Harris. New York, 1906-11.

Dewey, Davis Rich, *National Problems.* New York, 1907.

Dickason, David H., *The Contribution of B. O. Flower and the Arena to Critical Thought in America.* A doctoral dissertation of the Ohio State University. Columbus, 1940.

Dictionary of American Biography, The, Edited by Allen Johnson and Dumas Malone. New York, 1928-1936.

Faulkner, Harold Underwood, *The Quest for Social Justice.* New York, 1931.

Flory, Claud R., *Economic Criticism in American Fiction, 1792-1900.* Philadelphia, 1935.

Flower, B. O., *Progressive Men, Women, and Movements of the Past Twenty-five Years.* Boston, 1914.

Foerster, Norman (Editor), *The Reinterpretation of American Literature.* New York, 1928.

Gabriel, Ralph H., *The Course of American Democratic Thought.* New York, 1940.

Gordon, George, *The Men Who Make Our Novels.* New York, 1919.

Gronlund, Laurence, *The Coöperative Commonwealth.* Boston, 1884.

Guérard, Albert, *Literature and Society.* Boston, 1935.

Haney, Lewis Henry, *A History of Economic Thought.* New York, 1921.

Hartwick, Harry, *The Foreground of American Fiction.* New York, 1934.

Harvey, William Hope, *Coin's Financial School.* Chicago, 1894.

Hatcher, Harlan, *Creating the Modern American Novel.* New York, 1935.

Haworth, Paul, L., *The United States in Our Own Times, 1865-1920.* New York, 1920.

Hendrick, Burton J., *The Age of Big Business.* New Haven, 1919.

Henry, David A., *William Vaughn Moody.* Boston, 1935.

Hicks, Granville, *The Great Tradition.* New York, 1933.

Hicks, John Donald, *The Populist Revolt.* Minneapolis, 1931.

Hillquit, Morris, *A History of Socialism in the United States.* New York, 1903.

Hubbard, Elbert (Editor, beginning in 1896), *The Philistine, a Periodical of Protest.* East Aurora, New York, 1895-1915.

——, *Selected Writings of Elbert Hubbard.* New York, 1922.

Huth, John F., Jr., "Theodore Dreiser: 'The Prophet.'" *American Literature,* IX: 208-17 (May, 1937).

International Index to Periodicals, 1920 ——. New York, 1921 ——.

Josephson, Matthew, *The Robber Barons*. New York, 1934.

Knight, Grant Cochran, *American Literature and Culture*. New York, 1932.

Lewisohn, Ludwig, *Expression in America*. New York, 1932.

Lingley, Charles R., *Since the Civil War*. New York, 1920. Edition of 1926.

Lloyd, Henry Demarest, *Wealth against Commonwealth*. New York, 1894.

London, Jack, *The People of the Abyss*. New York, 1903.

———, *The War of the Classes*. New York, 1905.

Lorimer, George Horace, *Letters from a Self-Made Merchant to His Son*. Boston, 1902.

McMaster, John Bach, *A History of the People of the United States*. Volume VIII. New York, 1913.

Macy, John A. (Editor), *American Writers on American Literature*. New York, 1931.

Mitchell, Broadus, "American Radicals Nobody Knows," *The South Atlantic Quarterly*, XXXIV: 394-401 (October, 1935).

Moody, William Vaughn, *The Poems and Plays of William Vaughn Moody*, edited by John M. Manly. Boston, 1912.

Mumford, Lewis, *The Brown Decades*. New York, 1931.

———, *The Golden Day*. New York, 1926.

———, *The Story of Utopias*. New York, 1922.

———, *Technics and Civilization*. New York, 1934.

Myers, Gustavus A., *History of the Great American Fortunes*. Chicago, 1910.

Oberholtzer, Ellis P., *A History of the United States Since the Civil War*. Volumes II and III. New York, 1922, 1926.

O'Rourke, Constance Mayfield, *American Humor*. New York, 1931.

Parrington, Vernon Louis, *Main Currents in American Thought*. Three Volumes. New York, 1927-30.

Pattee, Fred Lewis, *American Literature Since 1870*. New York, 1915.

———, *The New American Literature*. New York, 1930.

Paxson, Frederic L., *Recent History of the United States*. Boston, 1922.

Poole, William Frederick, *An Index to Periodical Literature*, Third Edition. Boston, 1882.

Quinn, Arthur Hobson, *American Fiction: An Historical and Critical Survey*. New York, 1936.

Readers' Guide to Periodical Literature, The. Minneapolis, 1901-12. White Plains, New York, 1913 ——.

Readers' Guide to Periodical Literature. Supplement. White Plains, New York, 1916 ——.

Regier, C. C., *The Era of the Muckrakers.* Chapel Hill, 1932.

Riis, Jacob A., *Children of the Poor.* New York, 1892.

——, *How the Other Half Lives.* New York, 1890.

——, *A Ten Years' War.* Boston, 1900.

Rose, Lisle Abbot, *A Descriptive Catalogue of Economic and Politico-Economic Fiction in the United States, 1902-9.* A doctoral dissertation of the University of Chicago. Chicago, 1936.

Sanborn, Alvan Francis, *Moody's Lodging House, and Other Tenement Sketches.* Boston, 1895.

Schlesinger, Arthur Meyer, *New Viewpoints in American History.* New York, 1922.

——, *The Rise of the City.* New York, 1938.

Schmalhousen, Samuel D., *Behold America!* New York, 1931.

Sears, Minnie Earl, and Marion Shaw (Editors), *Essay and General Literature Index, 1900-33.* New York, 1934.

Seitz, D. C., *The Dreadful Decade, 1869-79.* Indianapolis, 1926.

Shaw, Henry Wheeler, *Everybody's Friend, or Josh Billings' Encyclopedia and Proverbial Philosophy of Wit and Humor.* Hartford, 1874.

Shurter, Robert L., *The Utopian Novel in America, 1865-1900.* A doctoral dissertation of the Western Reserve University. Cleveland, 1936.

Starke, Aubrey H., *Sidney Lanier: a Biographical and Critical Study.* Chapel Hill, 1933.

Steffens, Lincoln, *The Shame of the Cities.* New York, 1904.

Sullivan, Mark, *Our Times. The United States, 1900-25.* Volume I, *The Turn of the Century.* New York, 1926.

Tarbell, Ida M., *The History of the Standard Oil Company.* New York, 1904.

——, *The Nationalizing of Business, 1878-98.* New York, 1936.

Underwood, John Curtis, *Literature and Insurgency.* New York, 1914.

United States Catalog of Books in Print, The, Edited by George Flavel Danforth, Marion E. Potter, and successors. Minneapolis, 1900-11. New York, 1912 ——.

Van Doren, Carl, *Contemporary American Novelists.* Revised edition. New York, 1940.

Veblen, Thorstein, *The Theory of Business Enterprise*. New York, 1904.

——, *The Theory of the Leisure Class*. New York, 1899.

Walcutt, Charles C., *Naturalism in the American Novel*. A doctoral dissertation of the University of Michigan. Ann Arbor, 1937.

Warner, Charles Dudley, *Fashions in Literature*. New York, 1902.

Whitman, Walt, *Democratic Vistas*. Washington, 1871.

Wild, Henry Douglas, *Democratic Idealism in American Literature from Penn to Whitman*. A doctoral dissertation of the University of Chicago. Chicago, 1924.

Wyckoff, Walter A., *The Workers: An Experiment in Reality*. New York, 1898.

II. THE LESSER NOVELISTS

Adams, Frederick Upham, *President John Smith, The Story of a Peaceful Revolution*. Chicago, 1897.

Aldrich, Thomas Bailey, *The Stillwater Tragedy*. Boston, 1880. Edition of 1908.

Aristocracy. (Anonymous.) New York, 1888.

Armstrong, Leroy, *Washington Brown, Farmer*. Chicago, 1893.

Bachelder, John, *A. D. 2050*. Published anonymously. San Francisco, 1890.

Barr, Mrs. Amelia, *The King's Highway*. New York, 1897.

Barr, Robert, *The Mutable Many*. New York, 1896.

Bartlett, A. W. B., *A New Aristocracy*. Detroit, 1891.

Bartlett, George H., *A Commercial Trip with an Uncommercial Ending*. New York, 1884.

Bayne, Charles J., *The Fall of Utopia*. Boston, 1900.

Beard, Dan, *Moonblight*. New York, 1892.

Beck-Meyer, Nico, *A Story from Pulmantown* (sic). Chicago, 1894.

Bellamy, Charles Joseph, *The Breton Mills*. New York, 1879.

Bellsmith, Henry W., *Henry Cadavere*. New York, ca. 1897.

Benjamin, Chas. A., *The Strike in the B—— Mills*. Boston, 1887.

Bennett, Mary E., *Asaph's Ten Thousand*. Boston, 1890.

Bishop, William Henry, *The Garden of Eden, U. S. A.: A Very Possible Story*. Chicago, 1895.

——, *The House of a Merchant Prince*. Boston, 1883.

Boyesen, Hjalmar Hjorth, *A Daughter of the Philistines*. Boston, 1883.

——, *The Golden Calf*. Meadville, Penn., 1892.

——, *The Mammon of Unrighteousness*. New York, 1891.

——, *Social Strugglers*. New York, 1893.

Brooks, Byron A., *Earth Revisited*. Boston, 1894.

Bunner, Henry Cuyler, *The Story of a New York House*. New York, 1887.

Cahan, Abraham, *The Imported Bridegroom*. Boston, 1898.

————, *Yekl, A Tale of the New York Ghetto*. New York, 1896.

Campbell, Mrs. Helen, *Miss Melinda's Opportunity*. Boston, 1886.

————, *Mrs. Herndon's Income*. Boston, 1886.

Carlton, Waite, *A Silver Baron*. Boston, 1896.

Caryl, Charles W., *New Era*. Denver, 1897.

Caswell, Edward A., *Toil and Self*. Chicago, 1900.

Chamberlain, Henry, *6000 Tons of Gold*. Meadville, Penn., 1894.

Chavannes, Albert, *The Future Commonwealth*. New York, 1892.

————, *In Brighter Climes*. Knoxville, 1895.

Clark, Arnold A., *Beneath the Dome*. Chicago, 1894.

Clews, James B., *Fortune, a Story of Wall Street*. New York, 1898.

Collins, Robert Upton, *John Halsey, the Anti-Monopolist*, by Constance Reed. San Francisco, 1884.

Converse, Florence, *The Burden of Christopher*. Boston, 1900.

Cowan, James, *Daybreak, A Romance of an Old World*. New York, 1896.

Cowdrey, Robert H., *A Tramp in Society*. Chicago, 1891.

Craig, Alexander, *Ionia*. Chicago, 1898.

Crane, Stephen, *George's Mother*. New York, 1896.

————, *Maggie, A Girl of the Streets*. New York, 1892.

Crawford, F. Marion, *An American Politician*. Boston, 1885.

Cridge, Alfred D., *Utopia, or The History of an Extinct Planet*. Oakland, California, 1884.

Crocker, Samuel, *That Island*. Kansas City, Mo., 1892.

Cruger, Mary, *Brotherhood*. Boston, 1891.

Daniel, Charles, *Ai: A Social Vision*. Boston, 1892.

Davis, Rebecca Harding, *John Andross*. New York, 1874.

De Forest, John W., *Honest John Vane*. New Haven, 1875.

Deland, Mrs. Margaret, *The Wisdom of Fools*. Boston, 1897.

Dement, R. S., *Ronbar*. New York, 1895.

Denison, Thomas S., *An Iron Crown*. Anonymously published. Chicago, 1885.

Dodd, Anna Bowman, *The Republic of the Future*. New York, 1887.

Donnelly, Ignatius, *Caesar's Column*. By Edmund Boisgilbert. Chicago, 1890.

————, *The Golden Bottle*. New York, 1892.

Doughty, Francis W., *Mirrikh, or A Woman from Mars*. New York, 1892.

Douglas, Amanda M., *Hope Mills*. Boston, 1880.

Dowling, George Thomas, *The Wreckers, A Social Study*. Philadelphia, 1886.

Dreiser, Theodore, *Sister Carrie*. New York, 1900.

Duyster, G. F., *A Senator at Sea*. New York, 1894.

Edson, Milan C., *Solaris Farm*. Washington, 1900.

Eggleston, Edward, *The Mystery of Metropolisville*. New York, 1873.

Eggleston, George Cary, and Mrs. Mary Shell Bacon, *Juggernaut, A Veiled Record*. New York, 1891.

Emmons, Stephen H., *The Sixteenth Amendment*. New York, 1896.

Everett, Henry L., *The People's Program*. New York, 1891.

Fawcett, Edgar, *An Ambitious Woman*. Boston, 1884.

———, *An Heir to Millions*. Chicago, 1892.

———, *The Evil That Men Do*. New York, 1889.

Fiske, Amos K., *Beyond the Bourn*. New York, 1891.

Fitch, Thomas and Anna M., *Better Days, or A Millionaire's Tomorrow*. Chicago, 1892.

Foote, Mary Hallock, *Coeur D'Alene*. Boston, 1894.

———, *John Bodewin's Testimony*. Boston, 1886.

———, *The Led-Horse Claim*. Boston, 1883.

Foran, Martin Ambrose, *From the Other Side, A Social Study Based on Fact*. Cleveland, 1886.

Forbush, Zebina, *The Co-opolitan*. Chicago, 1898.

Ford, Mrs. Mary H., *Which Wins?* Boston, 1891.

Ford, Paul Leicester, *The Great K & A Train Robbery*. New York, 1892.

———, *The Honorable Peter Stirling*. New York, 1894.

Frederic, Harold, *The Lawton Girl*. New York, 1890.

———, *The Market Place*. New York, 1898.

———, *Seth's Brother's Wife*, New York, 1887.

French, Alice, *A Book of True Lovers*. Chicago, 1897.

———, *The Heart of Toil*. New York, 1898.

———, *Knitters in the Sun*. Boston, 1887.

Friedman, Isaac K., *Poor People*. Boston, 1900.

Fuller, Lieutenant Alvarado M., *A. D. 2000*. Chicago, 1890.

Fuller, Edward, *The Complaining Millions of Men*. New York, 1893.

Fuller, Henry Blake, *The Cliff-Dwellers*. New York, 1893.

———, *With the Procession*. New York, 1895.

Galloway, James M., *John Harvey, A Tale of the Twentieth Century*, by Anon Moore. Chicago, 1897.

Geissler, Ludwig A., *Looking Beyond*. New Orleans, 1891.

Giles, Fayette S., *Shadows Before*, or *A Century Onward*. New York, 1893.

Gilmore, Minnie L., *The Woman Who Stood Between*. New York, 1892.

Glasgow, Ellen, *The Descendant*. New York, 1897.

———, *Phases of an Inferior Planet*. New York, 1898.

Grant, Robert, *Face to Face*. Anonymously published. New York, 1886.

———, *Unleavened Bread*. New York, 1900.

Grigsby, Alcanoan O., *Nequa, or The Problem of the Ages*. Topeka, Kansas, 1900.

Grimshaw, Robert, *Fifty Years Hence*. New York, 1893.

Gunter, Archibald C., *Her Senator*. London, 1896.

Hale, Edward Everett, *How They Lived at Hampton*. Boston, 1888.

———, *Sybil Knox*. New York, 1892.

Hamblen, Herbert Elliott, *The General Manager's Story*. New York, 1897.

Harvey, William Hope, *A Tale of Two Nations*. Chicago, 1894.

Hay, John, *The Breadwinners*. Anonymously published. New York, 1884.

Herrick, Robert, *The Gospel of Freedom*. New York, 1898.

———, *The Web of Life*. New York, 1900.

Hertzka, Theodore, *Freeland, A Social Anticipation*. New York, 1891. A translation by Sir Arthur Ransom.

Heuston, Benjamin Franklin, *The Rice Mills of Port Mystery*. Chicago, 1891.

Hill, Beveridge, *The Story of a Canyon*. Boston, 1895.

Hillhouse, Mansfield Lovell, *Iola, the Senator's Daughter: A Story of Ancient Rome*. New York, 1894.

Holford, Costello N., *Aristopia*. Boston, 1895.

Holland, Josiah Gilbert, *Nicholas Minturn*. New York, 1876.

———, *Sevenoaks*. New York, 1875.

Hubbard, Elbert, *No Enemy (but Himself): The Story of a Gentleman Tramp*. New York, 1894.

James, Henry, *The Princess Casamassima*. London, 1886.

Keenan, Henry Francis, *The Money-Makers*. Anonymously published. New York, 1885.

Kerr, Alvah Milton, *An Honest Lawyer*. Chicago, 1892.

King, Charles, *A Tame Surrender*. Philadelphia, 1896.

King, Edward, *The Golden Spike*. Boston, 1886.

——, *Joseph Zalmonah*. Boston, 1893.

Kirk, Mrs. Ellen Warner, *A Daughter of Eve*. Boston, 1889.

——, *Queen Money*. Boston, 1888.

——, *Walford*. Boston, 1890.

Kirkland, Joseph, *Zury*. Boston, 1887.

Knapp, Adeline, *One Thousand Dollars a Day: Studies in Social Economics*. Boston, 1894.

Lawson, Minnie, *Money to Loan on All Collaterals*. Detroit, 1895.

Leggett, General Mortimer D., *A Dream of a Modest Prophet*. Philadelphia, 1890.

Leigh, Oliver H. G., *Dollarocracy, An American Novel*. Anonymously published. New York, 1891.

Leland, Samuel Phelps, *Peculiar People*. Cleveland, 1892.

Locke, David Ross, *A Paper City*. Boston, 1879.

Long, Lily Augusta, *Apprentices to Destiny*. New York, 1893.

Lubin, David, *Let There Be Light*. New York, 1900.

Lush, Charles Keeler, *The Federal Judge*. Boston, 1897.

Lynde, Francis, *The Helpers*. New York, 1899.

McCardell, Roy Larcom, *The Wage Slaves of New York*. New York, 1899.

McCowan, Archibald, *Christ the Socialist*. Anonymously published. Boston, 1894.

——, *Philip Meyer's Scheme*, by Luke A. Head. New York, 1892.

Macnie, John, *The Diothas, or A Look Far Ahead*, by Ismar Thiusen. New York, 1883.

Machar, Agnes Maule, *Roland Graeme, Knight*. New York, 1892.

Mackay, John Henry, *The Anarchists*, translated from the German by George Schumm. Boston, 1891.

M. A. M., *Engineer Jim*. 1889 (Place unknown).

Mason, Caroline A., *A Woman of Yesterday*. New York, 1900.

Matthews, Brander, *His Father's Son*. New York, 1895.

Maynard, Cora, *Some Modern Heretics*. Boston, 1895.

Mead, Mrs. Lucia Ames, *Memoirs of a Millionaire*. Boston, 1889.

Merwin, Samuel, and Henry Kitchell Webster, *The Short Line War*. New York, 1899.

Michaelis, Richard, *Looking Forward*. Chicago, 1890.

Mighels, Philip Verrill, *Nella: The Heart of the Army.* New York, 1900.

Miller, Joaquin, *The Building of the City Beautiful.* Cambridge, 1893.

Mitchell, John Ames, *The Last American.* New York, 1889.

Nitsch, Helen Alice, *Gentle Breadwinners.* Boston, 1888.

Nobody Knows. (Anonymous.) New York, 1888.

Olerich, Henry, *A Cityless and Countryless World.* Holstein, Indiana, 1893.

Payne, Will, *The Money Captain.* Chicago, 1898.

Peck, Bradford, *The World a Department Store.* Lewiston, Maine, 1900.

Phelps, Corwin, *An Ideal Republic.* Chicago, 1896.

Phelps, Elizabeth Stuart, *The Silent Partner.* Boston, 1871.

Pollock, Margaret Sherwood, *An Experiment in Altruism,* by Elizabeth Hastings. New York, 1895.

———, *Henry Worthington, Idealist.* New York, 1899.

Pomeroy, William C., *The Lords of Misrule: A Tale of Gods and Men.* Chicago, 1894.

Porter, Lynn Boyd, *Speaking of Ellen,* by Albert Ross. New York, 1890.

Post, Charles Cyrel, *Congressman Swanson.* Chicago, 1892.

———, *Driven from Sea to Sea.* Chicago, 1884.

Prince, Helen Choate, *The Story of Christine Rochefort.* Boston, 1895.

Ramsay, Milton W., *Six Thousand Years Hence.* Minneapolis, 1891.

Reed, Isaac George, Jr., *From Heaven to New York.* New York, 1876.

Rehm, Warren S., *The Practical City.* Lancaster, Pa., 1898.

Riis, Jacob A., *Nibsy's Christmas.* New York, 1893.

———, *Out of Mulberry Street.* New York, 1897.

Rivers, George R. R., *Captain Shays: a Populist of 1786.* Boston, 1897.

Roberts, J. W., *Looking Within.* New York, 1893.

Robinson, Harry Perry, *Men Born Equal.* New York, 1895.

Roe, E. P., *Barriers Burned Away.* New York, 1872.

———, *Opening a Chestnut Burr.* New York, 1874.

Roe, Mary Abigail (C. M. Cornwall), *Free, Yet Forging their Own Chains.* New York, 1876.

Rood, Henry Edward, *The Company Doctor.* New York, 1895.

Rosewater, Frank, '96: A Romance of Utopia. Omaha, Nebraska, 1894.

Ross, Clinton, The Silent Workman. New York, 1886.

———, The Speculator. New York, 1891.

Salisbury, Henry Barnard, The Birth of Freedom. New York, 1894.

Sanborn, Alvan Francis, Meg McIntyre's Raffle. Boston, 1896.

Sanford, Frederick R., The Bursting of a Boom, Philadelphia, 1889.

Savage, Richard Henry, The Anarchist: A Story of Today. Chicago, 1894.

Schindler, Solomon, Young West. Boston, 1894.

Scott, H. E., The Girl from Macoupin. Chicago, 1894.

Serviss, Garrett Putnam, The Moon Metal. New York, 1900.

Sheldon, Charles Monroe, The Crucifixion of Philip Strong. Chicago, 1894.

———, His Brother's Keeper. Boston, 1896.

———, In His Steps. Chicago, 1897.

Simpson, William, The Man from Mars, His Morals, Politics, and Religion. San Francisco, 1891.

Smith, Edgar Maurice, A Daughter of Humanity. Boston, 1895.

Smith, F. Hopkinson, Tom Grogan. Boston, 1896.

Smith, Marion Couthouy, Dr. Marks, Socialist. Cincinnati, 1897.

Some Great Cause: God's New Messiah. (Anonymous.) New York, 1900.

Stanton, Edward, Dreams of the Dead. Boston, 1892.

Stump, D. L., From World to World. Asbury, Mo., 1896.

Sullivan, James William, So the World Goes. Chicago, 1893.

———, Tenement Tales of New York. New York, 1895.

Swift, John F., Robert Greathouse. New York, 1878.

The Beginning. A Romance of Chicago as It Might Be. (Anonymous.) Chicago, 1893.

The Fall of the Great Republic. (Anonymous.) 1885.

Thomas, Chauncey, The Crystal Button. Boston, 1891.

Thurber, Alwyn M., Quaint Crippen, Commercial Traveller. Chicago, 1896.

Tibbles, T. H., and Mrs. Elia W. Peattie (the latter originally anonymous), The American Peasant. Chicago, 1892.

Tincker, Mary Agnes, San Salvador. Boston, 1892.

Tourgée, Albion Winegar, Murvale Eastman, Christian Socialist. New York, 1890.

Tower, Reverend F. E., The Advancing Kingdom. Hartford, 1891.

Townsend, Virginia F., *But a Philistine*. Boston, 1884.

Trammell, William Dugas, *Ça Ira*. New York, 1874.

Trowbridge, John T., *Farnell's Folly*. Boston, 1885.

Van Deventer, Emma Murdoch, *Moina, or Against the Mighty*. Chicago, 1891.

Vinton, Arthur Dudley, *Looking Further Backward*. Albany, N. Y., 1890.

Walch, Caroline C., *Doctor Sphinx*. New York, 1899.

Warman, Cy, *Snow on the Headlight*. New York, 1899.

——, *The White Mail*. New York, 1899.

Warner, Beverley Ellison, *Troubled Waters*. Philadelphia, 1885.

Warner, Charles Dudley, *The Golden House*. New York, 1885.

——, *A Little Journey in the World*, New York, 1889.

——, *That Fortune*. New York, 1899.

Waterloo, Stanley, *The Launching of a Man*. Chicago, 1899.

——, *An Odd Situation*. Chicago, 1893.

Webster, Henry Kitchell, *The Banker and the Bear*. New York, 1900.

Welcome, S. Byron, *From Earth's Center*. Chicago, 1894.

Wellman, Bert J., *The Legal Revolution of 1902*. Chicago, 1898.

Westcott, Edward N., *David Harum, a Story of American Life*. New York, 1899.

White, Hervey, *Differences*. Boston, 1899.

Wiggin, Kate Douglas, *The Story of Patsy*. Boston, 1889.

——, *Timothy's Quest*. Boston, 1890.

Wilbrandt, Conrad, *Mr. East's Experiences in Mr. Bellamy's World*, translated from the German by Mary J. Safford. New York, 1891.

Winslow, Helen M., *Salome Shepard, Reformer*. Boston, 1894.

Wolf, Emma, *The Joy of Life*. Chicago, 1896.

Woodbury, Helen Sumner, *The White Slave*, or *The Cross of Gold*. Chicago, 1896.

Woods, Katharine Pearson, *John, A Tale of the Messiah*. New York, 1896.

——, *Metzerott, Shoemaker*. Anonymously published. New York, 1880.

——, *The Son of Ingar*. New York, 1897.

——, *A Web of Gold*. New York, 1890.

Worley, Frederick U., *Three Thousand Dollars a Year*. Washington, 1890.

III. THE LESSER NOVELISTS: A SUPPLEMENTARY LIST

(Works of fiction, published after 1900, from which some evidence has been taken for use in the preceding study. For a completer list of the economic fiction of this period, see the thesis of Dr. L. A. Rose, listed above.)

Barr, Robert, *The Victors*. New York, 1901.
Beach, David N., *The Annie Laurie Mine*. Boston, 1902.
Betts, Lilian W., *The Story of an East Side Family*. New York, 1903.
Blake, Adam, *The Man with the Hoe*. Cincinnati, 1904.
Boyce, Neith, *The Forerunner*. New York, 1903.
Burr, Anna Robeson, *The Millionaire's Son*. Boston, 1903.
Carryl, Guy Wetmore, *The Lieutenant Governor*. Boston, 1903.
Daniels, Gertrude Potter, *The Warners*. Chicago, 1901.
Flower, Elliott, *Slaves of Success*. Boston, 1905.
Flynt, Josiah, *The Little Brother—A Story of Tramp Life*. New York, 1902.
Freeman, Mary Wilkins, *The Portion of Labor*. New York, 1901.
French, Alice, *The Lion's Share*. Indianapolis, 1907.
———, *The Man of the Hour*. Indianapolis, 1905.
French, Allen, *The Barrier*. New York, 1904.
Friedman, Isaac K., *The Radical*. New York, 1907.
Hall, Bolton, *The Game of Life*. New York, 1902.
Harriman, Karl Edwin, *The Homebuilders*. Philadelphia, 1904.
Herrick, Robert, *The Common Lot*. New York, 1904.
———, *Memoirs of an American Citizen*. New York, 1905.
———, *The Real World*. New York, 1901.
Hill, Frederic Trevor, *The Minority*. New York, 1902.
Hillman, Harry W., *Looking Forward*. Northampton, Mass., 1906.
Hopkins, Herbert M., *The Torch*. Indianapolis, 1903.
Josaphare, Lionel, *A Tale of a Town*. San Francisco, 1903.
Kemp, Matt. Stan., *Boss Tom*. Akron, Ohio, 1904.
LeFevre, Edwin, *The Golden Flood*. New York, 1905.
———, *Wall Street Stories*. New York, 1901.
Lush, Charles Keeler, *The Autocrats*. New York, 1901.
Lynde, Francis, *The Grafters*. Indianapolis, 1904.
Makin, Richard Lawrence, *The Beaten Path*. New York, 1903.
Merwin, Samuel, *The Whip Hand*. New York, 1903.
——— and Henry Kitchell Webster, *Calumet K*. New York, 1901.
Overton, Gwendolen, *Captains of the World*. New York, 1904.
Payne, Will, *Mr. Salt*. Boston, 1903.
———, *On Fortune's Road*. Chicago, 1902.

Phillips, David Graham, *The Cost*. Indianapolis, 1904.
———, *The Deluge*. Indianapolis, 1905.
———, *The Great God Success*. New York, 1901.
———, *The Master Rogue*. New York, 1904.
———, *The Plum Tree*. Indianapolis, 1905.
Riis, Jacob A., *Children of the Tenements*. New York, 1903.
Scott, Leroy, *The Walking Delegate*. New York, 1905.
Scudder, Vida D., *A Listener in Babel*. Boston, 1904.
Smith, Alice Prescott, *The Legatee*. Boston, 1903.
Smith, William Hawley, *The Promoters*. Chicago, 1904.
Swift, Morrison I., *The Monarch Billionaire*. New York, 1903.
Thorpe, Francis N., *The Divining Rod*. Boston, 1905.
Tilton, Dwight, *On Satan's Mount*. Boston, 1903.
Townsend, Charles, *The Mahoney Million*. New York, 1903.
Turner, George Kibbe, *The Taskmasters*. New York, 1902.
Van Vorst, Marie, *Amanda of the Mill*. New York, 1905.
———, *Philip Longstreth*. New York, 1902.
Wakeman, Annie, *A Gentlewoman of the Slums*. Boston, 1901.
Webster, Henry Kitchell, *Roger Drake, Captain of Industry*. New York, 1902.
Wilson, A. F., *The Wars of Peace*. Boston, 1903.
Wright, James North, *Where Copper Was King*. Boston, 1905.

IV. MAJOR FIGURES

Henry George

Books

Our Land and Land Policy. San Francisco, 1871.
Progress and Poverty. New York, 1879-80.
The Irish Land Question. New York, 1881.
Social Problems. Chicago, 1883.
Protection or Free Trade. New York, 1886.
The Condition of Labor. New York, 1891.
A Perplexed Philosopher. New York, 1892.
The Science of Political Economy. New York, 1898.

Articles

The Standard. New York. Editorial contributions during the time of George's editorship, January, 1887, to December, 1890.
"Labor in Pennsylvania." *The North American Review*, 144: 86-95 (January, 1887).

"The New Party." *The North American Review*, 145: 1-7 (July, 1887).

"How to Help the Unemployed." *The North American Review.* 158: 175-84 (February, 1894).

Biography, Criticism, Research

Babcock, W. H., "The George Movement and Property." *Lippincott's Magazine*, 39: 133-9 (January, 1887).

Bagot, John, "Progress and Poverty." *The Westminster Review*, 172: 371-5 (October, 1909).

Clark, Edward Gordon, "Henry George's Land Tax." *The North American Review*, 144: 107-10 (January, 1887).

Dewey, John, Introduction to *Significant Paragraphs from Henry George's Progress and Poverty*. New York, 1928.

Fairchild, Henry Pratt, "Henry George." *The New Republic.* 75: 321-2 (August 2, 1933).

Geiger, George R., *The Philosophy of Henry George*. New York, 1933.

George, Henry, Junior, *The Life of Henry George*. New York, 1900.

Gunton, George, "The Economic Heresies of Henry George." *The Forum*, 3: 15-28 (March, 1887).

Huxley, Thomas Henry, "Capital—the Mother of Labour." *The Nineteenth Century*, 27: 513-32 (March, 1890).

J. C. H., "Mr. Henry George and the Land." *The Dublin Review*, 14: 325-46.

McEwen, Arthur, "Henry George, A Character Sketch." *Review of Reviews*, 16: 547-54 (November, 1897).

Mackendrick, Alexander, "Henry George's Teaching." *The Westminster Review*, 177: 133-42 (February, 1912).

Nock, Albert Jay, "Henry George, Unorthodox American." *Scribner's Magazine*, 94: 274-9, 315 ff. (November, 1933).

Ryan, John A., "Henry George and Private Property." *The Catholic World*, 93: 289-300 (June, 1911).

Scanlon, T., "The Spencer-George Controversy." *The Independent*, 56: 1479-81 (June 30, 1904).

Shearman, Thomas G., "The Mistakes of Henry George." *The Forum*, 8: 40-52 (September, 1889).

Spencer, Herbert, "Unpublished Letters: Part II, The Henry George Controversy." *The Independent*, 56: 1169-74 (May 26, 1904). Part III, *Ibid.*, 1471-8 (June 30, 1904).

Tarbell, Ida M., "New Dealers of the Seventies." *The Forum*, 92: 133-9 (September, 1934).

Tolstoy, Lyof N., "Count Tolstoy on the Doctrine of Henry George." *Review of Reviews*, 17: 73-4 (January, 1898).

"Unearned Increment Tax and Land Ownership." *The Nation*, 89: 477-8 (November 18, 1909).

MARK TWAIN

Books

The Innocents Abroad. Hartford, 1869.

Roughing It. Hartford, 1872.

The Gilded Age (with Charles Dudley Warner). Hartford, 1873.

A Tramp Abroad. Hartford, 1880.

Life on the Mississippi. Boston, 1883.

A Connecticut Yankee in King Arthur's Court. New York, 1889.

The American Claimant. New York, 1892.

Following the Equator. Hartford, 1897.

The Man that Corrupted Hadleyburg. New York, 1900.

King Leopold's Soliloquy. Boston, 1905.

The $30,000 Bequest. New York, 1906.

What Is Man? New York, 1906.

Mark Twain's Speeches, with an introduction by William Dean Howells. New York, 1910.

The Mysterious Stranger. New York, 1916.

Mark Twain's Letters, arranged with comment by Albert Bigelow Paine. New York, 1917.

Europe and Elsewhere. Compiled by A. B. Paine, with an appreciation by Brander Matthews. New York, 1923.

Mark Twain's Notebook. Prepared for publication with comments by Albert Bigelow Paine. New York, 1935.

Mark Twain in Eruption, by Mark Twain. Edited and with an Introduction by Bernard DeVoto. New York, 1940.

Articles

"The Curious Republic of Gondour." *The Atlantic Monthly*, 36: 461-3 (October, 1875).

"To the Person Sitting in Darkness." *The North American Review*, 172: 161-76 (February, 1901).

"A Defence of General Funston." *The North American Review*, 174: 613-24 (May, 1902).

"The Czar's Soliloquy." *The North American Review,* 180: 320-6 (March, 1905).

Biography, Criticism, Research

Altick, Richard D., "Mark Twain's Despair: An Explanation in Terms of His Humanity." *The South Atlantic Quarterly,* 34: 359-67 (October, 1935).

Arvin, Newton, "Mark Twain, 1835-1935." *The New Republic,* 83: 125-7 (June 12, 1935).

Brashear, Minnie May, *Mark Twain, Son of Missouri.* Chapel Hill, 1934.

Brooks, Van Wyck, *The Ordeal of Mark Twain.* New York, 1920. Revised edition, 1933.

Chapman, John W., "The Germ of a Book: A Footnote on Mark Twain." *The Atlantic Monthly,* 150: 720-1 (December, 1932).

Clemens, Cyril, *Mark Twain and Mussolini.* Webster Groves, Missouri, 1934.

———, "Mark Twain's Reading." *The Commonweal,* 24: 363-4 (August 7, 1936).

Clemens, Will Montgomery, *Mark Twain, The Story of His Life and Work.* San Francisco, 1892.

DeVoto, Bernard, *Mark Twain's America.* Boston, 1932.

Dreiser, Theodore, "Mark the Double Twain." *The English Journal,* 24:615-27 (October, 1935).

Gibson, William M., *Mark Twain and William Dean Howells: Anti-Imperialists.* A doctoral dissertation of the University of Chicago. Chicago, 1940.

"The Gilded Cage." *Old and New,* 9: 386-8 (March, 1874).

Hamado, Masajiro, "Mark Twain's Conception of Social Justice." (Japanese) *Studies in English Literature,* 16: 593-616 (October, 1936).

Herrick, Robert, "Mark Twain and the American Tradition." *The Mark Twain Quarterly,* 2: 8-11 (Winter, 1937).

Johnson, Merle, *A Bibliography of the Work of Mark Twain.* New York, 1910.

Leisy, Ernest E., "Mark Twain's Part in *The Gilded Age.*" *American Literature,* 8: 445-7 (January, 1937).

Moore, Olin Harris, "Mark Twain and Don Quixote." *PMLA,* 37: 324-46 (June, 1922).

Paine, Albert Bigelow, *Mark Twain: A Biography.* New York, 1912.

Sherman, Stuart P., "The Democracy of Mark Twain." *On Contemporary Literature* (New York, 1917), pp. 18-49.

Wagenknecht, Edward, *Mark Twain: The Man and His Work.* New Haven, 1935.

Waggoner, Hyatt Howe, "Science in the Thought of Mark Twain." *American Literature,* 8: 357-70 (January, 1937).

Walker, Franklin, "An Influence from San Francisco on Mark Twain's *The Gilded Age.*" *American Literature,* 8: 63-6 (March, 1936).

Wyatt, Edith, "An Inspired Critic." *The North American Review,* 205: 603-15 (April, 1917).

HAMLIN GARLAND

Books

Under the Wheel. Boston, 1890.

Main-Travelled Roads. Boston, 1891. Also, with various additions, Chicago, 1893; New York, 1899, 1909, 1930.

Jason Edwards, An Average Man. Chicago, 1892.

A Member of the Third House. Chicago, 1892.

A Spoil of Office. New York, 1892.

Prairie Folks. Chicago, 1893.

Prairie Songs, Chicago, 1893.

Crumbling Idols. Chicago, 1894.

Rose of Dutcher's Coolly. New York, 1895.

Wayside Courtships. New York, 1895.

Boy Life on the Prairie. New York, 1899.

The Trail of the Goldseekers. New York, 1899.

The Eagle's Heart. New York, 1900.

The Captain of the Gray-Horse Troop. New York, 1902.

Hesper. New York, 1903.

The Tyranny of the Dark. New York, 1905.

Witch's Gold. New York, 1906.

Money Magic. New York, 1907.

Cavanagh, Forest Ranger. New York, 1910.

Other Main-Travelled Roads. New York, 1910.

The Forester's Daughter. New York, 1914.

A Son of the Middle Border. New York, 1917.

A Daughter of the Middle Border. New York, 1921.

A Pioneer Mother. Chicago, 1922.

Trail-Makers of the Middle Border. New York, 1926.

Back-Trailers from the Middle Border. New York, 1928.
Companions on the Trail. New York, 1931.
My Friendly Contemporaries: A Literary Log. New York, 1932.
Afternoon Neighbors: Further Excerpts from a Literary Log. New York, 1934.

Articles

"A New Declaration of Rights." *The Arena,* 3: 157-84 (January, 1891).

"The Alliance Wedge in Congress." *The Arena,* 5: 447-58 (March, 1892).

"The Land Question, and Its Relation to Art and Literature." *The Arena,* 9: 165-75 (January, 1894).

"Homestead and Its Perilous Trades." *McClure's Magazine,* 3: 1-20 (June, 1894).

"The Single Tax in Actual Operation." *The Arena,* 10: 52-8 (June, 1894).

"Sanity in Fiction." *The North American Review,* 176: 336-48 (March, 1903).

"The Passing of the Frontier." *The Dial,* 67: 285-6 (October 4, 1919).

"Limitations of Authorship in America." *The Bookman,* 59: 257-62 (May, 1924).

Biography, Criticism, Research

Hicks, Granville, "Garland of the Academy." *The Nation,* 133: 435-6 (October 21, 1931).

Hill, Eldon C., *A Biographical Study of Hamlin Garland from 1860-95.* A doctoral dissertation of the Ohio State University. Columbus, 1940.

"New Figures in Literature and Art: III. Hamlin Garland." *The Atlantic Monthly,* 76: 840-4 (December, 1895).

Raw, Ruth M., "Hamlin Garland the Romanticist." *The Sewanee Review,* 36: 202-10 (April, 1928).

EDWARD BELLAMY

Books

Six to One: A Nantucket Idyl. New York, 1878.
Dr. Heidenhof's Process. New York, 1880.
Miss Ludington's Sister. Boston, 1884.

Looking Backward, 2000-1887. Boston, 1888.
Equality. New York, 1897.
The Blindman's World. Boston, 1898.
The Duke of Stockbridge. New York, 1900.

Articles

"How I Came to Write *Looking Backward*." *The Nationalist*, I: 1-4 (May, 1889).
"Looking Forward." *The Nationalist*, 2: 1-4 (December, 1889).
"*Looking Backward* Again." *The North American Review*, 150: 351-63 (March, 1890).
"First Steps Toward Nationalism." *The Forum*, 10: 174-84 (October, 1890).
"The Progress of Nationalism in the United States." *The North American Review*, 154: 742-52 (June, 1892).
The New Nation. Editorial contributions of Bellamy from January 31, 1891 to December 30, 1893.
Introduction to the American Edition of *Socialism: The Fabian Essays,* edited by G. Bernard Shaw. Boston, 1894.
"The Progress of the Nationalists." *The Forum*, 17: 81-91 (March, 1894).

Biography, Criticism, Research

Baxter, Sylvester, "Edward Bellamy's New Book of the New Democracy." *Review of Reviews*, 16: 62-8 (July, 1897).
Flower, B. O., "The Latest Social Vision." *The Arena*, 18: 517-34 (October, 1897).
Gilman, Nicholas T., "Nationalism in the United States." *The Quarterly Journal of Economics*, IV: 50-76 (October, 1889).
Harris, W. T., "Edward Bellamy's Vision." *The Forum*, 8: 199-208 (October, 1889).
Higgs, William, "Some Objections to Mr. Bellamy's Utopia." *The New Englander*, 52: 231-9 (March, 1890).
Johnson, Oliver Warren, *An Answer to Chaos: The Coming Economic Life,* or *Edward Bellamy's Theory Reduced to Working Form*. Geneva, Ohio, 1933.
Laveleye, Emile de, "Two New Utopias." *Littell's Living Age*, 184: 387-98 (February 15, 1890).
Nationalist, The, edited successively by Henry Willard Austin and John Storer Cobb (Boston, 1889-92).

Phillips, W. Fleming, "Edward Bellamy—Prophet of Nationalism." *The Westminster Review,* 150: 498-504 (November, 1898).

Sedgwick, A. G., "Bellamy's Utopia." *The Nation,* 65: 170-1 (August 26, 1897).

Shurter, Robert L., *The Utopian Novel in America, 1865-1900.* A doctoral dissertation of the Western Reserve University. Cleveland, 1936.

Walker, Francis A., "Mr. Bellamy and the New Nationalist Party." *The Atlantic Monthly,* 65: 248-62 (February, 1890).

Woods, Katharine Pearson, "Edward Bellamy, Author and Economist." *The Bookman,* 7: 398-401 (July, 1898).

WILLIAM DEAN HOWELLS

Books

The Undiscovered Country. Boston, 1880.
The Rise of Silas Lapham. Boston, 1885.
The Minister's Charge. Boston, 1887.
Annie Kilburn. New York, 1889.
A Hazard of New Fortunes. New York, 1890.
Criticism and Fiction. New York, 1891.
The Quality of Mercy, New York, 1892.
The World of Chance. New York, 1893.
A Traveller from Altruria. New York, 1894.
My Literary Passions. New York, 1895.
A Boy's Town. New York, 1895.
Impressions and Experiences. New York, 1896.
The Landlord at Lion's Head. New York, 1897.
Literary Friends and Acquaintance. New York, 1900.
Literature and Life. New York, 1902.
The Son of Royal Langbrith. New York, 1904.
Through the Eye of the Needle, New York, 1907.
Seven English Cities. New York, 1909.
My Mark Twain. New York, 1910.
New Leaf Mills. New York, 1913.
Years of My Youth. New York, 1916.
The Vacation of the Kelwyns. New York, 1920.
The Life in Letters of William Dean Howells, edited by Mildred Howells. New York, 1928

Articles

The Editor's Study series, *Harper's Magazine,* beginning with the issue of January, 1886.

"Leo Tolstoi." An Introduction to Tolstoy's *Sebastopol,* translated from a French version by Frank D. Millet. New York, 1887.

"Are We a Plutocracy?" *The North American Review,* 158: 185-96 (February, 1894).

Introduction to Tolstoy's *Master and Man,* translated by A. Hulme Beaman. New York, 1895.

"Equality as the Basis of Good Society." *The Century,* N. S., 29: 63-7 (November, 1895).

"The Nature of Liberty." *The Forum,* 20: 401-9 (December, 1895).

"Who Are Our Brethren?" *The Century,* N. S., 29: 932-6 (April, 1896).

"The Modern American Mood." *Harpers Magazine,* 95: 199-204 (July, 1897).

"Edward Bellamy." *The Atlantic Monthly,* 82: 253-6 (August, 1808).

The Editor's Easy Chair series, *Harpers Magazine,* beginning December, 1900.

"Frank Norris." *The North American Review,* 175: 769-78 (December, 1902).

"John Hay in Literature." *The North American Review,* 181: 343-51 (September, 1905).

"Lyof N. Tolstoi." *The North American Review,* 188: 842-59 (December, 1908).

"The Novels of Robert Herrick." *The North American Review,* 189: 812-20 (June, 1909).

"Mr. Garland's Books." *The North American Review,* 196: 523-8 (October, 1912).

"Why?" *The North American Review,* 201: 676-82 (May, 1915).

Biography, Criticism, Research

Arms, George Warren, "Further Inquiry into Howells' Socialism." *Science and Society,* III: 245-8 (Spring, 1939).

———, *The Social Criticism of William Dean Howells.* A doctoral dissertation of New York University. New York, 1939.

Arvin, Newton, "The Usableness of Howells." *The New Republic,* 91: 227-8 (June 30, 1937).

Atherton, Gertrude, "'Why Is American Literature Bourgeois?" *The North American Review*, 178: 771-81 (May, 1904).

Bass, Altha Leah, "The Social Consciousness of William Dean Howells." *The New Republic*, 26: 193-4 (April 13, 1921).

Cairns, William B., Introduction to *Annie Kilburn* in Harper's Modern Classics. New York, 1919.

Cooke, Delmar Gross, *William Dean Howells, A Critical Study*. New York, 1922.

Erskine, John, "William Dean Howells." *The Bookman*, 51: 385-9 (June, 1920).

Firkins, Oscar W., *William Dean Howells: A Study*. Cambridge, 1924.

Garland, Hamlin, "Mr. Howells's Latest Novels." *The New England Magazine*, N. S., 2: 243-50 (May, 1890).

Grattan, C. Hartley, "Howells: Ten Years After." *The American Mercury*, 20: 42-50 (May, 1930).

Gronlund, Laurence, *The Coöperative Commonwealth*. Boston, 1884.

Howells, William Cooper, *Recollections of Life in Ohio from 1813 to 1840*. With an Introduction by William Dean Howells. Cincinnati, 1895.

"New York in Recent Fiction." *The Atlantic Monthly*, 65: 563-9 (April, 1890).

North American Review, The, 212: 1-20 (July, 1920), Commemorative tributes to William Dean Howells.

Quinn, Arthur Hobson, "The Art of William Dean Howells." *The Century*, 100: 674-81 (September, 1920).

Van Westrum, A. S., "Mr. Howells and American Aristocracies." *The Bookman*, 25: 67-73 (March, 1907).

FRANK NORRIS

Books

Yvernelle. Philadelphia, 1892.
Moran of the Lady Letty. New York, 1898.
Blix. New York, 1899.
McTeague. New York, 1899.
A Man's Woman. New York, 1900.
The Octopus. New York, 1901.
The Pit. New York, 1903.
A Deal in Wheat. New York, 1903.

The Responsibilities of the Novelist. New York, 1903.
The Third Circle. New York, 1904.
Vandover and the Brute. New York, 1914.

Articles

"Life in the Mining Region." *Everybody's,* 7: 241-8 (September, 1902).

Biography, Criticism, Research

Dell, Floyd, "Chicago in Fiction." *The Bookman,* 38: 270-4 (November, 1913).

Garland, Hamlin, "The Work of Frank Norris." *The Critic,* 42: 216-8 (March, 1903).

Leavick, M. B., "The Literary Work of Norris." *The Overland Monthly,* N. S., 45: 504-8 (June, 1905).

Martin, Willard E., "Frank Norris's Reading at Harvard College." *American Literature,* 7: 203-4 (May, 1935).

———, "Two Uncollected Essays by Frank Norris." *American Literature,* 8: 190-8 (May, 1930).

Preston, H. W., "The Novels of Frank Norris." *The Atlantic Monthly,* 91: 691-2 (May, 1903).

Reninger, H. Willard, "Norris Explains *The Octopus;* A Correlation of His Theory and Practice." *American Literature,* 12: 218-27 (May, 1940).

Walcutt, Charles Child, "Frank Norris on Realism and Naturalism," *American Literature,* 13: 61-3 (March, 1941).

Walker, Franklin, *Frank Norris, A Biography.* Garden City, New York, 1932.